The Myth of the Community Fix

The Myth of the Community Fix

Inequality and the Politics of Youth Punishment

SARAH D. CATE

OXFORD
UNIVERSITY PRESS

Oxford University Press is a department of the University of Oxford. It furthers
the University's objective of excellence in research, scholarship, and education
by publishing worldwide. Oxford is a registered trade mark of Oxford University
Press in the UK and certain other countries.

Published in the United States of America by Oxford University Press
198 Madison Avenue, New York, NY 10016, United States of America.

© Oxford University Press 2023

All rights reserved. No part of this publication may be reproduced, stored in
a retrieval system, or transmitted, in any form or by any means, without the
prior permission in writing of Oxford University Press, or as expressly permitted
by law, by license, or under terms agreed with the appropriate reproduction
rights organization. Inquiries concerning reproduction outside the scope of the
above should be sent to the Rights Department, Oxford University Press, at the
address above.

You must not circulate this work in any other form
and you must impose this same condition on any acquirer.

Library of Congress Cataloging-in-Publication Data
Names: Cate, Sarah D., author.
Title: The Myth of the Community fix : inequality and the politics of youth punishment / Sarah D. Cate.
Description: Oxford ; New York, NY : Oxford University Press, [2023] |
Includes bibliographical references and index.
Identifiers: LCCN 2022042457 (print) | LCCN 2022042458 (ebook) |
ISBN 9780197674291 (paperback) | ISBN 9780197674284 (hardback) |
ISBN 9780197674314 (epub)
Subjects: LCSH: Juvenile delinquents—United States. | Juvenile justice,
Administration of—United States. | Prison reform—United States.
Classification: LCC HV9104 .C36 2023 (print) | LCC HV9104 (ebook) |
DDC 364.360973—dc23/eng/20221123
LC record available at https://lccn.loc.gov/2022042457
LC ebook record available at https://lccn.loc.gov/2022042458

DOI: 10.1093/oso/9780197674284.001.0001

1 3 5 7 9 8 6 4 2
Paperback printed by Marquis, Canada
Hardback printed by Bridgeport National Bindery, Inc., United States of America

For Tim and Sue Cate

CONTENTS

Acknowledgments ix

Introduction The Limits of the Community-Based Reform Movement: Evidence from Pennsylvania, California, and Texas 1

1. Abandoning Public Goods: The Turn to Community in the Context of Inequality 17

2. Devolution, Not Decarceration: Expanding Punishment Closer to Home 39

3. Privatizing Punishment: Consequences of Foundation-Led Policymaking 76

4. The Individual Focus: The Limits of Behavioral Solutions to Structural Problems 112

5. Still Punitive: Rationalizing Punishment for the "Worst of the Worst" 147

Conclusion: Bringing Public Goods Back In 184

Notes 203
References 215
Index 247

ACKNOWLEDGMENTS

I would like to thank the many people who helped and supported me with researching and writing this book.

Above all, I would like to thank my family, who means everything to me. My dad, Tim Cate, taught me how to write and to love reading and researching. Sharing these pursuits with him continues to be an inspiration and joy for me. I appreciate his willingness always to be there to listen, discuss, and teach me. He carefully and tirelessly edited and insightfully discussed my work at every stage of this process. I owe unending gratitude to my mom, Sue Cate, the greatest person I know. She influenced me and this project in countless ways. She is an invaluable reality check for the research I do as someone who knows what it looks like on the ground—not to mention the daily, small, and enormous ways that she supports and loves me. My parents' compassion for and dedication to helping others informs and inspires my work. I have looked up to my brother, Aaron Cate, my whole life. He has positively influenced me more than anyone. His steady ease, confidence, and strength are a constant in my life, and I could not be luckier than to have him as my brother. Same goes for winning the lottery on the best sister-in-law, Sarah Dixon. She and my brother lead thoughtful lives of public service. Their work is exactly the model of what it takes to truly make the lives of young people better. To Beatrice Cate and Moses Cate, thank you for bringing so much happiness to me. I will always be grateful to you for being exactly who you are.

I want to especially thank and dedicate the final push of getting this book done to my uncle, Michael Cate. His humor and distinctive perspective on things are a bright light for me—always has been, always will be. I pay an enormous amount of respect and gratitude to him and my aunt, Joanne Cate, for all they have done for me.

In addition to my incredible family, which includes a lot of very special grandparents, aunts, uncles, and cousins whom I love dearly, I have also been fortunate to have time and again chanced to interact with the greatest colleagues and friends in the academic world.

This project began at the University of Pennsylvania, where I was blessed with incredibly talented and supportive advisors. My sincerest thanks go to Marie Gottschalk, who more than anyone helped shape this book. My research and teaching have benefited immeasurably from her scholarship and mentorship. Her voice is a constant in my mind when I write, research, and make decisions. I thank her for sharing her great intellect with me and for supporting me. Rogers Smith has been an essential adviser and role model. He has the ability to always cut right to the core of a research project and ask the most challenging questions. I am deeply indebted to him for his unwavering support, wisdom, and kindness. Adolph Reed Jr. has had an outsized impact on me, influencing my life, politics, and research in profound ways. There are so many times when communication with him and hearing his perspective have reassured and encouraged me when I have needed it most. Having him as a friend is one of the greatest fortunes in my life.

In addition to my advisors, there were also a number of people who generously read portions of the book and gave me important feedback. Thank you Alexandra Cox, Katie Rader, Anthony Grasso, and Heather Schoenfeld for taking the time to read and comment on chapters of this book. Thank you to the two reviewers who offered insightful feedback that significantly improved the book, and to my editor, Dave McBride for his support and guidance. Additionally, there are a number of people whose work significantly influenced this project that I would like to thank: Lisa Miller, Gordon Lafer, Touré Reed, Cedric Johnson, and Dino Guastella.

All of the hard work my teachers put into my decades of schooling deserve a great amount of thanks, particularly Mrs. Seeder, Mrs. Wolf, Mrs. Wells, and Mrs. Densmore from Helman Elementary School; Mrs. Wieczorek from Ashland Middle School; and Mr. Cornelius, Mr. McKinnon, Mr. Schoenleber, and Mr. Cicerrella from Ashland High School. Special thanks to Camille Morris and Kristina Voskes for being with me in most all of those classrooms and all the years since.

I am immensely grateful to the professors I had while at the University of Oregon, especially Daniel HoSang, who introduced me to the idea of attending graduate school and encouraged me and gave me the confidence to apply to PhD programs. I can only hope I have a sliver of the positive impact on any of my students that he had on me. Mary Wood, David Frank, Joe Lowndes, Gerald Berk, and Dan Tichenor were generous mentors who encouraged and guided my initial forays into research. I am also grateful to my many friends there who kicked off my scholarly pursuits in such a positive way: Joshua Plencner, Kathryn Miller, Nicolas Thompson, Katya Dunajeva, Jeremy Strickler, Brian Guy, and even earlier on, Ossie Bladine, Ryan Manfrin, James Keane, Laura Lynch, and Carrie Bateman. And to Anne Roney, Jackie Renteria, Jamie Escobar, and Isabel Crosby, thank you for always being right by my side then and now.

During my time in Philadelphia I benefited a great deal from the friendship of some of the most creative, funny, and smart people. To have shared such a unique experience and time of our lives together is something I will always cherish. Thank you, Chelsea Schafer, Evan Perkoski, Laura Silver, Emmerich Davies, Josh Darr, Ian Hartshorn, Doug Allen, Tim Weaver, Carly Regina, Joanna Wuest, Katie Rader, Danielle Hanley, Anthony Grasso, Ellen Donnelly, Allison Evans, Osman Balkan, David Bateman, Begum Adalet, Alexandra Schepens, Amy Steinmetz, and Helen Reed.

I am appreciative of all the support I received from my colleagues while at the University of Southern Mississippi, especially Marek Steedman. The stars aligned in a special way to allow me to join the faculty with Jill Abney and Laura Stengrim. Our writing group, including Allison Abra, was a big help in keeping this thing moving. More than that, your friendship means a great deal to me.

At Saint Louis University, I continued to benefit from supportive colleagues and friends. Morgan Hazelton, J. D. Bowen, Ellen Carnaghan, Bob Cropf, Wynne Moskop, and Ruth Groff, were generous in mentoring me. I owe a great deal of thanks to the smart and talented Dylan McConnell Curry and Andrea Villalpando, who contributed invaluable help for this book as research assistants.

I am abundantly fortunate that there are so many more people who have encouraged me and taken special interest in this project over the years, especially Claudia and Jack Dixon, Suellen and Scott Willi, and Paul Morris. Thank you.

Daniel Moak holds a unique and incredibly special place among those I owe the deepest of thanks to. His influence and support are on every page of this book. I deeply admire him as a scholar and person, and he made every step of this possible and more enjoyable. Thank you for the great happiness you bring to everything.

Finally, thank you to all those organizing and struggling to make the world a better place.

Introduction

The Limits of the Community-based Reform Movement: Evidence from Pennsylvania, California, and Texas

In February 2007, Texas newspapers broke a major story exposing the scandalous widespread abuse of young people in the state's juvenile prisons and the years-long agency cover-ups of this repeated abuse. At the time, Texas held the second largest number of juveniles incarcerated in the country and was facing lawsuits, negative media attention, and political and legal challenges from numerous prison reform organizations. Among the long list of complaints logged at the youth prison system in the state were patterns of sexual and physical abuse, overcrowded facilities, inmate suicides, and subjecting youth to solitary confinement. A retired inspector general for the Texas Youth Commission (the body that oversees the state-run juvenile prisons) stated in the *Dallas Morning News*, "[T]he TYC has established a dynasty of corruption that condones the mistreatment of youth in its care" (Swanson 2007).

Given the evidence of horrific abuse, the Texas governor and legislature enacted sweeping reforms to the juvenile justice system. In Brown County, a small rural county in west-central Texas and the location of a state-run youth prison, arrests of guards and administrators cascaded down. The Brown County state-run prison was one of the sites of the shocking abuse of young inmates and was closed down thanks to reforms passed to address the scandal.[1] The prison had been in operation for more than 30 years and had housed thousands of juveniles from across the state. These youths, far away from their homes, were frequently subjected to solitary confinement, routine strip searches, and brutal physical force. Closing the detention center exemplified a commitment in Texas to put an end to the abusive conditions of state-run juvenile prisons, limit the number of juveniles sent to these prisons, and improve the care they receive. Shutting down the facility, a youth prison located far away from any major city and the site of indescribable horrors of youth victimization, was a way to literally close the doors on the physical embodiment of all that was wrong with the juvenile justice system in Texas.

Texas earned widespread praise for the reforms that led to state-run prison closures and the establishment of community-based alternatives. The reforms the Texas juvenile justice system enacted in the mid-2000s and early 2010s prompted the *New York Times* (2011, 2015) to praise the state for making "impressive strides" and to call it a "juvenile justice model for the nation."[2] Conservative advocacy groups applauded the state for taking "the opportunity to fundamentally reform and reshape" the system and ushering in "a new era of cost-efficient and effective juvenile justice" (Levin and Moll 2011). Liberal public interest advocacy organizations expressed similar support for the changes, declaring the policy changes had "produced great results" and urging Texas politicians to continue down this path of reform (Granite Public Affairs n.d.).

Yet, less than a year after being shuttered, the Ron Jackson Unit II in Brown County was reopened. As part of the community-based reform legislation responsible for closing the facility, control of the prison was transferred from the state to the county and reopened as the Ray West Juvenile Center—which now holds more juveniles than prior to the name change.[3] Since the county has taken over the facility, it has subsequently leased out a part to a large private company that enters the contract with a trail of abuse allegations in its wake (Nash 2014).[4] In the privately controlled 115-bed unit in the prison, employees routinely use physical restraints on youth and put them in solitary confinement—a practice considered "cruel, inhuman, and degrading treatment" by numerous international human rights treaties and bodies.[5]

Across the state, the county-run prisons that are meant to replace the state-run facilities have seen injuries to youth increase by a third since the community-based reforms were passed (Texas Criminal Justice Coalition 2012, 15).[6] Meanwhile, in the remaining state-run prisons conditions of confinement have *worsened* since the community-based reforms were enacted, with increased rates of violence and some of the highest rates of sexual victimization in the country (Ziff-Rosenzweig 2020). Despite the changes ushered in by the reforms, the juvenile correctional facility in Brown County still stands as a fixture of Texas's juvenile justice system where youth from across the state are confined with often tragic outcomes. The 30-plus years of abuse and neglect have not ended.

The glowing endorsements for the community-based reforms that model reform states like Texas have received suggest that these states really turned the corner on the worst practices of youth incarceration. However, this enthusiasm belies the evidence on the ground that shows youth are not getting the support they need and are being harmed in ways that have long-term consequences. As of 2020—13 years after the enactment of the much-celebrated community-based reforms—two leading juvenile advocacy organizations in Texas yet again filed a complaint with the U.S. Department of Justice citing "grievous violations of children's constitutional rights" in its youth prisons (Johnson and Surtees 2021). While some state-run prisons closed, the county-based facilities expanded to replace them, entrenching youth incarceration at the local level and perpetuating the same abuses and negative outcomes that the reforms seek to ameliorate.

The experience of Brown County is not unique but is emblematic of the broader trends of reform sweeping the juvenile justice system. In response to the problems that plague juvenile justice facilities throughout the United States, many states are pursuing community-based reforms. This reform movement is premised on reducing the number of youth sent to state-run prisons and instead getting kids "closer to home" by devolving control to county probation departments and expanding programs at the local level, often through public-private partnerships, that address the individual behavioral needs of youth caught up in the juvenile justice system. The "community-based reform movement" refers to the broad adoption of these policies that are promoted and disseminated by large charitable foundations and by politicians from across the political spectrum.

The main features of the community-based reform movement—devolving responsibility to counties, increasing public-private contracts, and implementing individual behavioral programs—is emblematic of the broader shift away from the centralized provision of public goods in the United States. Changes like those in Brown County as part of the community-based reform movement are not fundamentally improving the lives of youth, particularly among racial minorities and the working class. The community-based reform movement in the criminal justice system has a number of negative consequences and does not offer a promising avenue for fixing the problems of mass incarceration.

The Pitfalls of the Community-Based Reform Movement

This book examines the juvenile justice systems of Pennsylvania, California, and Texas, three states key to understanding the community-based reform movement. These state-level case studies reveal four key findings: the community-based movement devolves rather than eliminates the negative effects of juvenile incarceration and diminishes democratic accountability; it privatizes policymaking decisions and juvenile prisons and programs; it individualizes the solutions to delinquency at the expense of structural solutions; and it perpetuates and expands punitive policies in the juvenile justice system.

First, the three cases show that, counterintuitively, community-based reforms actually diminish democratic input. "Community-based" is a vacuous term whose outcomes depend on the social and political context in which they are enacted. The term is vague and used to conjure positive feelings about a diverse range of social relations and contexts that rarely match the ideal of what the concept elicits in our imagination. The ideal of "community" is elusive because there is "no primordial, nature-like community that exists unproblematically apart from the warp and woof of dynamic social relations" and that is "unaffected by surrounding state and market systems" (Reed 1999, 15). In practice, the membership and interests of a "community" are narrowly defined by those who have power within existing social dynamics. Therefore, the inclusion of "community control" in policy proposals is often a way to employ populist language to reproduce unequal social structures. The ability to participate in a local community is not meaningful if the community lacks resources and is mired by durable, inegalitarian structures (Immerwahr 2015).

In a highly stratified and unequal social context, devolution often exacerbates inequalities and patterns of abuse and punishment levied on the most vulnerable. Shifting control from the state to the county in the community-based reform movement reconfigures the justice system but does not substantially reduce its reach or improve accountability. In this new configuration, policymaking is left to lower levels of government, exacerbating inequalities in punishment, diminishing democratic input, and undermining oversight. The state-level case studies on the juvenile justice system show that, much like scholarship on other types of social policy, devolution often obscures the control and responsibility of governance and leads to inequitable outcomes (Hacker 2004; Kettl 2000; Lieberman 1998; Lowi 1998; Mettler 1998; Nathan and Gais 1999; O'Connor 2001; Pierson 1994; Soss, Fording, and Schram 2008).

Second, the embrace of the community-based reform movement in the juvenile justice system expands the role of the private sector in juvenile justice policy. Charitable foundations, specifically the MacArthur Foundation and the Annie E. Casey Foundation, have played a large role in forging a remarkable convergence in juvenile justice policy around community-based reforms across the United States. Advocates for reform are motivated by several goals, such as reducing gaping racial disparities in incarceration rates, ending abusive conditions of confinement, repealing the most punitive policies driven by the "superpredator" panic in the 1990s, as well as cutting public expenditures to the juvenile justice system. However, in the past two decades reform advocates and states across the country have converged around the community-based movement, implementing similar legislation to reduce the number of juveniles sent to state-run prisons and to bolster community-based alternatives. In the juvenile justice system today, foundations have a great influence on the policy agenda and local practices through their substantial seed money, well-funded resource centers, and effective state- and county-level partnership strategies. Foundations, alongside state advocacy organizations, have successfully fused conservative antistatism to criminal justice reform to achieve powerful bipartisan alliances supporting the community-based reform movement.

Subsequently, the types of programs and services promoted in community-based reforms are largely provided by the private sector and encourage public-private partnerships. The overall growth of privatization in the juvenile justice system reflects the ascendance of neoliberal governance, where the state increasingly subsidizes the private market. Further, private companies and organizations that operate in the juvenile justice system resist efforts to reduce the size and reach of the system. Private prisons and companies are driven by a profit motive that requires them to maintain or expand the number of people under correctional control and the programs to "serve" them. These growing interests, in addition to a policymaking environment that heavily privileges the voice of the private sector, make it difficult for legislation to pass that would significantly shrink the juvenile justice system.

Third, the community-based reform movement is rooted in a long history of post–New Deal policy development that has sought to solve social problems through interventions targeted at individual behavioral inadequacies. This focus on individual limitations as the root of all social ills is central to the "neoliberal" era (Brown 2003; Katz 1989; Lafer 2004; Larner 2000; Soss, Fording, and Schram 2011; Weaver 2012). Community-based programs such as life skills training, mentorship, intensive supervision probation, and drug treatment, in addition to largely being provided by the private sector, all focus on changing patterns of behaviors of individuals rather than changing the economic, political, and social forces that create the conditions within which individuals operate. Targeting individuals' behavior to solve the problems of the juvenile justice system, whether through rehabilitative or punitive policies, has occurred alongside the broader shift away from material redistributive economic policies.

Finally, the community-based reform movement has not ended the use of punitive policies that are disproportionately leveled at racial minority and working-class youth. Emphasizing individual treatment, cost-efficiency, and a notion of "redeemable versus unredeemable" offenders facilitates the preservation and even expansion of punitive policies. The community-based reform movement has influenced U.S. Supreme Court decisions limiting the use of the death penalty and life without the possibility of parole sentences for juvenile offenders.[7] However, even as the Court has handed down favorable rulings, it relies on rationales that reinforce individualized and biological understandings of crime that have long buttressed punitive policies and that displace much-needed and more effective structural solutions to crime and mass incarceration. Exempting certain populations of offenders from punitive policies like life without the possibility of parole sentences based on their perceived "redeemability" has not been an effective way to end these practices and other harmful alternatives. Community-based reforms have failed to improve the treatment of juveniles caught up in the system and are failing to mount a fundamental challenge to the use of punitive policies. Despite the widespread adoption of community-based reforms, large numbers of juveniles continue to be sent into the juvenile justice system and are often held in abusive conditions of confinement.

Successful decarceration will require rejecting the idea that fixing juveniles will fix the criminal justice system. The reform effort needs to be democratized by reversing the privatization of both the policymaking process and the institutions and programs of the juvenile justice system. Ultimately, in order to meaningfully alleviate the suffering inflicted on youth in the juvenile justice system, criminal justice reform will need to be part of a broader effort to reduce inequality and increase the provision of public goods for everyone.

The Political Economy of Criminal Justice Reforms

This book uses a historical institutionalist approach to study the political economy of criminal justice reforms. This analysis contributes to a wider scholarship on social policy and American political development.[8] The contextualization of reforms within broader social policy developments reveals the ways changes in juvenile justice policy relate to a number of other policy realms, such as education, healthcare, and welfare. A rich scholarship has shown that in these other spheres of policy the rise of neoliberalism and the retrenchment of the public sector have intensified inequality and ratcheted up punitive governance (Gottschalk 2000; Katz 1995; Lafer 2017; Moak 2022; Reed 2020; Soss, Fording, and Schram 2008; Wacquant, 2009). These developments outside of the criminal justice system have a profound impact on shaping the successes and failures of juvenile justice reforms—a relationship that is frequently overlooked in many evaluations of juvenile justice policies. This book reveals the relationship that prison reform policy choices have to broader shifts in American policymaking, particularly the key features of neoliberal governance: antistatism, privatization, and the individualization of social problems.

The extensive literature explaining carceral expansion often concludes with explorations of reform and decarceration (Alexander 2010; Bernstein 2015; Forman 2017; Pfaff 2017; Schoenfeld 2018). However, in recent years scholars are increasingly centering the politics of prison reform in their analysis (Aviram 2015; Dagan and Teles 2016; Eason 2017; Goodman, Page, and Phelps 2017; Gottschalk 2015; Schept 2015). The rise of mass incarceration and evaluating efforts to end mass incarceration are closely connected since understanding the origins of this social problem is critical to informing strategies to reverse these political developments and their devastating effects. This book joins this effort to explore the struggles to scale back mass incarceration by analyzing how the most popular strategies for reform in the juvenile justice system are playing out on the ground with state-level case studies. Developments like post-recession austerity politics, the bipartisan embrace of criminal justice reform, and the liberal faith in the benevolence of community institutions have all created opportunities and challenges for addressing mass incarceration (Aviram 2015; Pfaff 2017; Schept 2015; Schoenfeld 2018). The strength of the state-level case study approach is that it allows for the exploration of how these reforms are playing out in various political, historical, and economic contexts. As part of a growing scholarship that critically analyzes these developments, this book excavates the ways that reforms under these conditions have intentionally and unintentionally damaged the most vulnerable populations and fall short of mounting the significant challenge required to substantially curtail the carceral state.

In linking juvenile justice system developments to larger developments in American social policy, the book also contributes to a growing critical literature on philanthropy (Arena 2012; Callahan 2018; Giridharadas 2018; Kohl-Arenas 2015; Reich 2018). The policy changes traced in this book, ones in which large nongovernmental entities are influencing a common policy convergence across diverse states, parallel findings scholars have explored in other policy realms, such as education, labor, and economic policy (Fong and Naschek 2021; Lafer 2017; Reckhow 2012). Like these other studies, the case of juvenile justice reforms similarly shows that large nonprofits and charitable foundations are networking across state governments to put into place particular policies, incentives, and lessons that tend to be antistatist, emphasize "efficiencies," and advocate for public-private partnerships. This pattern of technocratic, private-sector solutions to a variety of social problems is failing to ameliorate racial and class inequalities and, in many instances, is exacerbating them. The dominance of these private-sector solutions to problems like high juvenile incarceration rates pushes out or directly undermines solutions that call on the state to provide for the common good by establishing universal social provisions. Overall, the analysis of state-level juvenile justice reform policy contributes to a better understanding of post–New Deal American political development as well as clarifies what is needed to truly improve the lives of youth caught up in the carceral state.

Why Juveniles?

Juvenile justice policy is important to study given the significant normative consequences it has for the rights of youth and the standard of care they receive. It is also a policy area that sheds light on the broader politics of criminal justice reform and American policymaking. The juvenile justice system has a particularly large number of political advocates and organizations working toward reform. The public has become open and receptive to changes in the treatment of juveniles, and there has been a sustained drop in juvenile crime for almost three decades now. The juvenile justice system is also characterized by greater policy innovation because of the smaller size of the system and a more cohesive elite consensus driving reforms. The current moment in juvenile justice policy is one of significant reform, where legislative changes are being pursued across nearly every state in the nation.

The realm of juvenile justice is critical for understanding penal policy and American politics generally (Cavadino and Dignan 2006, 301). From 2010 to 2020 there have been roughly 50,000 youth incarcerated in the United States (Sawyer 2019; Sickmund and Puzzanchera 2014). While this is a small percentage of the overall incarcerated U.S. population (less than 1%), the United States is an extreme outlier when compared to other national approaches to juvenile justice. For example, the number of juveniles incarcerated in Sweden and Japan is negligible: fewer than 20 each (Cavadino and Dignan 2006, 301; U.S. Department of Justice 2013). Further, the punitive policies applied to juveniles in the United States, such as life sentences, sex offender registries, and solitary confinement, are exceptional (Deitch et al. 2009; Gibson and Vandiver 2008).

The treatment of juveniles reflects and fits into the larger penal philosophy and approach different countries pursue in criminal justice systems (Bateman 2011; Cavadino and Dignan 2006). In addition to serving as a critical barometer of the punitiveness of the larger criminal justice system, juvenile justice reforms are also becoming models for policies now pursued in the adult system. The community-based reform movement explored in this book, most prevalent and first started in the juvenile justice system, is now sweeping the adult criminal justice system. For all of these reasons, understanding juvenile justice system developments offers important evidence to understanding the broader political landscape and its impact on the prospects for meaningful criminal justice reforms.

Comparative Case Studies: Texas, California, and Pennsylvania

This book compares the development of juvenile justice systems in Pennsylvania, California, and Texas from the 1960s through 2010s. The state-level case studies connect juvenile justice policies to broader social policy trends, particularly the consequences of devolution and privatization and the nature of policymaking in the United States. The three states represent geographic, partisan, institutional, demographic, and cultural diversity. In the past, these differences led to divergent policy outcomes, but now all three have converged on the community-based reform movement. Since the early 2000s all three states have been repeatedly held up as "models for the nation," and well over half the states in America have followed their lead (Burrell 2014; Butts and Evans 2011; Griffin 2008; *New York Times* 2011, 2012, 2015).

Pennsylvania, California, and Texas are key states to study in order to understand carceral policy development. These three are responsible for incarcerating about one-quarter of the entire prison and jail population and one-third of all juveniles in custody in the United States (Sentencing Project 2013). Focusing on these three states demonstrates the effects of reform in very different political, economic, and historical contexts. Despite their institutional, political, and cultural differences, all three states have converged around reforms producing similar limitations.

Pennsylvania is ground zero for the community-based reform movement. From the founding of its juvenile justice system to today, the state remains the most decentralized and privatized system in the nation. Its juvenile justice system remains more locally controlled compared to the large centralizing and modernizing efforts states like Texas and California went through in the 1950s. However, in Pennsylvania this institutional configuration did not prevent punitive policies from passing (with more juveniles serving life without parole sentences than in any other state or country in the world) or prevent large numbers of juveniles from being incarcerated. In 2004, Pennsylvania was the first state chosen for the MacArthur Foundation's Models for Change program because of its decentralized and privatized features. The foundation has since extended the community-based reform model into California and Texas as well as 13 other states. Pennsylvania is the birthplace of the community-based reform movement, and it demonstrates some of the longer-term consequences of devolution and privatization, particularly the problems with fractured oversight and profit incentives in incarceration.

California took a different path in building up its enormous juvenile justice system, pursuing a centralized model. Despite this different developmental path, the state has pursued similar community-based reforms in recent years. The state has some of the most progressive prisoner rights groups in the country, most of which largely embrace the community-based reform movement. California began devolving its juvenile justice system to community-based alternatives in the mid-1990s. In the early 2000s the state was the site of one of the first piloted, county-level initiatives of the Annie E. Casey Foundation that has now expanded to over 250 localities in more than 39 states. These policies have resulted in the entrenchment of punitive policies at the local level, where county facilities are also beset with abusive conditions of confinement. California moved toward community-based reforms well after Pennsylvania, yet much like Pennsylvania, the state's investment in community-based reforms did not reduce the number of juveniles it incarcerated. California has substantially expanded county-level institutional capacity over the past two decades and increased the role of the private sector in the juvenile justice system.

Texas is a contrast to the robust progressive criminal justice reform movement in California. Texas is home to the vibrant conservative prison reform movement, which has also embraced and promoted the community-based reform movement. The state exemplifies how the foundation-led community-based reform movement has connected conservative antistatist goals to juvenile justice reforms through powerful bipartisan alliances. These political forces contributed to the state legislature passing one of the most widespread and recent experiments in the community-based reform movement. Since passing major juvenile justice community-based reforms, Texas has closed several state-run prisons but has also expanded secure facility capacity, county probation and county detention, the number of privatized prisons, and the use of punitive policies such as solitary confinement. Despite accolades as a decarceration "model for the nation," the state is still "Texas tough" (Perkinson 2010).

National-level studies looking at the increasing use of incarceration in the United States since the 1970s have helped explain why the United States became the world leader in punishment, imprisoning more citizens than any other nation. However, as the summaries above indicate, there are significant differences regionally and culturally in the development of criminal justice policies and the use of imprisonment that these national-level studies are unable to capture (Barker 2009; Gottschalk 2011; Lynch 2010; Neill, Yusuf, and Morris 2014; Page 2011; Zimring and Hawkins 1991). The constellation of policies making up "penal transformations" is "deeply tied to locale and to history" (Lynch 2010, 216). This project joins an important shift in the research of prisons from the grand narratives of the American punitive turn to specific geographically located descriptions of how particular punitive policies develop across the United States (Barker 2009; Forman 2017; Gilmore 2007; Lowi 1998; Lynch 2010; Page 2011; Perkinson 2010; Pfaff 2017; Scheingold 1991; Schept 2015).

State-level case studies are particularly useful for analyzing the process of devolution that characterizes the community-based reform movement in the United States today. The case studies trace the on-the-ground consequences of what happens to youth in these devolved systems, where youth navigate a complicated set of local policies and institutions, that are not captured in national surveys. The state-level case studies are also able to capture the relationship between national actors, like MacArthur and Annie E. Casey, and state-level advocacy organizations and politicians. The three states show how community-based reforms are adaptive to and compatible with both liberal and conservative political contexts. Given the current juvenile justice landscape, a grounded comparative case study approach offers a particularly useful means of discovering why different states have converged on pursuing community-based reforms and the impact these policies have on youth.

Overview of Book

The three state-level case studies provide an on-the-ground account of the consequences of devolution, privatization, the individualization of social problems, and the continued punitiveness of the community-based reform movement. The development of juvenile justice policy over time in Texas, California, and Pennsylvania suggests that there is a remarkable convergence across diverse states in juvenile reform today. The embrace of the community-based reform movement in the juvenile justice system is not significantly improving the treatment of juveniles but is further entrenching the punitiveness of the criminal justice system at the local level. The developments and limitations of the community-based reform movement are closely tied to major shifts in post–New Deal American policymaking.

Chapter 1 begins by laying out the relationship between juvenile justice policy and broader social policy. The overview of several major themes of post–New Deal policy developments—devolution, privatization, individualization of social problems, and punitiveness—provides the important context for understanding the effects of the community-based reform movement today. Each of these shifts in social policy marks a substantial departure from the idea of government for the public good. Leveraging this historical institutionalist approach helps to explain why the community-based reform movement mirrors these key themes, and it also helps illuminate why the reforms are largely failing to improve the experiences of youth caught up in the justice system.

Pursuing devolution, privatization, and individual solutions within the context of decades of austerity politics and the retrenchment of public goods makes today's community-based reform movement particularly inadequate and ineffective. Previous forays into community-based reforms in the 1960s, detailed in Chapter 1, largely failed to solve social problems like poverty, unemployment, delinquency, and racial inequalities. Today, this same strategy is being reemployed in a context even less conducive to solutions that rely on individual uplift and community-based responses.

This chapter provides the background for understanding why large charitable foundations have such a privileged position in American policymaking today and offers insight into why the politics of juvenile justice reform is dominated by technocratic solutions that sidestep considerations of political economy. The remainder of the book traces the key features of the community-based reform movement in three model reform states: Pennsylvania, California, and Texas. Each chapter delves into the major components of the community-based reform movement, providing evidence from the three case studies, and examines the limitations of this approach to addressing juvenile delinquency and juvenile incarceration.

Chapter 2 shows in detail what community-based reforms look like in practice and argues that these reforms lead to devolution, not decarceration. Shifting youth from large state-run facilitates to the "community" is entrenching punishment at the local level. The political and economic contexts of devolution play a critical role in shaping the outcomes of a turn to the "community." In all three states, the strategy of devolving control to the local level has occurred in the context of fiscal austerity, whereby public institutions and services have been substantially cut back and hollowed out. Thus, when policy reformers shift responsibility for handling youth offenders to local governments, they are doing so as these governments are struggling with a significant lack of resources to provide for youth. The community-based reform movement is not merely occurring in this context but is actively buttressing fiscal austerity politics since "cutting costs" and "improving efficiencies" has largely justified these reforms.

By tracing grant funds and the local-level policy changes that occur when community-based reforms are implemented, it becomes clear that reform efforts and funding get funneled into traditional punitive responses to youth offending such as more incarceration and probation. Looking at where and under what conditions youth are handled at the local level also reveals that the very same problems that occur in large state-run facilities are replicated at "community" facilities, but with even less oversight. The community-based reform movement relies on an imagined ideal of community support for youth that does not occur in reality. These reform policies are part of an austerity politics that provides little room for proposals to expand public goods and address economic inequalities and therefore perpetuates the same punitive and damaging policies that have long plagued the juvenile justice system.

Because the devolution approach has been part of a broader austerity politics and does not seek to bolster public institutions, it has been closely tied to increased privatization—a major pitfall of the community-based reform movement. Chapter 3 shows how the community-based reform movement contributes to increased privatization in the juvenile justice system. There are three main areas of private-sector growth in the juvenile justice system that are occurring as part of the community-based reform movement. The first is the privatization of the policymaking process. The MacArthur Foundation and the Annie E. Casey Foundation are central leaders in juvenile justice policy today, controlling research, grants, and policy proposals that have coalesced around technocratic, pro-privatization approaches to reform under the mantle of the community-based reform movement. These foundations are not beholden to democratic input. Therefore, this shift in unaccountable policymaking results in outcomes that are inequitable and create substantial obstacles to meaningful reform. This chapter details the ways in which leading foundations have worked alongside other national and state advocacy organizations to achieve bipartisan support for the community-based reform movement with little input from those most affected by these policies.

In addition to the privatization of the policymaking process there have been substantial increases in the privatization of both the "hard end" (secure detention) and the "soft end" (programs and services) of the juvenile justice system as a consequence of the community-based reform movement. In large part, these two forms of privatization are occurring because private actors like foundations and state and national advocacy organizations are actively calling for the greater involvement of private-sector service providers. Additionally, the process of devolution, in the context of austerity, creates incentives and pressures to contract out aspects of the carceral state to the private sector. Both for-profit companies as well as nonprofit service providers are involved in the privatization of the "hard" and "soft" ends of the justice system. The reach of this complicated web of nonprofit and for-profit organizations is growing within the system thanks to community-based reforms, with little accountability or transparency. Privatization is introducing more juvenile justice stakeholders with interests that often run contrary to downsizing the reach of the carceral state or investing in public institutions and oversight necessary to ensure more equitable and safer outcomes for youth. The community-based reform movement not only falls short of what is necessary to significantly change the system for the better, but it is also establishing policies and a governance structure that will make decarceration in the long run more difficult.

Privatization also divorces the juvenile justice system from considerations of political economy. Private actors like large foundations and major advocacy organizations have long supported research on solutions to social problems that emphasize individual behavioral deficiencies at the expense of systemic critique and large-scale public spending. The individualization of social problems ranging from poverty to unemployment, delinquency, and racial inequality has been both the cause and the product of a political landscape dominated by the interests of powerful elites and the waning power of a left-labor political coalition in the United States. Charitable foundations have long attributed delinquency to individual behavioral deficiencies at the expense of connecting the injustices of the juvenile system to economic and social inequalities. The attention of foundations and nonprofit and for-profit service providers is primarily targeted at changing youth behavior, not structural inequalities. Chapter 4 details how the focus on fixing the individual in order to fix the system animates the community-based reform movement with negative consequences for youth in Texas, California, and Pennsylvania.

The chapter begins with an overview of the way that juvenile justice policy has long operated within a paradigm of individual behavioral approaches to antidelinquency. Both punitive and treatment-based solutions to delinquency are rooted in a belief that the behavior of youth can and should be changed in order to prevent delinquency and reduce youth incarceration rates. This paradigm has failed in many previous iterations to curtail carceral growth. The foundation-led community-based reform movement does not depart from this long-established individualistic paradigm, creating a number of negative consequences. Youth continue to be stigmatized and positioned as the problem in need of solving, while the highly unequal social context they inhabit continues to be naturalized. Despite being pitched as an alternative and solution to high incarceration rates and abusive conditions of confinement, the treatment-oriented individual behavioral interventions at the core of the community-based reform movement are fundamentally compatible with and supportive of punitive approaches to delinquency. The illusion that community-based reforms are better at sorting "high-" and "low-"risk youth in order to target the youth that really need punishment is buttressing the continued and, in many instances, accelerated use of some of the most punitive and harmful policies within the juvenile justice system.

The final substantive chapter demonstrates how the continued portrayal of *some* youth offenders as unredeemable in the community-based reform movement has preserved and in some instances required the expansion of punitive policies. Chapter 5 details the ways in which punitive policies persist in a devolved, privatized, and individually focused juvenile justice system. Since the community-based reform movement is largely targeted at exempting particular youth from punitive policies rather than fully repudiating them, the reforms have largely reinforced the use of policies like juvenile life without parole sentences, long sentences, draconian sex offender laws, gang sentencing enhancements, and the harsh conditions of juvenile prisons. There continues to be bipartisan support for punitive approaches to "serious" offenders occurring alongside the support for the community-based reform movement. The idea that an investment in individual behavioral solutions to delinquency will prevent youth from becoming involved in the system and ending up subjected to punitive policies often serves to legitimize rather than challenge these very policies. As happened many times in the past, trying to address the damaging repercussions of punitive policies through prevention fails because it misidentifies the cause of these consequences—the punitive policies themselves. In the context and often in conjunction with the establishment of community-based reforms, all three states have continued to levy some of the most punitive policies in the world on youth caught up in the juvenile justice system.

The book closes by highlighting the key conclusions drawn from the three case studies and describes the larger contributions the findings have for understanding policymaking, political development, and criminal justice reforms. The state-level case studies demonstrate that policy decisions are highly contingent on local interests affecting the timing, context, and manner in which states adopt community-based reforms. However, the similarities between the cases also reflect the national convergence around the community-based reform movement, which increases investments in local institutions of punishment and control over juveniles.

The embrace of the community-based reform movement devoid of substantial ideological, political, and institutional change does not in and of itself correct the problems in the juvenile justice system because it fails to address the underlying philosophy of youth punishment and how it fits within the broader sociopolitical economic system in the United States. Much like the literature on the welfare state and the rise of neoliberalism, the case of juvenile justice development reflects a broad trend in American governance whereby control over public services is increasingly devolved to local authorities and contracted out to private companies and organizations. Similar to other social policy areas, such as education, healthcare, and welfare, the ideological justification and basis for the juvenile justice system have remained stubbornly focused on correcting the individual failings of juveniles. Structural interventions continue to be sidelined and ignored in discussions over how to handle juvenile offenders and reduce the number of youth in prison. Meaningful reform requires rejecting the longstanding belief that juvenile delinquency can be solved through individualized behavioral interventions and will need to reverse the privatization of both the policymaking process and the institutions of the juvenile justice system.

Ultimately, the continued punitive policies and negative repercussions of the community-based reform movement in the juvenile justice system are a product of the broader shifts in American social policy that have undermined the provision of universal public goods. The community-based reform movement reinforces the harmful idea that government cannot improve people's lives and therefore supports alternatives like the private sector and the "community" as substitutes to robust public spending. The antistatist, pro-privatization, individual uplift approach to social policy is a key contributor to the development of punitive policies, exemplified in the juvenile justice system, that control and repress those crushed by the neoliberal political and economic landscape. Thus, turning to these same forces in an attempt to "reform" the juvenile justice system and address its harmful effects is woefully inadequate and largely counterproductive. When the juvenile justice system is appropriately contextualized within broader shifts in patterns of American governance, it becomes clear that solutions will have to address the broader politics that contribute to and exacerbate the problems youth face—specifically the retrenchment of public goods and the antidemocratic role of the private sector.

1

Abandoning Public Goods

The Turn to Community in the Context of Inequality

There are four major features of the community-based reform movement today: the devolution of control from the state to county level, the privatization of the policymaking and policies of the juvenile justice system, the increased investment and belief in individualized behavioral interventions for youth, and the persistent use of harsh punitive policies to address delinquency. The turn to devolution, the private sector, the individual, and punishment all map onto major developments in American policymaking after the New Deal. A brief summary of these historical developments is important for establishing a wider understanding of the juvenile justice reform landscape today. Using a historical institutionalist approach entails incorporating the ways that "political developments always take place in prestructured environments" that are "composed of intersecting contexts generating and shaping political life" (Smith 2014, 129). Institutional and ideological developments in social welfare policy have been closely related to those in juvenile justice policy and help explain why the current reform terrain looks the way it does. This book examines how the policy changes in the criminal justice system fit into broader developments in American politics. Putting the reform policies into this wider historical and political context illustrates why the reforms continue to fail to improve the experience of the vast majority of youth and are reshaping the juvenile justice system in ways that make substantial decarceration *more* difficult.

The following overview of major changes in American social policy suggests that the resurgent popularity of community-based policies is not new and, in many ways, is a long-running product of the shift away from a conception of government for the public good. Each development—devolution to the community, privatization, the individualization of social problems, and punitiveness—is connected to the attacks on universally provided public goods and the ascendant role of the private sector in American governing structures.

While similar juvenile justice reform policies have been pursued many times before, the reforms today are occurring in a distinct political and economic context. Decades of conservative governance, the erosion of the public sector, and major shifts in the economy since the height of the New Deal all condition the specific social relationships and economic and political contexts under which policymakers attempt to reform the juvenile justice system today.

The Shift to Devolution

Community-based reforms in juvenile justice policy today are ubiquitous. There is a consensus that getting youth "closer to home" and reducing reliance on large state-run prisons should be a central goal of juvenile justice reforms. Policymakers and advocates from both the left and the right have embraced the promise of the "community," which is assumed to be more benevolent and democratic and is often counterposed to the punitive excesses of the American carceral state. The focus and popularity of "community-based" control is not new to juvenile justice policy development or American policymaking more generally. This section explores the assumptions about "community" and its associated politics. The embrace of the "community" is frequently coupled with a devolution politics that is antistatist and endorses an individualistic, "bootstraps" approach to solving social problems. The long history of the popularity of a community-based, devolved policy configuration in a number of other policy realms has contributed to the hollowing out of universal public goods, which has increased privatization and punitive policies. The rollback of alternatives to the carceral state means that when juvenile justice reformers support policies that embrace "the community" as the solution to the problems of the criminal justice system in the current moment, the outcome is ever greater privatization and punishment.

Capitalism, Civil Rights, and Community

At the height of the New Deal, Democrats framed the social problems of inequality, unemployment, and crime as the result of failures in the economic system. According to this problem identification, New Dealers believed the government needed to deal with the flaws of the economic structure, such as concentrated economic power (Brinkley 1996, 5; Cowie 2016; Katznelson 1989).[1] While there were a number of competing policy visions and ideals within the broad New Deal coalition, there was a general consensus that the government had a responsibility to correct the structural flaws of capitalism. The New Deal was an exceptional period of political development in which many landmark policies were enacted in the interest of the nonelite and organized around the concept of collective economic security (Cowie 2016, 9). However, in subsequent decades these core ideals were greatly contested and weakened over time, and faith in centralized governmental power to address a variety of social ills receded from dominance (Katznelson 1989).

The ascendant position of the capitalist class in the United States during and after World War II facilitated an unprecedented attack on the New Deal coalition—including a vibrant labor movement—and the welfare state. McCarthyism and the related assault on labor organizing influenced the rightward shift of the Democratic Party and liberal and left political organizations (Lichtenstein 1989; Moak 2022; Reed 2020, 43). Wartime politics both rehabilitated the corporate world and dampened left hostilities to capitalism. The defeat of the 1945 Full Employment Bill and the Wagner-Murray-Dingell Bill (national health insurance) and the passage of the Taft-Hartley Act in 1947 exemplified the U.S. capitalist class's effort to roll back the advances of the labor left. Not only did opposition to New Deal policies greatly strengthen, but many liberals began to move away from support for downward redistributive policies requiring direct intervention in the economy and toward supporting fiscal policy to stabilize and grow the economy (Brinkley 1996, 7; Katznelson 1989; Reed 2020, 146). Coming out of World War II, Democrats were increasingly divided between those committed to material redistributive policies and those advocating for community-based behavioral policies to address issues like inequality, unemployment, and crime. As many scholars have argued, the ultimate ascendance of the community-based behavioral approach that emerged in the mid-20th century subsequently stymied progressive developments in the ensuing decades as well as facilitated a punitive turn in American policy (Bertram 2015; Chen 2009; Flamm 2005; Gottschalk 2000; Hinton 2016; Katznelson 1989; Moak 2022; Morgan and Campbell 2011; Murakawa 2014; Soss, Fording, and Schram 2011; Weaver 2007).

In the 1960s liberals began to turn away from the New Deal style of top-down federalism and began promoting community development projects to address poverty, joblessness, and racial inequality.[2] Federal grants to local governments were intended to support community partnerships with neighborhood groups, which were seen as being more responsive to the poor (Kerstein and Judd 1980; Kettl 2000, 493). Critics complained that large centralized programs neglected the sensitivities of local needs and ways of life (Chowkwanyun 2015; Morris 2004).[3] Liberals of this era hoped to democratize the provision of social services by returning power to the community. The turn to community-based policies and pursuing devolution in American policymaking accommodated a fear of centralized state power coming from a variety of sources (Brinkley 1996, 174).

Actors from both the left and the right increasingly embraced "community-based" policy solutions as a reaction to the perceived limitations of large centralized social programs—even if they disagreed on what they considered these limitations to be.

The shifting support for devolution and community-based programs had a profound impact on reshaping American governing structures. Heavily influenced by philanthropic giants like the Ford Foundation, community-based programs during the Great Society overturned existing local government structures and processes (Roelofs 2007). Initiatives like the Ford Foundation's Gray Areas experiments, a model for subsequent War on Poverty policies, created community development corporations (CDCs) where for-profit entities were enlisted to uplift depressed areas of the nation (Kohler 2007). The use of CDCs blurred the distinction between the public and private sectors by creating shadow governing structures to the existing local governments and introduced for-profit and nonprofit sectors into local governing structures (Kohler 2007).

The Rise of the Right

Social policy devolution in a number of policy realms, partially in the form of community-based programs and policies, that began in the 1960s ultimately contributed to a rightward shift against the social democratic policies of the New Deal coalition (Lowi 1998).[4] The promotion of public-private solutions like CDCs weakened faith in government, a trend that intensified over the course of the following decades. In the 1970s a unified and well-organized business lobby went on the offensive to further unravel the New Deal expansion of public goods (Akard 1992; Lichtenstein 1989; Stein 2011). The divide among Democrats between the antigovernment strain from the New Left and the social democratic commitments from unions deepened, with the former gaining an ascendant position in American politics (Stein 2011, 250).

There was a similar divide within the civil rights coalition. Those advocating for more individualized solutions to racial inequality in the form of incorporation within the existing economic order achieved dominance, while those advocating for challenges to economic exploitation requiring robust public spending were on the retreat (Moak 2022; Smith 2012). There were still a number of Democratic actors who advocated for national economic planning, for regulations to challenge concentrated economic power, and for the expansion of public goods like national healthcare; however, by the end of the 1970s both parties had shifted toward support for tax cuts and the deregulation of industry (Akard 1992; Stein 2011).[5] The emboldened business lobby and strengthened right wing of the Republican Party directed their efforts at further retrenching the welfare state

(Hacker 2002, 2004; Pierson 1994; Pierson and Skocpol 2007). The conservative ascendancy of the era ushered in a wave of punitive policies in conjunction with the dismantling of the social welfare state.[6]

In the 1980s, the Reagan coalition consolidated a conservative attack on the welfare state that led to its further privatization, retrenchment, and reorientation—a process often labeled "neoliberalism" by scholars (Hacker 2004; Pierson 1994). A defining feature of the neoliberal order was the class character of the sweeping cuts to state budgets that placed heavy burdens on labor (Cahill 2014, 142). The Reagan administration pursued tax cuts (especially for the rich), deregulation (especially for financial markets), cuts to social spending, and the destruction of unions (Leopold 2015).

President Bill Clinton continued the neoliberal push against the social welfare state by declaring "the era of big government is over" and passing welfare reform in the 1990s (Cowie 2016, 205). The Personal Responsibility and Work Opportunity Act signed into law by Clinton had no jobs component, and the decentralized framework it established allowed states and counties to impose restrictive conditions on welfare qualifications, substantially shrinking the number of people receiving assistance and exacerbating inequalities (Wacquant 2009, 89). The bipartisan welfare reform effort devolved administrative authority over welfare from the federal to state and local governments and allowed states to use funds to contract with for-profit service providers (Katz 2002; Lieberman 1998; Mettler 1998; Soss, Fording, and Schram 2008). Devolution was a pivotal tool in retrenching social services and "neoliberals advocated for the devolution of as many state functions as possible" (Cahill 2014, 1).

The Concept of "Community" and Its Consequences

Juvenile justice system devolution is similar to welfare retrenchment in its reliance on the powerful symbol of "community." The word "community" brings to mind "warm fuzzy, romanticized images of people knowing, helping and caring for one another" (Crawford 1999; Lyons 1999; Muniz 2015, 118). But policy enacted under the mantle of "community-based" often falls short of these ideals since there is no "community" that exists outside of a deeply stratified social context. Despite "warm fuzzy" feelings otherwise, the interests and the defined membership of "community" are determined by members of society with the greatest amount of power, and therefore can often serve to reproduce existing inequalities. Yet, it remains a powerful discursive tool in policy debates, embraced by policymakers across the political spectrum.

Political actors from the right continue to hold up the value of the "community" as a general antistatist alternative to the state's providing public goods for citizens. Steven Smith and Michael Lipsky (1993, 215) find that, "in fiscal crises, conservatives have been able to use their command of the symbol of community as a weapon to curtail the welfare state, with disastrous results for vulnerable groups." Meanwhile, those on the left often position the "community" as an unequivocal good and as comprising a ready and able democratic body that should be empowered so that it can best provide for its members rather than being policed and punished by state authorities (Armstrong 2002; Scull 1984). The common thread between both right and left promotions of "community" has been a critique of centralized, universal programs as the best route to assure equality for everyone.

The embrace of community as an alternative represents a major shift from the policy proposals that emanated from the labor militancy that buttressed the New Deal coalition at its height in the 1930s. Two powerful political strains, the emergence of the New Left in the 1960s and Reaganism in the 1980s, converged on their promotion of "community-based" initiatives in the post–New Deal decades, with both favoring voluntarism to government action (Reed 1999, 124).[7] In the 1990s, the moral uplift and community initiatives promoted by the Democratic Leadership Council as solutions to inequality and its effects gave public-sector retrenchment "a stamp of liberal, race conscious" legitimacy (Reed 1999, 124).

As a number of scholars have argued, the promotion of devolution in the form of calls for greater state and local control, often described as "community control," has been a powerful tool used to undermine universal programs, particularly those most beneficial to low-income people (Miller 2016, 136; Parker and Barreto 2014). The provision of social programs at the state and local level, as opposed to the uniform national administration of social policies, creates a vast discrepancy in which those subjected to the former face invasive regulations and an "inferior form of citizenship" (Mettler 1998, 21). Scholars have shown that the strong national structure and universality of policies like Social Security have strengthened support for this form of social welfare provision. In contrast, heavily decentralized social welfare policies tend to be much less generous and are comparatively politically weak (Lieberman 1998). Ultimately, devolution has significant limitations because individual communities lack the power to address forces like capital flight and deindustrialization and mount the resources necessary to ameliorate economic inequalities (Katz 1995, 6). Arguments for "local control" have been used to undermine the equitable implementation of a number of policies, ranging from racial integration to unemployment assistance and healthcare (Katz 1995, 6; Miller 2016). Despite the well-documented role devolution has played in undermining universalistic policies, the notion of "community" has remained powerful, animating policy prescriptions from political actors and organizations on the left and the right.

The "community-based" model of 1960s antipoverty legislation did not live up to its democratic ideals because community groups and leadership were easily co-opted by elites and the programs did not address deeper economic and social inequalities (Chowkwanyun 2015; Kerstein and Judd 1980; Morris 2004). For example, community action programs (CAPs) established through the War on Poverty enabled Black constituencies to gain control of government in a number of cities. However, as Cedric Johnson (2017) and Adolph Reed Jr. (1999) have both trenchantly shown, this process displaced working-class politics and installed "race leaders" who did not have meaningful democratic constituencies. Rather than increasing democratic participation, the boards operating the CDCs were rarely elected, were comprised of appointed "stakeholders," and were chosen and filled by elites (Fong and Naschek 2021; Reed 1999). There are examples of self-empowerment coming to fruition thanks to CAPs such as the Black Panthers' establishment of free medical clinics to combat racial discrimination in healthcare (Nelson 2013). However, the strategy of self-sufficiency for medical care, which was always limited, was not a strong enough match to combat the forces of a marketized healthcare system that continued to underserve the poor and racial minorities. Contrary to some of its goals, the Black Power movement ultimately evolved into an "elite-driven ethnic politics," despite its association with self-determination (Johnson 2017). As Johnson argues, "black power militancy and the managerial logic of the Great Society were symbiotic." The "participatory democracy" advocated by the New Left in the form of decentralized communities ultimately remained a utopian dream, not a reality (Isserman and Kazin 1989).

Scholars have identified a similar process of elite co-optation and inequitable outcomes in devolved "community-based" carceral policy. Ana Muñiz (2015) finds in her study of gang-injunction policies in Los Angeles from the 1980s that not all voices were equal in community policy decisions. Organized business owners and homeowners' associations wielded extraordinary power in shaping urban policy decisions regarding crime and development (13). The majority of working-class Blacks and Latinos did not have the resources to be represented in "community partnerships," which were reserved for those with the power and privileges that allowed them to declare themselves community spokespeople (199). In his study of rural prison siting, John Eason (2017, 74) similarly finds that mayors and chambers of commerce were the most powerful actors that spoke for the interests of their communities. In a grounded case study of a jail expansion project in Illinois, Judah Schept (2015) finds that the false assumption that "community-based" policies will be nonpunitive and racially egalitarian can actually legitimize calls for carceral expansion. James Forman Jr. (2017) and Michael Fortner (2015, 29, 52) both show that community groups are not necessarily antipunitive and that in fact grassroots groups representing racial minorities throughout the 1970s and 1990s actively called for punitive responses to drug dealing and violence in urban inner cities like Washington, D.C., and New York City.[8]

Ironically, the promotion of the "community" often serves to weaken the very governmental programs and interventions that would create conditions of equality and empowerment (Chowkwanyun 2015; Kerstein and Judd 1980; Reed 2000). "Community control" is a vacuous concept and has vastly different outcomes depending on the social context and racial hierarchies in which it exists. In the case of juvenile justice policy, the current re-infatuation with "community-based" solutions comes at a time in which inequality has deepened and the economic position of local governments, thanks to deep and lasting cuts to public services, is exceptionally weak and unequal. Because of this particular context, turning to communities continues a trend of social policy privatization that mires localities in economic distress while also shifting responsibility to local governments at the exact time they are least equipped to take on greater responsibilities to care for their residents. In the context of austerity, far from the ideal of creating more equitable, democratic governance structures and providing a bulwark against invasive, punitive state power, turning to the community promotes an antistatist individual responsibility model of governance that is incapable of ameliorating social and economic inequalities or of dismantling mass incarceration.

The Rise of Privatization

In addition to devolution, another major feature of the community-based reform movement is increased privatization. There are three main types of privatization occurring as part of community-based reforms: privatization of the policymaking process and the "hard end" (residential services) and "soft end" (programs and services) of the juvenile justice system. Within these three avenues of privatization, both nonprofit and for-profit entities comprise a complex web of nonpublic actors in shaping and carrying out policy. The private sector plays an outsized role in influencing the convergence around community-based reforms and the individual behavioral focus in the juvenile justice system. In this policy realm, innovations in policy, standards of success, and seed money come from large foundations, giving them enormous power to set the policy agenda and shape local practices. In part because of the provisions in the reforms encouraging private contracts, but also due to the incentives and pressures of devolution, the institutions, programs, and services of the juvenile justice system are increasingly being turned over to the private sector.

All of these major forms of privatization are emblematic of larger shifts in American governance since the New Deal. The power of large foundations and private advocacy organizations has substantially strengthened, with profound impacts on who controls policymaking in the United States (Ferguson 1989). In conjunction with the growth of the private sector in American policymaking, institutions, services, and governing structures have also been increasingly contracted to the private sector through private-public partnerships and the marketization of public goods. The promotion of private solutions to complex social problems, like delinquency and youth incarceration rates, is not unique to this policy realm but a broad feature of shifts in social welfare policy. Further, these broader developments, such as the establishment of a robust nonprofit sector and the expansive commodification of public goods, significantly shape the ways that juvenile justice reform policies play out in the current political landscape. The widespread reductions in public spending incentivize and lead to privatization.

The Growth of the Nonprofit Sector and Foundations

The production of a robust nonprofit sector followed a development timeline similar to that of the devolution of social services as part of the turn to "community-based" policies (Faber and McCarthy 2005). A vastly expanded nonprofit sector has largely supplanted the once more powerful political force of unions, political parties, and other mass membership organizations representing working-class people (Edsall 1989; Fong and Naschek 2021). Policy shifts in the mid-1960s, particularly the Economic Opportunity Act of 1965 and amendments to the Social Security Act in 1967, channeled a significant amount of money to nongovernmental organizations (Hammack 1998; Morris 2004, 275; Smith and Lipsky 1993). These key policy developments from the Great Society fundamentally reordered the social service sector by eroding the distinction between public and private social provision and massively expanding the amount of federal money going to private nonprofits (Bertram 2015; Eliasoph 2013; Hammack 1998; Morris 2004, 299–300). The increased role and number of nonprofits operating in the United States is now a major feature of U.S. governance. Since its expansion in the 1960s, a majority share of the goods and services provided to the poor by the American state has been distributed through nonprofit agencies and commercial outfits (Katz 1995, 26). In the decades following the 1960s, privatization accelerated through the bipartisan neoliberal consensus that fueled welfare reform and the expansion of America's carceral system. Welfare reform expanded the marketization of social services, with nearly every state outsourcing Temporary Aid to Needy Families obligations to the private sector (Wacquant 2009, 105).

The number of nonprofits in the United States has grown exponentially in the past four decades. Over this time, these organizations have increased their assets by 1,000% (Faber and McCarthy 2005). Just between 1998 and 2008, the number of nonprofits registered with the IRS increased by 30% (Arena 2012, xxvii). Part of the growth can be explained by a shift in governance, where governments or foundations contract with nonprofits to provide services that were previously delivered by the state (Arena 2012). This development has blurred the line between private and public entities since more than 50% of nonprofits rely on government funding (Kwon 2013; Smith and Lipsky 1993).

Large foundations are also part of this growth in philanthropic activity, working side by side with smaller nonprofits and encouraging their expansion through grant funding and by promoting public-private partnerships. The rise in assets for foundations has coincided with the growing wealth disparity in the United States and the world (Dowie 2001). Shifting tax policy going back as far as the late 1960s has channeled money into tax-sheltered funds that go toward nonprofits and large foundations (Kwon 2013). For example, about half of the assets that foundations hold would be government money through taxation without the protection of trusts (Dowie 2001). There are also more financial vehicles today for the wealthy to exert influence, such as donor-advised funds (DAFs) and limited liability corporations (LLCs) (Fleishman 2007; Greenblatt 2019).[9]

As a number of scholars have shown, wealthy donors have increasingly gained the power and assets to influence common policy convergences across diverse states (Reckhow 2012; Roelofs 2003; Skocpol 2016). Structural changes such as eliminating limits on campaign contributions, the exponential growth of the assets held by large foundations and corporations, and the erosion of funding and support for public institutions and research have contributed to an increasingly privatized policymaking environment in the United States (Edsall 1989; Lafer 2017; Levine 2016; Roelofs 2007). These larger developments in American politics help to explain how nongovernmental organizations have become leaders in policymaking and are now major service providers in a number of policy arenas as well.

The Rise of the For-Profit Private Sector

In addition to the expansion of nonprofits and charitable foundations, there has also been substantial privatization in the form of expanded markets for for-profit companies. It is often difficult to distinguish between nonprofit and for-profit entities since they tend to operate with a similar market logic and they both rely on public subsidies. However, the rise of the for-profit sector in what had been government-provided services and institutions is a distinct and significant shift in American political development. The commodification of basic social provisions is a hallmark of neoliberal governance. In a number of policy realms, such as housing, healthcare, and education, the effects of post–New Deal social arrangements, particularly the move away from universal social provisions to a more particularized and decentralized welfare state, have led to privatization (Edsall 1989, 272).

John Arena (2012) provides an instructive example of the relationship between a nonprofit-dominated policymaking landscape and the expansion of for-profit service delivery in the realm of housing policy. Using the case of post-Katrina New Orleans, his analysis demonstrates how the nonprofit model that overtook public housing advocacy placed for-profit real estate interests above the interests of Black public housing residents. This critical examination of the workings of urban neoliberal policy shows how greater nonprofit capture increases the marketization of public goods. Since the 1970s federal public housing has experienced cutbacks and privatization alongside the "devolution of both authority and funds from the federal government to local authorities" (Arena 2012, 89). From an original stock of about 2.4 million housing units, between the mid-1990s and 2010 the federal government and local housing authorities eliminated roughly 200,000 public housing apartments (Arena 2012). The passage of HOPE VI during the Clinton administration in the 1990s was a critical tool in dismantling public housing, and it also encouraged privatization through promoting "public-private" partnerships.

Healthcare policy today is also heavily privatized, providing huge profits for privileged health industries and excluding majorities of Americans from access to affordable healthcare. The post–World War II development of a private welfare state was critical in pushing healthcare policy to a job-based system of delivery instead of universal healthcare (Gottschalk 2000; Katz 1995, 48). The signature blow to workers in the post–World War II era, the passage of Taft-Hartley in 1947, created major legal and administrative challenges to labor that encouraged investing their efforts into securing decentralized collective bargaining agreements and curtailed attempts to establish universal policies (Gottschalk 2000; Lichtenstein 1989; Navarro 2010). The Taft-Hartley Act helped cement many unions' commitment to fighting for private-sector benefits as opposed to demands for structural changes in the political economy (Gottschalk 2000, 44; Lichtenstein 1989).[10] By 1982, only about 33% of health services were delivered by the government; 44% were delivered by nonprofits and 23% by for-profits (Fong and Naschek 2021, 107). Developments in both housing and healthcare policy from post–World War II politics and the neoliberal consolidations of the 1980s and 1990s reflect the ascendant position of the private sector in American politics and its advocacy for the greater marketization of essential public goods.

Similarly, there has been substantial privatization in education policy, which Daniel Moak (2022) argues is rooted in the political developments and context of the establishment of the federal education state in the 1960s. The landmark Elementary and Secondary Education Act (ESEA), passed in 1965, included provisions that reflected the broader political shifts of this era away from robust universalistic policies to more particularized, means-tested policies centered on individual solutions to social problems. This political orientation that Moak shows was integrated into the ESEA and subsequent amendments set education policy on a trajectory that would result in greater privatization. Educational institutions and policies were increasingly positioned as the answer to problems of unemployment, poverty, racial inequality, and delinquency, with the decline of support for interventionist economic policies that would address structural inequalities at the root of these problems. When education policy, which 1960s liberals had put so much faith in, failed to solve these social problems, public education experienced a bipartisan attack that has contributed to privatization measures like the rise of school choice and the charter school movement (Moak 2022; Ravitch 2014; Reckhow 2012).

Like the community-based reform movement analyzed in this book, the education policy sphere has experienced the outsized influence of large foundations (particularly the Bill and Melinda Gates Foundation and the Walton Foundation) that have invested hundreds of millions of dollars in education reform that largely supports privatization measures (Reckhow 2012).[11] Additionally, public education is being aggressively marketized thanks to the power and interests of big business alongside these major foundations (*Moyers & Company* 2014). As Gordon Lafer (2017) shows, the nation's biggest corporate lobbies have successfully transformed education across all 50 state legislatures in their vision of the "corporate education agenda."[12]

The growing role of the for-profit sector in American social policy is closely tied to the broader privatization of policymaking and the rise of such nonstate actors as foundations, nonprofits, and corporations in shaping policy decisions. All of these features of privatization flow from major shifts in political power that occurred thanks to postwar politics that revitalized the capitalist class and seriously weakened the left-liberal coalition at the heart of New Deal politics.

Consequences of Privatization

Scholars have shown that the rising power of private foundations has a "corrosive influence on democratic society" because these foundations circumscribe the boundaries of public debate and act as political gatekeepers without any accountability (Arnove 1980; Jenkins 1986; O'Connor 2007, 3). Foundations, think tanks, and related nonprofits constitute a "policy formation network" at the national level, and as G. William Domhoff (2009, 970) argues, "there are limits to what challengers can achieve in terms of greater democratic participation and individual opportunity when they are beholden to a corporate-financed network of nonprofit organizations concerned with maintaining the current class structure and the huge privilege it delivers to the wealthy few." The foundation-led policy process tends to neutralize dissent and promote apolitical solutions to social problems that largely uphold the economic and social status quo (Arena 2012; Arnove 1980; Dagan and Teles 2016; Dowie 2001; Roelofs 2003). Flowing from its antidemocratic and depoliticized characteristics, policymaking in one area (such as the juvenile justice system) is often divorced from the broader political economy and wider political context, leading to inequitable outcomes.

The increased influence of corporate for-profit entities has grown alongside that of foundations and nonprofits, resulting in similar antidemocratic policy outcomes. Foundation- and business-led policymaking tends to support antistatist, pro-privatization, self-help policy solutions to complex social and economic problems that undermine the equitable and robust distribution of public goods (Arena 2012; Arnove 1980; Hertel-Fernandez 2019; Kohl-Arenas 2015; Lafer 2017; Reckhow 2012; Roelofs 2003). The privatization of public housing has been a huge boon for real estate developers and the for-profit housing industry and has had devastating consequences for millions of Americans who cannot afford a place to live. The highly privatized healthcare system in the United States provides inferior care and inflated prices compared to public systems (Gottschalk 2000; Himmelstein and Woolhandler 2008). Corporate "reformers" have profited substantially from privatizing education, with harmful consequences for students and teachers (Lafer 2017; Moak 2022; Ravitch 2014).

Efforts to increase the role of the private sector in the juvenile justice system are not new, but today the increased promotion of private-public partnerships comes in the context of an established and robust private sector further accelerating the role of private actors in juvenile justice policy. Earlier community-based efforts had different impacts because there was relatively less privatization of social policy compared to today. The popularity of community-based reforms in the juvenile justice system has been heavily influenced by the private sector, particularly through large foundations, and has resulted in an increased role of the private sector in carrying out the functions of the system, particularly through nonprofit and for-profit organizations. The shift in American governance toward greater privatization is closely related to the turn to "community" solutions and individual explanations and solutions to social problems.

The Individual Behavioral Turn

Another emerging consensus within the community-based reform movement today is an endorsement of individual behavioral solutions to the problems of juvenile delinquency and juvenile incarceration. The community-based movement is largely predicated on increasing treatment and individual behavioral programs for youth. Focusing on fixing juveniles in order to fix the juvenile justice system is a long-standing feature of antidelinquency policy and also part of another major reorientation of social policy since the New Deal. Emphasizing individualist solutions to a wide array of social problems—poverty, racial inequality, and unemployment—has been an animating feature of neoliberal governance. A strong individualistic ethic runs deep in American political culture but has particularly infused social policy development after the New Deal as part of the effort to devolve, retrench, and privatize public institutions and services.

This section details some of the key developments in social science research and shifting political ideologies that fueled culturalist and individual behavioral explanations and solutions for a wide array of social problems, from the rise of human capital theory in the 1950s to the "culture of poverty" in the 1960s and 1970s and the "underclass" theory of the 1980s and 1990s. Each iteration of the individual focus on the causes and solutions to crime, unemployment, racial inequality, and poverty played a key role in justifying the attack on universal public goods and promoting the view that social policy should be decentralized and tailored to individual needs. The section concludes with how these layered strains of ideological and policy developments have created a political landscape where individual uplift is embraced across the political spectrum and is thoroughly integrated into the criminal justice reform landscape through the community-based reform movement.

Culturalist Explanations of Inequality: 1950s–1990s

Social policy in the United States has a long history of attributing poverty to bad behavior, but this individualist view came back with a vengeance in postwar politics (Katz 1995, 3, 63). In the 1950s, economists at the University of Chicago popularized "human capital" ideology, in which explanations for failures in the economy were increasingly blamed on the deficiencies of workers themselves, and therefore interventions to address unemployment were targeted at improving the skills of workers rather than something like public job creation. As Jenny Breen (2011) incisively shows, the public vision of work from the New Deal was supplanted with human capital theory in the 1950s and 1960s, with profound implications for views of the value of work and workers. The study of economics became disassociated from politics and was increasingly devoid of an analysis of power and class (Katznelson 1989). The rise of human capital theory was exemplary of a major intellectual and political shift that Daniel Rodgers (2012, 3) traces, in which "conceptions of human nature that in the post–World War II era had been thick with context, social circumstance, institutions, and history gave way to conceptions of human nature that stressed choice, agency, performance, and desire."

The Cold War politics of the 1950s fostered a special regard for the rights of the individual, a distinctive feature of American liberal democracy that was contrasted to the stoked anxieties of communism (Mayeux 2020, 16). The liberal consensus during this period rejected economic security in the form of commitments like the right to a job, a living wage, and healthcare and instead emphasized personal security in the form of commitments like the right to personal expression, private property, and religious freedom (Reed 2020, 54). Post–New Deal democracy was defined by the autonomy of the individual and their distance from the state thanks to the mounting fear of totalitarianism and also the triumphant defeat of policies geared to socialize aspects of the economy and social life (Brinkley 1996; Mayeux 2020). Large charitable foundations played a critical role in the production and dissemination of individual behavioral solutions in public policy (Arnove 1980; Berman 1983). The Ford Foundation, Carnegie Corporation, and Russell Sage Foundation funded research in this vein starting in the 1950s, publishing a number of studies linking "the community" to issues of poverty and inequality and pushing policy research away from materially redistributive solutions (O'Connor 2001; Roelofs 2003).

Emanating from this increased focus on the individual, the "culture of poverty" theory soon followed, echoing many of the same assumptions and policy prescriptions that would heavily influence and shape the policies of the War on Poverty. In the early 1960s, anthropologist Oscar Lewis published his theory on the "culture of poverty," asserting that those living in poverty develop subcultures that make them unable to change their conditions and that they pass these behaviors and attitudes on to their children, ensuring continued intergenerational poverty (Katz 1995, 69). Increased attention to aspects of culture to explain social ills like crime, poverty, and unemployment pushed from view concerns about structural inequality (Gottschalk 2020). In Great Society politics, a consideration of the relationship between poverty and class relations, even in the limited terms of the New Deal, was largely vanquished (Katznelson 1989). Poverty increasingly became defined as a cultural rather than an economic condition (Cowie 2016; Woodsworth 2016). Thus, many of the CDCs and community-based initiatives within the War on Poverty funneled money to nonprofit and for-profit programs and services that employed a "self-help" style of social intervention geared toward moral rehabilitation.

The popular adherence to "culture of poverty" explanations for economic inequality was deeply bound up in conceptions about racial inequality. The language of "ethnocultural exceptionalism" in discussions of class inequality, exemplified in the work of Daniel Patrick Moynihan, was taken up by a diverse array of politicians, social scientists, and political activists (Johnson 2017). Adherence to Moynihan's formulation of the cause of racial inequality as a "racist virus" unattached to features of political economy effectively divorced racial disparities from economic inequality, as historian Touré Reed (2020) has carefully detailed. An emphasis on the psychological rather than economic features of racial inequality advanced social policy geared toward individual interventions and often "community-based" policies as the preferred remedies for persistent racial inequalities.

Charitable foundations, as early supporters of research on behavioral explanations and solutions to juvenile delinquency, promoted "community-based" policies to address the problem in this manner. Large recipients of foundation funding, Richard Cloward and Lloyd Ohlin's (1960) "opportunity theory" (a close relative of the "culture of poverty" theory) focused on the psychological damage of racial and economic inequality as a source for delinquent behavior (Fleury 2019). Their work played a significant role in shaping antidelinquency policy during the 1960s (Katznelson 1989). Rather than focus on the larger social and economic forces that contributed to the conditions of "slums," the theory highlighted the emergent delinquent subcultures at the community level as the problem in need of amelioration (Schmitt 2010, 69). As a number of scholars have shown, this perspective led to, paternalistic, and punitive approaches to antidelinquency (Hinton 2016; Murakawa 2014).

During the War on Poverty antidelinquency programs were combined with antipoverty "community-based" efforts focused on individual behavioral interventions (Austin and Krisberg 1981; Bakal 1998; Bernard 1992; Binder and Polan 1991; Curran 1988; Feld 1999; Klein 1979; Lemert 1970; Lerman 1984; Miller 1998; Polsky 1993; Sutton 1988). The focus on individual explanations and solutions to delinquency was part of the disassociation of crime from social arrangements and political and economic inequalities (Austin and Krisberg 1981; Beckett 1997, 48; Flamm 2005; Garland 2001; Klein 1979; Polsky 1993). The behavioral failures of youth were positioned as the core problem to be solved in reforming the juvenile justice system (Garland 2001; McDonald 1994; Muncie 2005; Wacquant 2009).

The subsequent devolution and retrenchment of social policy in the 1980s as well as welfare reform in the 1990s continued to be connected to a new iteration of individual blame in the form of "underclass ideology." Figures like Charles Murray, along with a number of scholars and policymakers, began to assert that policies from the War on Poverty, specifically the social welfare state, fostered dependency and antisocial behaviors that caused people to be mired in poverty (Katz 1995, 63; Reed 2020, 133). While many of these assertions, like those coming from Murray, advanced crude racial essentialisms, figures like William Julius Wilson helped to seemingly remove the racist tenets of the underclass theory and forge bipartisan support for this perspective in the 1990s (A. Reed 1999; T. Reed 2020; Katz 1995, 75). Both liberals and conservatives embraced underclass ideology, contributing to the bipartisan support for policies targeted at limiting public support and increasing punishments for inner-city Blacks and Latinos (A. Reed 1999, 183; T. Reed 2020, 134).[13] Underclass ideology drew a sharp distinction between "worthy" and "unworthy" poor, the latter being stigmatized and punished for their supposed deviant behavior (Wacquant 2009, 79).

Consequences of the Individual Turn

Decades of focusing on individual pathology as the source of social and racial inequality has had a deep impact on American governance (Katz 1995). Cuts to public housing and social welfare programs and the rise of mass incarceration during these decades were justified by the tenets of underclass ideology that blamed the cultural and moral inadequacies of poor people of color for their poverty and their entanglements in the criminal justice system (Reed 2020, 99). Individual explanations for gaping economic and social inequalities muted demands on the government to alleviate poverty through durable public-sector investments (Reed 1999, 179). Rather than transform structural inequality, the various versions of individual behavioral explanations for inequality instead naturalized the existing political and economic structure. As Reed argues, "in such accounts 'structure' appears as a reified, opaque background—a natural boundary, whose constraints are inexorable and beyond the possibility of human intervention" (123).

The individualized approach to delinquency likewise naturalizes the broader economic and structural context youth inhabit. Delinquent acts are not the product "of a singular and autonomous individual endowed with a warped will or vicious aims" but rather stem from a "network of multiple causes and reasons" that therefore require "remedies that are just as diverse and finely coordinated" (Wacquant 2009, 283). The programs advocated for in the community-based movement are frequently geared toward preventing as many youth as possible from entering the system by intervening in their individual behavior, but do not fundamentally challenge the core purpose of the system or punitive ideology. The resurgent popularity of community-based reforms to the juvenile justice system continues to focus on individual behavioral deficiencies rather than take a broader view of the causes and needed solutions to delinquency. The emphasis on individualistic explanations for juvenile crime reifies the idea that youth who are unable to fix their own personal deficiencies are the "really bad ones" who *do* deserve punishment.

The Punitive Expansion

The final feature of the community-based reform movement—the preservation and in some instances expansion of punitive policies—is less explicitly advocated for by reformers but is a critical component of recent policy changes. The rise of punitive governance goes hand in hand with all of the previously cataloged shifts in post–New Deal American governance. Many scholars have connected the rise of punitive policies in social policy to developments from the 1960s, showing the contemporaneity of devolution, privatization, the individualization of social problems, and punitiveness. This final section shows how punitiveness has been a key feature of changes in American politics and why it continues to infuse the juvenile justice system today.

During the 1980s and 1990s, social welfare retrenchment was coupled with the expansion of punitive policies (Gilmore 2007; Wacquant 2009, 69). As Loïc Wacquant (2009, 90) argues, the reduction of public services along with mass layoffs and lower wages of this era necessitated the "penal wing to 'mop up' the ensuing public troubles." When key federal legislation was rolling back the welfare state, most states were ratcheting up the construction of prisons and pouring state funds into the criminal justice system. Between 1980 and 1996, the national prison population tripled (Carson 2014). The buildup of mass incarceration has worked to control and segregate those dislocated and marginalized by a changing economy and public-sector cutbacks (Gilmore 2007; Johnson 2019; Lowi 1998; Reed 2020; Soss, Fording, and Schram 2008; Wacquant 2009). Fast-growing incarceration rates for youth stemmed from high arrest rates concentrated in geographic areas in economic distress (Wacquant 2009, 68). The very areas and populations that had been devastated by the upward redistribution of wealth and the divestment in public goods experienced the full weight of carceral machinery that was proliferating to unprecedented levels. The punitive repression and containment of the poor became a cheaper solution to the economic dislocation than investments in a broad array of public goods (Clegg and Usmani 2019; Pfaff 2017).

The most obvious expression of the punitive turn has been the rise of mass incarceration; however, the use of punitive sanctions has been ratcheted up broadly in social policy beyond just carceral policy. From welfare to education reform, the rise of punitive policies has been a defining feature of post–New Deal social policy. The collapse during the 1960s of the New Deal approach to governing led to a transformation of governance being increasingly organized around the control of crime (Garland 2001; Simon 2009). The 1980s and 1990s reshaped the purpose of government, and the "right to security" increasingly displaced commitments like a "right to employment" as the central function of the government.[14]

The dislocation wrought by major shifts in the economy was met with increased punishment and punitive management of the poor (Simon 1993; Soss, Fording, and Schram 2011). Jonathan Simon (2009) connects this rising "culture of fear" and the multifaceted War on Crime to the proliferation of security discourses and policies throughout American life, from gated communities to employer-mandated drug testing. Joe Soss, Richard C. Fording, and Sanford F. Schram (2011) show how welfare reform in the 1990s led to a new mode of poverty governance—one that marshals market principles but also disciplines poor people through paternalistic policies targeted at poor people's behavior. The turn to punishment was closely connected to the rise of "culture of poverty" and "underclass" theories, which blamed and stigmatized the poor for their economic and social position. Blaming the moral and behavioral failures of people for their poverty became a pivotal tool in advocating for welfare retrenchment and punitive public policy (Katz 1995, 70).

State legislatures throughout the United States in this newly evolving policy landscape enacted punitive welfare reforms, from punishing parents for their children's school attendance to punishing mothers for having too many children (Katz 1995, 19). Under the Reagan and Clinton administrations nearly every measure of public-sector retrenchment and privatization was paired with punitive policies. For example, as part of its sweeping 1994 Crime Bill that facilitated the most significant expansions of mass incarceration, the Clinton administration passed a "One strike you're out" provision that excluded felons from public housing, the punitive component of dismantling public housing (Arena 2012, 88). Similarly, cuts to public education have been accompanied by the expansion of punitive policies such as school closures and mass layoffs. Students since the 1990s have experienced the consequences of the rise of "zero tolerance" policies in schools, which strictly punish youth for in-school infractions (Skiba and Knesting 2002).

The juvenile justice system also experienced a major uptick in punitiveness aided by the moral panic over "juvenile superpredators" that led to the widespread passage of policies like "adult time" laws, juvenile life without the possibility of parole sentences, and gang enhancements. In the 1990s and 2000s most states reached all-time-high rates of youth incarceration as the prison population under the age of 18 ballooned. Since this high-water mark, there has been a significant drop in youth crime rates as well as incarceration rates; however, much of the punitive ethos and many of the policies have remained intact. This outcome is largely because the social and political developments related to punitiveness, namely devolution, privatization, and the individualization of delinquency, have all endured and deepened as features of American policy. Despite discourse to the contrary, reforms in the community-based movement that entail devolution, privatization, and an individual approach to youth crime have not replaced punishment as a cornerstone of juvenile justice policy but in fact have legitimized it.

Summary

The main features of the community-based reform movement being pursued today—devolution, privatization, individual treatment, and punishment—fit into major changes in post–New Deal American policymaking. All of these developments are co-constitutive with the declining support for robustly provided public goods and the stigmatization of the government. The political features explored in this chapter capture the ways in which postwar politics, the Great Society, and the rise and consolidation of neoliberalism contributed to a set of policies and ideological commitments that corresponded with public-sector retrenchment, the rising power of foundations and corporations in American politics, widening economic inequality, and the concentration of wealth among the most affluent (Cowie 2016, 10). When reformers pursue community-based solutions today they are doing so in a context that has been transformed by decades of devolution, privatization, the individualization of social problems and a rise of punitiveness in American politics. Not only do these conditions make "communities" more inegalitarian and unequipped to provide robust and equitable social protections to its citizens than at any time since the New Deal, but they demonstrate why going down this path of policy decisions is failing to improve the conditions youth face in the American criminal justice system.

The interrelated developments of devolving control to the community, privatization, and promoting individual behavioral modifications in the 1960s comprised a new policy consensus that replaced universalistic policies targeted at structural reform. The ascendancy of individual behavioral explanations for social problems ranging from juvenile delinquency to unemployment that gained traction in post–New Deal policymaking helped support devolution and community-based solutions. In many instances, the notion that individual failures were the cause of racial, social, and economic inequalities was the *reason* to increase community-based interventions, such as supporting programs targeted at moral uplift. The shift from material redistributive to culturalist views of the cause of and solution to a wide range of social problems in post–New

Deal policy legitimized the attack on universal public goods and ultimately contributed to the devolution and privatization of social policy.

The fact that devolution coincided with public-sector retrenchment and ideologies that emphasized individual blame was not an accident—these developments were and are interrelated. The notion of "community" often functions in much the same way as the notion of the "individual," with both being counterposed to universal policies, centralized state management of the economy, and a robust commitment to the public good. In the latter half of the 20th century, both the "community" and the "individual" as ideal units of focus uplifted the idea of "self-help" and narrowed the realm of acceptable government activity away from a political economy focus. Great Society policies were founded on the assumption that "community activity" could affect behavioral changes in the poor, which had displaced agitations for structural reforms that could achieve collective economic security (Katznelson 1989).

It is perhaps possible that a turn to community control might have been distinct from individual uplift ideology, particularly if increased community empowerment occurred in a context of egalitarian social relations. However, in practice, the turn to community control was and continues to be a powerful tool for entrenching inegalitarian social structures and undermining the public distribution of goods and services. Social policy devolution coincided with a dramatic attack on the public sector and an intensified belief in the paramount importance of individual autonomy. The rise of individualist behavioral explanations and solutions to social problems profoundly shaped American policymaking and American life. A popular way to deflect from pursuing structural reforms has long been to insist that in order to fix social problems you have to fix the behavior of people mired in inequality and economic distress. The construct of fixing the people to fix the system has been a central means in post–New Deal policy development to undermine the provision of public goods and to ratchet up punitive policies (Michaels and Reed 2020).

The focus on individual uplift and on community-based policies as central juvenile justice reform strategies is not *necessarily* or always connected to privatization. There certainly are individualized and community-based interventions that are publicly supported and carried out. However, as this chapter has detailed, the turn to the community and to individual explanations and solutions to social problems has been and continues to be intertwined with attacks on centralized publicly provided goods and supported by powerful political actors interested in expanding the private sector. This key link contributes to why these developments in social policy are in actuality intimately connected to privatization—both in terms of who has fought for them and how they have reshaped American governance and policy implementation.

The community-based reform movement examined in this book is emblematic of these broader turns in social welfare policy that have dominated since the decline of the labor-left coalition of the New Deal. Community-based reforms are shaped by a landscape characterized by decades of conservative governance and the upward redistribution of wealth. While turning to the private sector for service delivery is not new, thanks to decades of establishing a robust role for the private sector in social policy, the turn to community-based private providers in the current moment is often the *only* option a local government has because this infrastructure is readily available and public institutions and services have been drastically cut back.

Since the community-based reforms explored in this book continue these broader trends in social policy, they are entrenching a policymaking strategy that contributed to the rise of mass incarceration. Rising inequality, broad public-sector retrenchment, and major shifts in the economy created concentrated pockets of marginalized populations that the carceral state serves to suppress and manage (Clegg and Usmani 2019; Johnson 2017; Reed 2020). The legitimization of these broader changes hinges on ideologies that blame individuals for their increased marginality and stigmatize the government while valorizing the private sector. These developments ensure that the juvenile justice system continues to have a negative impact on the poor and disproportionately racial minorities. The effort in the community-based reform movement to address these effects—such as large numbers of youth being imprisoned and treated inhumanely—is doubling down on many of the features of neoliberal governance that contributed to these very conditions rather than challenging them.

The community-based reforms being pursued throughout the country do not invigorate calls for democratic control over and expansion of publicly provided, universal goods. Instead, they continue to stigmatize the government in contrast to preferred community-based solutions. They do not address the social, political, and economic contexts that contribute to which youth are caught up in the system and why. Instead, they continue to blame the problems of the juvenile justice system on the deficient behavior and immorality of the youth in the system. The reforms do not challenge the social construction of "delinquent behavior" nor its relationship to unequal social dynamics and structures and therefore continue to levy on youth some of the most punitive juvenile justice policies in the world. Subsequent chapters turn to state-level case studies to unpack the effects of devolution, privatization, individual treatment, and punishment in the community-based reform movement. These central features of reforms today are failing to ameliorate some of the most brutal outcomes of public-sector retrenchment, privatization, and vast economic inequalities that get reflected in the criminal justice system.

2

Devolution, Not Decarceration

Expanding Punishment Closer to Home

In 1976, the Pennsylvania State Legislature debated whether or not the state should devolve control for youth in the justice system from the state to the county level. Republican Pennsylvania senator Edward Howard strongly advocated for the passage of community-based reforms, which were subsequently passed and implemented, arguing, "[T]he chances for its [juvenile justice system] improvement, in my judgment at least, lie mainly with the hope of getting the problem a little closer to home... and discouraging commitments to the kinds of institutions which, like the Majority Leader, I strongly agree need urgent investigation" (Pennsylvania State Legislature 1976). The statement put forth a simple formulation for juvenile justice reform: bring youth closer to home. Almost 50 years later, this core ideal remains at the center of the resurgent community-based reform movement. Keeping youth closer to their homes is broadly agreed to be an important goal for juvenile corrections, as most research and common sense suggest youth have more positive outcomes when they remain connected to their families. From this commitment flourishes the vaguer but equally powerful notion of providing youth with "community" support. The notion of "community-based" supports conjures feel-good images of a young person being buoyed by robust supports, services, opportunities, and acceptance in their day-to-day lives. Yet, as the previous chapter detailed, the policy development and the political forces behind a community-based turn in service delivery more broadly in U.S. public policy have created a different reality, one in which there are fewer public supports and more punitive policies.

In Pennsylvania, the idea of holding juveniles in facilities "closer to home" grew alongside political developments that undermined funding for equitably distributed public goods, creating greater inequalities in the state and ultimately more punishment for the most economically marginalized youth. The faith of Pennsylvania legislators in 1976 that devolution was the needed fix for the juvenile justice system has proven to be misguided. In this chapter, I trace three consequences of devolving control to the local level in a context of fiscal austerity. I demonstrate that the community-based reform movement in the juvenile justice system, in contrast to the admirable goals and connotations of the reform agenda, has entrenched punishment at the local level, continued abusive treatment of youth in the system, and strengthened interests opposed to substantial decarceration. This chapter shows that despite the positive appearances of increasing "community control," the reform movement actually leads to a number of negative consequences as part of a broader austerity politics.

The community-based reform movement seeks to expand county-level juvenile justice institutions and limit the use of state-run secure prisons. The reliance on juvenile county probation departments is not a new configuration for the juvenile justice system. Both before and after the enactment of community-based reforms, county probation departments handled the vast majority of youth referred to the justice system. In all three states, fewer than 3% of youth referred to the justice system were sent to state-level prisons before the passage of community-based reforms. However, state-run prisons have been the central target of reforms in part thanks to widely publicized abuse scandals in these institutions. By targeting changes at reducing the number of youth sent to state-run prisons, the community-based reform movement addresses a small percentage of youth in the system, while expanding and entrenching the largest part of the system: county probation departments.

Large charitable foundations and state-level advocacy organizations and politicians from across the political spectrum broadly support the community-based reform movement because it is often sold as a cheaper and more effective way of handling youth and fixing the problem of abuses in state-run prisons. The focus on expanding community-based institutions is largely based on the idea that state-run youth prisons are the source of the worst problems in the justice system. However, the following evidence from the state-level case studies suggests there is nothing fundamentally better about institutions run by county probation departments. The very same problems of abusive conditions of confinement in state-run prisons also occur in county-run facilities. Relocating rather than eliminating the use of carceral institutions does not solve such problems as high rates of justice-involved youth and their abusive treatment in the system.

This is not an inevitable outcome of local control. Indeed, the main argument of this chapter is that the level of governance (state versus local) does not necessarily create particularly harmful or good outcomes. The context and broader political commitments of policy development are key determinants of these outcomes. Local control in the context of significant social policy retrenchment and without adequately repudiating punitive accountability leads to these negative outcomes. A central failure of the community-based reform movement is that it is premised on increasing the responsibility of county governments to address youth crime and incarceration when they are poorly funded, lack oversight and regulation, and are greatly unequal in representing the interests of those they govern. In this context, the community-based reform movement has exacerbated inequalities in who, where, and how youth are punished in the justice system.

This chapter begins by looking at the broader context for devolution, in which all three states have intensified the upward redistribution of wealth and cut back on public goods. The analysis then builds on this broader political economy focus to examine how it conditions the effects of establishing community-based reforms and what these have looked like in practice. The money funneled to the local level to increase community control over corrections has largely gone toward secure institutionalization and punitive probation. A close evaluation of these county institutions being expanded under community-based reforms suggests that they are plagued by the same problems of abusive conditions of confinement (such as physical abuse and the use of solitary confinement) as state-run prisons, but with even less oversight. Increased local control has perpetuated inequalities between counties in terms of resources and juvenile justice placements. Increasing county control has not even lived up to the ideal of bringing youth "closer to home." Finally, the community-based reform movement entrenches interests at the local level that are resistant to decarceration, making the goal of significantly reducing the number of youth handled in the justice system more difficult. Community-based reforms to juvenile delinquency are failing to address the problems of the juvenile justice system and are also entrenching the most harmful aspects of the system.

The Political Context of the Community-Based Reform Movement

States following the community-based reform movement are devolving control to the county level in a context where there are major inequalities among counties and decades of public-sector retrenchment. The turn toward devolution of the juvenile justice system is part of a broader trend in devolving the administration and funding of social services to the local level in the context of significant public-sector cuts. The community-based reform movement suffers both from being enacted in this wider context and by following a similar austerity logic of promoting "cost savings." The turn to community-based reforms has not challenged austerity but instead has taken the principles of cost-cutting and economic efficiency and applied these to juvenile justice policy. This section details how model states for the community-based reform movement have at the same time retrenched social policy. The states most aggressively devolving control over youth corrections to the local level, such as California, Pennsylvania, and Texas, despite significant variations in partisanship and institutional settings, are also simultaneously among those that have most aggressively divested in public goods. The "layering" of devolution on top of retrenchment and broadening inequality has resulted in youth facing gross inequalities in their treatment in the system depending on where they live (Orren and Skowronek 2004). Also, the notion of "the community" being able to support and provide for young people is belied by the reality of dramatic declines in funding for social services, education, health, and youth employment.

Public-Sector Retrenchment in California, Pennsylvania, and Texas

Given the close links between devolution, social policy retrenchment, and the rise of mass incarceration, it is concerning that the community-based reform movement of these three model states have all occurred alongside major public-sector cuts and rising inequality. California, Pennsylvania, and Texas have enacted regressive tax overhauls, made public-sector cuts, and experienced job losses and wage stagnation that contribute to greater inequality and increased economic marginalization for growing numbers of people. These factors create an inauspicious context for devolution as a solution to the problems with youth incarceration. They also exemplify the problematic compatibility community-based reforms have with this broader political orientation.

In California, the economic position of counties has been greatly hindered ever since the passage of an antitax revolt initiative in 1978 as well as the economic recession of the early 1990s.[1] These developments coincided with the ascendancy of "law and order" policies that fueled the rise of mass incarceration (Campbell 2016; Gilmore 2007). As Ruth Gilmore incisively documents, as the state of California cut back on public investments in education, jobs, and infrastructure, it significantly invested in correctional expansion. The state is turning to community-based reforms as a cheaper solution to delinquency when most communities, particularly the poorest counties in the state, are the least capable of providing services and support because of significant drops in revenue and cuts to expenditures.

In 2020, corporations in California paid less than half the amount in state taxes compared to three decades earlier (Kaplan 2020). Thanks to generous tax breaks to high-income households and corporations, estimates are that California loses more than $60 billion a year in revenue (California Budget and Policy Center 2020). In conjunction with the decline in revenue from corporations and the wealthiest in the state, California heavily depends on regressive taxes, including a sales tax that is among the highest in the nation. The result of these revenue-generating priorities and a strained state budget has been major drops in funding for education, public health, and public jobs. California used to be above the national average in education spending, but since the passage of Proposition 13 there has been a significant decline (Willis et al. 2018). As of 2019, California ranked 38th out of 50 states in per pupil funding (Quality Counts 2019). While California used to have among the nation's lowest childhood poverty rates, the state now is above average. Across the state, an estimated 2 million children face food insecurity (Call 2020).

In 2004, Californian voters overwhelming passed (83.7% support) Proposition 1A, which strengthened and stabilized local revenues. The measure prohibited unfunded state mandates which led to higher and more stable local government revenues, but also reduced resources for state programs. Under the proposition, revenues collected by local governments are protected from being transferred to the California state government for statewide use. The change to the constitution requires that local sales tax revenue be spent by local government (California Legislative Analyst's Office 2004). Reduced funding for statewide social programs has worsened regional inequalities. Many counties in California, particularly poorer ones, continue to struggle to pay for local services, and there are major inequities between counties in the state in terms of revenue and public expenditures.

On top of this revenue change, in the wake of the Great Recession, California cut services to public health, the elderly and disabled, K–12 and early education, higher education, and the state workforce (Johnson, Oliff, and William 2011).[2] At the same time the state passed community-based reforms it also dramatically slashed its budget for social services. Devolution of the juvenile justice system is one part of the trend toward an increasingly localized provision of goods and services. The effect of this shift has been to undermine statewide programs and services, resulting in a more unequal provision of goods (Lagos 2012). The deterioration of universal programs providing basic public goods along with devolution has contributed to intensified inequality in California—and in the juvenile justice system.

Like California, Texas has enacted tax policies that have facilitated the upward redistribution of wealth, leaving the poorest in the state to carry the heaviest burden in generating revenues. The state's long-held commitment to small government and local control over social policy means that when the state devolved greater control over juvenile corrections in the name of community-based reforms, they did so in the context of heavily burdened counties with few resources. A lack of stable and robust funding from the state and national government has left the poorest areas of the state the most vulnerable to inadequate services and supports.

Since 1991, Texas has almost exclusively reduced state taxes (Texas Comptroller of Public Accounts 2019). In 2017, the state ranked 48th out of 50 for lowest per capita state tax collections (Capps et al. 2001). Like California, Texas heavily depends on a sales tax as its major source of revenue, making it the state with the fifth most regressive tax code (Castro and Lavine 2013; Ramsey 2018). The state does not have a corporate income tax, and it is the most populous state with no personal income tax. In Texas, cities and counties pay for most essential services almost entirely through locally raised revenue from property and sales taxes (Every Texan 2020b). Yet, despite heavily relying on local revenues, local governments still spend less than the national average per capita (Castro and Lavine 2013). The result has been devastating for the funding of education and public health and has increased economic inequalities in the state. Coming out of the 2008 recession, its economy was stronger than most states, but Texas still chose to make significant spending cuts at the same time it enacted and implemented community-based reforms to the juvenile justice system. Texas was one of many states that made large cuts to expenditures, eliminated hundreds of thousands of jobs, and cut unemployment and retirement benefits (Aviram 2015, 51; Lafer 2017).

After the recession, Texas decreased its state funding for education and has increased the burden at the local level to shoulder the costs of education (Ramsey 2018). While community-based reforms were supposed to be replacing the need for state-run prisons, in 2011 Texas cut education funding by $5.3 billion (American Federation of Teachers 2018). From 2008 to 2018 Texas was the second-to-worst in the nation for cuts in funding per student (percentage change in state formula funding per student over this time was −16.2%). One result has been that local school districts had to cut a total of 135,000 jobs between 2008 and 2017 (Chávez 2017). In 2016, Texas was 42nd in the nation for per pupil funding, allocating $2,300 less a year per student than the national average (Texas State Teachers Association 2018).

In addition to education cuts and the increased burden at the local level to try to keep basic public services in operation, Texas has cut assistance to its poorest residents (the state accounts for 10% of all poor Americans) (Ura 2017). The number of people receiving cash assistance went from 479,000 in 1998 to 60,000 in 2017, even though poverty rates have not gone down. The state led the way in welfare reform, predating the federal changes in the 1990s. Texas, more than most states, heavily devolves social welfare policies to the local level (Capps et al. 2001). The local control of these policies without sufficient funding has exacerbated inequalities and weakened social provisions, such as having the highest rate of uninsured children in the nation.

In the absence of public funding for basic necessities, Texans also face a labor market in which jobs paying a middle-class wage have significantly declined since the early 1980s, while the share of low-wage jobs has grown at twice the rate of high-wage jobs (Every Texan 2020a). Finally, Texas is dead last in the nation in per capita mental health expenditures (National Alliance on Mental Illness 2011). A state budget crunch in 2003 resulted in more than $100 million being cut from the community mental health system (Romer 2008). As social services have been eviscerated, prisons have become the site "of last resort" for providing services such as mental health treatment (Phelps 2011, 35). It is in this context that the state has turned to community-based solutions to the abuses of the juvenile justice system—counties that have for decades seen reduced funding and increased responsibility to carry out basic governmental services.

While Pennsylvania in some respects has done better in initiating tax increases and public spending compared to Texas and California, overall the state shares many of the same broader economic characteristics of the other model states for the community-based reform movement. Every state has undergone budgeting challenges due to federal retrenchment and rising costs. Between 1979 and 2010 healthcare spending in Pennsylvania (in 2010 dollars) grew 350%, transportation by 220%, and education by 140% (Miller 2016, 154). In addition to rising costs and less federal support, Pennsylvania also relies heavily on local taxes and local spending for carrying out government services. It is also one of the most regressive tax states, largely due to its flat personal income tax. The poorest in Pennsylvania pay a greater percentage of their income in taxes than the richest (WHYY 2009). Pennsylvania ranks higher than Texas, California, and the national average on medical insurance coverage and childhood poverty but still spends less than the national average on public goods as a share of personal income.

The state falls into the same pattern of having devolved control of social services and the juvenile justice system to the local level in the context of widening inequality, with the vast majority of economic gains from the past several decades going to the wealthiest Pennsylvanians. It has the fourth largest reliance on local funding for education in the United States, at about the same level as Texas (Wood et al. 2008). The state's heavy reliance on local taxes leads to big differences in the revenue and expenditures of wealthy and poor counties. Like Texas and California, when Pennsylvania passed its landmark community-based reform (Balanced and Restorative Justice [BARJ] in 1995), legislators also slashed funding to welfare, and reductions have continued since (Pennsylvania Budget and Policy Center 2007). Local communities have more control over justice-involved youth, and they also have greater rates of poverty. Public-sector support and wages and the number of those insured have all gone down in the state, while from 2000 to 2019 the poverty rate increased from 8.6% to 12% and child poverty increased from 11.6% to 16.9% (Pennsylvania Budget and Policy Center 2007).

This political economic context puts into perspective what a turn to the community-based reform movement actually means in these states. It is one of many nodes of retrenchment and decentralization that are occurring more broadly in social policy and that are leading to fewer public goods, more punitiveness, and widening inequalities. In all three states, implementing community-based reforms has required an investment and expansion of county-level probation and detention programs. The pressure on counties to handle a greater number of juveniles as part of the community-based reform movement is pushing them to invest in punitive solutions at the expense of robust funding for a broad array of public goods. While counties secure money to expand existing jails and build new ones, they are simultaneously seeing dramatic cuts to public education, child support services, the health system, state and county parks, affordable housing, and cash to families (Durand 2012a, 2012b).

Implementing community-based reforms is fundamentally undermined by the commitment to austerity that undergirds the popularity of pursuing these "cheaper" alternatives. In Texas, Harris County Commissioner Steve Radack, in the debate over the 2007 community-based reform legislation, argued against increasing county control over juveniles who would previously have been sent to state-run prisons. He claimed the policies would worsen crowding in Harris County lockups, and were "another unfunded mandate to the counties," and would "just put the problem on the taxpayers of Harris County" (quoted in Murphy 2007). Alan Mayfield, McLennan County juvenile court judge, similarly framed his resistance to moving juveniles to the county level in economic terms, stating that if services were transferred to counties it would "shift the burden to local taxpayers who have quite enough burdens already" (quoted in Doerr 2008). Counties are rightfully wary of the long-term plan of how they might pay for the community-based services. In 2012, 75% of counties in Texas reported that their funding was insufficient or very insufficient to implement community-based programs (Texas Criminal Justice Coalition 2012, 3).

Devolution has left counties responsible for numerous social services and with strained budgets, forcing counties to make tough choices about what to fund (Nielsen 2011b). Without a clear vision to significantly shrink the carceral system, many counties predictably choose the well-trod route of jail and probation expansion, especially since the states in these community-based reform models have provided funding for these types of investments through specialized block grants, as the following section illustrates (Durand 2012b). Community-based reforms in this context do not challenge, but instead exemplify, what Loïc

Wacquant (2006, 109) describes as "the shift towards the penal management of social insecurity that is everywhere being generated by the social and economic disengagement of the state." The following sections detail the on-the-ground consequences of devolution in this context.

Expansion and Entrenchment of Local Capacity

The enactment of devolution in this political economic framework of austerity and retrenchment results in expanded and entrenched punitive capacity at the local level. One of the main goals of the community-based reform movement is to expand local facilities and programs so that they will *replace* the use of secure confinement (defined as an institutional setting where a youth is locked in a cell within a secure facility) and eliminate the punitive and abusive treatment of youth in state-run prisons. However, a closer examination at individual state developments shows that the community-based reforms have often *expanded* secure confinement and punitive alternatives at the local level. Devolving control and funds to the local level has not necessarily eliminated punitive and abusive conditions that youth in the juvenile justice system experience.

As the preeminent example of a devolved juvenile justice system that has most aggressively pushed for local control over juvenile justice policies, Pennsylvania demonstrates that community-based reforms do not necessarily mean less secure confinement. Despite being the state with the greatest amount of local control over its juvenile correctional system in the nation and the model for the community-based reform movement, as of 2017 the state had a juvenile incarceration rate above the national average (National Center for Juvenile Justice 2021). In fact, it was Pennsylvania's efforts to infuse punitive accountability into local, community-based institutions that earned it the distinction of being a groundbreaking model of juvenile corrections that states like Texas and California have since modeled reforms after.

While Texas and California more recently moved toward community-based reforms, ultimately the three cases show a common pattern: a punitive philosophy and approach to youth offending characterizes *both* the community-based and state-run configurations of the juvenile justice system. Since core punitive principles of juvenile corrections have not been fully repudiated, the community-based reform movement has had the effect of entrenching and expanding secure confinement and punitive probation at the local level. What these cases demonstrate is that a shift in the organizational configuration of the justice system alone does not substantially curtail the use of secure confinement or punitive probation. Funding allocations in community-based reforms have largely gone toward expanding secure confinement and probation at the local level.

Community-Based Budget Allocations

The clearest way to observe that the community-based reform movement has entrenched and expanded local secure confinement and punitive probation is to track the way budgets directed toward establishing these alternatives have been spent. In both California and Texas, the recent community-based reforms have established grant funds given to local jurisdictions to establish community-based alternatives. In both states, the majority of funds have been channeled into traditional forms of secure confinement and punitive probation.

In California, the core of the 2007 community-based reform bill was the establishment of the Youthful Offender Block Grant. YOBG provides funds to counties to deliver custody and care to youth offenders who previously would have been committed to the Department of Juvenile Justice and to "enhance the capacity of local communities to implement an effective continuum of response to juvenile crime" (California State Legislature 2007).[3] In addition to the YOBG, at least $100 million in lease revenue bonds from the Public Works Board was made available to counties for costs related to the construction or enhancement of "local youthful offender rehabilitative facilities" as part of implementing the community-based reforms enacted in 2007 (Dawood 2009, 4).[4]

A general breakdown of the allocations of the YOBG for counties exemplifies how punitive institutionalization as well as other traditional law enforcement tools have been supported and funded in the community-based reform movement. As part of the YOBG guidelines, each county submits a development plan to the Corrections Standards Authority (now the Board of State and Community Corrections [BSCC]) to detail how it will spend the grant funds. The BSCC oversees these reforms in both the adult and juvenile justice systems and is largely comprised of law enforcement actors appointed by the governor and the legislature.[5] The BSCC has readily approved jail renovation and construction plans, likely a result of the predominant law enforcement interests represented on the board.

In the first year of the grant fund (2007–2008), the largest proportion of the funds was allocated to secure confinement programs for "high-end" local youth (Dawood 2009, 17). That year, 15 counties (including nine of the 14 largest counties in the state) used the grant money to enhance or establish new long-term commitment units within juvenile halls (17). In addition to the expansion of secure and punitive institutional options, 28% of counties also used funds to contract with juvenile halls, camps and ranches, regional facilities, group homes, and out-of-state and other residential facilities (17). In 2008, 37 of the 58 counties used YOBG for "placements in secure and semi-secure facilities and in private residential care programs" (17).

These priorities have not changed since this initial investment of the block grant money. In 2013–2014, 2015–2016, and 2018 counties in California made similar funding choices. Since 2007, approximately $1 billion in funds has gone from the state to the county level through the YOBG. Counties continue to use the majority of the money for traditional secure confinement in the form of detention halls, camps, and ranches. The minimal amount of money going toward treatment and alternative programs is largely in the form of contracts with the private sector. Figure 2.1 shows a side-by-side comparison of investments in residential institutions (juvenile halls, camps, ranches, secure/semi-secure and day/evening treatment centers) and probation (electronic monitoring, house arrest, intensive probation supervision) compared to investments in alcohol and drug treatment and counseling (individual, group, and family) in 2016 and 2018. In both years, detention and probation costs amounted to about 80% of the total grant funding, while drug treatment and counseling totaled 2%. In 2018 counties spent over $78 million on secure confinement and residential placements (up from $67 million in 2016) and nearly $20 million on probation services. In 2018, less than 1% of all YOBG allocations went to drug and alcohol or mental health treatment. About 5% of the allocations went to risk assessments, life skills, mentoring, and vocational training (California Board of State and Community Corrections 2018).

In addition to the YOBG, there are two other major grant sources that funnel money from the state to the local level for juvenile justice services. The Juvenile Justice Crime Prevention Act, enacted in 2000, allocates general funds to local

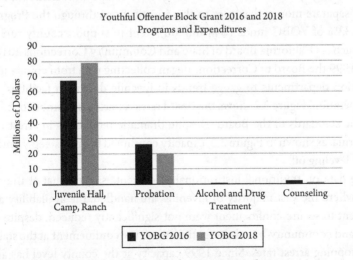

Figure 2.1 California youthful offender block grant 2016 and 2018 programs and expenditures Source: Data compiled from California Board of State and Community Corrections 2015.

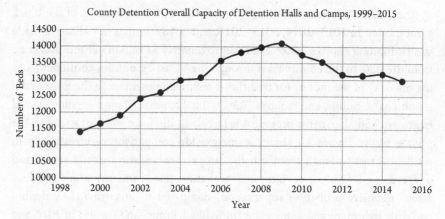

Figure 2.2 California County detention capacity 1999–2015 Sources: Data compiled from California Board of State and Community Corrections, Juvenile Detention Profile Series (www.bscc.ca.gov/s_fsojuveniledetentionprofile.php) and California Corrections Standards Authority Juvenile Detention Survey (www.bdcorr.ca.gov/fsod/juvenile_detention_survey/juvenile%20detention%survey.htm).

governments to support an array of services in county probation departments and community-based service providers. Since 2000, about $1.5 billion has been distributed to local service programs from state funds through this grant program. In 2005 Governor Arnold Schwarzenegger signed into law the Juvenile Probation and Camps Funding Program, which allocates around $200 million per year in state funds to county probation camps and ranches (Commonweal 2015). A large portion of YOBG funds goes to camps and ranches *in addition* to the separate money that goes to these institutions through the Program. In 2018, 33% of YOBG funds ($44 million) went to support county-run camps and ranches (California Board of State and Community Corrections 2018).

In 1999 the Board of Corrections began collecting data from county juvenile probation departments to gauge trends in juvenile detention facilities' design and operation. Figure 2.2 shows the Board rates capacity, or number of beds that met the standards of the Board. Despite dramatic reductions in arrest rates in California, as shown in Figure 2.3, capacity continued to grow steeply until 2008 before leveling off.

The data on traditional institutional placements suggest that at the county level, where the vast majority of juveniles are handled, the availability and investment in secure confinement were not significantly reduced, despite efforts to expand community-based alternatives to secure confinement at the state level and dropping arrest rates. Since 1999 capacity at the county level has actually increased by about 1,500 beds. The rated capacity data does not take into account the wide variety of other types of institutionalization and correctional

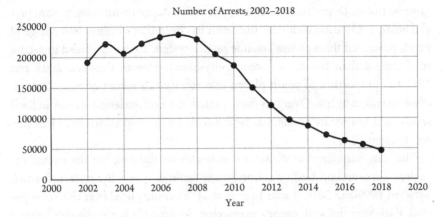

Figure 2.3 California number of juvenile arrests 2002–2018 Source: Data compiled from California Department of Justice statistical reports 2002–2018, http://oag.ca.gov/cjsc/pubs#juvenile Justice.

control that counties have expanded, such as semi-secure and private residential programs as well as house arrest, electronic monitoring, and intensive probation supervision. In 2009, California had the highest percentage of juvenile offenders in local custody in the nation, twice the national average (Clarke et al. 2009, 28).

A similar outcome has occurred in Texas, where grant money targeted in community-based reforms has largely been funneled to expand local secure confinement. The 2007 reform legislation in Texas promoted widespread commitment to community-based programs as an alternative to state institutions. Subsequently, the state has directed money to counties to expand local jails and myriad treatment programs and facilities. In 2007, the state allocated about $35 million to the Texas Juvenile Probation Commission to open 600 more community-based secure beds (Ward 2007b). The state provided an additional $12 million to local juvenile probation departments to place "low-risk, nonviolent offenders" in locally operated facilities (Copelin 2007b). In 2011, Ray West, chairman of the Commission, described the reorganization in plain terms: "I think the direction we will see the state go in the foreseeable future is to minimize the kids who go to TYC [Texas Youth Commission, the state-run prisons] and maximize the [use of] alternate placement facilities" (quoted in Emison 2011).

Funding allocations have mirrored the commitment described by West. Between 2008 and 2012 county expenditures on juvenile justice increased by 12%, with more funds going to both secure and nonsecure facilities than to community-based alternatives that would keep youth in their homes. During this period, funding for residential placements (out-of-home secure or nonsecure facility placements) grew three times more than the funding for community-based programming. In 2014–2015 a third of the total funds (36%) given by the Texas

Juvenile Justice Department to county probation departments went toward pre- and post-adjudication facilities. The result has been that a greater percentage of youth processed through the juvenile justice system are being placed in secure confinement than before the community-based reforms. Between 2005 and 2012 the proportion of youth placed in a county-run secure or nonsecure facility increased by 5%. Over this same period, the average length of stay in local secure and nonsecure residential facilities also increased (Carreon, Henneke, and Kreager 2015).

The state has closed down several state-run institutions, but the overall capacity of pre- and post-adjudication secure facilities across the state has grown between 1999 and 2016 thanks to growth at the county level over this same period. Each year the state agency overseeing the juvenile justice system keeps a registry of secure facilities in the state.[6] Figure 2.4 shows the changes in the rated capacity (number of beds available) throughout the state of all secure facilities for juvenile offenders. Capacity was actually declining in the years leading up to the 2007 community-based reform legislation, but by 2014 it had grown to its highest level in 15 years. Since the initial reforms passed in 2007, the state has opened five new county-run facilities.[7]

Since the 2007 legislation was enacted, county spending has been increasing for county juvenile probation and community-based corrections. The amount both county and state contribute to county probation departments has steadily increased since the 2007 community-based reforms.[8] In 2000 the state allocated $98 million to county probation departments; in 2014 it allocated $153.8 million (Texas Juvenile Justice Department 2014a). In 2007, 11% of the money allocated from the state for county probation departments went toward residential services (about $15.6 million). By 2014, the portion of the state funds going to residential services increased to 26% (about $34.7 million) (Texas Juvenile

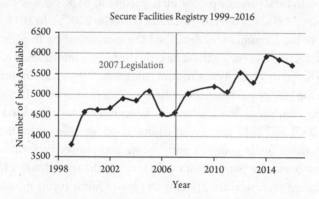

Figure 2.4 Texas Secure Facilities Registry 1999–2016 Source: Data compiled from Texas Juvenile Probation Commission statistical reports. Data unavailable for 2009.

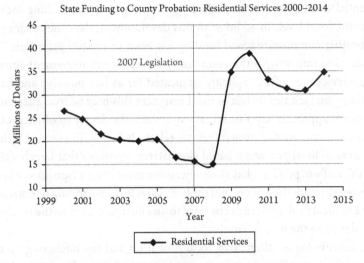

Figure 2.5 Texas State funding to counties for residential services 2000–2014 Source: Data compiled from "Allocation of State Funds to Local Communities" annual reports 2000–2014. Adjusted for inflation, annual allocations are in 2007 dollars.

Justice Department 2014a). Figure 2.5 shows the growth of money allocated from the state to counties to bolster residential services from 2000 to 2014.

The 2007 juvenile justice legislation set up specific grants for counties to use to handle young people who previously would have been sent to state-run institutions. As in California, the majority of this money has gone toward secure and nonsecure institutions, bolstering preexisting probation programs and alternative services that contain punitive conditions of community supervision. Between 2009 and 2011 the state awarded counties around $48.6 million through a diversionary fund (Grant H) to develop community-based probation programs and services for juveniles at risk of being sent to state-run prisons. Over these years about 93% of the funds went to residential services. Another diversionary fund (Grant C) provided $89.6 million to counties from 2010 to 2014. Sixty-three percent of the funds went to secure and nonsecure residential facilities, while the rest went to probation.[9] In Texas, pursuing the community-based reform movement has contributed to more county-run facilities, more money for secure confinement, and an increased capacity to incarcerate youthful offenders.

Community-Based Probation Expansion

As Texas and California embrace the community-based reform movement, the consequence in each state has been to funnel large portions of this money into residential institutionalization, effectively shifting and entrenching incarceration at the local level. In addition to this development, the other major source of allocating community-based funding has been to expand probation. This is a predictable outcome in the community-based reform movement since probation services are often explicitly advocated for as less punitive and harmful than state-run facilities. While in most instances this may be true, there are two flaws to this approach. The first is that it overstates the degree to which probation services are nonpunitive, even if they are relatively better. The second is that the wide array of local probation-based alternatives—policies that largely exist beyond the walls of prison—has always been the most likely disposition a juvenile processed through the system will receive. Therefore, expanding or entrenching the use of local probation runs contrary to an effort to minimize the reach of the carceral state in the lives of youth.

Far from being an alternative, local probation and the ratcheting up of punitive probation policies have been critical parts of expanding carceral power. As Michelle Phelps (2017) has termed it, "mass probation" has not operated as an alternative to incarceration but has been a codevelopment in the rise of the carceral state. Probation often serves as a "net-widener" by expanding supervision for lower-level cases, and in the juvenile justice system it remains the most common punishment (Phelps 2017). In addition, probation always comes with the threat of revocation, and as such it is a key facet of the "shadow carceral state" in which many individuals are sent to prisons through administrative agencies rather than criminal courts (Beckett and Murakawa 2012). Further, successful compliance with probation requires a stable job and a robust safety net of support, which is actively being rolled back in these states in the context of social policy retrenchment.

A brief description of how Pennsylvania was a model state in developing probation as an alternative community-based punitive accountability measure demonstrates that these policies were an outgrowth of the "get tough" changes of the 1990s. Large foundations, like MacArthur and Annie E. Casey, as well as the national government picked up on these model policies and have incorporated them into the community-based reform movement. In doing so, they are repackaging programs and policies that were integral to a punitive accountability correctional philosophy as new reform strategies.

Pennsylvania was an influential state in launching community-based probation programs like Intensive Supervision Probation (ISP) and electronic monitoring that were pitched as cost-effective and more rehabilitative alternatives to secure confinement. Juvenile ISP programs started becoming fixtures of probation departments in the 1980s. ISP was marketed as a central component of a new "get tough," surveillance-oriented probation system (Beatty 2002, 8). Similarly, electronic monitoring was a key part of a burgeoning movement toward intensive probation and parole in the 1990s. The use of electronic monitoring fit into a "new generation" of community penalties where different kinds of interventions, increasingly privatized, were mixed for more controlling and individualized sentences (Nellis, Beyens, and Kaminski 2013). Both ISP and electronic monitoring fit the new model of crime control based on efforts to target risks among groups of offenders and then apply the most cost-effective measures of handling them (Paterson 2013, 216). Both types of detention alternatives, while arguably better than secure confinement, are still strict, controlling, and punitive (Beatty 2002; Nellis, Beyens, and Kaminski 2013; Paterson 2013; Payne and Gainey 1998; Petersilia 2016; Renzema 2013).

Pennsylvania piloted an ISP in 1988 in Allegheny (Pittsburgh) and Philadelphia counties. ISP was billed as a cost-effective supplement (not alternative) to institutional placement for "serious, habitual and violent" juvenile offenders.[10] The Community Intensive Supervision Program in Allegheny, still in operation, uses electronic monitoring, weekly drug testing, and restitution. The MacArthur and Annie E. Casey foundations have both endorsed the use of ISPs.[11] As the model for the community-based reform movement, about 80% of the 67 counties in Pennsylvania have an electronic monitoring component to their juvenile probation services.[12]

When Pennsylvania implemented its sweeping reform legislation in 1995 that, in addition to ratcheting up punitive policies, also increased community-based services, probation departments grew significantly. As part of the community-based reforms, counties were given grants to expand specialized probation services, and across the state counties increased the number of probation officers they hired. About two years into the implementation of the grants, the number of juvenile probation officers grew from 1,000 to 1,500 (R. Steele, personal communication, September 21, 2020). The long-running investment in community-based, local probation in Pennsylvania and its establishment of piloted programs for alternatives to secure confinement has led to increased numbers of parole violations and over time more juveniles under some form of correctional control.

Overall the expansion of probation programs like ISP and electronic monitoring in Pennsylvania corresponded with an increasing percentage and number of juveniles under supervision who have been found in violation of their probation conditions. The state has increased required programming at the local level for youth, yet youth are *more* likely to violate probation, perhaps because they are more tightly monitored (Pennsylvania Juvenile Court Judges' Commission 2013). The Pennsylvania case suggests that over time, more robust investment in probation does not necessarily reduce the number of youth under correctional control and can even increase the severity of dispositions for those caught up in the system through increased parole revocations.

Despite these mixed results and concerns about the entrenchment of correctional control through a broadened reach of probation at the local level, both large foundations and the national government have advocated for these policies in their support of the community-based reform movement. Following the lead of Pennsylvania and its large foundation boosters, California and Texas, as part of embracing the community-based reform movement, have used large portions of reform grant money to expand probation, and specifically policies like ISP and electronic monitoring. Not only have community-based reforms failed to substantially curtail the capacity of secure institutionalization, but they are also leading to the expansion and entrenchment of punitive probation.

In Texas, the community-based reform legislation has contributed to the growth of probation departments and programs. The total number of staff employed by probation departments across the state doubled between 1997 and 2014, from about 4,000 to 8,000. The largest area of growth has been in certified juvenile detention officers, who work in secure facilities and halfway houses (728 in 1997 to 2,187 in 2014), suggesting that the growth of probation has in large part bolstered the most punitive aspects of departments. The growth in all juvenile probation officers from 1997 to 2014 is illustrated in Figure 2.6.

The expansion of programs and services in local probation departments in Texas also illustrates the growth of county capacity in the community-based reform movement.[13] There has been a substantial expansion of county probation departments and programs offered at the community level. These programs

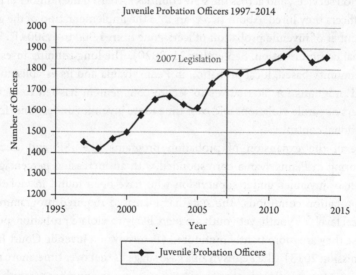

Figure 2.6 Texas juvenile probation officers (certified and uncertified) 1997–2014 Source: Data compiled from Texas Juvenile Probation Commission statistical reports. Data unavailable for 2009 and 2015.

serve more than 32,000 juveniles each year across 149 juvenile probation departments. Of these departments, 62% have an electronic monitoring program, and 74% have an ISP program, and most of the growth of these programs occurred *after* community-based reforms were enacted. While many of these programs are treatment-oriented, including 61% of departments that provide substance abuse treatment, the majority of the programs (including those that are treatment-oriented) are part of secure detention or conditions of probation that come with the threat of reincarceration.

As part of the 2007 legislation passed in Texas, the legislature also established the Intensive Community-Based Program (Grant X) to fund community-based programs for offenders under the supervision of the juvenile court. Between 2008 and 2011, the state awarded $19.8 million through this grant. In 2011, 37% of the Grant X money went to probation departments that used in full or in part their allocated funds for ISP programs and/or electronic monitoring (Texas Juvenile Probation Commission 2010).

This expanded role of county probation in the juvenile justice system has not always lived up to the decarceration goals articulated by community-based reformers because the expanded probation programs have corresponded with increases in probation revocations. In 2018, reports revealed Harris County struggling with overcrowding in its local juvenile justice center and a large rise in the number of juveniles ordered to be detained on a probation violation. In both 2016 and 2017, 73% of juveniles cited for a probation violation were incarcerated, compared to 40% in 2007. The county had experienced a decline in jailed probation violators after it adopted the Annie E. Casey Foundation's Juvenile Detention Alternative Initiative's principles in 2007, but the decline persisted for only about three years. In order to relieve overcrowding in the Harris County Juvenile Detention Center, officials approved a project to build a new juvenile detention facility in 2018 (Flynn 2018).

In California, a similar use of community-based grant funding has been funneled into probation, and particularly electronic monitoring and ISP. In the first year of the grant money flowing from the community-based reforms, 55% of all counties (including all of the largest counties in the state) used the YOBG in 2007–2008 to hire more probation officers, and 65% of counties used the funds for electronic monitoring and ISP. A similar trend has occurred in grant funding after this initial year of community-based investment, with counties continuing to use the funds for county probation and punitive programs. From 2013 to 2018 about $53 million of community-based funds went toward ISP and about $3.5 million went toward electronic monitoring. In contrast, over this same period just $2 million was spent on alcohol and drug treatment, and since then the allocation to these services has substantially gone down. In 2013, counties spent

$871,464 on alcohol and drug treatment, and in 2018 they spent $291,463, one-third of the allocation five years prior.

Providing grant money to counties to bolster probation does not fundamentally orient the juvenile justice system away from punitive accountability policies, nor does it necessarily reduce the reach of the carceral system in the lives of youth. Alternatives to secure detention like ISP and electronic monitoring were key components of the 1990s "get tough" approach to corrections; just because they are carried out by local probation departments as community-based programs does not make them nonpunitive.

State-Run Closed Facilities

The community-based reform movement is primarily targeted at eliminating harmful state-run youth prisons, so what happens to these facilities once they have been depopulated sufficiently to shut down? Tracking what has happened to these facilities exemplifies the clearest example of how community-based reforms have shifted the control of secure confinement rather than eliminated the use of these institutions.

One way Texas has devolved control of juveniles from the state to the county level has been to directly transfer facilities funded and operated by the state to counties. In 2011, the legislature passed Senate Bill 653 to reorganize the juvenile justice system. The measure merged the Texas Juvenile Probation Commission, which oversees county probation departments, with the TYC, which oversees state-run institutions, to create the Texas Juvenile Justice Department. An important provision in the merger legislation was that any of the shuttered state-run facilities could be transferred to counties of fewer than 100,000 people.

As a result of the provision, closed state-run prisons have been transferred to counties but remain in use. For example, the Ron Jackson Unit II facility was transferred from the state to Brown County, a small rural county located in west-central Texas, in January 2012 under a provision in the merger legislation.[14] The portion of the unit transferred to the county had capacity for 120 juveniles, yet Brown County typically has only one to eight juveniles housed at the county level. Brown County is planning to use part of the unit, renamed the Ray West Juvenile Justice Center,[15] to expand its current short-term facility to house juveniles transferred from other counties at a charge to those counties (Kirk 2012; Nash 2011, 2012). Crockett State School was closed down in 2011, then three years later was transferred to the City of Crockett and reopened. Three other facilities that closed as part of the community-based reform legislation have since gone through similar transformations.[16] Most of the state facilities that closed have been repurposed as county-run secure residential facilities and have been subsequently leased to private companies.

In California, the fate of closed juvenile prisons has similarly resulted in a shifting of punitive confinement rather than the elimination of the operation of these state-run prisons. The California state-run juvenile prison system began downsizing before the 2007 community-based reforms were enacted. Prior to 2007, two state-run prisons were shut down, and an additional eight have been shuttered since.[17] This is a notable victory for those who have long argued that state-run prisons are fundamentally flawed and incapable of providing positive interventions for youth. However, in the community-based reform movement the closures have not been a repudiation of punitive confinement and have instead served as a convenient source of expansion for the state-run adult system. Three of the closed prisons have been transferred for use in the adult corrections system. As there has been an increase in the percentage of youth directly transferred to the adult system since the community-based reforms were enacted, this is another way of shifting punitive institutionalization rather than eliminating it.[18]

The outcomes detailed in this section reflect the negative consequences of a narrowly construed community-based reform movement in the juvenile justice system. While closures in one area of the system look like a positive development, as a whole these model reform states continue to devote a considerable amount of money to punitive institutionalization, which is being shifted to the local level or adult system. Assumptions that enhancing "community control" will solve these problems obscures the reality that problems with abuse and the negative repercussions of prisons are being relocated, not eliminated.

Conditions at the County Level

As the previous section has demonstrated, the enactment of community-based reforms has not eliminated the use of punitive institutionalization or punitive probation. Instead, these reforms have helped funnel money to counties, who were already responsible for handling the vast majority of youth processed in the system, to further entrench and expand these institutions and services. The community-based reform movement hinges on the idea that youth sent to prison will be better served at the local level, where conditions are considered to be more conducive to rehabilitation and less abusive.[19] Matthew Cate, secretary of the California Department of Corrections and Rehabilitation from 2008 to 2012, claimed, "[R]esearch shows that most juvenile offenders are more successful in their rehabilitation when they remain in their local communities" (*CDCR Today* 2011). The text of Senate Bill 81 from 2007, the major juvenile community-based reform bill in California, similarly stated, "The legislature finds and declares that local youth offender justice programs, including both custodial and non-custodial corrective services, are better suited to provide rehabilitative services for certain youthful offenders than state-operated facilities. Local communities are better able than the state to provide these offenders with the programs they require" (California State Legislature 2007, 30). However, in the cases of the three leading model states for the community-based reform movement, county juvenile justice systems do not appear to live up to the high expectations of the reform promises. Instead, youth face similar patterns of abuse at the county level as in state-run prisons (but often with less oversight), they are routinely subjected to solitary confinement and the use of pepper spray, and there are great inequalities across counties in incarceration rates and how delinquent youth are handled.

Abuse in County-Run Prisons

Despite assurances of the superiority of local communities, the conditions of confinement in local facilities show a pattern of abuse similar to what occurs in state-run facilities. Margo Schlanger (2013, 168) refers to this problem as the "hydra risk," where the state may succeed in "chopping the head off of unconstitutional conditions of prison confinement" at the state level only to cause counties "to develop unconstitutional conditions of jail confinement."[20] In California, the impetus for passing sweeping community-based reforms to the juvenile justice system was the mounting legal challenges facing state-run youth prisons over problems with abusive conditions. While the process of devolution has helped the state comply with the legal changes directed at state-run prisons by depopulating these institutions, it has not resolved the underlying complaints of the lawsuits. Since the community-based reform movement has been implemented in California, counties have continued to be plagued with similar charges of abusive conditions of confinement related to the use of solitary confinement, excessive force, and abuse of disabled youth.

Just one year after the passage of community-based reforms in California in 2007, Los Angeles County entered an agreement with the U.S. Department of Justice to remedy conditions in its probation camps that had been investigated and found to be unconstitutional. The Justice Department investigation found that the camps failed to protect youth from harm and did not provide adequate suicide prevention and mental health services. Additionally, staff systematically physically abused youth, probation officers used pepper spray excessively, and there was a high incidence of youth-on-youth assaults, inadequate staffing levels, and inadequate investigations of abuse allegations (U.S. Department of

Justice 2008). The Los Angeles County Probation Department operates 19 detention camps housing approximately 2,200 post-adjudicated youth. To contextualize, just the camps (not detention halls or other institutions) run by Los Angeles County alone were about the same size as the *entire* state-run juvenile prison system at the time the community-based reform legislation was passed in 2007. Los Angeles County was not alone, as both San Joaquin and Sacramento counties have also been forced to sign consent decrees after devolution.

The serious issues that Los Angeles County was facing when the reform legislation passed continue to persist well over a decade into the establishment of community-based reforms. The county continues to struggle with providing adequate conditions of care, despite dropping arrest rates. Between 2015 and 2018 the rate of assaults on guards at Los Angeles County facilities more than doubled. In 2018, the Los Angeles juvenile justice department reported a major uptick in the use of pepper spray; between 2015 and 2017 several facilities in the county increased their use by 200% to 300% (Sanchez et al. 2019). A 2018 report by Los Angeles County listed major problems with the system, including deteriorated facilities, inadequate training of staff, lack of structured activities, little contact between youth and their families, excessive use of force, use of solitary confinement, use of chemical spray, and sexual and physical abuse. According to the 2018 report, many officers reported not showing up for work because of the chaotic conditions (Sanchez et al. 2019). In short, the problems at county facilities almost exactly mirror those found in state-run facilities, but county facilities incarcerate a far greater number of youth than the state-run prisons ever did.

In Texas, after passing community-based reforms, injuries in county juvenile facilities increased by more than a third between 2008 and 2011 (Texas Criminal Justice Coalition 2012, 15). According to data given to the Texas Criminal Justice Coalition in 2012, youth in county juvenile facilities were physically restrained (sometimes referred to as "use of force") 9,701 times, and there were 1,870 reported injuries (Texas Center for Justice and Equity 2021).[21] One of the major catalysts for pursuing community-based reforms in Texas was reports of sexual abuse to youth in state-run prisons. However, county-run institutions also experience these same problems of abuse. There have been multiple instances of guards at county-run facilities being charged with sexually abusing juveniles in custody.[22]

In Pennsylvania, most of the litigation and continued issues of abuse in a highly devolved and community-based system have occurred in privately run facilities, which will be detailed in the following chapter. But the county-run facilities also have problems with abuse. In 2018, Lancaster County was sued for ignoring reports of sexual abuse in its youth detention center, and the county has faced several federal lawsuits related to abuse (LancasterOnline

Editorial Board 2020). A report from Children's Rights Philadelphia-based Education Law Center in 2018 found "statewide patterns" of abuse in county-run youth residential facilities and a "shocking lack of oversight and accountability" (Palmer 2018). The outcome is similar in California and Texas; the greater local control (and in Pennsylvania private control) of youth prisons has not effectively addressed the issues of abuse that youth face in the juvenile justice system.

Solitary Confinement

In both California and Texas, the abusive use of solitary confinement in state-run facilities was a major impetus for passing sweeping community-based reforms. Solitary confinement has been found to increase violence in prisons and cause serious emotional and psychological damage (Haney 2003; King 1999; Reiter 2012; Rhodes 2004; Shalev 2013; Travis, Western, and Redburn 2014; Ward and Werlich 2004). Studies on the effect of prison isolation find that the conditions of solitary have serious psychological consequences, such as insomnia, depression, self-mutilation, suicidal ideation and behavior, and hallucinations (Haney 2003). Experts assert that young people are psychologically unable to handle solitary (Human Rights Watch 2012); because juveniles are still developing, the experience of solitary confinement can be traumatic and profoundly negative to their future growth and welfare (American Civil Liberties Union 2014; Gately 2014; Human Rights Watch 2012). A 2009 study by the U.S. Department of Justice found that juveniles held in solitary confinement committed half of the 110 suicides over a four-year period in the late 1990s. More than two-thirds of these youth were being held in juvenile facilities for nonviolent offenses (U.S. Department of Justice, Office of Juvenile Justice and Delinquency Prevention 2009).

While there is limited oversight of county facilities, a number of reports suggest that the use of solitary confinement at the local level is widespread. Devolution makes the tracking of this abusive policy and providing adequate oversight more difficult. For example, in California, the state-run juvenile prison system operates under one court order that prohibits all forms of isolation, but county juvenile halls do not operate under this same stipulation (Bundy 2014). Counties in California have had a number of different lawsuits related to solitary confinement, suggesting its use is widespread. The multiple lawsuits also illuminate the great difficulty in addressing abusive practices in the context of devolution. The dispersion of authority to 58 counties means legal challenges have to be brought against each individual county's use of solitary confinement rather than one lawsuit addressing an entire system.

In California, state regulators inspect juvenile facilities once every two years. In these inspections, the state checks whether juveniles are receiving the state-mandated one hour a day outside of their cells for exercise, but they do not track or count the number of days juveniles are in solitary confinement (Bundy 2014). Sue Burrell, an attorney working for the Youth Law Center in San Francisco who has been instrumental in suing a number of counties in California over abusive conditions of confinement, says that "law regulations have allowed juvenile solitary to be used in most county facilities that hold minors in California" (quoted in Bundy 2014).[23] Court documents from 2011 suggest that solitary confinement is frequently used for punishment in county-run facilities. The documents revealed 249 incidents of solitary confinement in just over a one-year period at five facilities in the state (Levin 2015). One report of youth held at Camp Scudder in Santa Clarita found that 43% of youth spent more than 24 hours in solitary confinement (Therolf 2015). Contra Costa County, Los Angeles County, and Kern County have all faced investigations and lawsuits over their use of solitary confinement and other abusive practices.[24]

Texas has similar issues with accountability and oversight at the local level. In an effort to better regulate and prevent abusive practices in the state-run prisons, the community-based reform legislation of 2007 set up the Office of the Independent Ombudsman. However, the ombudsman was neither mandated nor fully funded to carry out oversight of the more than 90 local juvenile correctional facilities (Carreon, Henneke, and Kreager 2015). (It oversees only the five state-run prisons, where a lack of funding has also been an issue, as detailed in Chapter 5.) Despite these challenges of fully tracking incidents of abuse at the local level, Texas also shows indications of the widespread use of solitary confinement in county institutions.

In 2011, youth in county juvenile facilities in Texas were sent to solitary confinement 37,071 times, and in 2012 36,820 times (Bernier 2013). There is not precise data on how many of these were short- versus long-term confinements, but data collected by the Texas Criminal Justice Coalition (2012) shows that thousands of assignments to solitary confinement in 2011 lasted longer than 24 hours. The rules governing commitment to solitary confinement vary greatly from county to county. A comparison of 13 counties in Texas found that the list of "major rule violations" that can qualify a youth to be put in 24-hour seclusion range from "disrespectful behavior towards staff" to "assault" (Texas Criminal Justice Coalition 2012). In 2017, reports about abusive conditions in a Dallas County facility, the Lyle B. Medlock Youth Treatment Center, described youth spending months and sometimes more than a year without going outdoors (Flynn 2018). Harris County's juvenile detention center has also faced legal action related to confining youth to their rooms for 23½ hours a day (Banks 2020).

A recent effort in California to further advance legislation outlawing solitary confinement has been limited by the broader commitments to austerity in the state. In 2013, Senator Leland Yee (D–San Francisco)[25] introduced a bill to limit the use of solitary confinement for juveniles. County probation heads and prison guard union representatives opposed the legislation on grounds that it was too expensive, would necessitate more training, and could lead to more lawsuits (Meronek 2013). The bill was revised to exclude a requirement for mental health caregivers to check in on youth in solitary because opponents in the legislature, such as Senator Ron Calderon (D–Los Angeles), deemed it too expensive. The bill was watered down but still did not pass.

In 2015, Senator Mark Leno (D–San Francisco) introduced another bill to restrict the use of solitary confinement for juveniles. This bill was successful in passing largely because this time around it was endorsed by the state association for county probation department heads after a provision was added that allows for "room confinement" (solitary confinement) to still be used in certain cases (Loudenback 2016). A particularly powerful endorsement for the bill came from Los Angeles County Probation Chief Jerry Powers, who supported the legislation but also acknowledged that alternatives for how to deal with juveniles that are sent to solitary confinement do not exist (Therolf 2015). For example, there are strict limitations on emergency hospitalizations, and hospitals quickly discharge youth who are experiencing mental health crises, leaving actors in the juvenile justice system few choices for how to handle youth in crisis. In response to the lack of adequate alternatives available for corrections officials, Powers commented, "[I]t's like Sacramento gives us no option. In some ways they are going to force us to violate the law on the first day it is passed" (quoted in Therolf 2015). The solitary reform bill did not address the deeper issues related to adequate mental health services. A central mechanism for eliminating the use of solitary confinement is having a suitable medical and mental health system. Since decades of austerity measures have hollowed out these public goods, whether or not legislators outlaw solitary, the practice of using seclusion will likely continue. The broader context of austerity and the commitment to passing reforms that save money means that an effort like this on solitary confinement will continually be dead on arrival. The efforts to curtail the use of solitary are promising, but devolution and the turn to community-based reforms are not effective solutions alone, especially in the context of public-sector retrenchment. Instead, youth continue to be routinely subjected to this harmful practice at the county level in the wake of community-based reforms.

Pepper Spray in County Facilities

Another example of continued abuse in devolved juvenile justice systems is the continued use of pepper spray on youth. Contrary to the notion that community-based facilities are intrinsically more rehabilitative, the evidence on the ground suggests that youth face abusive practices in these facilities in greater numbers and with less uniform regulations and oversight. The use of pepper spray, like solitary confinement, is widespread in California county facilities. California is just one of 14 states that allow the use of pepper spray in juvenile facilities,[26] and it is one of only five states that allow staff to carry pepper spray (Maass 2012). Most states and localities outlaw the use of pepper spray because it is physically harmful to youth and has a negative impact on staff-youth relations (Council of Juvenile Correctional Administrators 2011). Pepper spray, also referred to as OC (oleoresin capsicum), is a "chemical restraint that incapacitates individuals by inducing an almost immediate burning sensation of the skin and burning, tearing and swelling of the eyes" (Council of Juvenile Correctional Administrators 2011). Pepper spray can be particularly threatening to youth who suffer from asthma or who are taking psychotropic medications (which is a high percentage of youth in the juvenile justice system). Pepper spray use is often unmonitored and widely used in county-run juvenile detention facilities in California (California Rural Legal Assistance 2011).

San Diego County has some of the highest levels of pepper spray usage in the country (Maass 2012).[27] One detention center, the East Mesa facility,[28] averaged more than five pepper sprayings per week. While the county detention system is supposed to be holding "less serious" offenders than the state facilities, the use of pepper spray at state and county facilities is comparable (Maass 2012).[29] In 2014, a number of juvenile reform organizations sued San Diego County over its use of pepper spray in juvenile detention facilities, where, they argued, it had been used as an "all-purpose behavioral management tool" (Youth Law Center 2014; Thompson 2018).[30] San Diego County also received a negative inspection report of its facilities in 2016 from Disability Rights California (2016) regarding its use of excessive force, pepper spray, and restraints and inadequate accommodations for disabled youth. In 2019 an Inspector General report revealed that Los Angeles County was overusing pepper spray in its youth jails (Stiles 2019). In the same year, six officers in the county were charged with child abuse and assault due to allegations of unreasonable use of pepper spray. The dispersal of authority to the community level has not curbed the use of the harmful practice and has made it even more difficult to track, monitor, and address the issue.

The Texas state-run prison system also faced litigation for its practice of using pepper spray on youth, which was another key motivation for enacting community-based reforms that would move youth out of these facilities and into county-run institutions and programs (Rigby 2008). However, like the previous examples, the assumption that county officials would be less likely to use pepper spray was unfounded. In 2013, Texas county probation officials from across the state asked for *expanded* authority to use pepper spray since they now were handling more youth who would previously have been sent to state-run prisons. The existing rules authorized the use of pepper spray only during a riot and required pepper spray to be locked away. County probation chiefs wanted authorization to use pepper spray when youths become physically aggressive and to allow staff to carry pepper spray. Luis Leija, Calhoun County's chief juvenile probation officer and the president of the South Texas Chiefs Association (who supported the rules change), insisted that most counties did not intend to use the chemical restraints, but that "it's always good to have local control of what you do with your facilities" (quoted in Grissom 2013).[31] Reform advocates from the Texas Criminal Justice Coalition and the ACLU pushed back against the rules change, and ultimately the proposal was tabled. In this particular case, increased local control was aligned with calls to *expand* the harmful practice of chemical restraints. By granting more control to these community-based institutions, the state potentially opened the door to the expanded use of pepper spray. While local control does not always lead to worse outcomes, in the context of limited funding for real alternatives from broad public-sector retrenchment and with less centralized regulation and oversight of facilities, many jurisdictions will fall back on punitive forms of control of youth in facilities.

County-Level Inequalities

In addition to the ways in which county-run institutions can replicate the abusive problems of state-run institutions, devolution has also resulted in considerable inequalities in the administration of services and punishment at the local level. While this was true before the move toward community-based reforms, the reliance on increased local control is exacerbating the problem. This outcome is particularly pronounced given that the turn to local control is occurring in a context of broadening economic, social, and political inequalities. Miller (2016, 199) points out that at the local level budgets and taxing authority are so constrained it makes it difficult to enact redistributive and inclusionary policies. In all three model states, youth receive widely different treatment within the justice system depending on where they live, with the poorest youth receiving the brunt of punitive policies. The county in which a juvenile happens to live can influence their access to treatment programs and the likelihood they will face punitive sanctions, something scholars have referred to as "justice by geography" (Ball 2011; Feld 1991; Feld and Schaefer 2010; Krisberg, Litsky, and Schwartz 1984).

From 2004 to 2007 the state of California ran a juvenile justice data project as a partnership between the California Department of Corrections and the nonprofit Juvenile Law Center that collected economic data on juvenile placements (Hennigan et al. 2007). The working group collected data on the relationship between the median household income for each county and levels of commitments to local and state institutions. Counties that had the lowest median household incomes (below $35,000) in 2005 had about a four-times-higher rate of county placement and more than twice the rate of commitments to state prisons compared to counties where the median household income was above $47,000 (Hennigan et al. 2007). These findings reinforce the important link between carceral policy and political economy.

The report also found great regional variation in commitment rates. Counties in the north and central regions as well as smaller counties have higher rates of confinement in county and state institutions. These results are complementary because 82% of the poorest counties are small and disproportionately located in the north and central regions of the state (Hennigan et al. 2007). The correlation found in the data suggests that youth in the poorest counties are more likely to be incarcerated at both the state and county level. Devolution does not address these inequalities and in fact can make them worse. As the poorest counties continue to be left to their own devices and lack resources to fund social services, they tend to fall back on sending youth to state- and county-run prisons.

The criminal justice system has a great amount of county-by-county variation as a result of this broader process of devolution. For example, in Los Angeles the number of juveniles committed to adult court grew between 2003 and 2007, but in the Bay Area the percentage went down over the same time period. As of 2007, youth in Los Angeles County were four times more likely to get an adult commitment than in the Bay Area (Jannetta and Lin 2007). Leading up to the major community-based reforms of 2007, counties varied greatly in the number of juveniles they sent to state-run institutions for sex offense crimes. Small counties sent a far higher number of sex offenders than large counties (for example, Los Angeles committed proportionally fewer juvenile sex offenders than any other county), most likely because these counties lack appropriate programs and facilities for these offenders compared to larger counties like Los Angeles (Jannetta and Lin 2007). Centralized state-run prisons do not solve these deeper problems of the links between economic inequality and punitiveness, but these findings suggest that more devolution on top of broader trends in devolving and retrenching social policy fails to address the important relationship between broader political economy and carceral policy.

In Texas, reports show similar wide-ranging differences from county to county in percentages of youth who receive services. For example, in Cameron County 40% of youth assessed to be low-risk were placed in a treatment program, compared to 91% in Victoria County. The per capita income in Victoria County is almost two times that of Cameron County (Carreon, Henneke, and Kreager 2015). There is also wide variation from county to county in terms of other dispositions. The percentage of youth referred to the juvenile justice system within a county who are securely detained before adjudication ranges from as low as 15% to as high as 95%, and for those are adjudicated to probation the range is from 2% to 65% (Carreon, Henneke, and Kreager 2015). Turning over more control to counties that are increasingly unequal in terms of their resources and approaches to handling delinquent youth intensifies these inequalities and does not increase the support for the youth who need it most.

Pennsylvania's reliance on local control also corresponds with significant inequalities in the treatment of youth. For example, judges in Pennsylvania are given a great amount of discretion, and there are significant differences from one county to another in how they determine dispositions and where they might send youth. Despite guidelines from the state, there is little control over how counties carry out their juvenile justice policies. One example is the vast discrepancies county to county in youth receiving legal representation. Pennsylvania is one of just two states that does not provide funds for public defenders to represent juveniles. The burden falls completely on counties to run this part of the juvenile justice system, and so there are significant differences geographically in which youth get legal representation and which do not (Ecenbarger 2012).

Turning over more control to counties does not necessarily mean every county will invest in nonpunitive programs and services; in fact most measurements show that a majority of counties invest in traditional forms of punishment (Dawood 2009; Nieto 2008). Juveniles receive a wide variation of services and responses, highly dependent on which county they live in. Poorer counties suffer the most from retrenchment of state-funded programs and services. When youth from these communities are "returned home," they return to even more unequal and unstable contexts as a consequence of broader devolution and public-sector retrenchment.

The image of community-based programs promulgated by large foundations is of youth being connected to their families and receiving treatment and support. This is far from the reality on the ground. In practice, there is a diverse set of institutions, actors, and programs that constitute the "alternatives" to state-run prisons that often replicate the problems in these institutions. There are enormous problems with inequality and abuse at the local level, and—as the next chapter shows—this configuration of service delivery also opens avenues for privatization. The broader turn to community solutions is part of a larger political project in which universal public goods are scaled back, intensifying inequality and leaving the most marginalized with less safety and security and more punishment.

Regionalization

Because of the cost imperative and a broader commitment to austerity in the model community-based reform states, even the localization of secure confinement "closer to home" is failing to take root as both Texas and California are pursuing regionalization plans. A major exception to the "closer to home" promise of the reform effort has been the simultaneous and contradictory push for regionalization. As more responsibility has fallen on county probation departments to provide services for a wider range of juveniles, counties have been pushed to pool their resources to provide regional care options. While counties in many ways replicate the state-run prison system through these consolidations and consortiums, they do so with even less uniformity and with ad hoc oversite that will likely lead to similar problems with the system they are intended to replace.

In California, state grant funds have gone to regionalization efforts where counties combine their resources and each specializes in particular programs and services. For example, one county has a sexual offender program that neighboring counties send juveniles to rather than each county having its own. Several of these county consortiums exist across the state, such as the partnership between Ventura, Santa Barbara, and San Luis Obispo counties; a 15-county cooperative in northern California; and Humboldt County's New Horizons program, which meets the mental health needs of juveniles in neighboring counties (Nieto 2008). As more control is pushed to the county level and more pressure is placed on local probation departments to care for a wider range of youth, this has necessitated county partnerships.

The prevailing justification of cost savings and efficiency is driving regionalization and undermining the community-based and "closer-to-home" goals of the reforms.[32] For example, in 2015, Lake County, a small county in northern California, decided to close its juvenile hall, cutting 20 staff positions, to save on costs (Quirino 2015). The county found that contracting the services of neighboring Mendocino County was cheaper than keeping the Lake County facility open (the cost for a juvenile detainee at Mendocino is $150/day compared to $520/day at Lake County) (Quirino 2015). The Lake County facility was significantly more expensive in part due to high staff turnover.[33] As part of the contracting partnership Mendocino County will not handle any kind of visitation transportation for legal or family matters.[34] The Mendocino facility is 40 miles from Lake County and there is no public transportation between the two locations. Just as in state-run facilities, these youth are housed away from any support they may have at home. In 2020, Governor Gavin Newsom proposed that counties continue to take more of the youth held at state-run facilities. In response to concerns that counties are not equipped to handle these more serious youth, Newsom proposed annual competitive grants to counties of nearly $10 million so that they can create "hubs" to take in youth from state-run prisons who have "serious sex behavior or mental health treatment needs" (Thompson 2020). These consortiums, "hubs," and regionalization plans comprise a system design that is much closer to the state-run prison system in organization than the rhetoric of the community-based reform movement would suggest.

In Texas, the centrality of economic efficiency and cost savings is also contributing to regionalization developments and outcomes that are contrary to the "closer to home" promise of community-based reforms. Regionalization efforts are particularly pronounced in Texas, a state with 254 counties. It would be quite expensive for each county to provide the wide range of programs and services envisioned by the community-based reform movement, an impossibility in the context of the commitment to austerity in Texas politics. Therefore, unsurprisingly, counties have already started consolidating services into regional facilities. As Texas Representative Jim Dunnam (D) has pointed out, "[C]onsolidating services at some TYC institutions saves money" (quoted in Doerr 2008). Contrary to the predominant pitch about localization, Dunnam suggests that consolidation rather than dispersion of institutions is a cheaper route.

Texas has set up grant money for this process, the regional diversion alternatives (RDA) program. Counties can receive money to build capacity and forge collaboration to place youth within the region or in a nearby region instead of being committed to a state-run prison. Under the RDA program, counties will receive a reimbursement if they send a youth to a residential facility in a nearby county. Counties can also receive funds to initiate or expand existing programs and facilities to allow for these transfers. The state is divided into seven regions for these collaborations and intracounty transfers. Since Texas is such a large state, these seven regional consortiums cover a lot of ground. The western region, for example, spans east to west more than 500 miles (from El Paso County to Brown County) and north to south more than 350 miles (from Gaines County to Kinney County). For some youth in the western region, the closest regional facility is 300 miles away, the same distance it would be to be sent to a state-run prison prior to the community-based reforms. A report from 2019 found that county probation departments along the Texas border are incentivized to send youth *farther* from home under the RDA program. For these departments sending youth to facilities in Arizona, Oklahoma, or Colorado would allow parents to visit their children more often, but the regionalization program does not allow out-of-state placements. Instead youth are sent farther away to qualifying regional facilities (Texas Legislative Budget Board, 2019).

Overall, the evidence on the ground suggests that, contrary to the notion of bringing youth closer to home to reduce punitive incarceration and abusive conditions of confinement, the reality is that devolution as part of broader austerity measures is continuing or worsening these very problems. In practice, community-based solutions take the form of county-run prisons and probation programs, which are beleaguered by abusive conditions in an even less regulated context. As part of a political landscape of public-sector retrenchment that has created greater inequalities and burdens on counties to provide basic public goods, the turn to community is intensifying inequality and entrenching the role of the carceral state to punish and suppress the most economically marginalized youth. In addition to these negative outcomes, devolution is creating incentives that uphold the juvenile justice system rather than foster the conditions necessary to truly move away from carceral solutions to social problems like youth delinquency.

Entrenched Interests

This final section addresses another outcome of devolution and the increased flow of responsibility and funds to the local level: the entrenchment of interests at the local level that are invested in *maintaining* juvenile justice institutions. In all three cases, dynamics at the state and local level suggest that the promotion of community-based reforms can create incentives contrary to the retraction of the carceral state by empowering local probation departments, which, particularly in the context of broader austerity measures, tend to advocate for the maintenance and expansion of local facilities and programs. In a context where there is a scarcity of jobs and a lack of funding for public works, actors in these institutions are resistant to cutting or downsizing these programs and services. Additionally, when local probation departments are being asked to take on greater responsibility for more youth in a wider range of contexts, they are incentivized to advocate for increased funding to carry this out.

Pennsylvania illustrates the long-running consequences of pursuing community-based reforms that give a great deal of power to probation departments. Absent significant shifts away from punitive accountability (even if it is paired with principles of rehabilitation) and a lack of funding for other public services, these actors become invested in maintaining and expanding their role in juvenile corrections. Over time this further entrenches probation programs at the local level and creates powerful constituencies that advocate for their continuation. In Pennsylvania, probation officers heavily lobbied for the pioneering model of community-based reforms. The Pennsylvania Council of Chief Juvenile Probation Officers (PCCJPO) influenced the legislation of 1976 that set up generous reimbursements allowing counties to largely control and oversee juvenile corrections—which set the state on the path of a heavily devolved juvenile justice system. The PCCJPO then was a central lobbying power for the BARJ model implemented in the state in 1995—a central model for the community-based reform movement in juvenile corrections today. The PCCJPO has continually advocated for more funds and power for probation departments at the local level. Probation officers are highly professionalized in Pennsylvania, and their officer training program is a national model for juvenile justice training.

As probation departments in the state have over time become more entrenched and better funded, they have become an even more powerful political force. By taking on greater responsibility for juvenile corrections, probation officers in Pennsylvania have expanded their law enforcement capacities and roles. The central component of BARJ and its community-based philosophy is to mandate close supervision of court-involved youth as an absolute necessity. The PCCJPO has argued this increases the danger for officers. As a result, an increasing number of departments began arming their officers after BARJ was passed and implemented in the state. In the mid-1990s the state passed legislation providing firearms training for county probation officers, and counties began equipping probation officers with their own handcuffs, pepper spray, portable communications radios, and bullet-resistant vests (Pennsylvania Juvenile Court Judges' Commission 1999). In 2002, the state legislature passed a law (Act 215) giving juvenile probation officers the authority to conduct warrantless searches of a youth's person, vehicle, or property (Pennsylvania State Legislature 2002).[35] The number of probation officers in the state significantly grew after BARJ, and while the number has ticked back down a bit, county probation departments consistently request more funds (R. Steele, personal interview, September 21, 2020).

In California, similar moves toward community-based reforms have led to calls for expanding resources and facilities at the local level. Rather than pushing against carceral expansion, actors at the county level have pushed to grow existing institutions. For example, a major player in the California justice system, the State Sheriffs' Association, has repeatedly advocated for the expansion of facilities at the local level. In 2006 the California State Sheriffs' Association stated, "[W]e will be encouraging our local public safety partners, our corporate partners and our over 42,000 Associate Members to work with us to convince state Legislators that improving and expanding local detention facilities is a top priority" (33). During the 2000s, the Association called for a repeat of the major bond grant construction programs from the 1980s. The Association has advocated for a proactive "continuous growth" model rather than the "periodic crisis" model that they argue often leads to the cyclical crisis of local institutions getting dangerously overcrowded. The sheriffs have long supported funding local expansion and provided key research and political support for the community-based reform movement.

If Pennsylvania is any indication of what this could mean moving forward, as these groups help to pass community-based reforms and increase funds at the local level they are likely to continue to advocate for their continued funding and expansion. Ultimately, this leads to incentives that run contrary to more robust efforts at reducing the role and size of the juvenile justice system. Since the community-based reforms are almost entirely run by county probation departments, as previous sections demonstrated, this does not fundamentally change the way youth are handled in the system, and it can create incentives to expand the system in the longer term. Properly funded oversight for local lockups and probation is necessary to avoid abusive outcomes and continues to be inadequate, but these dynamics are far from an alternative to the existing system.

These outcomes are particularly pronounced in the context of fiscal austerity. As investments in public goods are significantly cut and regressive tax measures passed, shrinking the public coffers, institutions like the county juvenile probation departments aggressively push for their continued funding. The threat of losing important jobs at the local level is intensified when alternative prospects for public employment and program resources are so competitive, making local actors fight hard to maintain the status quo. The dynamics in Texas related to shuttering state-run prisons highlight this conflict. In the debates over choosing which state-run juvenile prisons to shut down in Texas, there was much resistance at the local level to closing a facility, highlighting the interests in maintaining jobs and institutions when there are severely limited prospects for employment in the context of public-sector retrenchment.

Texas Democratic state senator Juan "Chuy" Hinojosa, a key architect of the community-based reform movement, was one of the few politicians who criticized relying on state-run prisons as a source of economic development and jobs. He argued, "[B]y and large, our goal is to regionalize treatment. There are going to be some chambers of commerce complaining, but incarcerating youth should not be used as a tool for economic development" (quoted in Hernandez 2007c). And yet, in the same breath he assured his constituents that in his district, the Evins Regional Juvenile Center would not be susceptible to closing because it was an urban facility (Hernandez 2007c). Hinojosa asserted, "[W]e're not Pyote," referring to the rural prison where the abuse scandal that spurred reforms centered (Sunset Advisory Commission 2009, 112).[36] His statement conveyed that Evins was not part of the problem because of its geographic location and therefore was not liable to be closed (Hernandez 2007c). As for Pyote, West Texans protested the loss of 228 jobs, preventing the facility from closing until the end of 2010 (Ward 2007a).

While the state was ultimately able to overcome the three-year-long local resistance to closing the Pyote facility, the debate revealed the competition at the local level over siting prisons. And despite his assurances otherwise, it exposed the interest Hinojosa represented in ensuring facilities remain open for the benefit of local communities worried about funding and job losses. One of the reasons the state enacted the provision that the closed state-run prisons could be transferred to counties was to appease these local interests in keeping these institutions open. As Eason (2017) has argued, the construction of rural prisons is often a "last-ditch effort" to stem economic decline. The community-based reform movement does not adequately address these interests at the local level that often work against shrinking probation and secure confinement and may actually be further entrenching them. This tension is particularly heightened by the primacy of cost cuts and economic efficiency in the community-based reform movement. Major public investments would be a way to ensure jobs and resources are provided at the local level, potentially diffusing the source of why local actors resist facility closures, but this would run contrary to the promise of cost savings and the fiscal austerity commitments in the reforms.

Summary

Analyzing the way devolution plays out in the juvenile justice system requires consideration of the broader political context in which it is occurring. It is not accidental that devolution is occurring in the context of widespread public-sector retrenchment. The goals of the community-based movement in the juvenile justice system mirror the austerity goals of the broader turn away from universal guaranteed programs and services. Because the community-based reforms carry the same logic and *also* occur within the context of public-sector retrenchment, the ideal of turning to the community to solve the problems of the juvenile justice system is not met in the on-the-ground reality of reform in these three model states. Without robustly funded, public supported alternatives and greater equality (not growing *in*equality), the aspirations of the community-based movement will not be fulfilled. Instead, the money allocated to community-based reforms has largely gone toward punitive policies, such as secure confinement and probation, further entrenching these practices at the local level.

Despite constant assertions that counties are less punitive and abusive than the state in carrying out these policies, on-the-ground evidence suggests this is not the case. Counties replicate the very problems of the state-run system with greater numbers of youth and less oversight. Bolstering county probation departments in the name of the superiority of community-based solutions creates interests that run contrary to decarceration, especially when the reforms are paired with public-sector retrenchment and geared toward the goal of cost savings. The continued and expanded interests at the local level in maintaining these juvenile justice institutions are not incentivized to downsize, and in fact more public-sector retrenchment increases calls for juvenile justice system expansion. For many youth, their experience and treatment has not gotten better as a result of the reforms and, in some cases, has gotten worse.

The community-based reform movement remains narrowly tailored around in-system changes, and there is little imagination for expanded public institutions outside the justice system that would better support youth, like mental health services, public education, public employment, public health, and cash assistance to families. Instead of a more capacious vision of how youth could be supported outside of state-run prisons, the reforms call for turning over youth to local probation departments as the way to provide better support and treatment. This is a consequence of divorcing the goals of juvenile justice reform from broader changes to the political economy and positioning the reforms themselves as part of the broader effort to divest in public funds in order to cut costs. The next chapter shows that not only is the community-based reform movement detached from the role of public-sector investments in producing positive outcomes for youth; it is actually geared in the opposite direction—promoting the expansion of private solutions. In addition to the pitfalls of devolution in the context of public-sector retrenchment, the increased privatization of the juvenile justice system also fails to address the abusive treatment of youth and further introduces powerful interests in maintaining the juvenile justice system and even expanding its reach.

3

Privatizing Punishment

Consequences of Foundation-Led Policymaking

As part of a major scandal in the American juvenile justice system, Judge Mark Ciavarella was convicted in 2011 in Pennsylvania on a racketeering conspiracy charge for taking millions of dollars in kickbacks from a private prison he sent youth to for minor infractions (NPR Staff 2014). In his defense Judge Ciavarella stated, "[L]ook, this was a finder's fee. We needed this center built. I was always yelling at kids because that's what they needed because parents didn't know how to be parents and so forth. So what's the big deal now? I mean, everybody was celebrating me all these years and now they're not happy with me anymore just because I took this money?" (quoted in NPR Staff 2014). Significantly, Ciaverella asks "what's the big deal" with privatization? Indeed, the private sector does not have the corner on the market of corruption and abuse in the carceral state, particularly as public juvenile justice institutions adopt a similar market logic in an age of austerity (Aviram 2015, 99; Pfaff 2017, 80). However, in addition to the gut-wrenching immorality of profiting from youth going to jail for minor in-school infractions (as thousands of youth did in the case of Ciaverella), privatization is also a powerful force stymieing the prospects of significant decarceration. The increased role of the private sector in the justice system undermines the humane treatment of youth caught up in the system and diminishes accountability, transparency, and the democratic input in policymaking that is necessary to overturn the punitive carceral state. The community-based reform movement is driving juvenile justice policy toward privatization and by doing so pushing the system further away from a reform path that will significantly improve the treatment of youth in America.

The process of turning to community-based reforms and devolving control from the federal to the state and then to the local level is part of a broader shift in American public policy that has undermined universalistic policies. This policy trend of devolution and decentralization has occurred in conjunction with a retreat from providing robust public goods made equitably available to all. In the context of public-sector retrenchment, policy areas ranging from healthcare to education are being turned over to private service providers. Devolution creates opportunities for the private sector to expand its reach by negotiating contracts at the local level, often with even less oversight. Large foundations, nonprofits and for-profit companies are often advocates of this organization of service delivery and have become powerful leaders in guiding juvenile justice policy in this direction. While the juvenile justice system may not be categorized by all as a "public good," it is yet another governmental function and institution that is increasingly being shifted to the private sector in important ways and with negative consequences.

There is a growing consensus in the literature on mass incarceration that private for-profit interests were not the major source for prison expansion in the United States but have become a significant obstacle to reform (Gilmore 2007; Gottschalk 2015). The phenomenon of mass incarceration was not devised by private prison and security companies, but the rise of mass incarceration has given a number of for-profit companies an opportunity to profit from the growth of these institutions and services by commodifying the diverse elements of the carceral state. Between 1999 and 2010 the United States experienced an 80% increase in the number of people held in private prisons, even though the overall number of people in U.S. prisons increased by only 18% over this time (Aviram 2015, 99).[1] Companies running entire prisons to those providing phone services in prison or private bail have exploited the opportunities to profit from the correctional system and do not support the retraction of their particular sectors.

The dissolution of centralized policy provisions—in the service of promoting "community-based" solutions—creates a juvenile justice system that encompasses a wide array of public and private political actors and service providers. In this chapter, I map out the various forms of privatization that are occurring across states as a result of the community-based reform movement, specifically privatization in policymaking and privatization of the "hard end" (prisons) and "soft end" (community-based services) of the juvenile justice system. Additionally, I trace the on-the-ground consequences this has for youth in the justice system and for broader patterns of diminished democratic governance.

Development of Juvenile Justice Privatization

The use of private-sector contracts for facilities and community-based programs is a long-standing feature of the juvenile justice system, which has always had a much higher level of privatization than the adult system. In 2012, almost half of all juvenile facilities in the United States were privately operated, and in 2019 it was estimated that private facilities made up a larger share of youth confinement than public facilities (Pfaff and Butts 2019; Hockenberry, Sickmund, and Sladky 2015). Charitable and philanthropic organizations were instrumental in the Child Savers Movement at the turn of the century, imprinting on the nascent juvenile justice system a high reliance on the private sector. This was particularly pronounced in Pennsylvania, contributing to why the state to this day has the most privatized juvenile justice system in the country. The early "houses of refuge" and community-based programming for wayward youth crafted by Progressive-Era philanthropic reformers were often provided by private organizations (Platt 1977). The establishment of these private solutions was the product of moral crusaders who believed "troublesome" youth could be saved from the moral dangers of an increasingly industrialized urban society (4). The creation of the juvenile justice system was bound up in the development of private philanthropic solutions for fixing the morality of disproportionately working-class, immigrant, and racial minority youth, which ranged from psychological therapeutic interventions to harsh treatments and incarceration (Chávez-García 2012; Platt 1977; Ward 2012).

Juvenile justice reforms in the 1960s and 1970s also had a profound impact on private-sector contracting, pushing the juvenile system even closer to privatization. As described in Chapter 1, the culturalist versus redistributive vision of the War on Poverty was critical in promoting "community-based" programs that were linked to the adoption of financing formulas that increased private-sector contracts to carry out these programs.[2] Much like today, public-sector juvenile institutions were scathingly critiqued in the 1960s and 1970s, contributing to the promotion of private alternatives. This tendency was heightened given the popularity of community-based solutions being broadly advocated for in American social policy during this time. From 1970 to 1979 the percentage of youth held in privately operated long-term secure facilities went from 13% to 48% (Pfaff and Butts 2019, 367). Today, with the support of large charitable foundations, the community-based reform movement is enjoying a resurgence in popularity. These alternatives are being pursued with even greater fervor than they were 60 years ago.

The historical role of the private sector in the juvenile justice system has laid the groundwork for even greater expansion of privatization with bipartisan support today. Whether state legislatures are controlled by Democrats (like California) or Republicans (like Texas), there is bipartisan support for nongovernmental solutions to social problems, mirrored in policy reform efforts spanning from education and healthcare to welfare. Since there is not a robust, principled opposition to the commodification of a wide variety of public goods in either major political party, policy proposals that seek to bolster the private sector, like the juvenile reforms analyzed here, are readily embraced by actors across the political spectrum. This is particularly the case if the policy proposals are framed as improving efficiency and increasing community control.

Forms of Privatization Today

There are a number of different forms of privatization in the juvenile justice system today. One is the privatization of the policymaking process. The private sector largely dominates research on juvenile delinquency, the dissemination of reform models, writing legislation, and lobbying for reforms. Within this type of privatization there are two major groups responsible for these roles in policymaking: large charitable foundations and smaller but often related nonprofit advocacy organizations. Tax-free charitable foundations, think tanks, and nonprofits comprise a "policy formation network" at the national level that is distinct from democratic governance (Domhoff 2017). Foundations privatize policymaking by being powerful "political 'gatekeepers'" that shape policy and political possibilities (Jenkins 1986). Private foundations, nonprofits, and advocacy organizations are shaping juvenile justice policy and advocating for a greater role for the private sector to carry out the operations of the system.

The privatization of policymaking has subsequently led to the privatization of the facilities, services, and programs in the juvenile justice system. As scholars discovered in the aftermath of Massachusetts's decarceration experiment—a massive undertaking in the 1970s to close down state-run prisons—private service providers monopolized control of the "soft end" (programs and services in lieu of or in addition to secure detention) of punishment in the state, but they also were involved in the "hard end" (secure detention) of punishment (Armstrong 2002, 357). This ultimately undermined the long-term viability of the decarceration effort by developing strong vested interests in maintaining the size of the juvenile justice system. The argument for privatization is often framed as an alternative to the problems of large state-run institutions, yet private interests end up investing in the hard end of the juvenile justice system as well as the soft end. The community-based reform movement has contributed to increasing privatization in all three states of *residential services* (hard end) and of the *programs and services* (soft end) of the juvenile justice system.

These areas of privatization—policymaking, hard end, and soft end—comprise the role of both for-profit and nonprofit entities. It is often difficult to identify the difference between for-profit and nonprofit service providers in terms of their public identity and also how they operate. Contrary to the label "nonprofit," many of these organizations operate with a similar logic as for-profit organizations. As a number of scholars have noted, nonprofits (large and small) have adopted business methods and structures and focus on cost-effective delivery of services akin to for-profit businesses. Referred to as "sector-bending," the line between nonprofits and for-profits is blurred because they share a wide variety of approaches, activities, and relationships (Dees and Anderson 2003). Often a for-profit company also has a nonprofit component, and vice versa. Nonprofits and for-profits also often receive governmental funding, making the distinction between for-profit, nonprofit, and public unclear. Further, nonprofits often act like businesses operating according to pragmatism and short-term fiscal goals in order to compete with their peer organizations and secure foundation or governmental funding (Featherstone, Henwood, and Parenti 2004). Nina Eliasoph (2013) refers to the "decentralized web of nonprofit and for-profit organizations" as a key feature of American governance.

This complicated web is central to understanding the development of juvenile justice reforms and the changing composition of institutions, programs, and services that youth are subjected to in the system. A wide scholarship on the effects of privatization in the criminal justice system suggests that privatization is incongruent with decarceration and can often serve to expand the number of people under correctional control (Bakal 1998; Feeley 2002; Lucken 1997; Lundahl et al. 2009; McDonald 1994; Segal and Aviram 1978; Shichor and Bartollas 1990). Scholars have long argued that a major consequence of private-sector involvement in the justice system is that these entities have an interest in growing their clientele, acting as a force of entrenchment and expansion (Bakal 1998; DiMaggio and Anheier 1990; Lucken 1997; Segal and Aviram 1978). Whether a small nonprofit or a large for-profit organization, private-sector service providers want to maintain their place within the system, and they also often seek to grow their services. The three forms of privatization—policymaking, hard end, soft end—are interrelated and together show the ubiquitous role of the private sector that has been introduced into the juvenile justice system through the process of devolution in the community-based reform movement. Expanding the role of the private sector in juvenile justice policy is an obstacle to significant decarceration, threatens the humane treatment of youth in the system, and is corrosive to democracy.

Policymaking Privatization

The policymaking process in the juvenile justice system is increasingly being privatized through the nationalizing role of large charitable foundations, with profound implications for democratic governance and the nature of juvenile justice policy. The privatization of the policymaking process in the juvenile justice system diminishes democratic accountability and also causes greater privatization of the institutions (hard end) and services (soft end) of the system. The MacArthur Foundation and Annie E. Casey Foundation are central actors in providing research, grants, and policy proposals for juvenile justice reforms. The leadership of these large foundations has helped forge a consensus around a technocratic and pro-privatization approach to reform across diverse states. Large foundations are central to promulgating a model for the juvenile justice system that relies on public-private partnership in the delivery of services. Despite major political differences between Pennsylvania, California, and Texas, these three states are pursuing similar policies in the juvenile justice system in part because of the leadership from foundations that wield a great amount of power by dominating research and policy recommendations for addressing juvenile delinquency and providing a large amount of resources for grant funds.

Regardless of the motivations of these large organizations, their role in policymaking lacks any process of democratic input. These private entities exercise political and ideological control by "circumscribing the boundaries of public debate" (O'Connor 2007, 3). As Robert Arnove (1980) describes it, foundations have "a corrosive influence on a democratic society; they represent relatively unregulated and unaccountable concentrations of power and wealth which buy talent, promote causes, and, in effect, establish an agenda of what merits society's attention" (1). The most powerful actors in shaping juvenile policy today are not accountable to those affected by these policy choices. Two central tenets of meaningful accountability in policymaking are that people must have a clear sense of whom to hold responsible for policies and confidence their preferences can be implemented (Miller 2016). Foundation policymaking like that occurring in the juvenile justice system undermines both of these tenets. While much of the criminal justice literature, particularly that focused on the United States, promotes the view that mass publics has *too much* influence on criminal justice policy, resulting in more punitive outcomes, a number of scholars argue the very opposite (Barker 2009; Gottschalk 2016; Miller 2008, 2016).

Political scientists have found across multiple in-depth studies that the majority of Americans have little influence over what policies are adopted (Bartels 2016; Gilens and Page 2014). Thus, a growing literature supports the conclusion that it is democratic *deficits*, not excess, that lead to greater punishment in the United States (Barker 2009; Dzur 2011; Miller 2016). Lisa Miller's (2008, 2016) extensive analysis on this question provides strong evidence that a lack of input from America's public has led to more punishment and also state failure to protect vulnerable communities from violent crime. These findings suggest that insulating policymaking from mass public input, as foundations and other nongovernmental policymakers do, is detrimental for pushing policymaking toward more inclusive policies that address the lived concerns of working-class people. The technocratic, privatized method of crafting juvenile justice policy with little democratic input reveals one way in which the reform effort is perpetuating the political forces that helped give rise to the very policies creating the problems the reforms seek to redress.

Analysis from the three case studies shows that one of the major ways that foundations influence juvenile justice policy is by providing grant money and leveraging matching funds from the state to get their endorsed policies off the ground. Once the reform model, policies, and recommendations become established, financial support from the foundation is tapered off and funding is shifted to county or state budgets. Often the policies and procedures become permanent features of the system supported by public resources. Once entrenched, these experiments then become a guiding model for other states and localities to replicate. Through this process, these private actors exert a great deal of independent power over the direction of public policy.

For example, the MacArthur Foundation chose Pennsylvania as its core state for its "Models for Change" initiative, which emphasized leveraging public-private partnerships. When its community-based reform model was integrated there, the foundation expanded the model to three additional core states, then to 35 more states, greatly influencing new juvenile justice policy developments across the country. The Annie E. Casey Foundation also chose Pennsylvania as a model site for its Juvenile Detention Alternatives Initiative (JDAI) in 2011, under which four counties (Allegheny, Lancaster, Lehigh, Philadelphia) served as pilot sites. Building off this work, JDAI has become the standard of practice nationwide for how states handle the front end of the juvenile court process. As of 2018, JDAI has been replicated in more than 300 local jurisdictions across at least 39 states, the District of Columbia, and Puerto Rico (Guckenburg et al. 2019).

In addition to large charitable foundations, powerful advocacy organizations particular to each state have also rallied behind the community-based reform movement. These nonprofit organizations (some national and some state-specific) that also advocate for juvenile justice reforms help write legislation and lobby for the passage of reforms they support. While these organizations appear more grassroots than large foundations, often they too lack democratic input because of their institutional structure and their funding relationship to foundations.[3] These organizations often overlap with large foundations in that they may receive grant funds from the larger charitable foundations or work closely with them. The state-level case studies on juvenile justice reform reflect Roelofs's (2007) finding that "there is considerable collaboration among foundations and their networks of nonprofits" (480). The interrelated role of foundations in shaping policy and then supporting nonprofits to carry out these policies creates a powerful force that expands privatization in juvenile corrections.

For example, the California nonprofit Commonweal, an advocacy organization for justice-involved youth, receives funding from Annie E. Casey along with other foundations, trusts, and charities.[4] Commonweal was one of the key architects of the juvenile community-based reform legislation of 2007 (Senate Bill 81). The organization's director, David Steinhart, helped design SB 81 and is one of the Senate's appointees to the Board of State and Community Corrections, which oversees implementation of the reforms (such as voting to approve allocating block grant funding to jail construction for a particular county). He is also a lead trainer for Annie E. Casey's JDAI. In all three states, there are active and influential organizations like Commonweal that have significantly shaped policy development, even though they are not typically organically rooted in a democratic base of public support.

For the most part, these state-level advocacy organizations are progressive-oriented groups that have long championed the rights of youth in the justice system. In Texas, the policy sphere has been much more dominated by conservative advocacy groups like the Texas Public Policy Foundation (TPPF),[5] but TPPF has made strong alliances with progressive organizations. For example, Texas Appleseed,[6] a nonprofit public interest law center, has welcomed support for juvenile justice reforms from TPPF and publicly acknowledges that this has been a key to forwarding causes that the organization has tried to implement (Schill 2011). Texas particularly highlights the ways that large advocacy organizations have combined conservative antistatism with criminal justice reform to achieve this bipartisan alliance and push for privatization.

The alliance has largely been on the terms of the conservative approach to criminal justice reforms. In Texas, the conservative advocacy of the TPPF dominated the development of the community-based reform legislation, infusing it with pro-private-sector and antigovernment commitments. The organization's interest in reforming juvenile justice policy is based in a critique that the current system is a waste of taxpayer money and is ineffectual at promoting public safety (Levin 2014). The motivation to save taxpayer's dollars and shrink the government fits with the other initiatives the foundation has signed onto as a member of the State Policy Network, such as reducing state health and welfare programs and expanding access to charter schools and school vouchers.

Mark Levin, the director of the Center for Effective Justice at TPPF and a cofounder of Right on Crime, a conservative U.S. criminal justice reform initiative, has been instrumental in changing the way conservatives think about criminal justice policy. The changes TPPF advocated for in Texas have subsequently been nationalized through the work of Right on Crime, particularly in the South (Keller 2015). A number of scholars have detailed the ways cost-centered arguments have facilitated the embrace of prison reform among conservatives and helped forge an alliance between these actors and progressives supporting nonpunitive policies (Aviram 2015, 79; Dagan and Teles 2016; Pfaff 2017). The example of juvenile justice system community-based reforms highlights the other side of this alliance, which has been youth justice advocates' easy acceptance of a conservative logic of austerity and private solutions in juvenile justice policy.

This conservative bent of community-based reforms is a consequence not just of the power of groups like TPPF, though in Texas this was a major factor, but of the broader political developments these types of prison reforms fit into. The rightward drift of the Democratic Party along with the popularity of community-based approaches to solving social problems that is rooted in 1960s policy developments has moved political efforts away from considerations of political economy. This means that even progressive organizations are not necessarily rooted in a politics that would make them fundamentally opposed to TPPF's larger austerity goals; instead they have become eager partners in this style of reform and particularly framings that emphasize cost savings and privatization.[7] The community-based reform model espoused by large foundations like MacArthur and Annie E. Casey that have influenced the orientation of many state-level advocacy organizations is compatible with the TPPF reforms, creating a powerful and broad coalition of support for the community-based reform movement that increases private contracts.

Many of the most active of these organizations are public interest law groups, which originated through foundation funding and continue to be tied to large foundations. For example, Texas Appleseed (2021), which lobbied for community-based reforms, is funded by Annie E. Casey, the Ford Foundation, more than 20 other foundations and 12 corporate donors. Pennsylvania's Juvenile Law Center, one of the most influential state advocacy organizations in juvenile justice policy in the state, is a frequent recipient of MacArthur Foundation grant money. Organizations like these often rely on funding from foundations, so even if that is a small portion of their budget, the foundations can exert decisive control (Roelofs 2007). In California, an organization called Californians United for a Responsible Budget comprises a coalition of 70 grassroots organizations that work on prison reform. At least 55 (78%) of the member organizations of the coalition receive funding from large charitable foundations or corporations (Youth Law Center 2018). The organization itself is financially sponsored by Social and Environmental Entrepreneurs (2021), a nonprofit that supports other nonprofits and that was founded by Andrew Beath, a California corporate real-estate developer. Even unfunded groups are influenced by large foundations because they often make operational decisions hoping to secure grants from these entities (Roelofs 2007).

The interrelated role of large foundations and state advocacy organizations is profoundly shaping juvenile justice policy toward the goals of the community-based reform movement and increasing local control over juvenile corrections. These influential actors are not embedded in popular support, nor are they democratically accountable to the public. The privatized nature of the policymaking process is pushing out democratic input that is needed to ensure policy changes reflect the interests of the people whose lives are profoundly impacted by them. The following section explores how private policymaking is shaping policy on the ground.

The Annie E. Casey Foundation and Camp Kilpatrick, Los Angeles

Counties in California have directly adopted the Annie E. Casey Foundation's most popular community-based reform program, known as the "Missouri Model," exemplifying the privatization of policy development and implementation and the ways it diminishes democratic accountability.

Exhaustively promoted by the foundation, the model comes out of the foundation's work in Missouri, where it established small youth facilities providing 24-hour treatment heavily inflected with a message of individual uplift. Santa Clara County and Los Angeles County in California, among others, have followed this foundation model for reshaping their juvenile justice detention centers (Nieto 2008, 22).

For example, Camp Kilpatrick of Los Angeles County was closed in March 2014 but was replaced by a new facility designed to follow the Annie E. Casey model. The new facility opened in 2016 after the county spent roughly $53 million of community-based grant money on renovations and changed its name to "Campus Kilpatrick." Following the Missouri Model design, youth at the new facility are supposed to be housed in small group settings and given education, counseling, and vocational training (Cohn 2014). Campus Kilpatrick is set to become the prototype for the entire Los Angeles County justice system (the largest in the nation). The camp is referred to now as the "L.A. Model" and is expected to become a nationwide model (Newell and Leap 2013; Sagona 2014).

The decision to pursue these particular reforms followed a common policymaking path. In 2015, a charitable foundation funded a "juvenile probation outcomes study" that highlighted high recidivism rates of youth sent to camps and the need for youth to have more behavioral treatment options (Herz et al. 2015). An advisory committee flew to Kansas City to observe the Missouri Model used there, and then Los Angeles officials chose to implement the plan back in California to address the concerns raised in the study. While there is nothing outwardly objectionable to this routinized method of policymaking, it is one in which policy decisions are largely removed from public view and input and it resulted in the decision to allocate millions of dollars to pursue the foundation-led community-based model.

Just two years after the newly renovated Campus Kilpatrick facility opened, it faced scrutiny after a member of the California Probation Department's independent oversight commission released a critical report (*Los Angeles Daily News* 2018; Wells 2018). According to the report, Campus Kilpatrick is not applying the principles of "therapeutic, trauma informed care" and has discontinued the small group sessions at the heart of the L.A. Model. The costly renovation was intended to support these ideals (in fact the architectural firm that received the bid designed the facility in this image), but it appears the design of the facility may not be the essential factor in achieving the goals of the L.A. Model.

One main contributor to these problems is understaffing—the facility has struggled to attract workers given its location and the condition of work there. The foundation-led community-based reform movement pays little to no attention to adequate pay and conditions of work in order to attract enough quality employees. This is one consequence of policy decisions that do not effectively incorporate the public or even key stakeholders like correctional workers into the decision-making process. In fact, the Annie E. Casey model for reform is predicated on increasing contracts with community-based service providers where there is little standardization of employment protections, pay, or training compared to public employees. In response to the report, the county is considering trying to get around labor contracts that mandate work shifts do not exceed 56 hours (Wells 2018).

While these facilities in California are publicly run, the shape they are taking and the funding directives are largely influenced by private entities. In 2019, Governor Newsom included in his budget an allocation of $8 million for the creation of "therapeutic communities" within the existing state-run facilities and $1.2 million to train Department of Juvenile Justice staff to carry out the rehabilitative mission of the agency. The proposal draws directly from the Missouri Model and is supposed to create smaller divisions within existing facilities to create small groups for youth in the prisons. While foundations and policymakers likely believe they are operating in the best interests of youth, such decisions are almost entirely removed from any democratic input.

The buildup of youth prisons in the first place was done without the input of those most impacted by their construction. The community-based reform movement is replicating this pattern of undemocratic policymaking and inequitable and punitive outcomes. The example of Campus Kilpatrick suggests the reforms have been directed toward measures like a facility makeover but fail to address the bigger problem of youth being sent to a prison, whether a small or large facility. The community-based reforms also ignore the needs and treatment of workers in these facilities who are central to determining the day-to-day treatment of incarcerated youth. The case of Campus Kilpatrick shows that the foundation community-based reform model is being plucked up and applied with little regard to the unique circumstances on the ground. It also suggests there is very little community input in these community-based reforms.

The MacArthur Foundation and Young Adult Courts in California

Another major development coming from foundation leadership has been an emerging interest in the creation of young adult courts (YACs) that hold people 18 to 25 years old in separate prisons intended to cater to their particular needs. The interest in YACs is directly connected to the MacArthur Foundation's research on the brain development of adolescents and a key example of how foundations create "common wisdom" and steer policy developments in profound ways (Roelofs 2007). MacArthur has dedicated millions of dollars to this line of research through its creation of the Research Network on Adolescent Development and Juvenile Justice. Housed at Temple University in Philadelphia, this network examines the neuroscience behind adolescent brain development. These studies have found that brains continue to develop well into one's mid-20s.[8] The neuroscience and brain maturity arguments for juvenile reform have become common among reformers. Advocates draw from this research to argue that people in prison up to the age of 25 deserve the rehabilitative, therapeutic interventions being targeted at youth offenders. Both counties and the state-run prison system in California have cited this research in proposals to open YACs. While the facilities themselves are not privately run (thus far), their construction and promotion is influenced by private actors, and the services *within* the prisons are largely provided by the private sector.

In 2015, San Francisco County created a new YAC, the first of its kind in the country, to serve eligible adults 18 to 24 years old, drawing from adolescent brain development research. The website of the California Superior Court, San Francisco County (2019) asserts, "[T]he prefrontal cortex of the brain—responsible for our cognitive processing and impulse control—does not fully develop until the early to mid-20s." The San Francisco YAC reports a success rate of about 45% from its first cohort. The court has received praise from the likes of the *New York Times* and Brent J. Cohen, a former senior policy adviser in the Obama Department of Justice.

Relying on research supported by the MacArthur Foundation, recent developments at the state level have followed these same policy trends. In 2016, the California legislature passed Senate Bill 1004, which created a pilot program in five counties to send 18- to 21-year-olds to juvenile halls instead of adult county jails. The proposal had bipartisan support and the backing of the Chief Probation Officers of California. On the heels of this pilot program, in 2018 the legislature also passed Senate Bill 1106, the Transitional Age Youth Pilot Program. Explicitly relying on "mounting brain research of treatment options for youthful offenders," the new legislation expanded the initial pilot program (Chief Probation Officers of California 2018).

In 2019 the state officially adopted a seven-year pilot program to divert young male offenders (18 to 25 years old) from adult prison to a juvenile facility. The enacted 2018–2019 budget allocated $3.8 million for the New Young Adult Pilot Program, with plans to expand funding to $9.2 million in 2020–2021. The "diverted" men will be held at the O. H. Close Youth Correctional Facility in Stockton in two newly opened 38-bed units (California Department of Corrections and Rehabilitation 2019). The units are supposed to have intensive behavioral programming largely provided by private nonprofits. The facility currently partners with The Last Mile, a private nonprofit that provides programs that teach "skills that include entrepreneurship, front-end coding, web and mobile app development and quality assurance" to people in the prison. The nonprofit is active in 12 facilities in California, Indiana, Kansas, and Oklahoma and seeks to "change lives through tech." In 2019 The Last Mile received a $2 million grant from Google to further its work (Goldeen 2019). In addition to the tech giant, the nonprofit also partners with a number of private entities, such as the software company Slack, the Kellogg Foundation, the Chan-Zuckerberg Initiative, and FreeAmerica (The Last Mile 2019).[9]

This rising popularity of YACs comes with a number of troubling consequences. The neuroscience research on adolescent brain development and juvenile justice policy forges a link between biology and culpability—echoing the reactionary Lombrosian view of criminality. These proposals are rooted in the presumption that one's brain development is determinative of the type of programming one deserves. (Those older than 25 presumably would not benefit from these interventions because their brains are "fully developed.") Additionally, this may lead to institutional expansion (as it has already led to newly opened housing units in California's prison system), or at the very least to the shuffling of people within the system to fill beds.

It is unclear what shape these young adult programs and facilities will take in the coming years. However, the model of the pilot program and the idea of young adult prisons are derived from the most powerful actors in shaping juvenile justice reforms: large foundations. The emphasis on brain maturity is an example of the ways in which foundations significantly shape and limit the boundaries of policy debates. The assertions about brain maturity have become ubiquitous in the community-based reform movement. This directs reforms toward carving out exceptions for youth (rather than holistically challenging policies directed at all people in the justice system) and relying on biological criteria to determine who deserves punishment and treatment.

The desire of the MacArthur Foundation to pursue and fund this vein of research is a decision that deeply affects policy outcomes and was made without the input and consideration of anyone outside of MacArthur. There are countless lines of inquiry that could be pursued with millions of dollars of support in attempting to improve the treatment of youth, but the role of foundations in policymaking places these decisions out of the public domain. Despite some of the larger concerns, the trend of creating YACs is picking up steam across the country. In 2016, following the lead from San Francisco, about six more courts opened in other jurisdictions in the United States.[10] The popularity of young adult offender programs is a quintessential example of the effects of the privatization of the policymaking process.

In California, the establishment of privately run prisons in the juvenile justice system has not been nearly as prolific as in Pennsylvania (the most privatized system in the nation) or Texas, which is more quickly moving in this direction. There has been stronger opposition in California to private prisons and more support for regulations that have deterred these developments in the youth system thanks to the state's more progressive political landscape and public-sector unions. Most of the private prisons in California (a small percentage of all prisons) are for housing adults or are immigration detention centers.[11] Despite this difference between the cases, in California private entities, in the form of large foundations, still significantly shape the design and developments of youth prisons, with little to no democratic involvement from those most affected by these policy decisions. While California has less facility privatization, the state and counties are still heavily influenced by private actors.

The variety of ways that the policymaking process is controlled by private entities, infusing policy development with pro-privatization incentives, helps to explain the ways the community-based reform movement has contributed to the privatization of residential services (hard end) and the programs and services (soft end) of the juvenile justice system. Privatization goes well beyond contracting out an entire prison to a private entity, as the complex role of foundations and nonprofits shows. Yet, in the community-based reform movement there have been a number of ways in which this very direct and specific form of privatization is occurring. The following section shifts to an exploration of hard-end privatization, referring to the private control of juvenile prisons and the implications of this type of privatization.

Hard-End Privatization

While the vast majority of privatization in the juvenile justice system is occurring outside of prisons, the community-based reform movement has significantly impacted the privatization of residential facilities themselves. In Pennsylvania and Texas, greater county control of juvenile institutions has led to increased contracts with private prison operators. Pennsylvania is the most privatized juvenile justice system as a result of the longer-term consequences of pursuing the community-based reform model. The vast majority of incarcerated youth in the state are held in private prisons. Texas has been quickly moving in this direction because of the broader bipartisan support for privatization and the general conservative context of the state. Although California has not privatized the hard end of the juvenile justice system to the same degree, private actors do heavily influence the policy design of its youth prisons. The privatization of youth facilities not only fails to eliminate the use of remotely located prisons but introduces for-profit actors into their operation, often with negative consequences for youth, and entrenches their use.

Privatization of Youth Prisons in Pennsylvania and Texas

Pennsylvania is a critical example of the long-term consequences of pursuing the community-based reform movement and its relationship to high levels of privatization. When the state passed its landmark Balanced and Restorative Justice legislation in 1995, a precursor to the community-based reforms that are resurgent today, it began expanding private contracts. As more counties got control over facilities, they contracted with private companies to run them. Private takeovers of juvenile facilities is a statewide trend; only a minority of Pennsylvania counties still operate their own juvenile centers (Miller 2012). In 1998 the state's Department of Public Welfare made a deal with Cornell-Abraxas, part of GEO Group, Inc. (one of the world's largest private correctional companies), to open up secure detention facilities in the state. GEO Group also has the GEO Care segment, which comprises privatized mental health and residential treatment services business, reflecting the private sector's emergence in community-based treatment alternatives. GEO Group (2014) considers itself the "nation's leader in safe, secure alternatives to detention and reentry services for offenders released to community treatment and supervision." BI Incorporated, part of GEO Care, is the largest provider of electronic monitoring products and services in the United States, a major component of community-based "secure alternatives." Today the company operates 10 facilities in Pennsylvania.[12] These prisons are located outside small towns and far from major population centers.[13]

As part of the 1995 reforms, the state directly tapped existing youth service nonprofits to become even more active in the juvenile justice system by licensing private providers through the Department of Public Welfare to expand their services to include secure detention. One large private provider, Northwestern Human Services, was initially started with federal funding for community mental health centers in the early 1960s. When the state pursued its major juvenile justice reforms in 1995, it licensed Northwestern Human Services to open a secure detention unit as part of its education and human services. Similarly, after the 1995 legislation the state expanded its contracts with Alternative Rehabilitation Communities, Inc. (ARC) (2016a), a community-based nonprofit that has been providing services in Philadelphia since 1975 to include secure detention. As of 2016, ARC had 11 residential programs in Pennsylvania.[14] In 2014, the company had 320 employees, $6.4 million in assets, and $14 million in income (GuideStar 2016). In 2012, ARC took over the Schaffner Facility in Dauphin County.[15]

In Texas, the 2007 community-based reforms laid the groundwork for devolving control of the juvenile justice system to counties while also promoting the expansion of private contracts.[16] In the same legislative session in which the landmark community-based legislation was passed, thanks in part to heavy lobbying from GEO Group, Jerry Madden (a Republican sponsor of the community-based reforms) also introduced legislation to raise the cap on private prison beds allowed in the state (including in the adult system) (Gotsch and Basti 2018). The authors of the bill, which passed unanimously, argued that it is cheaper to contract with private companies than with counties and that private facilities can offer better education and other programs than counties that currently have limited programming.

In the hearing for the prison privatization legislation, a representative from Corrections Corporation of America (CCA), Laurie Shanblum, argued that private prisons were a "better bang for your buck" and advocated for expanding state jail contracts (Texas House of Representatives 2007). Levin at the TPPF, who helped draft and pass the juvenile community-based reforms, also testified at the hearing in support of the bill and privatization more generally. He advocated for "unlocking competition in corrections" because the state is the consumer in the realm of criminal justice policy and "competition can work in corrections" (Texas House of Representatives 2007). In Texas, each community-based reform legislation had bipartisan cosponsors who also received campaign donations from the private prison industry.[17] The political action committees of Geo Group and CCA, the two largest private prison operators in the United States, ranked in the top 10 donors of Representative Madden's 2006 election cycle (Reinlie 2008). Senator John Whitmire, a Democrat who cosponsored juvenile community-based reforms and voted for the prison privatization legislation in the same session, was the recipient of the most private prison industry money in the senate from 2002 to 2004 (Institute on Money in State Politics 2006, 31).

The legislation expanded the number of private beds in the state and asserted that private contractors are superior to counties in terms of cost and services. The timing of this claim is important given that it came in the same legislative session where the major initiatives in both the adult and juvenile justice systems were appropriating more money for county institutional expansion. The goals of cost savings and shifting populations of offenders out of state-run institutions drove both county-level expansion and increasing private contracts. The state shifted resources to the county level at the same time that it advocated for increasing private contracts.

In 2011 the Texas legislature passed Senate Bill 653, a continuation of the community-based reform movement started in 2007 that pushed the reconfiguration of the system even more clearly toward privatization. The new legislation merged the state agencies operating state-run prisons (the Texas Youth Commission) and overseeing county facilities (the Texas Juvenile Probation Commission) into one new agency, the Texas Juvenile Justice Department. Senate Bill 653 expanded existing law and authorized the Texas Juvenile Justice Department to cooperate and contract with private agencies for programs and facilities. The legislation stated that funding for prevention and intervention services should come from "a competitive process" between "private service providers, local juvenile boards, municipal and justice courts, schools, and nonprofit organizations" (Texas State Legislature 2011). The bill also authorized the State Board of Education to grant detention, correctional, or residential facilities the ability to start charter schools for juveniles on probation (Daly 2011; Texas State Legislature 2011).

Like Pennsylvania, the transfer of control of facilities from the state to counties in Texas has led to privatization as a number of counties have chosen to contract out the operations of their facilities to private entities. Brown County, Houston County, Navarro County, and Jefferson County all took over state-run facilities as part of the merger provision in the community-based legislation and have since contracted with private entities. For example, Crockett State School was transferred to the City of Crockett in 2011 as part of the community-based legislation and was then reopened. The Texas facility has been renovated and renamed the Davy Crockett Regional Juvenile Facility (Washington 2014). A private company called Cornerstone Programs now operates the institution.[18]

Similarly, the Al Price Juvenile Correctional Facility closed in 2011 and was subsequently leased out by Jefferson County to the Evolution Academy Charter School. The deal fell through when the school failed to pay its utility bills (Moore 2017). Since then, a number of private companies have bid on the facility, including CCA. In 2017 the county agreed to a 20-year lease with The Dream Center, a Pentecostal community residential drug treatment company out of Los Angeles. The Dream Center owners have raised millions of dollars for renovations through other nonprofits and the use of Federal Home Loan Banks. One big expense is removing the barbed-wire fence you can see from the highway. The owners said "they're brainstorming ideas to increase the curb appeal while keeping the safety feature." They have also said they are "going to take a play on the prison atmosphere and have ID cards for the visiting students look like mugshots and have jumpsuits made" (Aldrich 2017). The facility transfer provision in Texas is a direct way that the state has devolved control of juvenile institutions to the county level and to private entities. Further, since the reforms were enacted, counties have opened up seven *new* facilities; two of them are private.[19] The expansion of new facilities, public and private, provides many avenues for private-sector subcontracting like bids to construct the prisons themselves (Eason 2017, 119).

As a result of the community-based reform movement, devolution opened up avenues for the private sector to broker contracts at the local level, where there is less scrutiny and oversight than at the state level. For example, the transfer of the Brown County prison from the state to the county and its subsequent lease to a private company has been suspected of being the result of a sweetheart deal. The county judge Ray West, who the facility was named after when it was taken over by the county and who brokered the deal with the private company, is facing allegations that he failed to use a competitive bidding process (Seibert 2017). While this is not an inevitable outcome of devolution and community-based reforms, the expanded discretion for county probation departments to spend grant money and reconfigure their justice systems does open up the potential for outcomes like those in Brown County.

State-run facilities transferred to counties are a key provision in the community-based reform movement, and in the context of promoting privatization this has led to an increase in private youth prisons. As the previous chapter detailed, these prisons are not being eliminated from use but are being transferred to counties and private companies to operate. The move to privatize whole facilities is a concerning development and one that is not accidental but a direct outcome of the community-based reform policies. Counties have limited restrictions on who they can contract out facilities to. Privatization in the context of austerity with limited oversight puts thousands of youth in danger of abusive treatment in for-profit prisons and fuels interest for expansion in the juvenile justice system.

Privatization of Prisons and Abuse

The private sector's increased role in the hard end of the juvenile justice system poses a significant challenge to scaling back the reach of the carceral state in the lives of youth; it is also a major threat to their equitable and humane treatment. Public carceral institutions are also abusive, lack oversight, and are supported by actors incentivized for expansion, not retraction, as has been well supported by these case studies, but privatization plays a uniquely harmful role in attempting to reverse these unacceptable outcomes. Privatization often leads to cost-cutting (such as hiring few guards, paying them as little as possible, and failing to properly train them) in order to maximize profits, which leads to dangerous conditions of confinement and creates situations ripe for corruption and abuse (Pfaff 2017, 83). When privatization is pursued for the goal of cost-cutting, as it often is, this can lead to less accountability and oversight, which can also increase levels of abuse (Cate 2021). Further, incentives to make money from correctional services can lead to abusive and corrupt practices rather than serve the best interests of youth involved in the system.

The community-based reform movement has targeted limiting the placement of youth in abusive state lockups, but the growth of private prisons goes against this goal. Private prisons are often plagued with instances of abuse. These institutions are in some contexts more susceptible to these outcomes because of a lack of oversight and the motive to cut costs to maximize profits. In studies on adult private prisons, these institutions have been found to have substantially higher rates of violence and higher staff turnover rates than public prisons (Aviram 2015, 107; Pfaff 2017). Prison guards working in private prisons have lower salaries than public prison employees (who are also underpaid and overworked) and less training, which undermines the safety of the youth (CorrectionalOfficerEDU 2016; Ferdik and Smith 2017; Thompson 2011b; Zoukis 2018).

Private providers, policymakers, and scholars can point to the failures of public institutions and claim private prisons are no worse (Pfaff 2017), but this does not make this a promising avenue for carceral reform. In Texas, the killing of a boy in the Granbury Regional Juvenile Justice Center is an example of how these abusive and dangerous conditions can persist in private prisons. The death of this juvenile and the center's repeated negative compliance audits largely stemmed from a lack of personnel. The privately run facility had cut positions in order to ensure profits. As a result, youth in isolation were not routinely checked, which eventually led to the boy's death (Clarke 2012). The private sector is indeed *no better* than the public, and in many instances is significantly worse because of incentives to maximize profits and a greater lack of accountability.

As was detailed in the previous chapter on devolution, shifting control to the local level with the goal of cost savings has led to a lack of oversight over the wide constellation of facilities and programs at the county level. This lack of accountability and oversight exacerbates potential problems with inequities and abuse. A particularly dark consequence of Pennsylvania's exceptionally privatized system and lack of oversight was the "Kids for Cash" scandal that broke in 2008. In Luzerne County, judges received kickbacks for sending youth to private juvenile facilities. Judges Michael Conahan and Mark Ciavarella received at least $2.6 million in payments from two private juvenile detention centers for imposing harsh sentences on juvenile offenders to ensure they would be sent to the detention centers. From 2003 to 2008 the judges sent 2,500 youth in 6,000 cases to private for-profit prisons for minor offenses committed at school (Jordan 2015).

When the "Kids for Cash" scandal finally broke thanks to the hard work of the Juvenile Law Center (the nation's first comprehensive nonprofit law firm exclusively for children), the state responded by investigating and prosecuting the judges as well as addressing the issue of inadequate legal representation for minors. The Juvenile Law Center has been deservedly commended for its work in exposing the scandal. However, the scandal points to the consequences of a devolved and privatized system in the context of austerity. This egregious violation of the law and deep corruption was detected and brought to light by a nonprofit firm that was tipped off to what was happening after years of malfeasance, not by any formalized state system of oversight.

In response to the scandal, the Pennsylvania legislature unanimously voted in 2009 to create the Interbranch Commission on Juvenile Justice to investigate the Luzerne case and to discuss ways to prevent similar events from occurring. In the hearings, it was suggested that the Commission should recommend creating an office of ombudsman. However, the Commission did not ultimately make this recommendation because, as the final report stated, "the statewide juvenile justice system as currently constituted can be improved without additional bureaucratic structures" and because the resources to create the office could be put to "more productive uses" (Interbranch Commission on Juvenile Justice 2010, 41). Even after the scandal, the state has resisted efforts to create a stronger oversight mechanism at the state level to oversee county operations.[20]

The lack of adequate oversight and the use of private juvenile institutions continue to be problems in the state. In 2016, at Wordsworth Academy Inc., a nonprofit residential treatment facility in Philadelphia, 17-year-old David Hess died by suffocation in an altercation with guards that was ultimately ruled a homicide, yet no charges have been filed related to the death. This is not an isolated case; dozens of sex crimes and allegations of abuse had been reported at the facility for years before Hess was killed (Terruso and Palmer 2018). After

Hess's death the facility was finally shut down. The large network of services and facilities operated by Wordsworth (serving over 5,500 kids in Philadelphia) was then acquired by Public Health Management Corporation, another nonprofit based in Philadelphia. Wordsworth declared bankruptcy, which may prevent it from paying compensation to victims whose lawsuits are still pending.

Then, in 2019, the *Philadelphia Inquirer* published a report documenting extensive abuses at the Glen Mills school, where court-ordered juveniles have been sent since 1826. One of the original "houses of refuge," the school is the oldest of its kind in the nation and has been lauded throughout its tenure as a model institution—receiving accolades from the U.S. House of Representatives, the Pennsylvania State Assembly, numerous U.S. states, and countries around the world (WHYY 2019).[21] The school has been accused of abusive practices numerous times throughout its long tenure but has managed to escape any severe recourse or closure. The most recent litany of abuse charges alleging boys have been seriously beaten and that this serious violence has been covered up by officials has initiated a U.S. Department of Justice investigation and led to a class-action lawsuit in part led by the Juvenile Law Center against the state. In response to the abuse scandal, the state has revoked the license of the school (which it has appealed) and counties have stopped sending youth there (Lozano 2019; 3 CBS Philly 2019).

These abuse scandals were exposed and condemned, but the use of private institutions has largely gone unchallenged. If the *Philadelphia Inquirer* had not conducted its investigative reporting, the youth at the facility might still be suffering abuse (Gartner 2019). The state continues to privately contract for detention facilities and has not devoted significant funds to oversight. The reliance on private service providers has deep roots in the state. The latest turn to the community-based reform movement is therefore unlikely to fundamentally challenge this long history of abusive conditions faced by juveniles. Far from isolated anecdotes, cases like those at Glen Mills are indicative of historically persistent problems related to privatization and devolution. In sum, these longstanding issues suggest the limitations of the community-based reform movement as a panacea.

Private prisons are not unique in having abuse problems. As has been thoroughly detailed, public institutions at both the state and county level have also been the site of such scandals. However, the turn to privatization is not solving these underlying issues and, in several ways, is exacerbating the conditions that lead to abuse and creating new types of abuses. Privatization is a key component of the larger effort to reduce costs. This leads to perverse profit motives in these facilities and encourages cost-cutting measures (like reducing personnel) that make abuse and negligence more likely. The move to privatization is not accompanied by necessary public investments in oversight and regulation because these would cost states *more* in order to assure the safety of youth in facilities. Finally, as these private companies establish a foothold and then expand their presence (as in Pennsylvania) they become major players in shaping juvenile justice policy and are strongly motivated to maintain and expand their reach, even when arrest rates significantly go down.

Privatization as an Obstacle to Decarceration in Pennsylvania

One consequence of the expanded and institutionalized role of private organizations is the way they become an entrenched force that seeks to grow over time. Pennsylvania provides insight into the longer-term consequences of high rates of privatization of the hard end of the juvenile justice system. In the state, the percentage of youth sent to private institutions has continued to grow, despite major declines in arrest rates. Figure 3.1 captures the trend only after 2001, when the state and counties had already substantially increased their use of private contracts; however, since this time the percentage of youth sent to private institutions has continued to grow. As of 2015, 57.5% of youth in Pennsylvania placed out-of-home were sent to a private institution. "Out-of-home placements" is a broad category that includes youth sent to groups homes, drug treatment, boot camps, wilderness camps, state-run facilities (secure and nonsecure), foster care, and other placements, but the majority of the youth in this category go to juvenile justice institutions at the county level.[22]

Despite a drop in the number of delinquency dispositions (those arrested or referred to the juvenile justice system) in the state from 45,504 in 2005 to 24,139

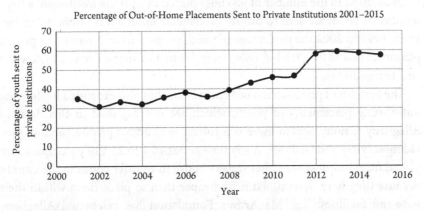

Figure 3.1 Placement in private institutions in Pennsylvania, 2001–2015 Source: Data compiled from reports by the Juvenile Court Judges' Commission 2001–2015 (only years consistent data were available), https://www.jcjc.pa.gov/Research-Statistics/Pages/AnnualReports.aspx.

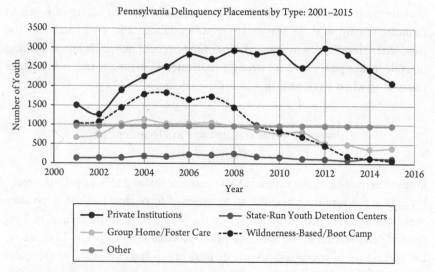

Figure 3.2 Placement in private institutions and state-run detention centers in Pennsylvania Source: Data compiled from reports by the Juvenile Court Judges' Commission 2001–2015, https://www.jcjc.pa.gov/Research-Statistics/Pages/AnnualReports.aspx.

in 2015, the number of youth in private institutions has *grown*. There were about 600 more juveniles sent to private institutions in 2015 than in 2001, despite the fact that about as half as many youth were processed in the justice system over this time. Figure 3.2 shows the number of youth sent to private institutions in comparison to youth sent to state-run youth detention centers and other forms of placements.[23]

This trend is occurring in Pennsylvania at the same time that the number of youth arrested is significantly declining, as illustrated in Figure 3.3.

In addition to the number of juveniles placed in a private institution, a large number of youth are sent to private placements upon release from detention. From 1997 to 2002 the percentage of youth released from detention to private placements more than tripled, rising from 9% to 35% in just five years (Zawacki and Torbet 2004).

The breadth of privatization in Pennsylvania has also expanded by drawing out-of-state placements of youth, which are not captured in this data. In Allegheny County, where there is a robust network of private vendors providing services and facilities, at any time about 10% to 25% of participants are placed from out of state. Other states choose to transfer youth to the county because they have determined it is cheaper than to place them within their state-run facilities. The MacArthur Foundation has celebrated Allegheny County for achieving such a high level of transfers, attributing the phenomenon to the private vendors being "so superior" that neighboring states want

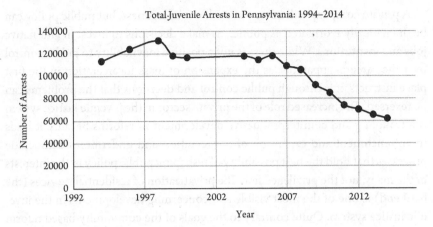

Figure 3.3 Total juvenile arrests in Pennsylvania, 1994–2012 Source: Data compiled from FBI arrest statistics 1994–2012 (Puzzanchera and Kang 2014).

to take advantage of them (Aryna et al. 2005). The out-of-state transfers are a boon for private vendors, but the practice undermines the ideal of community-based programs that are supposed to keep youth closer to their families and highlights the ascendant motive for *expansion,* not decarceration, of institutions and programs.

A major negative consequence of hard-end privatization is that private-run facilities want to stay in business and will be motivated to expand in order to increase profits. For example, many for-profit prison contracts have "guaranteed profit" or "bed occupancy" requirements, ensuring that a certain percentage of the facility (as high as 80% to 100%) is occupied at all times (National Juvenile Justice Network 2015). This puts these actors and their interests at odds with the goals of decarceration. John Pfaff (2017, 93) argues that private prisons are not unique in pushing for expansion and that "as long as someone, public or private, is benefiting from servicing prisons, that person will push back against reforms." While Pfaff is correct that public institutions, employees, and public-sector unions also seek to preserve jobs and contracts, there are a number of ways that the public sector can rein in or redirect these incentives that the private sector cannot. Public institutions ideally can be held democratically accountable. When masses of people organize, they can redirect policy toward the greater good and push against particularized special interests. While U.S. policymaking often falls short of this ideal, public control of institutions is the best way to achieve these ends. Public control offers a superior position to accommodate the powerful interests for job preservation and institutional maintenance that can stymie decarceration efforts and is capable of channeling these demands into outcomes that better serve the public.

A private company will never put itself out of business, but public policy can be dramatically reoriented as politicians make decisions to invest in alternative jobs and institutions. While there is not a positive inevitability to public control over the carceral apparatus, as the expansion of mass incarceration in the first place instructs, it is through public control and decisions that the problems can be reversed. The increased role of the private sector in the juvenile justice system is a troubling and counterproductive development in reforms because it leads to entrenchment and expansion of incarceration and undermines democratic processes that hold the best possibility of reshaping public policy in the interests of the many, not the privileged few. The privatization of residential services (the hard end) is one of the most visible and concerning developments in the juvenile justice system. Quite contrary to the goals of the community-based reform movement, private prisons do not reduce the abusive treatment of youth nor their confinement in remote locations far from family and support. Instead, the privatization of the hard end of the juvenile justice system introduces powerful interests into the system that are motivated to expand their reach, making this process a significant obstacle to razing the carceral state.

Soft-End Privatization

While the increased privatization of youth prisons is one of the most visible forms of privatization in the justice system, it is not the most wide-reaching form of privatization. The greatest area of expansion is in the extensive network of community-based programs and services provided in states to carry out a range of functions, from behavioral interventions to assessment tools and software management—what scholars refer to as "soft end" privatization. In all three states the establishment of community-based programs and services outside of detention in practice means private contracts. Community-based organizations are largely nonpublic, either nonprofit or for-profit organizations that carry out a range of programs and services, from those embedded in detention centers to those provided for youth outside of prisons. These programs and services are ultimately an inadequate substitute for the vast disinvestment of government-sponsored policies and institutions (Reed 1999, 127).

The community-based reform movement has explicitly directed states to increase their partnerships with this wide network of nonprofit and for-profit entities providing these services. For example, in Texas, TPPF was integral to the construction and passage of juvenile reforms in the state in 2007 and 2011. Since then, the organization has pushed aggressively for private-public partnerships in the juvenile justice system and in 2014 published an article arguing that the juvenile justice system is primed for such partnerships. TPPF outlined a vision for the system that it called an "outcome-based model" in which rehabilitation programs are funded by private capital, administered by a private nonprofit, and contracted for by the government (Cohen 2014). The organization captured the ideal behind the move in a number of states to bolster community-based services, which entails reorganizing the system into this type of public-private collaboration.

Even without the powerful influence of a conservative advocacy organization like TPPF in Texas, the community-based reform legislation in California has also stipulated increased privatization, particularly in terms of contracting out the services and programs in the juvenile justice system, another indication that privatization is a bipartisan effort. The landmark community-based legislation in California, Senate Bill 81, increased privatization by shifting juvenile corrections from a casework model to a brokerage-based model. The older casework model was dependent on probation officers supervising youth in the community. Under the new arrangement, probation departments were directed to expand their contracts with nongovernmental organizations (Macallair 2007, 3). Instead of delivering direct services, under the brokerage system probation departments contract with nonprofit agencies to deliver a variety of services (3). The community-based legislation of 2007 reduced California's reliance on state institutions by housing and monitoring juveniles at the county level through contracts with private service providers. In this new model of the juvenile justice system, private-sector organizations assumed a dominant role in the actual delivery of services, while the public sector assumed the responsibility of oversight in delivery (Macallair et al. 2011).

Since this broader structural change to the juvenile justice system in 2007, the state has continued to funnel money to the county level to support these private-sector contracts. For example, Governor Newsom spearheaded the establishment of the Youth Reinvestment Fund in 2018, which allocates funding to nongovernmental organizations to provide programs and services that will divert youth away from the juvenile justice system. As of 2019, there was about $37.3 million available, and 85% of the funds go to community-based organizations (Youth Reinvestment Fund n.d.).[24] Governor Newsom also included in his 2019 budget $5 million to increase grants for community-based programs (Petek 2019). These large sums flowing to community-based programs are integral to the community-based reform movement and exemplify the ways in which the soft end of the juvenile justice system is being privatized.

In addition to the explicit advocacy for contracts with privately run community-based organizations, a number of other factors have contributed to the increased soft-end privatization as a result of the community-based reform movement. One factor is the way the reforms have been implemented using no-strings grant funds that require quick implementation. The lack of specificity to what the grant can be spent on and the wide definition of community-based programs have allowed counties a great deal of latitude in spending the money. As the previous chapter illustrated, in practice most counties have spent the money on traditional forms of punishment like expanding secure confinement and probation. Within funds going to probation, the wide range of programs, from electronic monitoring to sex offender treatment, is often provided by nonprofits or for-profit companies.

As part of the process of devolution that occurs thanks to community-based reforms, each county has been given the task of building up its own programs and services, resulting in many turning to the ready-made services and programs provided by the private sector. For example, a key provision in the community-based reforms implemented in all three states is the establishment of risk assessment tools. Rather than each county developing its own risk assessment tool, and in the absence of a standardized state-created and -disseminated tool, most counties predictably turn to the private sector to purchase these.

Finally, the larger context of policy devolution contributes to privatization. As detailed in the previous chapters, the community-based reform movement is being layered on top of years of public-sector retrenchment, leaving many counties (particularly poor ones) without resources to carry out basic functions of government. In this context, privatization continues to be a viable solution given the dearth of public institutions and services to turn to in reform implementation. For example, in Texas 90% of foster care is privatized. There are not easily accessible public social services dealing with youth that can be used to bolster community-based responses to youth delinquency. The existing service providers in many counties are dominated by nonprofits and for-profit entities as a result of the broader shift in American public policy toward subsidizing private-service providers. In Pennsylvania, the long-running consequence of establishing nonprofit services to address "delinquent" and "wayward" youth made these entities easy to enlist in the juvenile justice community-based efforts. The result of these aspects of the community-based reform movement is that the private sector has expanded its role in the juvenile justice system.

Evidence-Based Programs

Privatization of the soft end of the juvenile justice system has largely gone hand in hand with the promotion of programs targeting the individual deficiencies of juveniles. The emphasis on these interventions will be explored in detail in the following chapter, but notably these community-based programs are largely provided by nonprofit and for-profit entities. There is a strong relationship between private service providers and the ascendancy of evidence-based programs premised on individual uplift. The private sector has become thoroughly integrated into policy proposals for the juvenile justice system through the promotion of evidence-based programs. For example, the Office of Juvenile Justice and Delinquency Prevention, part of the U.S. Department of Justice responsible for strengthening the juvenile justice system, has established a "Model Programs Guide" that provides information about evidence-based programs. The Office has determined 52 "effective" evidence-based programs. All but three programs were developed and are disseminated by a nonprofit or a for-profit company.[25]

One of the reasons that Pennsylvania is considered a leader in juvenile justice reforms is its support for the private sector's development and dissemination of evidence-based programs. In 1996, Pennsylvania partnered with the Office of Juvenile Justice and Delinquency Prevention and the Centers for Disease Control and Prevention to contribute funding to the Blueprints Project at the Center for the Study and Prevention of Violence at the University of Colorado. The Center was originally founded in 1992 with funding from the Carnegie Foundation and is currently funded by the Annie E. Casey Foundation. The Pennsylvania Commission on Crime and Delinquency and with the Pennsylvania Juvenile Court Judges' Commission (2008) have contributed millions of dollars to the Blueprints Project and invested in over 140 evidence-based programs in more than 100 Pennsylvania communities (Schneider 2007). Blueprints model programs are a variety of behavioral intervention programs run by for-profit and nonprofit organizations. (Eight of the 12 model programs are run by for-profit companies.) Table 3.1 lists the Blueprints programs and the type of service provider that runs them.[26]

Table 3.1 **Blueprints model programs**

For-profit	Nonprofit
Multidimensional Treatment Foster Care	Strong African American Families Program
Functional Family Therapy	Big Brothers Big Sisters of America
LifeSkills	Nurse-Family Partnership
Multisystemic Therapy	Olweus Bullying Prevention
Positive Action	
PATHS (Promoting Alternative Thinking Strategies)	
The Incredible Years	
Project Towards No Drug Abuse	

The Blueprints program, funded by large charitable foundations, was one of the early leaders in the effort to identify and disseminate evidence-based programs. Through its online registry of evidence-based programs, the organization has been at the forefront of evidence-based programming since the 1990s. It is a trusted resource used by governmental agencies, schools, foundations, and community organizations throughout the United States to determine which programs will "reduce antisocial behavior and promote a healthy course of development" (Mihalic and Elliott 2015). The promotion of evidence-based programs has melded with the label "community-based," and both are synonymous with "cost-effective" approaches to delinquency. The model programs determined by the Blueprints program have proliferated throughout the country and are a cornerstone of the community-based reform movement. Pennsylvania, California, and Texas have included the promotion of evidence-based programs in their respective pieces of juvenile reform legislation. Both the MacArthur and the Annie E. Casey foundations include the use of evidence-based programs as pillars of their core reform initiatives.

As a result, in Pennsylvania the number and percentage of juveniles ordered to participate in "competency development" programs (prosocial skills, moral reasoning skills, academic skills, workforce development skills, and independent living skills) have continued to grow over time. From 2004 to 2013 more than 75% of juveniles under supervision were ordered to participate in a "competency development" activity, which draws from the evidence-based program list (Pennsylvania Juvenile Court Judges' Commission 2013).[27] Pennsylvania has led the nation in the use of some of the most popular evidence-based programs. For example, the state contracts with Multisystemic, Inc., a private, for-profit corporation that oversees the dissemination of multisystemic therapy (MST), an intense community-based treatment program for juveniles (Multisystemic Therapy Services 2007). In 2014 there were 40 MST teams serving 54 counties in Pennsylvania (EPISCenter 2014). As of 2017, there are licensed MST programs in 34 U.S. states and 15 countries provided by thousands of clinicians serving hundreds of thousands of youth (M.S.T. Services n.d.). Given the growth of the number of youth required to participate in these programs and the fact that these programs are mostly run by nonprofit and for-profit organizations, this is a substantial area of private growth in the juvenile justice system.

In California, after the initial allotment of the YOBG to establish community-based alternatives, about 60% of counties established new programs, many of which are contracted from private entities. These privatized alternatives include day and evening treatment programs and counseling programs and indicate how recent reforms have funded the proliferation of soft-end privatization. Similarly, in Texas the majority of programs and services within probation departments are largely privately contracted for or privately run. Table 3.2 shows the percentage

Table 3.2 **Percentage of privatization of probation programs and services in Texas, 2018**

Program Type	Percentage of Programs Privately Contracted or Privately Run
Anger management	56
Drug court	40
Educational	29
Electronic monitoring	68
Experiential education	45
Family preservation	60
Female offender	25
Home detention	25
Intensive supervision/case management	3
Life skills	40
Programs for parents	47
Sex offender	78
Substance abuse prevention	42
Substance abuse treatment	55
Victim mediation	75
Vocational	50

of privatization of probation programs and services in Texas county probation departments as of 2018. In total, about half of all probation programs and services are privately operated or privately contracted for in Texas. Therefore, when the community-based reform money mostly goes to bolstering probation services, this leads to major avenues of increased private contracts.

Electronic Monitoring

Electronic monitoring provides another clear example of how the community-based reform movement is expanding a key growth area for the private sector. As the previous chapter detailed, investment in programs like electronic monitoring and intensive community supervision probation has been a major part of the establishment of community-based reforms. A majority of counties in Pennsylvania, California, and Texas have an electronic monitoring program, and a majority of counties in Texas and California used community-based grant funds to expand electronic monitoring. In Texas 68% of electronic monitoring programs are provided by a private company; this is not unusual. Electronic monitoring is a major growth area for private for-profit companies in the justice system, despite virtually no evidence that it is effective (Weisburd 2015). Studies show that despite claims to the contrary, in the juvenile court system electronic monitoring does not lower incarceration rates, save costs in the long run, or further rehabilitative goals. Instead, most research shows electronic monitoring has a "net-widening" and "net-deepening" effect on youth and contributes to the "adultification" of juvenile corrections (Weisburd 2015).

Yet, in the move to promote community-based alternatives to prison time, electronic monitoring is quickly expanding and is being dominated by for-profit companies. In just the past decade, the use of electronic monitoring for youth has roughly doubled in the United States.[28]

In the adult system, the First Step Act, signed into law by President Donald Trump and supported by the private prison lobby, includes provisions for "home detention" (which requires electronic monitoring), one of the fastest-growing areas of the private prison industry (Kofman 2019). The largest private prison companies, such as GEO Group and CCA, are aggressively acquiring companies that provide services central to community-based alternatives like electronic monitoring, halfway houses, treatment programs, and prison healthcare services (Stillman 2014). Since 2005 the two companies have invested $2.23 billion in acquisitions in this sector of the private prison industry. From 2011 to 2015 GEO Group spent more than $450 million specifically on acquiring companies that provide electronic monitoring and alcohol monitoring services (Joseph 2016). Electronic monitoring alone has become a multimillion dollar industry.[29] Today, every state except New Hampshire has some form of electronic monitoring for juveniles in the justice system (Weisburd 2015). In California, 51 of the 58 counties have an electronic monitoring program for juveniles (Coen et al. 2017). In Los Angeles County alone there are 450 to 500 youth on electronic monitoring every day (Weisburd 2015).

According to a 2014 study, every state except Hawaii requires those on electronic monitoring to pay at least part of the costs associated with wearing the devices (Kofman 2019; NPR 2014). Families often have to foot the bill for the costs of electronic monitoring for youth offenders (Mack 2018). While policies and fees vary a great deal from county to county, families can be responsible for exorbitant costs related to electronic monitoring. For example, in Alameda County, California, families are charged $15 per day when their child is being monitored (and on average youth are monitored for weeks or months at a time), and if the device is damaged the family can be billed hundreds of dollars for replacement costs. Further, if a youth is incarcerated in Alameda County as a result of a violation while being monitored, the family is still charged for electronic monitoring for the nights their child is in custody (Weisburd 2015). This contributes to a trend in carceral development that Aviram (2015, 144) refers to as "pay-to-stay" policies, whereby people are increasingly forced to pay for their own punishment. Soft-end probation programs like electronic monitoring are a major growth area for-profit companies and they result in negative outcomes for youth.

Risk Assessments and Case Management Software

In addition to the growth in numbers of youth required to participate in community-based programs like electronic monitoring, there is also increased privatization of risk assessments and other case management services. Risk assessments are heavily pushed in the reform models put forth by the Annie E. Casey and MacArthur foundations. In Pennsylvania, California, and Texas, the majority of counties have purchased risk-assessment tools since passing community-based reforms. Pennsylvania was the trial location for many of these assessment tools, and while some risk-assessment tools are created and run publicly, most are privately created and purchased through private contracts. In 2000, Pennsylvania was the first state to contract with MAYSI-2 (a for-purchase mental health screening tool), which is now used in 46 other states (Aryna et al. 2005; National Youth Screening & Assessment Partners 2021).[30] From 2004 to 2015 the MAYSI-2 Project was funded by the MacArthur Foundation as a part of its nationwide reform program, and today the tool has become "the primary method nationwide for behavioral health brief screening in juvenile justice programs" (National Youth Screening & Assessment Partners 2021).

In California across multiple years of funding, community-based block grant allocations have been used to purchase risk-assessment tools in the majority of counties. From 2013 to 2018, counties spent millions of dollars on these tools (California Board of State and Community Corrections 2014, 2015, 2018), mostly from Assessments.com, a private company that provides "proprietary predictive tools and innovative technology to help corrections agencies assess, predict, sort, and manage their populations" (AngelList 2015).[31] The company has contracts with more than 100 state and county agencies throughout the United States and brought in $1.5 million in revenue in 2014 (AngelList 2015).[32] The privatization of risk-assessment tools is an example of how state and local governments are contracting out the screening process of youth. Further, the tools are diminishing the human interactions used in screening processes that are increasingly replaced by employees having to enter information into computer systems that use algorithms to sort youth.

Another avenue for privatization is case management software for corrections departments. In 2019, Alameda County made a deal to contract out the administration of all aspects of its juvenile supervision to Tyler Technologies, Inc. (Business Wire 2019a).[33] Representatives from the county probation department lauded the efficiencies and cost savings the company would be able to deliver by replacing a manual, paper process. The contract was also part of the county's effort to "increase collaboration between justice partners to better achieve common goals and improve safety" (Business Wire 2019b; Trimble 2019). Tyler Technologies is the largest and most established provider of integrated software and technology services for the public sector in the country. They have over 10,000 sites in all 50 states and a number of countries, including contracts in 24 counties in California. Since 2012, Tyler Technologies has experienced double-digit revenue growth every quarter and made Forbes's list of "Most Growth Companies." It continues to forge more contracts and expand despite having a trail of more than a dozen lawsuits and numerous news reports concerning its problematic track record (Farivar 2016; Wadsworth 2019).[34]

In addition to the negative consequences of introducing for-profit interests into the justice system, another consequence of the privatization occurring in the community-based reform movement is that these providers are not as stable or consistent as public providers. Community-based organizations have a great deal of turnover because they often cannot sustain their programs in the long term. These organizations receive start-up funds but do not always flourish, either because they cannot secure additional years of public funding or they are unsuccessful (Nieto 2008). In 2008, the Public Safety Committee in California cited the high turnover in these programs as one reason that juveniles leaving Camp Gonzales in Los Angeles County face problems related to reentry (Nieto 2008). It is very difficult to trace the various community-based organizations and the number of youth they serve because of turnover and the lack of transparency at the local level. While there are large long-running nonprofits, like some of those in Pennsylvania, this is just a small percentage of the wide network of providers. Many of these nonprofits and for-profits may do a good job of serving youth, but they lack transparency and they have an interest in maintaining and growing their presence in the justice system, running against longer-term goals of downsizing the juvenile justice system. Further, they are insufficient substitutes for more robust and consistently funded public goods and services.

From the wide range of probation programs to screening tools and software management, the most diverse and largest area of growth for the private sector in the juvenile justice system is in the soft end, which is supported and expanded through the community-based reform movement. These nonprofits and for-profits comprise a complex web of services and providers that is largely out of the view of the public. The concerning increase in privatization in the juvenile justice system is occurring without meaningful public input or oversight and under the cover of the popular support for community-based services. However, many of these services are imbued with a punitive logic and work in concert with hard-end responses like incarceration. A full account of the role of the private sector in juvenile corrections requires attention paid to the interrelated bolstering of private contracts in both the soft and hard ends of the juvenile justice system.

Summary

Privatization is a key piece of the puzzle for understanding the developments in American governance over the past 60-plus years, and in juvenile justice policy specifically. The process of contracting out more portions of the juvenile justice system to the private sector is closely connected to the retrenchment of public goods. The foundation, nonprofit, and for-profit sectors that advocate for community-based reforms are so powerful because there has been an enormous concentration of wealth among the small group of people who can create multimillion-dollar foundations and they operate in a political system that privileges their interests above the voices of ordinary people. The path into mass incarceration was greased by these antidemocratic developments: attacks on the welfare state, the decimation of unions and other democratic organizations that represented large swaths of working-class Americans, and the upward redistribution of wealth. As a number of scholars point out, the bipartisan forces pushing for policies that contributed to mass incarceration are a critical but incomplete part of the story. Marie Gottschalk (2006), Lisa Miller (2008), and Vanessa Barker (2009) all show that the lack of *resistance* to these policies is a uniquely American phenomenon stemming from a deficit of robust democratic practices and equitably resourced society that helps explain the rise of mass incarceration.

Removing carceral policymaking from the input of those it affects most contributes to punitive and inequitable outcomes, and this is being intensified in the current foundation-led community-based reform movement. The lack of support for noncarceral solutions to social problems is widespread in the age of austerity, where there is little political will to fund and support universalistic policies that provide security for working people. While many Americans do support noncarceral alternatives, current social movements are not powerful enough to force policymakers in this direction. In the absence of mass movements of working people, the nongovernmental policy landscape is dominated by foundations and their related network of nonprofit advocacy organizations. This privatization of the policy process has led to growing privatization in the hard and soft ends of the juvenile justice system, adding even more stakeholders with interests in maintaining or expanding the system of mass incarceration.

Many prominent scholars of mass incarceration rightfully downplay the role of private prisons in explaining the rise of mass incarceration. Private prison companies did not devise mass incarceration in secret and then singularly impose these policies on Americans, but they do pose a challenge to meaningful reform. If the goal is to fashion institutions to be responsive to the needs of the people (not profits) and to have robust regulation and oversight, then forfeiting them to the private sector is counterproductive. Even if public institutions do not currently always serve the public good, keeping them in the public realm is the best way to ensure they someday might. A wealth of scholarship suggests that robust public control and funding in a number of other policy realms, particularly education and public health, is the best way to ensure institutions are equitable and adequately serve the public. Similar findings apply to the justice system as well.

Understanding the broader economic and political context is imperative for understanding the limitations and pitfalls of privatization. Private-sector expansion is tied to the effort to scale back public goods, so it is unlikely to be accompanied by robust public oversight. The turn to private-sector contracts is facilitated by cost-saving imperatives (even if this is misguided, as the private sector often ends up costing as much as or more than publicly provided goods) and so is rarely part of an effort to *increase* expenditures on oversight and properly paid and trained personnel. Public investment is necessary to reverse the pathologies in *both* the public and the private sector of the carceral state. Public-sector employees in the justice system will resist decarceration, just like private companies will, but this can be mitigated by a broader concentration on the labor market and providing adequate replacement employment to assuage the understandable resistance to losing jobs. There can be public solutions to these problems that ensure everyone benefits from juvenile justice reforms. The private sector offers few solutions that are not fundamentally in the interest of the private sector.

The private sector's role in juvenile corrections is a long-standing aspect of the system and is intimately connected to the view that the way to fix the juvenile justice system is by fixing the juvenile, not political and economic inequalities. Behavioral interventions, as opposed to universalistic public goods, are the preferred policy prescription of large foundations and their related nonprofit advocacy organizations and also happen to be the type of programs and services that nonprofits and for-profits are best positioned to provide. Charitable foundations have long contributed to this focus of the system at the expense of connecting the failures of the juvenile justice system to broader state failures to provide adequate support to all youth. The next chapter turns to this recurring feature of the juvenile justice system that traps reforms into a limited set of options that continually fail to solve the most profound problems with the juvenile justice system and its negative impacts on youth in America.

4

The Individual Focus

The Limits of Behavioral Solutions to Structural Problems

The Annie E. Casey Foundation says that among their values and philosophy is that "lasting changes can only result from internal choices made by the young people themselves" (Mendel 2010, 38). This emphasis on "internal choices" in community-based reforms is tied to larger changes in social policy in the United States in which major social problems are distilled down to individual explanations and solutions. The reification of external realities and the emphasis on individual change is not new. In 1940, the first director of the California Youth Authority, Karl Holton, described his philosophy for juvenile corrections similarly: "[W]e've got to teach the children that they must live in the world as it is" (quoted in Deutsch 1950, 118). Since the 1940s major shifts in political and governing structures have intensified individual behavioral approaches to youth delinquency. From Holton's leadership to today there has been a substantial upward redistribution of wealth and decades of public-sector retrenchment, creating gaping inequalities and concentrating policymaking power in the hands of the select few, such as large charitable foundations. Placing the burden on individuals to remedy the attendant problems that arise from massive inequalities and diminished democratic structures has been a crucial part of justifying and naturalizing these larger structural changes. Reforms premised on fixing youth in order to fix the juvenile justice system have arguably failed many times in the past and will likely continue to be insufficient solutions to ameliorating high youth incarceration rates and abusive conditions of confinement. As Pfaff (2017, 5) cautions, "reforms built on misconceptions will disappoint at best and fail at worst." A central misconception in the community-based reform movement is that correcting the individual behavioral, moral, and skills deficiencies of youth will be an adequate solution to the problems of delinquency, high rates of youth imprisonment, and abusive conditions of confinement.

The community-based reform movement pioneered by Pennsylvania, California, and Texas, with its endorsement of individual behavior approaches to delinquency carried out by local probation departments, has received widespread praise for shifting the juvenile justice system to a more therapeutically based orientation (Burrell 2014; Butts and Evans 2011; Thompson 2013).[1] Yet, the story on the ground shows a different picture, with most reform dollars flowing to prisons and punitive probation. While appropriations to treatment have been dwarfed by money going to traditional punitive policies, an examination of these individual behavioral programs and the philosophy behind them is a critical part of understanding juvenile justice system developments. A considerable amount of money has gone toward the crown jewel of the reform effort, community-based programs, but what exactly are these, and what do they mean for youth in the system? This chapter looks closely at the philosophy that undergirds these programs, what they provide for youth, and how and by whom they are administered. Ultimately, these interventions continue a long tradition of aiming to "fix" juveniles at the expense of larger structural explanations and solutions to delinquency. This individualized behavioral modification strategy in the community-based reform movement stigmatizes the "juvenile offender," disproportionately harms poor youth and youth of color, and fails to curtail punitive policies and carceral state expansion.

The community-based reform movement is premised on the assumption that local institutions are more benevolent and rehabilitative than state-run prisons and therefore need to be expanded (Schept 2015). It is through this belief in the rehabilitative and therapeutic capacity of the community that reformers advocate for the expansion of treatment programs provided by community-based organizations. Often the reforms expand privatization in the juvenile justice system because they are provided by the private sector, as the previous chapter detailed.

The type of treatment provided in community-based reforms in Pennsylvania, California, and Texas has several distinct features. First, it focuses on changing youth in order to reduce delinquency, lower youth incarceration rates, and curtail the use of prisons with abusive conditions. Pursuing changing youth as a solution to these problems tends to undermine or push out approaches that would challenge broader inequalities rooted in political economy. The second is that these programs are supposed to save money and reduce recidivism. This narrows the policy landscape to proposals that focus on cost and variables related to reoffending rather than on the qualitative assessments of youth's experiences in the programs. Third, the discourses of "treatment" and "positive youth development" in the community-based reform movement largely leave intact and, in many instances, expand punitive policies. Often the individual behavioral community-based programs promoted in the reforms are part of punitive dispositions or tied to punitive consequences, not alternatives to these policies. The "self-help" style of individualized interventions continues to stigmatize the juvenile offender as a broken, immoral subject in need of personal transformation, which contributes to continued punitiveness in the system.

This chapter begins by briefly detailing the cyclical nature of crisis and reform in juvenile justice policy from the 1940s to the 2000s that has operated within the paradigm of individual behavioral approaches to antidelinquency—whether ratcheting up punishment or expanding community-based treatment. Following this historical background, the chapter closely examines the consequences of the current foundation-led reform efforts continuing to adhere to an individualistic reform philosophy in three sections: the absence of political economy in individualized approaches, the embrace of narrow reforms, and the perpetuation of punitive policies in the focus on the individual.

Cycles of Crisis and Reform: 1940s–2000s

The history of juvenile justice development suggests that attempts to devise new types of behavioral modification strategies to root out "delinquency" will not curtail carceral expansion (Bernard 1992). Reinvigorating principles of rehabilitation and increasing community control are not counterpoints to punitive policies and high levels of incarceration. The rehabilitative ideal has always relied on a penal philosophy that justifies punitive policies (Grasso 2017). A brief consideration of earlier reform efforts in Texas, California, and Pennsylvania reveals that attempts to change the behavior of individuals has done little to diminish the expansive punitiveness of the system. In all three states, periodic disenchantment with large centralized state-run institutions led to efforts to implement community-based reforms. Much like today, these reforms were primarily predicated on better treating youth for their individual behavioral defects, but they failed to curtail the rise of incarceration and the abusive treatment of youth. The cycle of crisis and reform in the juvenile justice system has vacillated between treatment and punishment but, in all instances, has remained focused on individual behavioral approaches.

The 1940s: Cure Delinquency to End Abuse

While there had been cycles of crisis and reform in the juvenile justice system since its inception in the late 1800s, this brief historical analysis begins in the 1940s, when California, Texas, and other states challenged state-level incarceration problems with individual behavioral community-based reforms. In the 1940s

California had the highest juvenile incarceration rate in the country; abused and neglected children were held indiscriminately with delinquents in a wide constellation of county-run institutions and state-run reform schools (Macallair 2003). Widespread incidents of abuse in the state-run juvenile prisons created the impetus to reorganize the control of the system.[2] In response, Republican governor Earl Warren created a new agency, the California Youth Authority (CYA), in 1941, to control the three state-run juvenile reform schools, arguing that a more modern, centralized style of management would be the key to finally ending decades of abuse and scandals (Macallair et al. 2011). Holton, the first CYA chairman and director, pioneered community coordinating councils (county-based entities that organized various agencies and volunteer organizations to combat delinquency) and the proliferation of forestry camps based on a nonpunitive philosophy for delinquent boys (Roberts 2004). Conceptualizing the problem of abuse in prison as a product of prisons' size and institutional philosophy (a familiar refrain in reform strategies today), these alternatives were supposed to be small, camp-like schools. Holton promoted benevolent goals for the juvenile justice system, but he maintained that the problem with delinquency was the deficient behavior of youth themselves.

A strong belief in the power of science to identify causes of and cures for delinquency animated the policy reforms and had particularly harmful repercussions for Mexican and African American youth, who were disproportionately labeled "delinquent" and subjected to punishment (Chávez-García 2012).[3] The reforms ultimately expanded institutionalization, pathologized criminality, curtailed structural demands on the state, and continued the abuses and marginalization of youth. A decade after the 1940s reforms were implemented, all of the new camps exceeded the capacity they were designed for, institutionalization rates did not decline, and abuse scandals continued (Deutsch 1950).

In the late 1940s Texas underwent a similar development of its juvenile justice system. In 1949, Governor Beauford H. Hester, members of the Texas Training School Code Commission, and key legislative leaders all supported a bill to develop a new state agency, the Texas State Youth Development Council (TSYDC), to address accounts of abuse against juveniles in large state-run institutions (Bush 2010, 94).[4] The agency was commissioned to reduce the number of youth held in state-run prisons and also help local governments institute community-based prevention and rehabilitation programs (93). The Texas Training School Code Commission announced the new agency would be "the most extensive youth program ever developed" (93). In 1950, the newly minted agency's leadership was sent to the White House Conference on Children and Youth, where it was hailed as "a model worthy of emulation by other states" (93). The primary goal of restructuring the institutions in Texas was to promote individualized treatment. This central goal followed a national trend of promoting an ideal of rehabilitation that emphasized individual psychological deficiencies as the cause of delinquency.

Like California, less than a decade after the reforms were instituted the incarcerated juvenile population in Texas rose. Budgetary concerns and social pressure to address growing anxiety about the threat of juvenile offenders led TSYDC to become a version of the regime it sought to replace. Failing to "cure" delinquency through community-based alternatives, TSYDC instead functioned to oversee an expanding number of juvenile institutions (Bush 2010, 96).

Behavioral Change through the 1960s Community-Based Movement

In the 1960s, a familiar crisis emerged: nationally the numbers of youth in the juvenile justice systems had continued to rise and abuse scandals in state-run prisons spurred calls for reform. The "rights revolution" of the 1960s and 1970s extended criminal offender protections to youth, and juvenile courts became more professionalized and formalized (Bernard 1992). A growing concern about rising delinquency led the federal government to comprehensively address youth crime and incarceration for the first time.

In 1961, President John F. Kennedy established the President's Committee on Juvenile Delinquency, tasked to study and develop programs and policies to combat delinquency. The committee's work led to major federal antidelinquency legislation, such as the Juvenile Delinquency and Youth Offenses Control Act of 1961. The guiding principle behind the Committee's work was heavily influenced by social scientists Richard Cloward and Lloyd Ohlin, who emphasized the psychological causes of delinquent behavior. The emphasis on individual causes and solutions to delinquency supplanted efforts to address social and economic contributors to patterns of delinquency (Moak and Cate 2022). The influence of this broader turn toward individual explanations for social ills imprinted on the first major federal intervention into juvenile justice a focus on behavioral explanations and solutions to delinquency that influenced developments at the state level (Moak and Cate 2022). Reforms in the 1960s targeted the behavioral roots of delinquency to address both youth crime rates and abuse in scandal-ridden youth prisons. In the 1960s Texas and California earned the praise of the federal government and became models for the nation for investing in community-based reforms, small regional facilities to replace large state-run prisons, and "life skills" programs aimed at curing juveniles of their psychological shortcomings.

In the 1960s, under the leadership of Allen Breed, "the CYA pioneered work on offender classification, expanded vocational and educational programs, virtually created the enterprise of reentry, prevention, and embarked on a major program to subsidize communities to treat youthful offenders at the local level" (Krisberg 2011, 1). California was the leader in these innovations, and professionals from around the world came to the state to learn about them (Krisberg 2011). In 1961 the CYA piloted the Community Treatment Program, which pushed to place wards in community settings. By 1967, there were four times as many delinquents sent to community programs compared to those sent to state reformatories (Scull 1984). The Community Treatment Program was lauded by President Lyndon Johnson's Commission on Law Enforcement and the Administration of Justice Commission in 1967 (Greenwood et al. 1983, 72; Smith 1972, iii).

In Texas, the federal government funded the Greater Houston Action for Youth (GHAY), a model of the type of programs that were supposed to replace training schools.[5] Robert Sutherland, the director of the University of Texas Hogg Foundation for Mental Health, promoted the psychological premises of opportunity theory (espoused by Cloward and Ohlin) and was the main champion of GHAY's application for federal support (Bush 2010, 139). The project spent a great portion of its money on a media campaign that broadcasted the urgency of fighting juvenile delinquency and promoted a narrative that psychological disorders in individuals and families were the main causes of juvenile delinquency. GHAY's reports promoted the prevailing thought at the time that the urban poor's imprisonment was the consequence of their own moral and psychological failings (Bush 2004, 140–147). Consequently, the programs promoted the development of life skills and therapeutic services to help cure juveniles of their psychological shortcomings. The program in Houston reflected the prevailing beliefs in the "power of laws to change individual behavior, the power of behavioral science to uplift individuals and communities, and the possibility that social problems could be ameliorated without major changes to the political economy" (Austin and Krisberg 1981, 187). Additionally, reforms in Texas were also spurred by the *Morales v. Turman* (1977) case, which resulted in preliminary injunctions that pressured the state to increase community-based programs and improve procedural fairness.[6]

Texas embraced the rehabilitative rationale behind the programs espousing the tenets of opportunity theory, but aspects of the theory that concentrated on the psychological rather than socioeconomic causes of delinquency ultimately legitimized the expansion of incarceration in the juvenile justice system. By pathologizing delinquency, the reforms during this time promoted a personal responsibility ethic that was foundational to justifying incarcerating large numbers of juveniles in the following decades. The belief that youth who committed crimes were psychologically, morally, or behaviorally deficient fed into arguments that they needed punitive discipline and to face consequences for their personal failures. The ultimate outcome of programs like GHAY in Texas and the Community Treatment Program in California was an increasing use of detention to "treat" those who failed in community programs (Klein 1979, 150).

About a decade later, in 1976, Pennsylvania also passed significant community-based reform: Act 148. Much like California and Texas, there was bipartisan agreement that the state-run prisons were "broken" and that community-based interventions would be a superior solution. After Act 148 passed, state subsidies for community programs targeting individual interventions nearly doubled, from about $65 million to $114 million, much of which went to private service providers (Aryna et al. 2005). Between 1981 and 1984 the number of youth in community placements increased by 20% and increased in day treatment programs by 52% (Aryna et al. 2005). Act 148 is responsible for building up the most extensive and diverse set of local and community-based programs in the nation, all premised on the idea that individual behavioral interventions could decrease youth incarceration rates and instances of youth being abused in prisons (Griffin 2003).

The federal government's piloted antidelinquency interventions in places like Texas and California and the rise of community-based reforms of the 1960s and 1970s were critical in setting juvenile justice policy on a trajectory of heavily emphasizing individual, psychological, and behavioral explanations and solutions to delinquency at the expense of considerations of structural explanations and solutions (Collier and Collier 1991; Pierson 2000; Pierson and Skocpol 2002). The reforms sought to modernize and "humanize" the juvenile justice system, curbing the most abusive practices—but they did not challenge the notion that youth caught up in the system were psychologically deficient and needed programs of individual uplift. The changes did not address economic, racial, and social inequalities as sources of patterns of behavior considered delinquent. Instead, by focusing on individual explanations and measures of delinquency, the reforms codified and scientifically rationalized these structural inequities through the use of intelligence tests and psychological screenings (Bush 2010; Chávez-García 2012). Through all of these changes, these states became increasingly committed to principles of fiscal conservatism as well as a strong commitment to punishment and individual responsibility. Consequently, the number of juveniles incarcerated rose in all three states. This framework for the juvenile justice system has largely gone unchallenged ever since.

Individual Fix and Punishment in the 1980s and 1990s

The investments in treatment and community-based reforms did not prevent a punitive uptick in the 1980s and 1990s which was in many ways seamlessly layered on top of the principles of rehabilitation and individualized treatment. As Schoenfeld (2018, 2) argues in her analysis of prison expansion in Florida, there is "no such thing as a clean historical slate." Prior policy choices and discursive frameworks shape future institutional development. The two approaches—rehabilitation and punishment—were both based on the assumption that delinquency was caused by individual deficiencies. States around the nation worked to prevent delinquency but also increased punishments for youth offenders in a wave of "get tough" changes to the juvenile justice system.

While continuing to invest in treatment and community-based reforms to the system, California significantly increased its use of incarceration for youth in the 1980s and 1990s.[7] Between 1979 and 1982 the number of youth detained in California increased by 30% and the state had the nation's highest rate of youth detention in the country (Krisberg et al. 1986, 24). By 1991 California had the nation's highest pretrial detention rate for juveniles and was responsible for incarcerating 30% of the nation's youth in detention centers (Schwartz and Barton 1994, 47). The emphasis on preventing delinquency through individualized behavior programs had failed in a context of widening inequality and greater punitive approaches to crime. In response, states doubled down on an individual approach by adding into the juvenile justice system severe punitive consequences that heavily emphasized personal accountability.

Texas also dramatically increased punishments for youth while maintaining a commitment to community-based rehabilitation (Mears 2000). The state coupled the focus on individual uplift and personal responsibility that was highlighted from the 1950s to 1970s with increasingly punitive policies.[8] The emergent push for punishment subordinated principles of care, treatment, and rehabilitation even though these were not unequivocally repudiated (Fritsch and Hemmens 1995, 564). The Texas Youth Commission described this period of transformation as a "back to basics" philosophy where public safety and punishment for criminal acts would be balanced with the need for rehabilitation. Tougher sanctions and the many punitive policies passed in this period resulted in a nearly 300% increase in youth incarceration throughout the state from the early 1990s to the 2000s. The "get tough" philosophy of the era remained focused on individual interventions by emphasizing the need for strict punishment as a key tool for shifting behavior.

In Pennsylvania, the punitive turn in the 1980s and 1990s was layered atop the community-based reforms that caused the devolution of control to counties from the 1970s. The community-based reforms in Act 148 were in no way a counterpoint to the "get tough" movement in Pennsylvania. In fact, they helped streamline and legitimize the many punitive policies the state passed during this era by combining the two philosophies into one "balanced" approach for juvenile corrections. In 1995, the Pennsylvania legislature passed 15 crime bills specifically affecting the juvenile justice system in some way.[9] Pennsylvania is unique in that its most significant community-based reform legislation was folded into its most significant punitive "get tough" bill. The Balanced and Restorative Justice (BARJ) legislation created these punitive changes *and* promoted devolution and community-based reforms to corrections. Pennsylvania's continual commitment to community-based reforms did not stop punitive policies from expanding. The strategy of "fixing" youth through community-based individualized interventions complemented the ratcheting up of juvenile life without parole sentences and youth incarceration rates.

These states did not choose between punishment or rehabilitation but instead combined them in order to legitimize and expand the juvenile justice system. As Ashley Rubin (2016, 16) argues, "penal change is not a series of ruptures, but a series of accretions in which new layers are repeatedly added atop other, older layers." The administrators of the juvenile justice systems in California, Texas, and Pennsylvania never fully abandoned the principles of individual responsibility and rehabilitation, but these ideals had been directed in a substantially more punitive direction. The two seemingly opposing policies for addressing juvenile delinquency often developed complementarily because they both emphasized individual behavioral deficiency as the core to solving delinquency and contributed to sidelining political economy and social explanations for youth crime and incarceration rates. Despite the cyclical and repeated failure of individual behavioral interventions to stem the tide of rising youth incarceration rates and repeated abuse scandals, the current community-based reform movement largely is repackaging these old approaches.

This historical background provides the context for the ideological commitment in the juvenile justice system to individualized approaches to delinquency. The following section transitions to a focus on the current community-based reform movement and its effects. Rogers Smith (2014, 129) explains that "political developments always take place in prestructured environments" and suggests that "these environments are best seen as composed of intersecting contexts generating and shaping political life." The broader shift in American governance away from demands on the state to provide for the public good and toward a belief in individual and community-level uplift has conditioned the approach and outcomes of reforms in the juvenile justice system today (Bell 2019; Crawford 1999). While the policies and tools for handling youth offenders have new names and new networks of private service providers, they largely repackage an individualized approach to addressing delinquency that was born out of these larger developments (Bernard 1992). The individualized approach within the community-based reform movement is ignoring political economy explanations and solutions to delinquency, narrowing the range of possible policies to pursue, and perpetuating a punitive philosophy in youth corrections. Ultimately, as the following grounded analysis of these three leading states suggest, as long as the community-based reforms remain focused on fixing the juvenile to fix the system, they will not be up to the task of significantly reducing the number of youth caught up in the system or improving their treatment.

Absence of Political Economy Framework in Individualized Approaches

Efforts to provide treatment and positive supports for youth are a positive development in juvenile justice reforms, especially if they can be channeled into adequately funded public institutions and services. However, the use of individual interventions often *supplants* efforts to address and remediate structural inequality. As Chapter 1 cataloged, the move from material to cultural and individual explanations and solutions to social problems was central to the retrenchment of public goods and has facilitated a significant rise in inequality. The long-standing individual behavioral focus of juvenile justice reforms has largely gone unchallenged in the community-based reform movement, and these reforms have contributed to public-sector retrenchment and privatization.

One of the major features of the individualized approach to delinquency is that these policy proposals either ignore or naturalize features of the political economy. Typically, the emphasis on fixing the individual through their own personal uplift suggests that the context in which they live in—one of vast economic inequality, concentrated poverty, and public-sector retrenchment—cannot be changed or is not the problem to be solved in an attempt to reform the juvenile justice system. The "self-help" treatment orientation of the vast majority of community-based reform programs reifies existing economic and social structures of inequality and perpetuates the belief that those caught up in the justice system are there because of particular moral, skills, and behavioral deficiencies. This mischaracterization of the source of high youth incarceration rates and high arrest rates leads to inadequate solutions.

"Self-Help" Treatment

The philosophy behind the most popular treatment programs in the community-based reform movement largely emphasize "curing" and "fixing" juvenile offenders. Programs for inmate rehabilitation have become narrowly focused on reentry-related life skills programs (Phelps 2011, 33). These community-based interventions tend to emphasize "character building" and provide job-training opportunities. Programs such as these contribute to an understanding that the juvenile must correct their attitudes and behavior to best fit into society and implicitly characterize juvenile probationers as lacking morals and character. This type of programming has been described as a "responsibilization technique," whereby offenders are treated as "active subjects who have choice and responsibility, and are expected to bring about changes in their own lives" (Lynch 2000, 41; Nurse et al. 2018; Werth 2013, 224). What fades from view or is actively obscured is consideration of the social, political, and economic obstacles faced by juveniles (Bosworth 2007, 74). Self-help policy solutions are fundamentally conservative—even though they are often also embraced by liberal advocates and policymakers. Self-help interventions conform to an antistatist politics that often absolves government and public institutions of their role in creating patterns of inequality (Reed 1999, 12).

In California, many of these individual uplift programs are funded at the county level by the Youthful Offender Block Grant thanks to the community-based reforms enacted there. In 2018 alone, counties spent $1.2 million on pro-social skills programs and $1 million on life skills, group counseling, parenting education, mentoring, job readiness, and vocational training (California Board of State and Community Corrections 2018).[10] In Texas, the number of individual uplift programs provided by juvenile probation departments has substantially grown over the past 10 years as a result of community-based reforms. For example, "life skills" programs offered in juvenile probation departments in Texas have increased from 22 in 1999 to 659 in 2012 (Arrigona and Gonzales 2013). These interventions are not provided by professional mental or public health service providers but rather by a network of private providers with a wide range of philosophies and approaches to treating youth. While rehabilitative programs were once provided by public social workers in the carceral setting, now they are contracted out to nonprofit and for-profit entities (Schoenfeld 2018, 230). Many of these programs are religiously oriented and emphasize a self-help style of treatment. The devolution of these services has shifted the responsibility of rehabilitation from the state and onto individuals themselves (230).

These self-help programs encourage inward introspection and treat the challenges youth face as unalterable forces that they have to adapt to. For example, a youth who is labeled a "low-risk" offender using the Youth Level of Service/Case Management Inventory (YLS/CMI) risk assessment tool in Lancaster County, Pennsylvania, might be assigned to a short-term weekend program called P.U.L.S.E. (Providing Uplifting Learning Skills to Excel). The program uses evidence-based practices to foster "self-reflection" and "equip participants with new tools for managing life's challenges" to ultimately have youth "elicit internal motivation... to create positive change within themselves" (Lancaster County, Pennsylvania n.d.).

Pennsylvania has explicitly worked to expand programs like these through an organization called the Juvenile Justice System Enhancement Strategy, which is tasked with promoting evidence-based interventions. The Pennsylvania Commission on Crime and Delinquency (2012) describes the need for these interventions:

> Juveniles under supervision come with a myriad of challenges, but none are as prevalent or present as great a risk for getting them in trouble than cognitions that lead to negative behavior. These "thinking errors" include, among others, the tendency to rationalize and justify antisocial or delinquent behavior, difficulty interpreting social cues, underdeveloped moral reasoning, a sense of entitlement, a failure to assess consequences of actions, a lack of empathy for others, and poor problem-solving and decision-making skills. Such skills can lead to rigid responses to stressful situations.

A consequence of positioning behavioral and moral traits as the cause of delinquency is that these programs often pursue interventions targeted at correcting "thinking errors."[11] Nurse et al. (2018, 16) find through a meta-analysis of these programs that the cognitive behavioral therapy programs "used in the facilities are devoid of language about the role of social structure in shaping young people's lives" and "actively discourage young people from discussing the role that sociostructural forces might play." One of the most popular and widely disseminated evidence-based programs in juvenile justice reforms is actually called Thinking for a Change. It has over 10,000 individuals trained as facilitators, and the curriculum has a number of positive interventions about listening to others and problem-solving. But the core emphasis in the program is "cognitive self-change" based on research on cognitive restructuring theory (techniques to break negative thinking patterns), which perpetuates the focus on individual behavior.

The community-based reform grant money in Texas going toward programs that are intended to divert youth away from state-run prisons also focuses on correcting the psychological and behavioral deficiencies of juveniles. About 66% of these community-based diversion grants (Grants X and U) went to departments funding the following programs: anger management, behavior modification therapy, cognitive behavioral programs, life skills, parenting classes, family preservation, mentoring, youth empowerment, and youth advocate programs.[12] Many of these programs are contracted with private companies and focus almost exclusively on individualized behavior modification. For example, 13 counties contract with WhyTry, a private company that sells products for "resilience education." Vicki Spriggs, the executive director of the Texas Juvenile

Probation Commission from 1995 to 2011, is featured on the WhyTry website supporting the program.[13] According to the website, "WhyTry motivates youth to overcome challenges in school and life. WhyTry is proven to reduce truancy, change behavior, and improve academics." The program teaches youth life skills and claims that the mastery of these skills "empowers students to take control of their future." The message of WhyTry is that juveniles are responsible, through attitudinal and behavioral solutions, for their successes and failures.

The list in Table 4.1 is not exhaustive, but these are popular behavioral intervention programs, like WhyTry and Thinking for a Change, that youth in the model community-based reform states and throughout the country are required to participate in. The programs listed are contracted for mostly by county probation departments, but sometimes also state juvenile justice departments. The common thread within these programs, as evidenced by their mission statements, is the focus on individual change and transformation. None of the leading programs is capable of, or geared to, effect any change on the structural context in which youth operate or the constellation of policies that criminalize and punish youth in the justice system.

The wide network of programs geared toward this self-help style of intervention is largely provided by nonprofit or for-profit organizations. Many of the programs attempt to do the best for juveniles in extremely challenging circumstances. However, by ignoring larger structural contexts and myopically focusing on individual betterment, the programs perpetuate the idea that problems like delinquency and poverty are caused by individual failure. These programs, whether intentionally or not, take the onus of responsibility off governing structures and the political choices that created deep inequalities and patterns of policing that are reflected in the unjust outcomes of the juvenile justice system. The responsibility that is instead put on individuals is then frequently connected to punitive outcomes. These behavioral change programs are supposed to be an alternative to punitive accountability, but when they fail to remedy problems they could never alone fix, youth bear the consequent punitive responses that come from their failure to change.

Personal, Not Structural, Changes: Individual Approaches to Youth Unemployment

Job training and skills training are similar to individual behavioral solutions in the community-based reform movement in naturalizing patterns of inequality, considering these immutable "facts of life" that youth must overcome. The emphasis on job training in community-based reforms attempts to ensure youth have a fair opportunity to fit in with the existing economic system. This tactic

Table 4.1 **Individualized behavioral programs: Mission statements**

Name	Mission Statement	Type of Organization and Where It Operates
SADD (Students against Destructive Decisions)	"Empowers and mobilizes students … to engage in positive change through leadership and smart decision-making." (Students Against Destructive Decisions 2022).	Nonprofit, National
SNAP for Boys Program (Stop Now and Plan)	"Helps troubled children and their parents learn how to effectively manage their emotions and 'keep problems small.'" (Youth Crisis Center 2022).	Nonprofit, National
ReWired for Change	"To empower at-risk youth living in underserved communities in a variety of ways." (ReWired for Change 2010).	Nonprofit, National
I Choose Me	"To promote the long-term wellbeing of youth through a comprehensive mentor-focused, family-centered, community-based approach that builds support systems in order to create self-sufficiency." (Metro Community Ministries, Inc. 2022).	Nonprofit, California
Project towards No Drug Abuse	"Addresses topics such as active listening skills, effective communication skills, stress management, coping skills, tobacco cessation techniques, and self-control—all to counteract risk factors for drug abuse relevant to older teens." (National Institute of Justice 2011).	Nonprofit, California
Stand Tall	"To reduce recidivism by providing intensive case management services for youth … [and] building social skills and self-esteem." (HealthRIGHT 360 2022).	Public, California
Incarcerated Men Putting Away Childish Things (IMPACT)	"Offers male accountability seminars." (Nonprofit Metrics LLC 2022).	Private, California

(*continued*)

Table 4.1 **Continued**

Name	Mission Statement	Type of Organization and Where It Operates
Weaving Our Community Threads	"To involve juvenile offenders in activities that provide skill-building and relationship-building with law-abiding adults, while contributing to the community." (Goss 2006, 9).	Nonprofit, Pennsylvania
JUMP (Juvenile Probation United with Mental Health Programming)	"Assists families in achieving an improved level of individual and family functioning." (Pennsylvania Juvenile Court Judges' Commission 2004c, 1).	Public, Pennsylvania
PSST (Parental Survival Skills Training)	"Stronger parents can better help their teenagers make good decisions about drugs and alcohol." (Parent Survival Skills Training 2022).	Nonprofit, Pennsylvania
E³ Power Center (Education, Employment, Empowerment)	"Neighborhood-based, holistic approach to preparing … youth for achievement of long-term educational, career and personal goals, including self-sufficiency." (City of Philadelphia 2022).	Nonprofit, Pennsylvania
Change Happens!	"Helping people to empower themselves." (Change Happens 2022).	Nonprofit, Texas
CoNEXTions	"To prepare youth to take the NEXT step, to connect youth to healthy, law-abiding relationships with their peers, families, and communities." (Texas Juvenile Justice Department 2017b).	Public, Texas
Project M2: Mobilizing Mentors	"Improve youth outcomes in at-risk youth mentoring programs by establishing and strengthening collaborative community approaches." (Office of Juvenile Justice and Delinquency Prevention 2022).	Public, Texas
SOS (Second Opportunity for Success)	"Youth and families learn valuable skills to improve their relationships, their school performance, and their behavior." (Lena Popo 2022).	Nonprofit, Texas

takes as a given the lack of sufficient employment for youth and therefore targets the individual behavior of juveniles, their "marketable skills," to best equip them to navigate an inadequate and unequal labor market. The discourse about juvenile offenders lacking marketable skills and education as the explanation for their delinquency feeds into the notion that the unemployed lack jobs because of their own personal deficiencies rather than inadequacies within the labor market itself. Large foundations have tended to support prison reforms that promote this "supply-side" explanation of unemployment (Gottschalk 2015). Lafer (2004) and Moak (2016) provide extensive analyses on the inability of education and job training alone to ensure youth get jobs. In a labor market context where jobs are scarce, improving skills may help that individual, but it cannot solve the structural lack of employment for many youth (Lafer 2004).[14]

The heavy emphasis on skills training as a solution to youth unemployment and delinquency disregards structural unemployment. However, large foundations have made job and skills training a key part of their explanation and solution for the problem of delinquency. In Pennsylvania, major community-based reforms sponsored by charitable foundations have invested in youth job training as a central intervention for incarcerated youth. In 2005, the MacArthur Foundation launched the Philadelphia Reintegration Initiative as part of its Models for Change program.[15] The initiative is targeted to solve what MacArthur has determined are the core problems for Philadelphia's delinquent youth: "academic failure, disconnection from school, and lack of job preparation and marketable skills" (Griffin and Hunninen 2008, 3).[16] The Stoneleigh Foundation (2013b), a cosponsor of the Initiative, invested in the effort believing that "academic failure and lack of marketable job skills are known pathways to delinquency."

The Philadelphia Reintegration Initiative works with the best-known private residential facilities and partners with Lehigh Career and Technical Institute, one of the nation's largest secondary vocation schools, to bring more job training into detention centers across the state. The goal of the program is to employ youth as supervised apprentices in the day-to-day clerical, groundskeeping, and food service operations of the prisons themselves. Thanks to the MacArthur Foundation, the Pennsylvania Association of Career and Technical Administrators (PACTA), and state investments to expand job training in detention centers, by 2012, 26 facilities across the state offered 73 career technical education programs (Schwartz 2013).

In Texas, a similar emphasis has been placed on job training in the community-based reforms as a tool of rehabilitation and an anti-recidivism measure. The Texas Juvenile Justice Department utilizes a workforce development program that consists of partnering with private employers and community-based organizations to provide job training for incarcerated youth. For example, in the Prison Industry Enhancement program youth receive job training and employment experience (Texas Juvenile Justice Department 2017a). The emphasis on "marketable skills" as a key to antidelinquency has also contributed to the proliferation of nonprofits providing these services. Active in four reentry centers in Texas, Jails to Jobs (2021) is a nonprofit that aims to reduce recidivism among formerly incarcerated youth by focusing on "workforce development," "character development," and "spiritual development." The nonprofit partners with about 10 different Christian churches and dozens of private employers, among them Chipotle Mexican Grill, Home Depot, and Intel (Jails to Jobs 2021). Jails to Jobs identifies character and job training as key to the success of formerly incarcerated youth.

Similarly in California, the Free Venture Program seeks to provide rehabilitation for incarcerated youth through work experience and job-skills training. Under the program the state contracts with private industry business owners to provide this work experience. Only 20% of the wages earned are given to the youth, who work while incarcerated. Businesses that partner with the state through the program earn tax credits and are able to lower labor costs (for example, they do not have to provide any benefit packages to the workers) and, as the state advertises, they get access to "a reliable, motivated labor force ready to work immediately" (Joint Venture Program 2021).

In addition to sidelining considerations of structural inequalities, the job-training programs pursued as part of community-based reforms do not show strong evidence of working to reduce delinquency or youth unemployment. The programs have had few evaluations, mostly conducted by the programs themselves or the foundations supporting them. Most outcome measures suggest low rates of program completion, and there are no measures of long-term employment outcomes or quality of employment assessments.[17] Further, there is little to no evidence suggesting whether career education contributes to a greater likelihood of postsecondary enrollment or long-term employment (Staklis and Klein 2010). Other reforms have attempted to make youth more employable through changes in how their records are reported or in their physical appearance. For example, California provided funds for youth to remove tattoos to make them more attractive to employers. The core limitation of these reforms is that they focus on giving youth a chance at employment in a context in which there is a significant lack of jobs.

All of these individual interventions targeting increasing youth's marketable skills, addressing the barriers created by a criminal record, and having tattoos removed ignore the availability and pay rates of jobs for youth. These approaches do not address the ways in which the political economy constrains opportunities in the first place (Gottschalk 2015). Overall, unemployment for youth in Pennsylvania, California, and Texas, as in all other U.S. states, is consistently high. In 2016, Pennsylvania tied Rhode Island with the worst youth

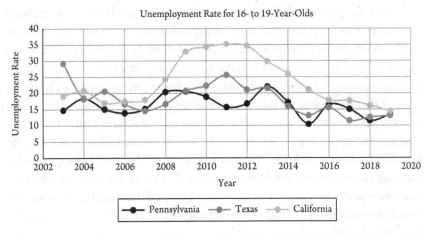

Figure 4.1 Unemployment rate for 16- to 19-Year-Olds, 2003–2019 Source: Data compiled from U.S. Bureau of Labor statistical reports 2003–2019, https://www.bls.gov/lau/ex14tables.htm.

unemployment rate in the Northeast and ranked 33rd nationally. In 2012, California had the highest rate of unemployment of those age 16 to 19 (34.6%) of any state in the nation (Maciag 2013). This is compared to 1977, when youth unemployment was much lower because 20% of California's job growth was funded by state and federal programs guaranteeing employment for youth who wanted work (Gilmore 2007, 48–49). Figure 4.1 shows unemployment rates for the three states between 2003 and 2019 for 16- to 19-year-olds. While the rate has fluctuated, anywhere from 1 in 3 to 1 in 10 youth looking for a job have been unable to find employment in these states over this time period.

The overall unemployment rate suggests that even if the job training efforts were effective (which little evidence suggests they are), they remain insufficient to address a labor market in which employment for youth is relatively scarce. Even youth who find work face a historically low minimum wage. In Texas and Pennsylvania, the minimum wage is just $7.25 per hour. California is moving toward a $15 per hour wage by 2022. In all three states, about 20% of people age 18 to 24 have incomes below the federal poverty level (Annie E. Casey Foundation 2020b). The insufficient labor market also affects the families that support young people, a factor again apart from the individual character of youth themselves.[18]

Because the community-based reform movement focuses on individualized solutions it fails to address deep and growing inequalities and an economic structure that explains why so few people are able to secure good-paying jobs. The obstacles to youth becoming "responsible, law-abiding citizens" are attributed to the individual juvenile's moral and personal failures rather than the fundamental flaws in the social and economic structure. Rather than address persistently high youth unemployment through something like public job programs, the community-based reform movement doubles down on efforts to mold the worker as a solution to unemployment. These individualized approaches to solving delinquency or youth unemployment are inadequate. In addition to being a core feature of an approach to delinquency that has failed for decades, the individualization of social problems contributes to naturalizing social and economic structures rather than challenging and upturning them. The high rates of incarcerated youth and the abusive conditions of American prisons are caused by complex social, political, and economic developments, and therefore solutions to these problems must be equally complex and structurally oriented. Instead, the community-based reform movement takes most strategies off the table and homes in on the individual fix.

The Embrace of Narrow Cost-Effective Reforms

The individual focus on the cause and solution to myriad problems related to the juvenile justice system has significantly narrowed the range of policy proposals and strategies for pursuing meaningful reforms. In the foundation-led community-based reform movement the promotion of risk assessments and evidence-based programs is paramount. Both policies reinforce the idea that individual behaviors are the cause of delinquency and, if corrected, can be the key to solving the problems of the juvenile justice system. Risk assessments and evidence-based programs are also closely related to an emphasis on cost and recidivism reduction, which exerts even more limitations on political possibilities. Individual behavioral interventions are often hailed as the cheaper and more effective way to handle youth in trouble with the law than locking them up. Putting a premium on cost savings is one of the most common and limiting features of the reform landscape today. The rationale that risk assessments, evidence-based programs, and recidivism reduction strategies will save money has proven to be politically powerful in garnering wide bipartisan support for these proposals. However, fitting reforms into an austerity discourse has made it even more difficult to pursue policy proposals that might require spending, such as ones that could ameliorate abusive conditions of confinement. The emphasis on individual interventions that can save money and reduce recidivism forfeits a whole range of policy proposals, specifically those that would significantly reverse public-sector entrenchment and persistent economic inequality—major variables that drove mass incarceration in the first place.

Cost Savings and Recidivism Reduction

The emphasis on recidivism reduction in the community-based reform movement has a particularly limiting effect on what programs are supported and how they are evaluated. When policies are channeled through the discourse of cost savings and recidivism reduction, attention is not paid to the qualitative experience of youth in the system. Gottschalk (2015, 106) argues, "[T]he single-minded focus on recidivism has diverted public attention from other important yardsticks by which to gauge the performance of correctional systems." Focusing on how to ensure a youth does not commit another crime as the goal of prison reforms perpetuates false ideas of what is driving high youth incarceration rates. Crimes committed by people released from prison are not a major driver of incarceration rates (Gottschalk 2015). Additionally, the skills and behavioral changes made in prison are not the major predictors of staying out of trouble with the law once released. The numerous restrictions and exclusions from mainstream society those leaving prison face are far greater contributors (Alexander 2010; Gottschalk 2015; Middlemass 2017). Focusing on reducing recidivism feeds into the individualizing tendency of the most popular reforms.

The Texas Public Policy Foundation, a leading organization in drafting and supporting community-based reforms in the state, often links recidivism reduction and cost savings to individualized approaches to delinquency. Jeanette Moll (2011) from TPPF asserted that "delinquent youth that learn a marketable skill are far less likely to re-offend and much more likely to be productive citizens who contribute to, rather than drain, Texas's budget." However, recidivism statistics in Texas since the 2007 reforms belie Moll's assertion. Probation recidivism rates have remained steady even though juveniles are participating in community-based programs (Texas Juvenile Justice Department 2012b).[19] The one year reoffense rate for "low-risk" juveniles who entered a community-based program in 2011 was the *exact same* as for juveniles who did not enter a program (Texas Legislative Budget Board 2013).

Recent community-based reforms in Pennsylvania also advance the idea that prevention and recidivism reduction can reduce the costs of the juvenile justice system. In 2013, Governor Tom Corbett revealed a plan to invest $10 million in community-based prevention and intervention programs for juvenile offenders. The programs the initiative invested in were evidence-based programs promulgated in partnership with foundations and the federal government that heavily emphasize individual uplift through behavioral interventions.[20] The 2013 community-based reforms set out to "intervene early on in an individual's life of crime by bolstering the front end of the criminal justice system, such as local probation and parole and law enforcement" (Wetzel 2012).

The main supporters and architects of the reforms and leaders in the juvenile justice system emphasized cost savings and cost efficiency as the primary policy goals of the community-based plan. Governor Corbett explained the rationale behind the reforms: "As we examined our resources, we realized we needed to take a closer look at the juvenile system. If we can prevent at-risk youth from becoming offenders, we can reduce the likelihood that they will spend time behind the bars of our country and state prisons, costing taxpayers billions of dollars each year" (quoted in Wetzel 2012). Similarly, Mark Zimmer, the chairman of Pennsylvania Commission on Crime and Delinquency, stated, "[W]e know the best way to prevent juvenile crime is through early identification and intervention. This long-term strategy benefits Pennsylvania's at-risk youth, while providing a greater return on taxpayers' investments" (Pennsylvania Office of the Governor 2013, 3). John Wetzel, Pennsylvania's secretary of corrections, described the reforms succinctly: "[O]ur goal is to reduce the future criminality of the offender—turning tax burdens into taxpayers" (Wetzel 2012). These endorsements of community-based reforms effectively aligned the interests of juvenile offenders with the interests of "the taxpayer" in a key strategy to forge a strong bipartisan consensus around the reforms. Investing a mere $10 million (given the Pennsylvania Department of Corrections budget by this time was over $2 billion) as a way to both save money and help juvenile offenders proved to be politically popular. The emphasis on individualized approaches to solving the delinquency problem in Pennsylvania is closely tied to the effort to reduce costs and conforms to a narrow range of proposed solutions—individual, not structural, changes that require relatively little public expenditure.

Community-based initiatives aimed at recidivism and cost reduction like that in Pennsylvania and Texas do not repudiate the use of traditional forms of punishment (detention and parole) because in this reform model these are still required once delinquency *does* happen or happens again despite the intervention. The state continues to position punitive accountability as the appropriate response to delinquency. The community-based reforms privilege targeting reducing delinquency as a means to prevent having to pay for these expensive responses to delinquency. Policymakers and reformers continue to advocate for individualized behavioral interventions, often carried out by the private sector, as the only valid solution to preventing delinquency, despite a lack of evidence they are effective in achieving this goal. These basic understandings of delinquency and the role of the juvenile justice system result in perpetually investing in prevention *and* punishment. The investment in behavioral interventions perpetuates the idea that high youth incarceration rates are caused by the individual deficiencies of youth. This perspective ignores structural conditions that lead to delinquent acts and fails to challenge how and why certain behaviors are considered criminal in the first place or question if they should be handled by the criminal justice system.

Risk Assessments: Race and Naturalizing Inequality

One major example of the heavily promoted cost-effective individualized approaches in community-based reforms is the proliferation of risk assessment tools. Risk assessments, primarily supplied by private companies to counties and states for purchase, are in many ways the first step in the behavioral approach to delinquency and juvenile justice reform. The ascendance of risk discourse concentrates on individual personal deficiencies, making economic, social, and political structures seem less important as targets of intervention (Gray 2009, 450). The use of risk assessments does not challenge or change the dispositions youth receive but serves to better sort the "right" youth into different dispositions. The investment and emphasis on risk assessments reflect a belief that the problems of the justice system, such as abuses and excessive use of confinement, can be solved by more accurately sorting *who* gets different types of dispositions—as the MacArthur Foundation has described it, ensuring "the right services for the right youths" (National Youth Screening & Assessment Project 2009). The hope is that risk assessments can minimize "low-risk" youths' exposure to unnecessary incarceration, but there is nothing about the tools themselves that ensures this outcome. Also, implicit in this goal is fine-tuning the identification of "high-risk" youth to receive more punitive dispositions, an effort that runs contrary to significant decarceration.

The use of actuarial risk assessments has been a feature of juvenile and adult justice system processing since the 1970s. More recently the tools have become commercially available and integrate complex algorithms and a wide range of factors. However, research finds that this newer generation of tools tends to be less effective and less reliable.[21] In fact, the more complicated and time-intensive tools emerging on the commercial market may not be as effective at sorting offenders, and they also have discriminatory outcomes. The MacArthur Foundation has been an important booster of this new generation of risk assessments and has made their use integral to community-based reforms. Risk assessment tools can widely vary in what they measure, but generally they are intended to inform a decision about whether youth are in need of secure custody. The more recent generation of assessments promoted by foundations in the community-based reform movement is also used to inform treatment plans by assessing the proper interventions for a youth to mitigate their risk of reoffending (Vincent 2012).

A popular tool that is used in Pennsylvania is the YLS/CMI. The tool is promoted by the MacArthur Foundation and is purchased through a private international company, Multi-Health Systems, Inc. (n.d.), which reports about $24 million in revenue annually (Owler 2021). The YLS/CMI measures both a youth's risks and needs and is used to determine the appropriate level of supervision for the youth. This particular risk assessment tool measures 42 risk/need factors in the categories of offense history, family circumstances, education, peer relations, substance abuse, recreation, personality, and attitudes (Pennsylvania Commission on Crime and Delinquency 2012).[22] Youth are labeled low, moderate, high, or very high risk based on the assessment. The assessment conjectures that youth who are high risk tend to lack prosocial skills and emotional regulation. While factoring in prior arrest records is fairly standard in the consideration of a youth's disposition, the introduction of attitudinal questions focuses the assessments even more on criminal propensity *and* susceptibility to treatment.[23]

Youth who score low on these assessments are often recommended to be diverted from prison, while high-risk "antisocial" youth are recommended to be given more punitive dispositions, such as prison time or intensive supervised probation. Overall, these assessment variables disadvantage poor and racial minority youth who are more likely to be labeled as coming from a "dysfunctional family" and scoring as "high risk" (Hager 2015). Unsurprisingly, the factors that are entered into assessments like these, such as prior arrest history (including that of the youth's parents), tend to reproduce patterns of inequality (Harcourt 2015). Poor and racial minority youth are more likely to get "high risk" dispositions and thus be channeled to the more punitive end of the system (Angwin et al. 2016; Harcourt 2015). The way that risk assessments problematically correlate with race and gender is a major concern as they are likely to increase the severity of sanctions poor and minority youth receive (Harcourt 2015; Pfaff 2017, 199).

The use of risk assessments to determine appropriate treatment is also concerning because it continues to distinguish "deserving" from "undeserving" youth in treatment plans. Grasso (2017, 396) documents the long-standing relationship that the rehabilitative ideal has had to punitive policies because of its reliance on distinguishing "curable offenders from incorrigible ones." Ward (2012, 228) documents that during the Progressive Era, the rehabilitative agenda for youth corrections was discriminatorily enacted. White youth were often determined to be "salvageable" and afforded rehabilitative opportunities denied to Black youth. Elizabeth Hinton (2016) demonstrates this same dynamic played out in the 1960s, when the federal Office of Juvenile Justice grants targeting white youth were more rehabilitative than the punitive policies (such as police in schools) that Black youth experienced. Similarly, in Texas, reforms from the

1970s included the use of IQ tests for offender classification that were supposed to humanize and modernize the justice system but ended up offering a scientific rationale for patterns of inequality.

Similar to prior reform efforts, assessments today are popular because they are extolled as "objective" measures that can bring rationality and fairness to the system. However, this assumes that the propensity to commit a crime is a natural process that can be studied and predicted in a fair and objective manner. There is little evidence that risk assessments are able to accurately predict future behavior or a propensity to benefit from treatment versus punishment. A study by the National Council on Crime and Delinquency found that the P.A.C.T. tool, used widely in California, performed relatively poorly, showing less than a 5% difference in recidivism rates across the three risk levels and having equity problems in regard to which youth were placed in facilities (Baird et al. 2013). The state-run prison system uses the California Youth Assessment Screening Instrument (CA-YASI), which has also been found to be unreliable and inaccurate at identifying high-risk youth (Washburn and Menart 2019; Skeem et al. 2017). Even if these snapshots of an individual's life were evidence of their behavior, which is contestable, they likely do not have a predictive power to determine if someone will commit a crime in the future. They are also not capable of determining if a person is capable of benefiting from programming. Additionally, the variables measured by risk assessments are widely found among the broader population (for example, poor performance in school, low self-esteem, use of drugs) and therefore fail to have much explanatory power in understanding the relatively small number of youth who are arrested and incarcerated.

In most instances, risk assessments are measuring law enforcement behavior, not getting at the root of someone's individual moral and intellectual capacities. There is a substantial literature documenting the discriminatory patterns of policing in the United States that have for generations disproportionately targeted racial minority and poor youth (Alexander 2010; Johnson 2022; Reed 2020; Tonry 2011; Ward 2012). Therefore, as Bernard Harcourt (2015, 237) argues, "using prior criminal history has become a proxy for race." Treating a history of contact with the police as determinative of a youth's propensity to commit a crime or their moral aptitude is misguided. Moreover, it is problematic to assume that moral and intellectual capacities are the cause of criminal offending, arrest, and conviction.

The assessments fail to account for policies that are outside of an individual youth's behavior, such as patterns of policing and definitions of what constitutes a crime, and instead attribute the outcomes of these policies to individual behavioral failures that the youth must correct. Further, they make factors external to a youth's behavior largely immutable as variables that must be "mitigated" rather than directly addressed.[24] These assumptions carry forward the culture of poverty theory, which hinges on the idea that "a hierarchy of norms of social behavior exists and is objectively discernable," a theory with a misguided tendency to "reduce the social world to aggregates of good people and bad people" (Reed 1999, 187).

Risk assessments channel solutions (whether punitive or rehabilitative) into policies targeting the behavior of youth, not the broader political, economic, and social structures they inhabit. While using risk assessments may make sense for particular jurisdictions to determine how to process youth, it is not a reform measure that can substantially change the justice system and correct its negative impact on youth. Further, the use of risk assessments imbues the justice system with a scientific rationality that de-emphasizes the socially and politically constructed notions of who is a risk and who is not. Such interventions reflect a narrow range of policy prescriptions being pursued in attempts to reform the juvenile justice system that mostly focus on sorting youth and attempting to solve their behavioral issues. Risk assessments direct the evaluation of youth toward their psychological and emotional fitness, subsequently directing interventions into this same realm, a limited and inadequate terrain for solving intractable social problems.

The Evidence-Based Movement

Risk assessments push the trajectory of the community-based reforms toward a heavy emphasis on individual behavioral solutions to delinquency. The focus on these solutions has been closely tied to the rise of promoting evidence-based programs as the gold standard of youth interventions. As discussed in the previous chapter, the development of evidence-based programs was supported by large foundations and is disseminated through the community-based reform movement and provided by nonprofit and for-profit organizations. In addition to being a major growth area for the private sector in the juvenile justice system, privileging evidence-based interventions is a limiting and technocratic, individual-based response to delinquency.

Everyone in the policymaking world, from professional associations, foundations, and the federal government, has accepted the evidence-based paradigm (Clear 2010). However, as Todd Clear stated in his 2009 presidential address to the American Society of Criminology, "the evidence-based policy paradigm is, at its core, extraordinarily conservative" (6). By directing policy only to "proven" solutions to delinquency, the political possibilities for the justice system are substantially narrowed into a conservative retrospective approach to policy. Evidence-based programs rely on an individuated and neoliberal approach to reform and are founded on a positivist epistemology (Schept 2015,

122–128). Juvenile justice programs are measured primarily by their ability to reduce recidivism, increase academic performance, and improve the emotional, behavioral, and moral soundness of youth. These categories for evaluating interventions ignore the broader qualitative experience of youth in the system and fail to address concerns about what is best for them beyond their chances of being caught up in the justice system in the future.

As mentioned in the prior chapter, the Blueprints Model programs developed and disseminated by large foundations are the leaders in delinquency prevention interventions. The evidence behind these model programs reveals the limited impact they have on addressing the greater concerns about large numbers of youth being processed in the juvenile justice system and their treatment in the system. There is a surprising lack of evidence for why these interventions are privileged above other programs and approaches to addressing delinquency and the injustices of the juvenile justice system. Evaluations of the Blueprints programs vary greatly, conducted either by the programs themselves or by the Blueprints project.[25] The evaluations mostly focus on measuring the effect of the programs on academic performance (grades and test scores), drug and alcohol use, attitudes, behavior, recidivism, and parenting skills, as indicated in Table 4.2. On these measures, all of the programs report some level of success. However, the different studies use a wide variety of methods for evaluating the programs, and the companies and organizations provide different levels of detail in explaining the findings in the studies.

A common theme among all of the outcome measures is that they do not specify comparison populations, nor do they provide any data on the connection the improvements they report may have on problems related to the juvenile justice system. The chosen metrics of evaluation—academic performance, interpersonal skills, and drug use—suggest that delinquency stems from individual behavioral deficiencies. The programs affirm the idea that there is a rational connection between misbehaving youth and youth caught up in the justice system. Therefore, promoting this constellation of programs positions "curing" delinquency as the solution to a punitive and wide-reaching juvenile justice system. Todd Clear and Dennis Schranz (2011) argue in their comprehensive evaluation of prison programming that while these interventions are valuable, they are not an effective strategy for reducing prison populations. Further, in this approach, there is no interrogation of the breadth of behaviors that are criminalized and patterns of policing that disproportionately target poor and minority youth; instead these criminalized behaviors are naturalized as problems that need to be solved through individual interventions.

Despite the fact that evidence-based programs have become the gold standard for where money should be invested in community-based reforms, there is a surprising lack of consistency in what counts as evidence and what

Table 4.2 **Blueprints Model program evaluations**

Program	Evaluator	Measurement	Findings
Big Brothers/Big Sisters	Internal	Attitudinal, academic grades	No difference between baseline and follow-up for attitudinal or academic grades
Positive Action	Internal	Testing performance	Increases testing performance
Family Functional Therapy	Internal	Recidivism rate	Lowers recidivism rate
Multisystemic therapy	Internal	Recidivism rate	Lowers recidivism rate
LifeSkills	Blueprints	Drug use	Reduces drug use
Project towards No Drug Abuse	Internal	Drug use	Reduces drug use
Strong African American Families Program	Blueprints	Drug use	Reduces drug use

Note: The academic grades of youth in Big Brothers/Big Sisters stayed the same between baseline and follow-up (Valentino and Wheeler 2013). The study does not specify to what degree testing performance for Positive Action (2016) improved for the youth studied. Two studies on the effect of Family Functional Therapy (FFT) on recidivism were conducted in 1998 and 1997. In 1997, those who participated in FFT had a recidivism rate of 20% and youth who received no treatment had a recidivism rate of 50%. In 1998, those who participated in FFT had a recidivism rate of 32% and youth who received no treatment had a recidivism rate of 40% (Sexton and Alexander 2000). Multisystemic Therapy Services provides a meta-analysis of 100 studies on the effects of the program. The summary published by the company reports that over all of these studies the median decline in rearrests is 42%, and there is a median decline of 54% in out-of-home placements for youth who receive MST (Multisystemic Therapy 2015). However, the company does not provide information on the uniformity of the studies, whether or not they are measuring against control groups, or how long after receiving MST the studies track recidivism rates. LifeSkills does not provide a specific time period, but it claims the program reduces the use of tobacco, alcohol, marijuana, and methamphetamines (Blueprints for Violence Prevention 2016). Studies on Project towards No Drug Abuse (2016) published by the company report a decrease in drug use among high schoolers. All 31 of the studies cited on the company's website are coauthored by Dr. Steve Sussman, who directs the program. The evidence for Strong African American Families Program comes from one study conducted in rural Georgia that claims the program improved parenting skills and reduced alcohol use for participants (Blueprints for Healthy Youth Development 2016).

as the measure of success. This approach significantly narrows the range of policy proposals considered and pursued while also reinforcing an individual focus on how to solve delinquency and other problems within the juvenile justice system. Advocating for community-based policies that lower costs and reduce recidivism has proven to be politically popular, but these goals are often incompatible with efforts to improve the treatment of youth and substantially diminish the punitive reach of the juvenile justice system. New technologies and programs geared toward accurately sorting youth and changing their behavior, like risk assessments and evidence-based programs, are incapable of adequately addressing the numerous factors rooted in political economy that contribute to high incarceration rates, abusive conditions of confinement, and the use of harmful punitive policies.

Still Punishing the Individual

Despite frequently being positioned as an *alternative* to punitive policies, the behavioral intervention approach in the community-based reform movement does not fundamentally challenge the punitive paradigm because it also adheres to an individual responsibility ethic. In both rehabilitative and punitive incarceration policies, there is a belief that "offenders are personally responsible for their reformation and that coercive state institutions are capable of enacting positive social change" (Grasso 2017, 395). Thus, whether the strategy is to teach a youth to behave differently through a life-skills program or give a youth a long sentence to learn accountability, the underlying goal is to change the individual. This individual focus helps explain why even though there appears to be a shift in the orientation of the juvenile justice system compared to the height of the "superpredator" moral panic in the 1990s, there is actually significant continuity in perpetuating a stigmatizing and punitive ethos toward youth offenders within the community-based reform movement.

The way that policymakers describe youth offenders continues to denigrate "juvenile delinquents," who are often described as being deeply psychologically flawed. The reinvigoration of an individual treatment approach, despite its limitations, could be channeled into public provisions to address mental health care in response to the discourse that youth are "more broken than ever"; instead, because of the larger developments in public-sector retrenchment and privatization, individuals are channeled into privatized programs and services within the justice system. The individualized treatment approach has been combined with punitive policies in an increasingly privatized policy sphere under the banner of community-based reforms, often further entrenching and legitimizing punishment, not replacing it.

Individual Blame and Stigmatizing the Juvenile Offender

The emphasis in the community-based reform movement on youth being behaviorally deficient is counterproductive to substantially reshaping the treatment of youth caught up in the juvenile justice system because it continues a long history of stigmatizing youth. While the political landscape has decisively turned toward an openness for juvenile justice reforms, politicians and advocacy organizations driving the community-based reforms continue to describe "juvenile delinquents" as nonproductive, troubled, and broken. The juvenile justice system, particularly in the vision of the community-based reform movement, is continually positioned as capable of turning juveniles around and of creating responsible, productive citizens. The optimism expressed about the malleability of youth and their particular propensity for change in turn justifies individual interventions. A repeated emphasis on the ability of juveniles to "turn around," based on a commonsense wisdom about youthfulness, implicitly suggests that the juvenile, not the social structure around them, needs to change (Cohen 2007; Klein 1979; Norman 2013; Quinney 1973; Rusche and Kirchheimer 1968; Scheingold 1991).

The mission statements of the Pennsylvania, Texas, and California juvenile justice systems adhere to this "turn around" discourse as part of their community-based reforms. In Pennsylvania, the BARJ mandate that guides the system states as one of its central goals, "help[ing juvenile offenders] develop into productive and responsible members of their communities" (Pennsylvania Commission on Crime and Delinquency 2021). The function of the Texas Youth Commission is described as taking "juvenile lawbreakers and send[ing] back as many functioning, productive citizens as possible" (*Dallas Morning News* 2007). The California Division of Juvenile Justice (2021) states as their mission "[T]o provide opportunities for growth and change by identifying and responding to the unique needs of our youth." In support of the community-based reforms in Texas, Representative Jim McReynolds (D-Lufkin) confidently asserted that "there are ways to turn them [juveniles] around" and, by changing them, keep them out of trouble (quoted in Graham 2010). Similarly, Judge Ray West of Texas described juvenile delinquents as "kids that have fallen by the wayside that we're trying to turn into productive citizens" (quoted in Kirk 2012).

The discourse animating the community-based reform debates often replicates the negative subject position of the juvenile offender even as it is contextualized within a more treatment-oriented discourse. Depicting youth as increasingly in need of treatment versus increasingly in need of punishment is a significant improvement. However, it perpetuates the expansive role of the criminal justice system and it continues to target interventions toward the individual failures of youth instead of developing policies to change the social and political context where juveniles find themselves. If the juvenile delinquent remains fundamentally in an "othered" subject position, loaded with conceptions of risk and danger—even if they are given behavioral interventions along with punishment—it is difficult to escape the "get tough" policies that are founded on these perceptions.

The Mental Health Panic: "More Broken Than Ever"

The precise way that youth are stigmatized has shifted over time and gone through a number of iterations of moral panics in which youth become defined as a threat to society. Juvenile justice policy reforms have repeatedly been based on a notion that the system needs to adapt to the changing nature of juveniles. The first federal interventions into juvenile delinquency from the 1950s and 1960s were founded on arguments that delinquents were more dangerous than ever before and that delinquency was a rapidly growing problem that needed to be addressed (Moak and Cate 2022). In the 1990s the widespread rhetoric of "juvenile superpredators," defining youth offenders as again more dangerous than ever before and uniquely deranged and damaged, fomented support for punitive policies (Fagan and Zimring 2000; Feld 1999; Mendel 2000). Recently, policymakers and practitioners coalescing around the community-based reform movement have tended to define the juvenile delinquency problem of today in a discourse about rising rates of mental health disorders. This is a different understanding of the problem; however, both articulations pinpoint the trouble with youth themselves and depict a new generation of youth as being different from the previous generation, with unique challenges and needs. In the broader political context of individualizing social problems and retrenching social welfare programs, this turn to a focus on mental health is not tied to expanding public goods in order to support the health and well-being of youth but instead treats individual pathologies as the source of high incarceration rates and disorder in youth prisons.

In Texas, policymakers often describe youth caught up in the juvenile justice system in terms of their mental health challenges and depict them as troubled and broken. Judge Mary Ann Turner of Montgomery County, Texas, claims she "has seen a growing number of young people in trouble with the law because of behavior related to a mental health disorder" (Lee 2009). Similarly, Judge Ray West of Brown County states, "[O]ver the past few years it has become very evident that a large percentage of juvenile offenders suffer from various mental illnesses" (quoted Nash 2012). And the chief juvenile probation officer of Randall County, Jane Anderson King, said, "[N]ow, kids are more broken than ever" (quoted in Cervantes 2012). Cherie Townsend, the executive director of the Texas Juvenile Justice Department in 2012, reported interagency findings that 52% of youth in the system have mental health problems and that "the numbers are increasing and the percentages are increasing" (quoted in Weissert 2012). The inclusion of more psychological and psychiatric testing in Texas's community-reform legislation (Senate Bill 103) was a response to and perhaps also a driving factor in identifying the increased prevalence of mental health disorders (Copelin 2007a). Examining the connection between mental illness and criminal charges is not inappropriate, nor are attempts to address mental health concerns among youth populations. However, the repeated references to the growing mental health problems of juveniles contribute to the perception that there is an increasingly difficult population of juveniles the system must handle. Historically, the belief that "juveniles are worse than ever before" has fueled the expansion of the juvenile justice system (Bernard 1992).

Some community-based reformers hope that defining the problem of delinquency as a product of mental illness may lead to less punitive responses. However, as these quotes and Texas Juvenile Justice Department statistics show, many of these juveniles continue to be processed through the justice system rather than the public health system. The result has been attempts to solve the juvenile justice mental health problem by infusing more treatment and behavior modification programs *into* the justice system. The reform discourse has called for more attention to mental health issues but has not explicitly been directed toward mental health funding or public health funding. In all three states, mental and public health funding has suffered from the trends of public-sector retrenchment and has actually *been reduced* in conjunction with efforts to increase "community control." Further, the focus on mental health has helped probation departments to justify funding for traditional forms of juvenile justice responses through a therapeutic-oriented discourse (Grissom 2012b; Phelps 2011, 61).

Ultimately, an individual focus is inadequate because it fails to attend to the complex causes of high rates of youth incarceration and the poor treatment of youth in the system. Further, the individual focus is particularly inadequate in the context of austerity and public-sector retrenchment, which have eliminated noncarceral solutions to problems like mental health issues. While the community-based reform movement attempts to ameliorate the worst punitive excesses within these carceral solutions, the lack of other public-sector approaches to these social problems fuels the continued use of punitive policies.

Treatment Integrated into Punishment

In most instances, counties adopting community-based reforms have coupled programs aimed at modifying the individual behavior of juveniles with the punitive elements of probation and secure confinement. Folding goals and programs of helping juveniles into punitive practices has helped to legitimize county probation (Bosworth 2007, 74; Werth 2013, 238). Punishment coupled with treatment is better than punishment alone, but adding treatment to the punitive apparatus is not an adequate solution to the negative effects of punishment. Further, there is little evidence that treatment in a punitive context and in the style of self-help interventions is actually effective or helpful to youth (Clear and Schrantz 2011). Rehabilitative resources have been used as mechanisms of supervision and control and can mediate carceral processes rather than eliminate them (Lynch 2000, 58; McKim 2014; Werth 2013, 238). Folding these types of interventions into punitive sanctions does not provide a significant change of experience for youth in the system.

For example, youth referred to the Texas Juvenile Justice Department may be assigned to P.A.C.E. Youth Programs, Inc., a private faith-based vendor that aims to "transform young people into responsible citizens" as a part of their probation disposition.[26] The Harris County Juvenile Probation Department has contracted with P.A.C.E. to assign over 2,000 youth to its intervention program and in 2007 was awarded the Unsung Heroes for Houston Children's Award from Children at Risk, a nonprofit that champions the well-being of children (GuideStar 2021). The program is nested in the Probation Department, and juveniles in P.A.C.E. do not get an exemption from the strict controls and consequences of probation. Youth still are at risk of probation violations, which can be minor infractions such as not attending school or breaking curfew and can lead to incarceration. This therapeutic program does not replace the punitive conditions of probation but is instead an intensive 12-week program that requires juveniles to comply with strict regulations of conduct.

Self-improvement programs like P.A.C.E. are integrated into sites of institutionalization (not necessarily in lieu of incarceration or probation) and can come with substantial fees. In Denton County, Texas (2014a), if a juvenile is court-ordered to take anger management, they must pay for the class at a rate of $445 (the related parenting class costs $305). If a juvenile participates in a life skills program, such as the Denton County Courage to Change Program available to youth in a secure residential facility, this might include "kitchen duty and housekeeping" (Denton County, Texas 2014b). Much of the funding for programs like life skills and anger management is not meant to replace punitive institutionalization but rather to infuse this punishment with these types of self-help interventions.

Within the Texas state-run prison system, as a result of major community-based reforms, treatment programs have been combined with secure institutionalization. In 2007, the Texas juvenile justice system implemented CoNEXTions, a general treatment program based on admission assessments for youth committed to state-run prisons.[27] CoNEXTions uses the Positive Achievement

Change Tool (provided by the private company Assessments.com) to assess juveniles when they enter the system, with the goal of improving their "thinking skills" in order to reduce recidivism (Texas Juvenile Justice Department 2013). Based on the assessment, youth are assigned to a variety of behavioral intervention programs that are developed by private companies that contract with the state.[28] The CoNEXTions program exemplifies the compatibility of self-improvement treatment goals with punitive institutionalization and demonstrates the opening it has given to private companies specializing in these types of programs.

These programs blame delinquent behaviors of all kinds on psychological shortcomings of youth involved in the system. The commitment to funding programs focused on behavioral modification continues to legitimize the punitive aspects of the system and expands the size and funding of probation departments since they are seen as best able to administer these services. Self-help individualized behavioral programs are not really alternatives but rather different formulations of policies in the juvenile correctional system that have been features of the institution dating back to the 1960s reform moment. When youth fail within this system of behavioral interventions they are seen as truly deserving punishment, which, as the following chapter addresses, helps explain why the reforms have failed to tackle some of the most punitive practices in the juvenile justice system.

Summary

The current enthusiasm for taking a more benevolent approach to handling youth in the juvenile justice system in the community-based reform movement is a significant improvement from the moral panic over juvenile "superpredators" that reached its height almost 30 years ago. The popularity of community-based reforms and their focus on rehabilitating youth reflects a comparatively kinder approach to misbehaving youth. As a demonstration of this shift, in the 2016 and 2020 election cycles both Democratic nominees Hillary Clinton and Joe Biden were excoriated for their association with the superpredator theory and its attendant "get tough" policies that had a devastating effect particularly on poor and racial minority youth (Gearan and Phillip 2016; Gillstrom 2016). Yet the brief analysis of the cyclical nature of juvenile justice system crisis and reform since the 1940s suggests the community-based reform turn is less of a departure from the get-tough 1990s than it might first appear. As the juvenile justice system has developed over time, its institutions have accrued greater capacity, technologies have changed, and, most important, the broader political context in which these policies emerge has changed. However, a key thread that connects both the rehabilitative and punitive approaches that have been layered atop one another is the emphasis on individual uplift and the idea that the system can be fixed by fixing the youth within the system.

The 1960s community-based reforms set the juvenile justice system's development on a trajectory of emphasizing individual, cultural, and moral explanations and solutions to delinquency. This development coincided with a similar turn in social policy more generally. As a number of scholars have documented, the turn away from redistributive economic policies and toward cultural explanations of social ills in the 1960s and 1970s stymied future progressive developments (Katz 1995; Moak 2022; A. Reed 1999; T. Reed 2020). These broader developments were critical in reshaping public policy by increasing public subsidies to nonprofit and for-profit community-based service providers and ushering in a retreat of the state from providing a wide range of public goods. Today the resurgent popularity of the community-based approach is able to build upon these institutional changes and even more heavily lean on the private sector to carry out the treatment functions of the juvenile justice system. The increasing privatization of the juvenile justice system is driving these policies even more thoroughly into the self-help style of individualized interventions.

The robust construction and dissemination of evidence-based programs, with a heavy focus on recidivism reduction and cost savings, has disciplined policymakers and juvenile justice practitioners into a narrow set of approaches to treating youth. Not only does the evidence-based movement significantly limit the range of possibilities and innovations in addressing both youth crime and incarceration rates, but it ignores the qualitative experiences of youths in service of actuarial goals. In the context of decades of neoliberal governance, the resurgent popularity of community-based reforms, even more so than in prior decades, naturalizes structural inequality. Because of the hegemonic belief that individuals are responsible for their own successes and failures, (growing) structural inequalities are rendered largely invisible. Juvenile justice interventions take the existing political, economic, and social range of inequalities as a given and attempt to ameliorate the worst outcomes of these conditions. It is considered well beyond the purview of juvenile justice policies to address rising inequality, weaknesses of the labor market, and the many facets of economic struggles that youth face in their life before and after entering the justice system. These realities are treated as insurmountable problems that will never be solved and thus can only be mitigated.

Most ironic, while the community-based reform discourse is one of rehabilitation, benevolence, and care for justice-involved youth, the focus on individual behavioral interventions is fundamentally compatible with and conducive to punitive approaches to delinquency. Upon closer examination, the interventions are not primarily targeted at fully repudiating punitive policies but rather are about ensuring the policies are not overused or targeted toward the "wrong kind" of youth. Because the community-based reforms give youth a chance, they isolate future failure as the youth's own and therefore legitimize the consequent punishment of those who repeatedly "fail." The bifurcation of low-level offenders from "truly dangerous" youth has been one reason that in some instances the community-based reform movement has facilitated the ratcheting up of punitive policies. While the treatment youth receive is undermined by stigmatizing views of the juvenile offender, the primacy of cost-cutting, and recidivism reduction, many youth, even in model reform states, still are subjected to extraordinarily punitive policies.

5
Still Punitive

Rationalizing Punishment for the "Worst of the Worst"

The revitalization of individualized treatment has been at the forefront of the community-based reform movement that seeks to reduce the punitive excesses of the juvenile justice system by investing in "developmentally appropriate" alternatives. However, in practice investing in treatment has not led to a clear repudiation of punitive responses to juvenile delinquency. For many decades, rehabilitative and punitive practices in the juvenile justice system have not necessarily been contrary approaches and in fact often have developed in support of one another. For example, in 1973 the superintendent of the Gatesville juvenile prison in Texas, where youth were forced to work in sewage and garbage ditches, defended the practice, arguing, "[I]f this helps this child go back to his dormitory and behave a little better, we think it is therapeutic" (Kemerer 2008, 154). With almost parallel logic, in 2012 the Texas Juvenile Justice Department executive director responded to criticism for using and expanding solitary confinement for youth by saying, "[W]ithout order and security and safety, you can't have rehabilitation and education" (quoted in Grissom 2012a). Punitive discipline is frequently framed as "rehabilitative" or necessary for rehabilitation, and punitive accountability is often seen as necessary when rehabilitative measures fail. Overall, the community-based reform movement has not displaced the development and rise of tough punitive policies in the juvenile justice system but has instead reinforced it.

The developments traced in the previous chapters help explain why the community-based reform movement has bolstered punitiveness in the juvenile justice system. This reform effort is focused on front-end behavioral intervention policies geared at reducing the number of youth who will become "delinquent" in the first place. Similarly, the reforms are focused on better determining which youth are "serious" offenders through risk assessments and other tools to sort youth within the justice system. The efforts to better sort and classify youth from low to high risk and distinguish serious from nonviolent reinforces rather than challenges a punitive ethos. Throughout the development of the American carceral state, efforts to distinguish curable from incorrigible offenders have justified harsh punishment (Grasso 2017). The logic of individual treatment is a conduit to greater criminalization as it diverts attention away from socioeconomic causes of behavior and justifies punitive accountability (Wacquant 2009, xxii).

Particularly in the context of neoliberal governance, the emphasis on individual uplift is likely to comport with punitive impulses. The emphasis on cost-efficiency in the criminal justice reform landscape leads policymakers to selectively focus on certain types of offenders that are and are not worthy of correctional expenses, enforcing the need for circumscribed use of punitive sanctions based on cost (Aviram 2015, 57). The community-based reforms thus uphold the process of bifurcation in which correctional systems are geared toward managing certain populations of low-risk offenders outside of prisons in rehabilitative programs and then subjecting populations of violent and serious offenders to incarceration (Seeds 2017). This process continues to portray some offenders as unredeemable, making the preservation and even expansion of punitive policies necessary (Schoenfeld 2018, 208).

Although some youth are being exempted from the most punitive policies available to handle youth offenders, the community-based reforms have largely left intact harmful punitive practices like juvenile life without parole sentences, long sentences, draconian sex offender laws, and gang sentencing enhancements. As a number of scholars have pointed out, any significant reduction in the U.S. prison population is going to require states to address people convicted of serious crimes (Gottschalk 2015; Pfaff 2017). In sidestepping these tougher questions, there continues to be bipartisan support for punitive sanctions for serious offenders at the same time that community-based alternatives are expanded. Further, youth left in state-run prisons who have not been moved to community-based alternatives are experiencing increasingly violent prisons and the expansion of abusive policies like solitary confinement.

This chapter begins by detailing national developments in sentencing that have shifted the policy landscape toward support for limiting the use of some of the harshest sentencing policies for youth, such as life without the possibility of parole (LWOP) and the death penalty. Each state has adapted in different ways to the opportunities afforded by this changing legal landscape, but overall states have fallen back on punitive ways of implementing the court's rulings. The chapter then shifts to three key policy areas—adult transfers, sex offenders, and gang sentencing enhancements—that exemplify the ways in which the enactment of community-based reforms have not displaced a punitive ethos and have frequently developed alongside increased punitiveness. This bifurcation of increased punishments for some youth while bolstering nonincarceration policies for others has largely failed on its own terms. Youth subjected to the most punitive policies are no more likely to be serious offenders than before the reforms, and therefore persistent inequalities and racial disparities have remained constant in the juvenile justice system. The last section details the worsened conditions for youth still being sent to state-run facilities, making them more likely to be subjected to violent, chaotic, and punitive experiences.

Adaptations to National Developments in Punitive Policies

As the national context has shifted away from the 1990s "superpredator" hysteria over juvenile offenders, there have been major legal developments that have challenged the use of the most punitive polices for juveniles, such as mandatory life sentences and the death penalty. Despite declining support for treating youth like adults and exacting extraordinary punishments on these youth, the move away from these policies has been slow and incomplete. Objections to these punitive policies have been brought forth by progressive legal reform nonprofits, but these objections have been channeled into technical legal objections and are largely pinning hope on U.S. Supreme Court decisions. This is a limited strategy, particularly in decentralized juvenile justice systems where local judges and law enforcement have a lot of power and discretion in determining how to carry out these rulings. This section details the changes driven by key Supreme Court cases and the ways in which states have responded to these legal developments.

There have been significant national developments coming out of the Supreme Court over the past 15 years that have challenged the most punitive policies levied on juveniles. In 2005, in *Roper v. Simmons* the Supreme Court prohibited states from giving the death penalty to offenders under the age of 18. *Graham v. Florida* (2010) extended *Roper* and prohibited states from giving LWOP for a non-homicide offense to youth under 18. The Court ruled in *Miller v. Alabama* (2012) that states could not have *mandatory* LWOP sentencing for youth convicted of murder (Feld 2013).[1] Most recently, in 2016 the Court made the ban on automatic LWOP sentences for juveniles retroactive in their ruling in *Montgomery v. Louisiana* (Melamed 2016a).

The Supreme Court decisions have relied on neuroscientific findings that juvenile brains are different from and less developed than adult brains as a rationale for excluding youth from mandatory LWOP and the death penalty. The MacArthur Foundation's massive investment in this research has led to nearly every major reform organization and the Court asserting that punishment for youth should be "developmentally appropriate" as a rationale for curbing these most extreme sentencing policies. In all of these cases the Court has curtailed the legal authority of states to enact some of the harshest policies available for youth offenders and opened up space for significantly shifting away from applying these "get tough" punitive policies to youth. However, in the context of increased devolution and community-based reforms, the Court decisions give a great amount of leeway for states and individual judges to determine what to do in resentencing youth and changing laws to adapt to the rulings.

In the leading community-based reform states policymakers and practitioners at all levels have been adept at complying with the rulings by replacing tough laws with nearly as tough laws, limiting the overall effect of the openings provided by the Supreme Court rulings. Two major factors are driving these developments. The first is the absence of a clear repudiation of punitive policies within the prevailing community-based reform movement. Instead, the challenges have been based on carving out exceptions to *who* these policies apply to. The second is that the community-based reform movement seeks consensus among diverse actors and largely maintains the status quo power structure within juvenile justice policy development. Securing the support of actors who still promote the value of punitive accountability, as do many district attorney associations and lawmakers, requires not challenging their efforts to reestablish harsh policies to replace those ruled unconstitutional by the Supreme Court.

While the shifting reform landscape and the Supreme Court cases have made significant challenges to these policies, they largely have left intact the political dynamics perpetuating their minimally curtailed use and, in some instances, helped bolster their continued and expanded use. Over the course of the past 20 years and the implementation of community-based reforms, all three model states have continued to levy some of the harshest policies against youth offenders, and often these policies were ratcheted up at the same time that devolution policies were enacted. As a result of the bifurcation process described in the previous chapter, community-based reforms can even legitimize punitive policies rather than challenge them. All three model states are hailed as leaders in reform *while also* leading the nation in some of the most punitive policies applied to juveniles.

In Pennsylvania, the establishment of community-based reforms occurred in the context of the buildup of an exceptionally high rate of juvenile LWOP sentences. Recent legal challenges to this practice have not fundamentally changed the punitive approach in the state to these serious youth offenders. In California, attempts to rein in the use of LWOP and long sentences have been lacking, and each effort to provide these youth with a path out of their long sentences comes with exceptions and largely leaves the policies intact while also attempting to carefully carve out which juveniles they will apply to. There is more momentum in California for reforming the practice of trying youth as adults, with promising developments occurring at both the state and local level, but the devolved juvenile justice system continues to perpetuate major inequalities. Texas has not seen similar attempts at rolling back these policies, which suggests community-based reforms are entirely compatible with efforts to reduce *or* increase the use of punitive sentences and trying youth as adults. In all three states community-based reforms were initiated either in conjunction with "get tough" laws (particularly in Pennsylvania and California) or were seamlessly layered on top of punitive policies (as in Texas). These community-based reform model states have increased community control and also increased punitiveness for serious and high-risk youth inside state-run prisons.

Pennsylvania and Juvenile LWOP Sentences

No state better demonstrates the compatibility of the community-based reform model with harsh punitive policies for select juvenile offenders than Pennsylvania. Pennsylvania passed a major "adult time for adult crime" law in the *same* piece of legislation that transformed its juvenile system into the community-based model. Since implementing a groundbreaking decentralized, community-based model of youth corrections, the state has continued to levy LWOP sentences at one of the highest rates in the country. As such external forces as U.S. Supreme Court cases, not community-based reforms, have pushed the state to reform its sentencing policy, the state has remained committed to a "get tough" approach. For all the talk of reform in the juvenile justice system there has been very little movement on the treatment of serious offenders. Most of the community-based legislation is premised on addressing wayward youth who need "to learn a lesson" and "be put on the right track," but there has been no serious discussion of what to do with youth charged with serious crimes. The notion of treatable versus untreatable youth, promulgated through the proliferation of risk assessment and scientific data collection, has legitimated the harsh sentences for youth who are "objectively" deemed high risk and beyond treatment.

Pennsylvania is exceptional in sentencing more juveniles to LWOP than any other state in the nation or any country in the world. The state incarcerates about one in five of all juvenile lifers in the United States ("Youth Should" 2010). There are over 500 people in Pennsylvania serving LWOP sentences for crimes they committed while a juvenile. Of these, about 300 are from Philadelphia County (Mitman 2016). In fact, Philadelphia County has the highest percentage of juveniles sentenced to LWOP in the country (Fair Punishment Project 2016). And around 71% of those serving juvenile LWOP sentences in Pennsylvania are Black (Pennsylvania State Legislature 2012b).[2]

In response to the legal changes coming from the Supreme Court decisions on LWOP, the Pennsylvania legislature passed Act 204 in 2012, which established new mandatory minimums for youth who previously would have received mandatory LWOP sentences. The Act put the state in compliance with the *Miller v. Alabama* Court ruling that determined states could not have mandatory LWOP sentencing for youth convicted of murder. Act 204 replaced mandatory LWOP sentences with 35-year mandatory sentences while retaining the ability for judges to use longer sentences or LWOP on a case-by-case basis.[3] In Pennsylvania, judges can still give juveniles a LWOP sentence or a sentence up to 100 years; this is just no longer a mandatory sentence (Hambright 2012).

Despite various states' forays into community-based reforms, the prevailing commitment nationally has been to retain long mandatory minimum sentences for serious juvenile offenders. Pennsylvania, Florida, and Louisiana combined imprison 40% of all juvenile lifers in the country, and all three states decided not to make their new sentencing policy retroactive until the Supreme Court forced them to. These three states replaced mandatory LWOP with a mandatory sentence of 35 years. Only Texas and Nebraska set a mandatory minimum higher than this, at 40 years (Rovner 2014). Most other states set mandatory minimums at 25 or 30 years. Because the legal decisions have been narrowly targeted at juvenile offenders, the Court has not fundamentally challenged the use of the death penalty and LWOP broadly. The justification for excluding youth from the harshest penalties because they are "different," whether intending to or not, cements the notion that these harsh policies *are* appropriate for adult offenders. These sentences are still sanctioned as constitutional and acceptable punishments, just not for all youth and not on a mandatory basis.

The debate over the bill to establish long mandatory minimums to replace mandatory LWOP in Pennsylvania encapsulated many of the themes regarding the perpetuation of a zero-sum notion of justice, the bipartisan desire to preserve the most punitive policies available, and the promotion of cost efficiency as a paramount concern in juvenile justice reforms. Act 204 received strong bipartisan support: seven Democrats and three Republicans sponsored the legislation. The final vote on the legislation was 174–20 in the state house and 37–12 in the state senate in favor of the bill.[4] While the mandatory minimums may continue to be severe, the *mandated* sentence of LWOP for juveniles has ended in Pennsylvania. However, in the legislative debate over the 2012 legislation, it was clear in the arguments made by legislators that the same "get tough" principles that supported the "adult time" law in the first place continued to shape the new legislation.

Representative Curtis Thomas, a Democrat from Philadelphia who was the only outspoken critic of the legislation, detailed a number of reasons he opposed the bill, foremost being that the new mandatory minimums violated the U.S. Constitution as a cruel and unusual punishment for juvenile offenders.

Thomas even called for a vote on the constitutionality of the bill, which was overwhelming voted down, 166–28. In response to the constitutionality criticism, Representative Bryan Barbin, a Democrat from Cambria County, argued that the mandatory minimums were rational because they had been set by consensus in the Pennsylvania legislature; he added, "As for me 35 years is appropriate. . . . [I]f I am wrong, God will judge me, but the collective voice of the General Assembly is a rational basis" (Pennsylvania State Legislature 2012b).

Other support for the bill echoed the sentiment that 35 years was not overly harsh. Representative Anthony DeLuca, a Democrat from Allegheny County, said in support of the bill, "We talk about cruel and unusual punishment. Tell that to the victim whom they might have murdered or raped or the families who never get over that the rest of their lives. I call that cruel and unjust punishment. We need to talk about the victims" (Pennsylvania State Legislature 2012b). DeLuca's argument touched on the core rationale that continues to guide legislation over serious juvenile offender sentences: that severe and long punishments are necessary for supporting victim's rights. The centrality of a zero-sum equation between victim's rights and punishment for offenders has been the long-standing cornerstone of "get tough" policies and was reaffirmed in the 2012 legislation. Victim's rights advocates have already expressed opposition to changes to LWOP sentences in Pennsylvania. State victim's advocate Jennifer Storm stated that the families of the victims "are not happy" about proposed changes and told her LWOP is "absolutely" still the right sentence (Melamed 2016a). The community-based reform movement does not challenge the uniquely powerful role of victim's rights organizations in shaping sentencing decisions—a critical component of the buildup of mass incarceration in the first place (Forman 2017; Gottschalk 2006; Schoenfeld 2018; Wacquant 2009).

The Pennsylvania District Attorneys Association was a major force in pushing steep mandatory minimums and retaining the option of LWOP sentences for juveniles convicted of murder. In defense of this position, Lancaster County District Attorney Craig Stedman argued, "[I]t is critical for the protection of the public that Pennsylvania preserved the option to make sure that the worst of the worst have no possibility of ever being released to kill again" (quoted in Hambright 2012). The District Attorneys Association also opposed making the 2012 ruling retroactive in Pennsylvania (Yates 2016). The opposition to the legislation was premised on the need to protect the public and ensure victims' rights. Since the community-based reform movement is often pursued with the support of the District Attorneys Association, the reform effort offers little meaningful pressure against these conservative and powerful pro-punishment actors.

Since the state passed the 2012 legislation, the Supreme Court changed the terrain by making retroactive the ban on automatic LWOP sentences (Melamed

2016a). States like Pennsylvania, Florida, and Louisiana that did not make their changes retroactive will now have to decide how to handle juvenile offenders serving LWOPs. The combination of the great amount of leeway in sentencing decisions and devolution has led to major inequities across jurisdictions in Pennsylvania. So far there have been major county-level differences in how judges are handling the resentencing of juveniles serving LWOP sentences. One Chester County judge converted all juvenile LWOP sentences to "time served to life" sentences, which immediately gives these inmates the possibility of parole (Melamed 2016b). In Monroe County, a judge resentenced two inmates to LWOP (Yates 2016). As of 2018, about 300 of the 521 juvenile lifers in Pennsylvania have been resentenced, and 95% of them have received new sentences longer than 20 years (Melamed 2018). The Juvenile Law Center has been tracking the resentencing and reports that "it's still very county-dependent." For example, because Bucks County has a particularly harsh judge, no one there has received less than 40 years, while in Philadelphia County the average sentence has been 31 years to life (Melamed 2018).

The debate over mandatory LWOP reforms shows that Pennsylvania continues to have a bipartisan commitment to viewing sentencing policy as a zero-sum balance between victim's rights and punishing offenders. Further, because of the highly devolved and locally autonomous configuration of juvenile justice policy in Pennsylvania, compliance with the Supreme Court's decisions is contingent on the disparate philosophies of individual judges. The community-based reform movement not only fails to challenge the use of extreme punitive sentencing policy, but it also legitimizes these responses to serious offenders by "proving" (through risk assessments and failed behavioral interventions) that these youth are irredeemable and contributes to the highly unequal distribution of these punitive policies in a devolved system. A stubborn commitment to "get tough" rhetoric and policies demonstrates the ineffectual impact of community-based reforms on significantly curtailing punitive policies. It is the same politicians who are simultaneously upholding the most punitive juvenile sentencing laws in the world while also supporting community-based reforms. Pennsylvania's investment in therapeutic programs at the local level legitimizes its continued use of punitive policies, allowing the state to be both committed to rehabilitating youth *and* holding them accountable through some of the world's harshest sentencing policies.

California and Parole Hearings

The state of California has also largely left LWOP intact despite the U.S. Supreme Court rulings.[5] In recent debates over increasing parole hearings for juveniles sentenced to long terms in prisons, the "most serious" offenders—specifically those given an LWOP sentence—have been excluded from reforms. This trend reflects the persistent unwillingness to address the treatment of all youth in the justice system. Instead, policy changes are channeled into concerns about procedural fairness and ensuring that the right youths receive harsh punishments.

In 2013, the California legislature passed Senate Bill 260 requiring the Board of Parole Hearings to review the cases of juvenile offenders who committed their crimes before they were 18 years old, once they had served 15 to 25 years and depending on their offense. Every major reform organization in California and many national groups, more than 80 organizations in total from both ends of the political spectrum, supported the legislation.[6] Opposition to the bill came from about 20 police associations and district attorney associations as well as crime victim groups. The legislation is typical of popular reform measures today that appeal to fiscal conservatism, personal responsibility, and neuroscience research on youth brain maturity (California State Legislature 2014).

The continued commitment to punitive accountability in the legislation is reflected in the bill analysis, which states, "SB 260 holds young people responsible for the crimes they committed and creates a parole mechanism in which they must demonstrate remorse and rehabilitation to merit any possible release on parole as determined by BPH [Board of Parole hearings]" (California State Legislature 2014). The reform legislation is directed at a small number of juveniles, excluding anyone sentenced under Jessica's Law (first-time child sex offenders), one-strike rape offenses, three-strikes offenses, and youth given an LWOP sentence. Even for the small number of youth granted a parole hearing due to the legislative changes, the hearing does not occur until a youth has served 15 to 25 years, which in most countries would be the longest sentence available to any offender. As of 2017, of the people who were granted a parole hearing, 62% were denied parole (Barlow 2019).[7]

Juveniles convicted of LWOP sentences were initially barred from getting a parole hearing, until in 2013 the legislature passed Senate Bill 9, which allows some juvenile lifers to apply for a new sentencing hearing.[8] If the juvenile gets a hearing, this does not mean they will receive a different sentence, and even if they are given the possibility of parole, this does not mean they will be approved by a parole board for release. The Fair Sentencing for Youth (2016) organization described the legislative change succinctly: "SB 9 is a hard road—but it is a chance for a chance." The reform policies in California continue to mostly hold the line on this most punitive policy and may further legitimize its use given the perception that appropriate measures are in place to ensure only the most deserving youth receive these sentences.

The opposition faced by these important, but arguably limited, changes to the most punitive policies reflects the degree to which the political terrain has not shifted as much as the advocates of the community-based reform movement may suggest. The resistance to take a more aggressive stance on sentencing reform and the staunch opposition to these changes indicate that the reform movement has yet to penetrate the more deeply held punitive impulses of powerful actors in the system, such as district attorney associations and victim's rights organizations. Policies like juvenile LWOP are incredibly damaging and put the United States well outside international practices of handling serious youth offenders. As many leading scholars suggest, reforming these harshest policies may be one of the most critical changes needed to significantly downsize the carceral state (Gottschalk 2015; Pfaff 2017). Rather than fundamentally challenging the use of punitive policies such as juvenile LWOP, reformers have sought to pursue a path of least resistance, which is to exclude certain offenders from these policies while leaving the policies in place for the "worst of the worst."

Texas and the Death Penalty

Texas has also adapted to the U.S. Supreme Court rulings with important but limited changes to its most punitive policies. As of 2005, Texas had by far the largest death row for juvenile offenders, holding 29 (40%) of the national total of 72 juvenile death row inmates (Death Penalty Information Center 2015). Since 1973, the state has been responsible for executing 13 of the 22 people who were executed for crimes they committed as a juvenile (Death Penalty Information Center 2015). In 2005, after the *Roper* decision, Governor Rick Perry commuted the sentences for twenty-eight 17-year-old juveniles on death row and gave them life sentences with the possibility of parole in 40 years (Ferguson 2012).

Because Texas used the death penalty as opposed to LWOP sentences for serious juvenile offenders (unlike Pennsylvania, Louisiana, and Michigan, which have large populations of juveniles serving LWOP sentences) it was much easier for the state to come into compliance with the *Miller* and *Graham* decisions. The state had already passed a law in 2009 that set the maximum sentence for juveniles at the possibility of parole after 40 years, so after *Miller* in 2013 the state just extended this sentencing policy to 17-year-olds (who in Texas were not considered juveniles and were still eligible for mandatary LWOP and therefore out of compliance with the Court ruling). A couple of Democratic representatives came out against the new law, arguing 40 years was too long for a juvenile and was essentially an LWOP sentence. However, the final vote on SB 2 (2013) passed with just one dissenting vote in the state senate and 113–23 in the state house (Grissom and Serrano 2013; Hudson 2013).

Texas has made moderate improvements to its most severe punishments. Abolishing the death penalty and mandatory LWOP for juveniles is a major victory for juvenile justice advocates. However, the alternative sentences continue to be among the harshest in the nation (Grissom and Serrano 2013; Hudson 2013).[9] The state's adaptations to the Supreme Court rulings reveal the persistence of the tough model despite the state's passage of sweeping community-based reforms. The Supreme Court cases have not had as significant an impact on scaling back very long sentences as some reformers hoped they would, and the primary focus on community-based reforms has not proven to be a powerful counterforce to continued punitiveness.

The Community-Based Reform Movement's Treatment of the "Worst of the Worst"

States have unevenly applied the changes afforded by a shifting national landscape that has begun to repudiate the unbridled use of extraordinarily punitive policies for youth. Because the community-based reform movement has not taken direct aim at the powerful interests in keeping punitive policies on the table, each model state has experienced the ratcheting-up of punishment for serious offenders, specifically those convicted of crimes that qualify for adult transfers, sex offenders, and youth labeled gang members. In California and Pennsylvania, the harshest "get tough" policies for youth offenders were passed and implemented in conjunction with investments in community-based reforms. In Texas, a more recent turn to community-based reforms has been layered on top of punitive policies and has not been part of repudiating or limiting these practices. In all three states the employment of community-based reforms has not limited the development and continued practice of categorizing some youth as "serious" and in need of harsh punitive accountability.

Adult Transfers

The community-based reform movement and the research by large foundations has gone a long way in framing youth as uniquely (even biologically) different from adult offenders in order to carve out exceptions for their treatment. This has been a powerful justification for the U.S. Supreme Court cases that created particular exemptions for youth offenders, but the strategy of promoting "developmentally appropriate" punishments has not been effective in ending the use of adult transfers. All three model states continue to try youth as adults and house them in adult prisons. Juveniles sent to adult facilities have higher rates of suicide, higher rates of recidivism, are more likely to be victims of violence, have less access to education and programming, and are often subjected to solitary confinement (Austin, Johnson, and Gregoriou 2000; Human Rights Watch 2012; Lahey 2016; Le 2019). In Texas, the majority of youth who have been certified as adults and who are housed in adult county jails are held in isolation for long periods of time (Deitch, Galbraith, and Pollock 2012).[10] Despite the talk of "treating youth like youth," the community-based reform movement has had little effect on the practice of trying youths as adults because these policies are still used for the "most serious" youth. Dropping arrest rates has had the biggest impact on lowering the number of youth processed as adults, but overall how the system processes youth and designates some as needing to be transferred to the adult system has not significantly changed.

In California, several statutory changes increasing the number of youth sent to adult prisons occurred alongside the first community-based reforms in the state. Legislation from 1996 (the same year the state passed a major juvenile devolution initiative) stipulated that juveniles who were given an adult sentence could no longer be housed in the juvenile state-run system once they reached the age of 18. Then, in 1998, the legislature enacted measures to exclude all youth over 18 from being held in the juvenile justice system. In 2000, the legislature passed a law requiring that juveniles 16 years of age or older who are convicted in an adult court be housed in adult prisons. Further, Proposition 21 from 2000 mandated the automatic transfer of youth as young as 14 to adult court for certain crimes. The statutory changes in 1996, 1998, and 2000 meant that many juveniles who previously would have been held in juvenile state-run facilities now went directly to adult facilities. Since the late 1990s the population of youth sent to state-run institutions in California was reduced by pushing youth to county institutions *and* transferring youth to the adult system (Jannetta and Lin 2007).[11]

The total number of juvenile offenders directly filed to adult court has been declining since 2008 but is still about the same given this disposition in the early 2000s, when the policies listed above drove up direct filings. Figure 5.1 shows the number of youth directly filed to adult court from 2002 to 2016.

The recent declines in numbers of youth directly filed to adult court is occurring in the context of historically low juvenile arrest rates. Thus, while a very small percentage of juveniles who are arrested get directly remanded to adult court, this percentage continued to increase over time in California.[12] Juveniles who come in contact with the juvenile justice system had a greater likelihood in 2016 than in the early 2000s to be directly filed to adult court. There is little evidence this is because juveniles are being arrested for more serious offenses.[13] Figure 5.2 shows the percentage of juveniles arrested that get directly filed to adult court from 2002 to 2016.

The data on juveniles sent to the adult system calls attention to measures beyond state incarceration rates that are important in evaluating progress in juvenile community-based reforms. While the number of youth arrested and processed in the juvenile justice system has declined, the state has increased its

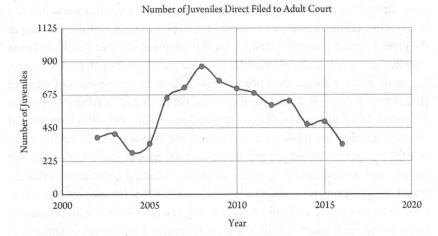

Figure 5.1 Number of juveniles directly filed to adult court in California, 2002–2016 Source: Data compiled from California Department of Justice statistical reports, oag.ca.gov/cjsc/pubs#juvenileJustice.

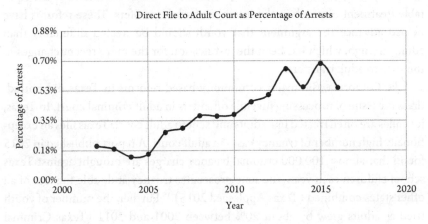

Figure 5.2 Direct filings to adult court as percentage of arrests, 2002–2016 Source: Data compiled from California Department of Justice statistical reports, oag.ca.gov/cjsc/pubs#juvenileJustice.

punitiveness. Despite the massive drop in arrest rates, in 2015, well into the implementation of community-based reforms, the number of youth given an adult disposition (416) was essentially the same as in 2005 (422). If arrests were to go up, the state would likely experience growth in the number of youth incarcerated and youth sent to adult prisons.

Fortunately, there has been some significant pushback in California on direct transfers, one of the major mechanisms by which youth get sent to adult court.[14] In 2016 voters approved Proposition 57, which ended the practice of prosecutors using direct filing where they alone determine whether a youth should be tried in the adult criminal court and instead requires a judicial transfer hearing in the juvenile court. Since the changes were implemented fewer youth are being transferred to adult court, but major regional disparities still exist; some counties use vastly more transfers than others, regardless of the seriousness of offenses (Lafferty et al. 2017; Ridolfi, Washburn, and Guzman 2017). After Proposition 57 passed, the California legislature passed Senate Bill 1391, which prohibited all adult transfers for those 14 and 15 years old (Cohen 2020). Additionally, in 2020 the newly elected progressive district attorney in Los Angeles, George Gascon, announced sweeping policy changes, including a declaration that he would not prosecute juveniles as adults (Queally 2020). Developments such as these are encouraging and reflect the growing disenchantment with processing youth in the adult court, but they will likely remain a patchwork of changes at the county level until the state develops a more sweeping end to the pathways of trying youth as adults, particularly in the event that arrest rates were to rise. The community-based reform movement has mostly focused on low-level offenders and promoting greater local control, neither of which is conducive to the equitable treatment of youth in the instance of adult transfers. These reforms have helped advance the argument that youth should be treated differently than adults, though, which has been the justification for the more recent changes in the state to adult transfers.

Like California, the major community-based reforms in Texas did not address the issue of processing juvenile offenders in adult criminal court. In Texas, juveniles are often treated like adults and sent to adult court. Texas files an exceptionally high number of truancy cases in adult court. A report published in 2015 found that almost 100,000 criminal truancy charges are brought against Texas school children each year. The state prosecutes truancy at double the rate of all other states combined (Texas Appleseed 2015).[15] Further, the number of youth tried as adults grew by about 20% between 2001 and 2011 (Texas Criminal Justice Coalition 2012, 23). Youth certified to the adult court are predominantly Black and Hispanic (about 80% of the annual commitments), despite making up about 65% of the state's youth population. The legislative changes in 2007 have not made any significant change to the practice of certifying juveniles as adults, as Figure 5.3 indicates, and unlike California, there has not been a more recent effort to push for changes to this practice.

Texas ranks fifth among U.S. states holding the greatest number of youth in adult prisons (Human Rights Watch 2012). Texas also has a "once an adult, always an adult" transfer law, which requires any juvenile who was criminally prosecuted in the past to be prosecuted in the adult court if they are later charged with another criminal offense, regardless of whether or not the offense is serious (Johnson 2010). Community-based reforms passed in 2007 and 2011 did not

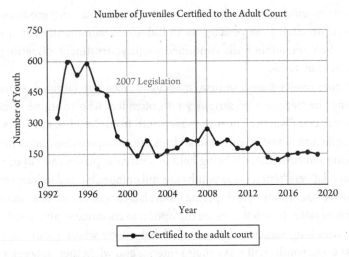

Figure 5.3 Juveniles certified to adult court in Texas, 1996–2019 Source: Data compiled from Texas Juvenile Justice Department annual statistical reports, 1996–2019, https://www.tjjd.texas.gov/index.php/doc-library/category/338-reports-to-the-governor-and-legislative-budget-board.

amend any policies for juvenile violent offenders. In 2019, a 12-year-old was charged with capital murder in Texas and could face up to 40 years in prison if convicted (Chuck 2019). The tough laws Texas has for handling serious juvenile offenders, such as blended sentencing (when juveniles serve time in the juvenile justice system and then are transferred to the adult system), have gone untouched and have not been criticized in the reform debate in Texas. The community-based reforms in Texas were targeted at those convicted of misdemeanors and drew distinctions between the "type of youths" in state-run prisons and those that could be in programs in local communities (Murphy 2007). Scott Fisher, chairman of the board of the Texas Juvenile Justice Department (TJJD), stated in conjunction with the passage of one of the community-based reforms, "[T]he institutionalization of juveniles is a necessary thing for violent, habitual perpetrators" (quoted in Hunt 2011). Rather than questioning the need for expansive institutionalization, the 2007 reforms focused on ensuring the "right" individuals went to institutions in the "right" location.

In 2018, the newly appointed executive director of TJJD, Camille Cain, decided to certify as adults 35 youth considered the "most violent" and transfer them out of the juvenile system to the adult system in order to try to solve the issue of increased violence and disorder in the state-run juvenile prisons. The youth were sent to the Youthful Offender Program at Clemens Unit, outside Houston. From there they were transferred to a location in Hunstville (a former death row wing) because the Clemens Unit was the site of an abuse scandal (McGaughy 2019). While the push for community control and the improved treatment of *some* youth within the system can help lay the groundwork for incursions on adult time policies, as in California, community-based reforms can also be compatible with continued punitive treatment of serious youth offenders, as in Texas.

The community-based reform movement has not targeted significantly reforming the treatment of serious youth offenders who continue to be given adult sentences. Even the effort to move youth from the adult system back into the juvenile justice system does not address the core questions and debates over sentencing reforms. Though being held in a juvenile prison instead of an adult prison is relatively better, these youths are still being subjected to long sentences and abusive conditions. The Supreme Court has carved out narrow exemptions, but all three states have left in place the option to continue to give youth LWOP and decades-long sentences. There are debates over where (adult vs. juvenile prisons) these youths will serve their sentence and when they may get a chance at parole, but lengthy sentences for youth continue to be a reality in all three states.

Juvenile Sex Offender Legislation

Similar to the debates over juvenile LWOP, the death penalty, and adult transfers, the community-based reform movement has largely left untouched the treatment of juvenile sex offenders. In fact, these youth, routinely excluded from community-based reforms, comprise a class of offenders that is experiencing an expansion and ratcheting up of punitiveness. Gottschalk (2015) has shown that policies geared toward sex offenders is a major growth area in the carceral state and encompasses a new wave of expansion that is not being critically examined at the expense of long-term decarceration goals. The construct of the "sexual predator" is part of a long-running tendency to create typologies of offenders who are vilified and scapegoated as *the* threat to society and that must be rooted out therapeutically or punitively because they are psychologically and morally deficient (Lancaster 2011; Leon 2011; Wacquant 2009, 31).[16] Typologies like these continue to justify punitive policies and also continue to make inequitable social and economic relations invisible. Despite research that suggests sex offender registries, civil commitments, and long sentences are ineffective at curbing sex offenses and pose troubling breaches of civil liberties, these policies have not faced substantial critiques as part of the movement for reforming the juvenile justice system.[17]

The community-based reform model states California and Texas continue to subject youth to sex offender registries despite evidence that the practice is harmful to individuals and does not improve public safety (Human Rights Watch

2013). In Texas, all registered juveniles are listed on a public website, a practice that is particularly dangerous for them and has no proven effect on preventing sexual abuse (Barajas 2013; Beitsch 2015). In 2011, there were 3,600 juveniles on the Texas state registry for sex offenders (Lee 2009). The state does not have age limits for the registry, so in 2011 eleven 10-year-olds were listed (Lee 2009).

In 2021, California revised its lifetime sexual registry requirements, but without fundamentally challenging the use of registries for juveniles. The law shifts away from blanket lifetime registries to a tiered system (where the top tier still requires lifetime registry). For juveniles, there are two tiers: one requires a minimum of 5 years on the registry and the other a minimum of 10 years. Only after this minimum amount of time has been met can a juvenile petition to terminate their registry requirement (California Department of Justice 2021). This legislative change could result in tens of thousands of offenders being able to petition to be removed from the registry; however, it largely keeps the use of registries intact (Munger, Zhang, and Liao 2018). The petitions will be handled at the county level, which could result in major inequities in approval rates across the state. The new law makes important and promising incursions on the use of registries for juveniles but does not repudiate their use.

The foundations most responsible for promoting the community-based reform movement do not significantly address the issues surrounding juvenile sex offenders in their models. Similar to the approach to juvenile LWOP and mandatory minimums, neither MacArthur nor Annie E. Casey make changing these policies central to their reform effort.[18] The community-based reforms these foundations espouse are predominantly targeted at low-level offenders. Questions about what to do with serious offenders, especially sex offenders, are highly contested and often unpopular in a policy environment that remains quite committed to a punitive accountability and a victim-centered approach to corrections. To the extent that these foundations point out the harmful effects of these policies (such as LWOP and sex offender registries), they mostly focus on carving out juveniles as "exceptional" and focus on exempting those under 18, despite the fact that studies find similar negative effects for adults on offender registries (Tofte and Fellner 2007).[19]

The MacArthur Foundation's first community-based model state, Pennsylvania, has led on some of the most punitive strategies for addressing juvenile sex offenses. Pennsylvania's policies and legislative debates over sentencing for juveniles convicted of sex offenses demonstrate its continued tough approach to the supposed "worst of the worst" offenders in the state. Pennsylvania has been one of a number of states that have passed punitive laws to deal with juvenile sex offenders over the past two decades. In 2003, the Pennsylvania legislature passed Act 21, which requires the State Sexual Offenders Board to assess juvenile sexual offenders that are about to turn 21 (and therefore age out of the juvenile justice system) and consider them for involuntary civil commitment. Many states have adult sex offender civil commitment legislation, but Pennsylvania was the first to pass civil commitment legislation for juvenile sex offenders (Lawrence and Barnes 2014). The legislation requires that a juvenile be committed if they are charged with a qualifying sexual crime and they exhibit "having a mental abnormality as defined in Section 6402 (relating to definitions) or personality disorder, either of which results in serious difficulty in controlling sexually violent behavior."[20] A youth can be recommitted yearly for up to 99 years (Lawrence and Barnes 2014).[21]

The 2003 legislation passed unanimously in the state senate and 197–3 in the state house. In addition to garnering bipartisan support, the bill was also supported by the Pennsylvania Coalition against Rape as well as the state's district attorneys. In the floor debate there was just one voice of dissent, that of Representative Greg Vitali, a Democrat from Delaware County, who argued that the law was "something you may expect in Stalinist Russia.... [T]o be able to be confined year after year after year as an adult for an act you may have committed as a 14-year-old is kind of frightening" (Pennsylvania State Legislature 2003). Vitali's colleagues pushed back, describing his objections as "outrageous," and strongly supported the bill. Representative Dennis O'Brien, from Philadelphia County, echoing the "adult time for adult crime" line, responded, "We are talking about juveniles who have been convicted of very serious offenses very late in their life, probably from the age of 17 through 21" (Pennsylvania State Legislature 2003).

Defense for the legislation was spurred by a case in central Pennsylvania in which a violent offender reportedly told a judge they were going to commit another crime, but the judge was forced to release the youth. As a local newspaper put it, "[A] rapist identified as someone with homicidal tendencies continues to fantasize about raping 4- to 6-year-old girls but will be released from prison Friday on his 21st birthday" (Bowman 2003). The discourse supporting the legislation harkened to the "superpredator" rhetoric; Republican representative Peter Zug framed the legislation as "protecting our children, protecting our neighborhoods, protecting our Commonwealth from predators—in this case, a sexual predator," and Representative Mauree Gingrich, a Republican from Lebanon County, described sex offenders as posing a "grave danger to our communities" (Pennsylvania State Legislature 2003). While the defense of the bill described those convicted of a sex offense in pathologizing and stigmatizing terms, the requirement that youth would receive treatment while incarcerated was key to the bill's success. The provision of treatment is also the justification for a lack of legal protection and representation in involuntary commitment decisions, because a civil commitment is not a criminal conviction. Civil commitments are a policy that exemplifies the way discourses of individual pathology and the need for individual treatment serve to justify punitive policies.

From 2004 to 2018 there were about 452 referrals of juveniles to the Sexual Offender Assessment Board, and 68 of these youth were committed to the Sexual Responsibility and Treatment Program (Domback and Lawrence 2018). As of 2014 there had only been six discharges and only one of the youth left the program because they "successfully" completed their treatment (Lawrence and Barnes 2014).[22] In the following four years, there were just three youth discharged from the program (Domback and Lawrence 2018). It is possible that, *so far*, youth within the program have been held for as long as 14 years.[23] Of all youth committed to the program over this period, the "successful" treatment rate is 0.02%, so the average length of stay will continue to grow over time.

A recent legal development that limited the punitive reach of sex offender laws has excluded offenders in the Act 21 Program. In 2015, the Pennsylvania Supreme Court ruled that lifetime registration for juveniles in the provisions of the Sex Offender Registration and Notification Act was unconstitutional. The ruling caused Pennsylvania state police to stop registering juvenile offenders and removed the names of those juveniles currently in the database. However, the court left intact the registration requirements in the Act for juveniles in the "Act 21 Program" (the 2003 legislation) who are classified as "sexually violent delinquent children" (Pennsylvania Juvenile Court Judges' Commission 2015). Similar to the state's policies on juvenile LWOP, in response to court rulings the state continues to carve out the continued use of something like a juvenile sex offender registry for the "worst" offenders, who in this case exhibit "mental abnormality."

The continued use of sex offender registries and expanding use of civil commitments signal a troubling area of carceral expansion that perpetuates the problematic conceptions of crime and crime control that contributed to the rise of mass incarceration. Reforms targeted at "deserving," low-level youth offenders, like those in the community-based reform movement, do not address the continued and, in some instances, increased punishments for classes of offenders deemed "serious," "dangerous," "pathological," and ultimately "undeserving." In the effort to isolate the true serious offenders, the community-based reforms pursued in these three model states have continued to perpetuate practices in which poor and minority youth are disproportionately swept up into the justice system, revealing the distinct class and racialized character of the individualized approach to solving social problems like crime.

Gang-Affiliated Youth

Like the exemptions of youth charged as adults and with sex offenses, youth considered gang members also continue to experience harsh punitive policies within the community-based reform movement. The focus on reserving punitive policies for the "worst of the worst" juveniles has entrenched and naturalized the ways that penal policies are geared toward managing marginalized populations in order to preserve and make possible a widening unequal economic structure. In California, the buildup of community-based reforms has explicitly excluded gang-affiliated youth, and the state has continued to ratchet up punitive treatment of youth labeled gang members. The use of gang injunctions is connected to the broader developments of austerity politics and is a tool to smooth development efforts in cities. The effort to remove, suppress, and contain jobless youth is justified by scapegoating the specter of the gang member, who must be punished and banished. The community-based reform movement has not challenged the development and rent intensification imperatives (efforts to increase rents and real estate values) at the heart of gang injunction policies, and therefore model states continue to disproportionately target poor and racial minority youth for punitive policies.

Establishing ever more sophisticated tools for determining which youth are "high risk" versus "low risk" and reinscribing notions of the "worst of the worst" offenders is exacerbating the racial and class character of the juvenile justice system. As the previous chapter demonstrated, the focus on individual interventions has been at the expense of addressing broader political economic inequalities that are a critical part of understanding why the United States developed such an extensive penal apparatus. By relying on the goal of better determining *which* youth deserve harsh punishments and which deserve alternatives, the community-based reforms themselves do not repudiate some of the most punitive policies in the juvenile justice system. The continued exclusion of gang-affiliated youth and their exceptionally punitive treatment is a critical way that the community-based reform movement has failed to address policies that are the foundation of a punitive and expansive juvenile justice system.

California has some of the most exceptionally punitive policies targeting youth labeled gang members. In 1987 the state created CalGang, a database of suspected gang members. In 2000 voters passed Proposition 21, the Gang Violence and Juvenile Crime Prevention Act, ushering in a wave of punitive policies including zero tolerance policies for gang crimes and gang sentencing enhancement measures.[24] The state also started using gang injunctions, which are essentially restraining orders covering entire neighborhoods where alleged gang members are not allowed to engage in behavior that would otherwise be legal (for example, congregating in groups of two or more or simply being in public) (Muñiz 2015, 7). Gang injunctions are an example of the ways in which increasingly punitive policies buttress broader public-sector retrenchment and the intensification of the upward distribution of wealth. As Muñiz details in *Police, Power, and the Production of Racial Boundaries*, gang injunctions are used to remove "undesirables" to smooth development efforts. These policies push marginalized individuals out of the way of certain neighborhoods as a tool of rent intensification (40). The use of the term "gang" is highly subjective, as are the criteria for inclusion in the database and for becoming an alleged gang member. The term has been used to classify and intensify punishments disproportionately for poor and racial minorities. According to CalGang, about 86% of gang members are Hispanic or Black.[25]

Texas has also used the label of "gang affiliation" as a tool for ratcheting up punishments for poor and racial minority youth. In 1996, the Texas legislature allowed the creation of "gang books" (catalogs of gang members and related information to help criminal investigations) (Johnson 1998, 2–13). In 1998, Texas used its first gang injunction. It continues to use TXGang Database, which includes divisions for those 17 and older and those 16 and under (Texas Department of Public Safety 2019). Pennsylvania does not have a statewide database for suspected gang members nor a formal use of gang injunctions; however, antigang programs in Philadelphia use some of these tactics, such as keeping a database of gang members and doing sweeps (Ewing 2017).

In recent years, the use of the gang databases and injunctions has been increasingly challenged on civil rights and antidiscrimination terms. In Texas, a proposed gang injunction in south Houston from 2016 was opposed by the ACLU, and the city eventually dropped the plan to use one (*Austin Chronicle* 1998; George 2016). The use of a gang database has been under fire in California; in 2016, the state auditor issued a report that found the California gang database included many entries that lacked substantiating evidence, that people on the list were not being purged as required by statute, and that juveniles (about 70% of those on the list) were not being notified of their entry on the database in order to have the opportunity to challenge the classification (California State Auditor 2016). Since the report there have been efforts to improve accountability for the list, and the number of names has substantially decreased from 2017 to 2020. In 2020, Los Angeles County issued a moratorium on adding new names to the database. However, the database is still in use, and gang injunctions also continue to be used by law enforcement. As of December 2020, there were 46 active gang injunctions targeting over 80 neighborhoods in the city of Los Angeles alone (Feuer n.d.; Los Angeles Police Department n.d.; Muñiz 2015).

There is promising momentum for curbing the use of gang databases and injunctions; however, none of this momentum is coming out of the community-based reform movement. In fact, the turn to greater community control is exacerbating the increasingly disparate use of injunctions and entries into gang databases from county to county (Garcia-Leys and Brown 2019). Giving juveniles and others on the list a better chance at petitioning for removal may be having a limited impact (Garcia-Leys and Brown 2019). For example, in 2018

6,007 people were added to the California gang database, while only 11 requests for removal from the list were granted (Garcia-Leys and Brown 2019).

Creating more exceptions for who is subject to these policies may eventually be an effective way of chipping away at their use; however, in order to fully end these practices it is likely that deeper critiques of their use beyond issues of procedural fairness will be needed. Challenging the notion of the "worst of the worst" offender that animates support for policies that target gangs will be an essential part of this effort. CalGang and gang injunctions are harmful not only because of the racist targeting of the policies but also because they presuppose that greater surveillance and punishment for the "really bad ones" is an effective way to fight crime. When the community-based reform movement ignores the rent intensification imperative of gang injunctions and the broader relationship between policies targeted at containing and suppressing the marginalized in an increasingly unequal social and economic context, this significantly limits its impact. As of 2020, violence in Los Angeles had begun to tick up, and as long as the deeper political economic causes of the persistently high rates of violence (compared to any other industrialized nation) are not addressed, policymakers at city, state, and national levels will continue to fall back on ineffective and harmful policies like these (Miller 2016).

Who Gets Punished? Persistent Inequalities

While the community-based reforms may not have taken direct aim at repudiating the punishment of serious offenders like those given adult sentences, charged with sex offenses, and considered gang members, they have focused on clarifying the "type" of youth who deserves to be in state-run versus local facilities. Despite widespread advocacy within the community-based reform movement to tackle racial disparities, the continued use of punitive policies and the methods of determining which youth deserve these punishments (such as risk assessments and gang labels) have ensured that poor and racial minority youth continue to be subjected to the most punitive policies: LWOP, long sentences, and being sent to state-run juvenile prisons. Both the MacArthur and the Annie E. Casey foundations include addressing disproportionate minority contact (DMC) as a pillar of their respective community-based reforms. The main strategies proposed by reform advocates like MacArthur and Annie E. Casey to address racial disparities attribute these inequalities to interpersonal prejudice and tend to ignore economic inequality. As a result, their proposed solutions are primarily focused on data collection, cultural sensitivity training, dialogues, and expanding private nonprofit community-based programs, despite little evidence that these approaches lead to greater equality (Griffin 2008;

Griffith, Jirard, and Ricketts 2012; Kempf 1992; Pennsylvania DMC Youth/Law Enforcement Corporation n.d.; Torbet, Hurst, and Soler 2006).[26]

In Texas, the 2007 community-based reforms did little to address the problem with the overrepresentation of Black and Hispanic youth in state-run institutions. Black and Hispanic youth continue to be sent to these institutions at a disproportionate rate.[27] In 2012, white youth committed more felonies (3,777) than Black youth (3,245), yet *more* Black youth (264) were sent to state-run institutions than whites (164) (Texas Juvenile Justice Department 2014b). While Black and Hispanic youth in Texas make up about 55% of the population, they comprise about 80% of the youth sent to state-run prisons. Just as before the 2007 reforms, the modal juvenile in state-run institutions is there for a nonviolent offense and disproportionately more likely to be a youth of color. Figure 5.4 shows the breakdown of youth sent to Texas state-run prisons by race and the persistent distribution before and after the implementation of community-based reforms.

Similarly in California, the youth sent to state-run prisons continue to be disproportionately Black and Hispanic since the implementation of community-based reforms, as indicated in Table 5.1.

As of 2012, a comprehensive study on DMC in Pennsylvania found that minority youth are three times more likely to be arrested and more than two times more likely to be incarcerated than white youth (Griffith, Jirard, and Ricketts 2012).

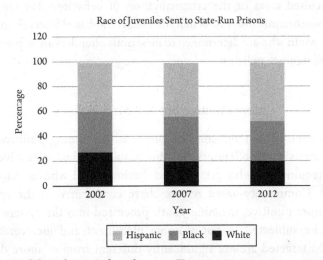

Figure 5.4 Breakdown by race of youth sent to Texas state prisons Source: Data compiled from Texas Juvenile Justice Department annual statistical reports, 2002, 2007, 2012, https://www2.tjjd.texas.gov/publications/default.aspx.

Table 5.1 **Breakdown by race of youth sent to California state prisons**

Race	2002	2019
White	13%	6%
Hispanic	51%	53%
Black	28%	36%
Other	7%	5%

The community-based reform movement has failed to change the disproportionate punitive treatment of racial minority youth in the juvenile justice system because it has largely misidentified the causes of these unequal racial outcomes. For example, a 1992 study on DMC in Pennsylvania found that 75% of the youth in the study were from families with an annual income of less than $24,000.[28] Families who made less than $8,000 a year had the highest rates of detention of the entire sample. Yet, these findings were buried in the appendix, and the overarching conclusion was that "youths are treated differently in juvenile justice depending on race" (Kempf 1992, 4). Rather than address the development imperatives driving gang injunctions or the ways the juvenile justice system criminalizes youth joblessness and other consequences of public-sector retrenchment, the reforms aim to fix the behavior of individuals—both of youth and practitioners. However, racial sensitivity training and diversity initiatives are not capable of fundamentally restructuring patterns of policing that target disenfranchised areas or the criminalization of behaviors that are largely a product of economic distress. When the behavioral-based interventions do not work, the youth who are determined to be serious offenders are subjected to unchallenged punitive policies.

More Punitive, but Not More Serious

The community-based reforms are premised on aiming punitive policies toward serious youth offenders, but this has not worked to resolve the persistent inequities of who gets labeled "serious" and who is subsequently punished. Community-based reforms have contributed to the system becoming more punitive, meaning youth processed into the system are *more* likely to be subjected to out-of-home placement and incarceration. Yet, the youths targeted are *not* significantly different from or more dangerous than those prior to the enactment of the reforms. The idea of sorting the youth committing serious crimes from the "rehabilitatable" youth does not fundamentally challenge the use of punitive policies, nor does it achieve the impossible goal of finding the "really bad ones." While sorting technologies (such as risk assessment algorithms) and policies have become more advanced, the belief that discerning "good" from "bad" youth will fix the problems within the juvenile justice system continues to be a fallacy that guides the community-based reform movement.

The results on the ground in the three model states suggest this strategy has largely failed in achieving a less punitive system. Contrary to the promotion and rhetoric of community-based reforms, a smaller percentage of juveniles in California were being monitored in their own home in 2011 than in 2004. Further, a greater percentage of juveniles were sent to secure county facilities and other public and private facilities in the years following the reforms. In Texas, the drop in juvenile arrest rates is obscuring the reality that the way the system is processing youth is actually becoming *more* punitive. Comparing the pre-community-based reform period with what is happening today, more youth who are referred to the juvenile justice system are being placed out-of-home and incarcerated. Between 2005 and 2012, the total percentage of youth in county-run secure or nonsecure facilities increased 5 percentage points (Carreon, Henneke, and Kreager 2015). In Pennsylvania in 2019 compared to 2002, a greater percentage of youth referred to the system were sent to state secure facilities (9% in 2019 compared to 5.5% in 2002), even though fewer youth were referred in total (Center for Juvenile Justice Training & Research 2002; Pennsylvania Juvenile Court Judges' Commission 2019).

Overall, youth being arrested today are facing more serious consequences (Males 2019). This is not because "more serious" offenders are being arrested and processed. The opposite trend is actually occurring in Texas, as a smaller percentage of the youth caught up in the system are in for a serious crime than they were prior to the 2007 reforms (Males 2019). Since the community-based reforms were enacted in Texas, the state has not succeeded in pinpointing more serious offenders to be sent to state-run facilities. Most of the youth in state-run institutions continue to be sent there for nonviolent offenses. For example, in 2007 violation of probation charges constituted 41% of the youth sent to state-run facilities. After eight years of implementing the community-based reforms, the percentage of youth committed to state facilities for a violation of probation *increased* to 51%. The remaining juveniles were sent for felony charges; however, only about 30% of them were convicted of a violent felony (Texas Juvenile Justice Department 2014b). This means that *after* the implementation of community-based reforms about 70% of all youth sent to state facilities are sent for probation violations or nonviolent offenses (Carreon, Henneke, and Kreager 2015).[29]

Arrests Drop, but Punishment Does Not

The most encouraging change that has occurred in the juvenile justice system has been the dramatic drop in arrest rates for youth over the past several decades. Fewer youth are being referred to the juvenile justice system today than in the early 2000s, leading to a reduction in the size of the system across the board. In California in 2002, 191,579 youth were arrested compared to 43,181 youth in 2019. In Texas in 2002, 140,085 youth were arrested compared to 49,562 youth in 2016.[30] In Pennsylvania in 2002, 106,077 youth were arrested compared to 37,821 in 2018 (Pennsylvania Office of Attorney General Josh Shapiro 2021). The total number of juveniles processed in the juvenile justice system has gone down because overall arrest rates are down. The fall in arrest numbers is a trend that all states in the nation are experiencing (and is occurring internationally). There is no evidence the drop in arrest rates is due to the community-based reforms passed in California, Texas, or Pennsylvania, particularly since the legislative changes did not address practices related to arrests and the downward trend of arrest rates predated the implementation of community-based reforms (Barmann 2019; Palomino and Tucker 2019; Pfaff and Butts 2019).

There are few explanations for why the arrest rates are going down, and little consensus on any factors being the key to this development (Forman 2017; Pfaff 2017).[31] Since the trend is occurring across the board despite significant differences in policies from county to county, state to state, and country to country, it is unlikely that one particular policy is driving the change. It would be of great value to better understand these trends, but it is important to note that the community-based reform movement is in many ways riding the wave of this larger trend rather than producing it, and thus the two developments should be disentangled (Pfaff and Butts 2019). The drop in arrests has led to an overall shrinking of the number of juveniles processed in the juvenile justice system, from a historic high in the 1990s, but all three states still process a large number of juveniles and subject them to punitive policies, particularly compared to international counterparts.

Despite dropping arrest rates, *how* youth are processed has remained fairly constant, which largely tracks with the persistent disparities in who gets punitive dispositions. Figures 5.5 and 5.6 show the dispositions youth receive in California and Texas. The percentages have remained consistent across the years before and after major community-based reforms were enacted. As these figures show, the percentage of juveniles sent to state institutions in California and Texas was never more than 2% of all wardship dispositions prior to the community-based reforms.[32]

The majority of youth are given a disposition in their home or a relative's home, which can be punishments like electronic monitoring, house arrest, or

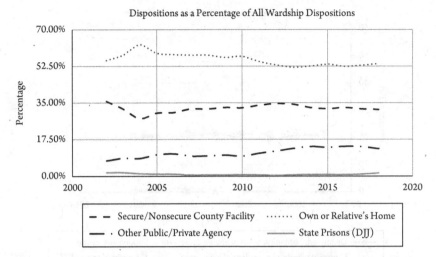

Figure 5.5 Dispositions as a percentage of all wardship dispositions in California, 2002–2018 Source: Data compiled from California Department of Justice statistical reports, oag.ca.gov/cjsc/pubs#juvenileJustice.

intensive probation supervision. These figures suggest that were arrest rates to go up, the community-based reforms have not created any changes that would prevent the incarceration numbers from going back up again. While it is difficult during a downward trend to imagine that arrest rates will ever climb back up, given the lack of clarity on what is driving this trend and a history of volatile arrest rates, it would be wise to consider the possibility. In the 1970s there was broad consensus that the decarceration trends in the American prison system would continue. Very few people predicted the carceral boom that came in the subsequent decades (Gottschalk 2006; Wacquant 2009). Given the lack of clarity on what is driving the current welcome drop in arrest rates, it is important to keep this history in mind, especially since the community-based reform movement has not changed the distribution of dispositions within the juvenile justice system.

The most punitive policies in the reform model states have remained largely intact in conjunction with the rise of community-based reforms. There have been substantial challenges to the use of these policies, but policymakers in all three states continue to fight to maintain the option of LWOP, long sentences, adult transfers, sex offender registries, civil commitments, and gang injunctions for the most serious youth offenders. While the community-based reforms have been aimed at identifying the "worst of the worst" offenders in order to get right *who* is subjected to these policies and *where* they will serve their time (adult prison, juvenile prison, or local jail), the community-based reform movement continues to reinforce the idea that these policies are still necessary. The

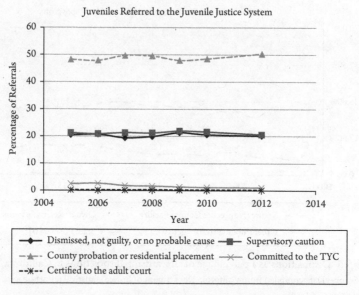

Figure 5.6 Dispositions as a percentage of referrals in Texas, 2005–2012 Source: Data compiled from Texas Juvenile Justice Department annual statistical reports, 2005–2012, https://www2.tjjd.texas.gov/publications/default.aspx.

efforts to shift some juveniles out of adult prisons and to exclude some from the most punitive policies have been successful, but the system still remains quite punitive. Despite rhetoric that the reforms have succeeded in more accurately targeting policies, the same youth are being subjected to serious punishments—disproportionately poor and minority youth. While those carved out of the system are a testament to positive improvements in juvenile justice policy, the experience of youth who remain caught in the carceral dragnet is in many instances getting more punitive and more dangerous.

Conditions in State-Run Facilities

The major motivation for pursuing community-based reforms is to address the abusive treatment of youth in state-run prisons. In all three states, increasing local carceral capacities and devolving control for youth from the state to the local level were justified on the grounds of limiting the youths' exposure to these harmful institutions. However, well into the implementation of the community-based reform movement, it is clear that the youth who continue to be incarcerated in state-run institutions face persistent and in many instances worse conditions of confinement. By focusing on moving youth out of these facilities rather than more fundamentally addressing abusive conditions the community-based reform movement has failed to fix the problems plaguing the state-run system.

Increased Violence and Abuse

Despite significant drops in the number of youth sent to state-run prisons, the youth remaining in these facilities continue to be subjected to the same abuses that spurred reforms in the first place. In most instances, these youth are experiencing *increasing* rates of violence and abusive conditions. In California, according to a 2019 report published by the Center for Juvenile and Criminal Justice, from 2016 to 2018 use-of-force incidents in state-run prisons increased threefold and the rate of youth subjected to beatings rose by 49% (Loudenback 2019; Washburn and Menart 2019). In just one year (2017–2018) there were more than 1,330 injuries to youth in state-run facilities (that's more injuries than there were youth in the prisons) (Alfonseca, 2019). From 2016 to 2019 an average of 33 youth per 100 in the state-run prison system were involved in a violent incident each month (Washburn and Menart 2019, 26). One state-run juvenile prison, the O. H. Close School, has been identified as having the eighth most use-of-force incidents in the California prison system, putting it in the company of adult maximum security facilities (Washburn and Menart 2019, 26). In California, efforts to comply with the *Farrell* litigation, a 2004 lawsuit that resulted in requiring the state to reform its juvenile system into a rehabilitative model, have largely been unsuccessful, and the facilities continue to be dangerous and fail to provide adequate treatment for youth (Ajmani and Webster 2016; Macallair, Males, and McCracken 2009, 17).

Persistent problems with abuse of youth in Pennsylvania facilities were extensively detailed in Chapter 3 since so many of these facilities are privately run. However, the state-run facilities also have issues with abuse. Repeated lawsuits have revealed that state-run facilities in Pennsylvania have problems with staff abusing youth, unlawfully using physical restraints, and causing numerous injuries (Bonk 2020; Pilnik et al. 2019). In Texas, since the community-based reforms passed in 2007 juveniles are even more likely to experience violence in state secure facilities (Grissom and Aaronson 2012). In 2012, reports showed persistent and in some areas growing rates of violence in juvenile state secure facilities. In the five-year span after the legislation was passed, youth-on-youth assaults had more than tripled at secure facilities, and attacks on staff members had also increased (Grissom and Aaronson 2012). From 2010 to 2013, the use of pepper spray in state-run facilities also significantly increased (Deitch et al. 2013). At the Giddings State School, the number of youth injured in assaults quadrupled from 2007 to 2011 (Grissom and Aaronson 2012). Pennsylvania

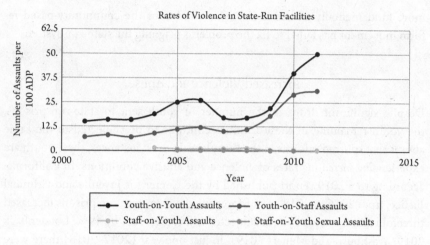

Figure 5.7 Rates of violence in Texas state-run facilities, 2001–2011 Source: Data compiled from interactive graphs from Grissom and Aaronson (2012), http://www.texastribune.org/library/data/tjjd-youth-violence-up/#tabs-2. Data for Staff-on-Youth Sexual Assaults" available only for 2005–2010.

and Texas, like California, indicate that the experience of youth in state-run facilities has by many measures deteriorated in the aftermath of the community-based reform movement.

The number of sexual assault incidents in Texas's state-run facilities has dropped (one of the main spurs of the reforms), but the rate of youth-on-youth assaults has doubled. Even at the peak of the highest incidences of staff-on-youth sexual assaults in 2005, the rate was 0.3 assaults per 100 ADP (average daily population) (about 13 confirmed cases). As of 2010, the rate had dropped to 0.17 per 100 ADP (about 3 confirmed cases). Over the same time frame youth-on-youth assaults grew from a rate of 25 per 100 ADP (about 580 cases) in 2005 to 50 per 100 ADP (about 695 cases) in 2010 (Grissom and Aaronson 2012).

Figure 5.7 is not intended to minimize the gravity of the problem of staff-on-youth sexual assaults in Texas state institutions (which hardly register on the graph). However, it does highlight the rates of other types of violence (youth-on-youth assaults, youth-on-staff assaults) that have not been addressed in the reforms and have always made up a much larger percentage of the incidents of violence in state-run institutions. The proposal to lower the youth-to-staff ratio in the reform debates would have potentially reduced these forms of violence, but was dropped for cost-savings purposes.

Inadequate Oversight and Staffing

One major reason for the failure of community-based reforms to improve the conditions of state-run prisons (and all facilities in the states) is the prioritization of cost savings. A core tension in the reforms persists in which reform actors do not want to allocate money to the state-run agency, but since state-run prisons remain open they continue to be sites of abuse and increasingly worse places for the youth sent there. As detailed in Chapter 3, lawmakers in Pennsylvania have been reluctant to fund oversight measures even in the wake of repeated incidents of abuse in private facilities. While there are several bodies in California that patch together oversight of juvenile state-run prisons, there is not a monitoring body that serves as the primary oversight authority for the Department of Juvenile Justice (Washburn and Menart 2019, 83). The chief goals of protecting "the taxpayer" and cutting costs have prevented Texas from making significant changes to improve oversight and conditions of confinement for juveniles.

Texas's community-based reforms created two administrative oversight positions, the Office of the Independent Ombudsman and the Office of the Inspector General. Additionally, the legislation created a crisis hotline and allocated money to put surveillance cameras in the state-run facilities. Almost immediately, however, the goal of cost savings undercut this set of plans for reducing abuse. Less than one month after the reforms were signed into law by the governor, Senator Juan "Chuy" Hinojosa (Democrat) and Representative Jerry Madden (Republican) publicly criticized the ineffectual role of the ombudsman, Will Harrell. The legislators accused Harrell of not conducting enough face-to-face interviews and for not going on enough visits to juvenile facilities (Hernandez 2007b). Harrell responded that he did not have enough money to set up regional offices, let alone the employees to staff them, and was using his personal cell phone to conduct his job due to a lack of resources (Hernandez 2007b). Since 2011, the Office of the Independent Ombudsman has increased site visits and the number of youth interviewed, but from 2014 to 2020 the Office's budget decreased about 20% (dropping from $1,124,389 to $901,289) (Texas Juvenile Justice Department 2021a, 2021b).

Another part of the effort to improve oversight and reduce abuse in Texas was to invest $18 million to ensure that surveillance cameras captured nearly every corner of the state facilities. However, as of 2012, TJJD interim executive director Jay Kimbrough acknowledged the videos were never monitored around the clock as intended (Ward 2012). Similarly in California's state-run prisons there are few cameras present or functional, which has hampered the state's ability to assess assault incidents (Washburn and Menart 2019). Even if the oversight mechanisms were well funded and operated, they only cover state prison facilities. This means that the thousands of youth held in local facilities are left without a strong oversight mechanism (Davis, Irvine, and Ziedenberg 2014). This has particularly negative consequences given that the reforms are premised on holding more youth at the local level. As Chapter 2 cataloged in detail, these facilities are rife with the same issues of abusive conditions of confinement.

Another cost-based reason the reforms have failed to improve abusive conditions of confinement is the underfunding of correctional officers. In Texas, as part of the deliberations over the 2007 community-based reforms, legislators debated the issue of how low the guard-to-youth ratios should be to help reduce instances of guard-on-inmate violence. With the support of the Texas State Employees Union, Kimbrough suggested reducing the 12:1 ratio to 6:1. Representative Madden, a key supporter of the legislation, responded that he had "75 to 100 million reasons," as in additional dollars, "not to shoot for a 6:1 ratio" (quoted in Copelin 2007b). The final version of Senate Bill 103 that became law stuck to the 12:1 ratio. The primacy of keeping costs down rather than the safety of juveniles and guards in the system ultimately shaped the 2007 legislation. This has had particularly negative consequences as turnover rates and understaffing are key contributing factors to the increased rates of violence in state-run prisons in the years after the community-based reform legislation was implemented.

In late 2016 Texas experienced another sex abuse scandal that spurred a renewed conversation about reform. In response to abuse allegations, Governor Greg Abbott sent in the Texas Rangers to the remaining five state-run facilities. The Rangers arrested a number of employees for abusing youth (McCullough 2018). Reports suggested that the systematic sexual abuse of youth and suicide attempts of youth in state-run prisons were in part caused by high staff turnover rates, low pay for correctional officers, and budget shortfalls. In the wake of the scandal, TJJD argued that it needed a significant increase in its budget to comply with the Prison Rape Elimination Act (about $170 million), but instead got a $17 million budget *cut* (Grissom 2016). Legislators and major organizations supporting the community-based reforms (such as Texas Appleseed and Texans Care for Children) remain opposed to increasing the budget at the state level to solve these problems. As Representative James White, Republican chairman of the Texas House Corrections Committee, stated in the wake of the scandal, "I don't give a damn how low the [correctional officer] pay is, there is no excuse for an adult to sexually assault a child" (quoted in Grissom and Ambrose 2017a).

The persistent underfunding of TJJD has led to high staff turnover and vacancies, which are contributing to greater violence in state-run prisons (*Katy [TX] News* 2019). In 2020 the TJJD had a staff turnover rate of 41.2%, the highest of any large state agency (Texas State Auditor 2020). Juvenile correction officers make $393 less per month than adult correctional officers. Many argue that the gap in pay is contributing to high turnover, instability, and abuse in juvenile facilities (Grissom and Ambrose 2017a, 2017b; McGaughy 2019; Ward 2017). TJJD and state employees' unions that represent correctional workers have asked for greater funding to get the state in compliance with federally mandated ratios of youth to juvenile correctional officers and to raise wages to retain staff (Texas State Employees Union 2021). However, like all state agencies, TJJD has been under pressure from the governor and other lawmakers to *reduce* its budget (Texas State Employees Union 2021).

California also continues to have staff-to-youth ratios that fail to comply with best practices and which put youth and staff in danger. In 2018 the California Department of Juvenile Justice reported an average 15% vacancy rate for juvenile correctional officers over the prior year. At two state-run prisons, Chad and O. H. Close, 23% of staff hired in 2015 left within two years of being hired (Washburn and Menart 2019). Issues related to understaffing are a major problem for the effort to provide treatment to youth in state-run prisons (Matsuda, Hess, and Turner 2020). Understaffing also diminishes oversight and supervision of youth; for example, a girl in a Pittsburgh prison attempted suicide due to "neglected supervision" (Frederick 2017). The failure to adequately pay and retain personnel in prisons is a major contribution to the continued and increased rates of violence and harm inflicted upon youth held in these state-run institutions.

Punitive Response: Solitary Confinement

Cost-cutting and reducing budgets are top priorities within the community-based reform movement, which has cut off other important measures to address abuse in prisons. Instead of properly funding these institutions, the state-run prison system has doubled down on some of the most harmful and punitive policies—such as solitary confinement—as the solution to increased violence. Yet solitary confinement itself has been found to increase violence in prisons and cause serious emotional and psychological damage (Haney 2003; King 1999; Reiter 2012; Rhodes 2004; Shalev 2013; Travis, Western, and Redburn 2014; Ward and Werlich 2004).[33] The persistent and expanding use of solitary confinement suggests the juvenile justice systems in these model states have not truly abandoned one of their harshest practices (Burke and Simpson 2015).

The California state-run prison system continues to rely on solitary confinement as a strategy to decrease violence and gang activity (Washburn and Menart 2019). From 2016 to 2018, the state's Department of Justice reported maximum stays in solitary confinement (a lockdown unit called the "Behavior Treatment Program") of nearly 13 months, 20 months, and 23 months at the three remaining prisons (Washburn and Menart 2019). The response to violent incidents or riots in the state-run system is to use lockdowns and more isolation.

During lockdowns youth spend much of their day in their cells and are unable to access school, religious services, or other programming (Washburn and Menart 2019, 29). From 2017 to 2018 the California corrections department reported that at least 968 class periods were canceled because of lockdowns as a response to security issues. The number of suicide attempts in the state-run prisons increased threefold from 2016 to 2018 (Loudenback 2019; Washburn and Menart 2019), yet suicidal youth are often put in isolation cells—a response that negatively affects mental health.

Since the passage of community-based reforms in 2007, the TJJD has continued to use solitary confinement for disciplinary purposes. One year after the reform bill passed, Harrell, the newly appointed TYC ombudsman, reported that the state was using isolation as a form of punishment and had increased its use of solitary since the reforms (Sandberg 2008). The 2007 community-based reforms did not change the rules on solitary, but there was some hope that with more oversight, the state institutions would adhere to regulations already on the books, such as providing intensive services to youth placed in solitary. In 2008, Harrell reported that TYC had turned two prisons into "de facto segregation camps where hard to manage youth languish in individual cells up to 23 hours a day" (Sandberg 2008). Harrell indicted TYC for applying policies from the adult prison system to the juvenile justice system and declared, "[I]t is straight-up isolation for the sake of punishment" (quoted in Sandberg 2008).

Two incidents of "uprisings" at the remaining state-run facilities in Texas in 2012 caused policymakers to double down on the use of solitary confinement (Grissom and Aaronson 2012). In October 2012, juveniles at Gainesville threw rocks through windows and tried to get on the roof of the facility, and in July 2012, 14 youth at the Giddings State School refused to go to bed and tore apart their dorm rooms. In both cases, the juveniles were pepper-sprayed and taken to detention areas. Policymakers blamed the incidences on the lenience of the changes coming out of the 2007 legislation and advocated for more consequences for "unruly" youth.

In response to the two "uprisings," the TJJD board voted in 2012 to implement a new solitary confinement program, the Phoenix program, and lifted the 42-day maximum stay cap on the amount of time juveniles could be sent to the existing solitary confinement programs in every state-run institution. The Phoenix program[34] is located in a section of one of the remaining state-run facilities, the McLennan County Juvenile Correctional Facility[35] in the small, rural town of Mart.[36] The program consists of single-cell rooms with a higher level of security to segregate the "troublemakers" from the rest of the juvenile population (Grissom 2012a). As you enter the wing there is a painting of a red phoenix rising from flames on the wall with "I will rise" painted above it (Grissom 2012a). Youth in the Phoenix program are kept in a locked security unit at all times and must wear mechanical restraints (shackles) when moving around the wing (Deitch et al. 2013, 51–52). If the youth leave the Phoenix area, their ankles are shackled too. In 2012, youth referred to the Phoenix program were held there for an average of 66 days (Grissom 2012a). Two thick security doors separate the security unit from the rest of the facility.

A report in 2013 by TJJD Independent Ombudsman Debbie Unruh detailed video evidence of guards fighting with juveniles in the Phoenix program on three separate occasions. One video showed the staff "slamming [the youth] to the floor where the staff pins the youth and makes repeated punches in the youth's ribs" (Independent Ombudsman for the Texas Juvenile Justice Department 2013; Michels 2013). Unruh conducted youth and staff interviews that indicated the practice of staff fighting with youth was common on the second shift (Independent Ombudsman for the Texas Juvenile Justice Department 2013). Yet, the defense of the disciplinary programs has been animated by the persistent bifurcation of offenders and the mythology of the "worst of the worst." Kimbrough characterized the juveniles in the remaining state-run institutions as "a different crowd now. Now we've got the worst of the worst" (Bell 2012).

Between 2009 and 2012, youth committed to the TJJD state-run institutions were, on average, referred to a security unit 48 times during their commitment (Deitch et al. 2013). Each secure facility has a security unit where juveniles can be placed in isolation either because they are engaged in "certain dangerous or disruptive behaviors" or because they self-refer to the unit out of fear of being assaulted by another youth (Deitch et al. 2013). There were 93 youth with more than 300 referrals to security during their stays in TJJD, suggesting they spent a large portion of their time in the security unit. Youth who did not commit any major rule violations were referred to security on average 23 times, suggesting security units are used routinely for even minor infractions (Deitch et al. 2013). A study published in 2014 cited a "stunningly high number" of placements in security units (Clarke 2014). In response to the reports on the heavy reliance of referrals to security units in Texas juvenile facilities, Jim Hurley, the TJJD spokesperson, defended the necessity of solitary confinement, stating, "When a youth is being disruptive or is assaulting somebody or has created a situation that is not safe, it's important to have a place to put the youth while they calm down" (quoted in Bernier 2013).

Despite the commitment to better "order and security" to deal with the remaining juvenile state prison population that is "the worst of the worst," the state continues to be plagued by scandal and has ratcheted up these punitive policies. In 2019, Gainesville experienced six days when inmates assaulted guards and organized a mass disturbance. One of the grievances expressed by the youth was the lack of enough correction officers to ensure stability and programmed time outside of cells. As of November 2019, the facility had experienced a substantial uptick in youth-on-youth assaults (more than doubled from 2017). The use of restraints and pepper spray also more than doubled over this time (Blakinger 2019).

In 2019, Senator John Whitmire (D–Houston), a main proponent of the community-based reforms, proposed centralization as a solution to the chaotic and violent nature of state-run prisons. Whitmire's proposal is to consolidate all of the youth held in the five remaining state-run juvenile prisons into a recently closed adult prison, Bartlett State Jail (McCullough 2019). The adult facility was closed following a federal lawsuit relating to sexual assault and ritual hazing against Corrections Corporation of America, which had a contract with the state to operate the facility from 2011 to 2017 (Osborn 2014). The senator proposed the closed juvenile facilities following the consolidation could be used to house geriatric prisoners. Reform organizations in the state have criticized the proposal as antithetical to the "closer to home" approach the community-based reforms have emphasized thus far. The proposal demonstrates the facility shuffle approach to reform and indicates the cyclical nature of the decentralization-centralization approach that is also occurring in California through the county regionalization plans.

Measuring the success of reforms by tracking the decline in youth sent to state-run facilities only partially accounts for the developments youth are experiencing on the ground. A qualitative assessment of the treatment of these youth in state-run prisons is necessary to give a fuller picture of the successes and limitations of community-based reforms. The misconception that the youth incarcerated in these institutions are now really the "bad ones" has legitimized the punitive and abusive practices used within these prisons, such as solitary confinement. Because of an unwillingness to adequately fund these facilities and establish robust oversight, many youth continue to suffer and the very conditions that spurred reform have worsened.

Summary

After more than a decade of implementing community-based reforms there continues to be violence and abusive conditions in the juvenile justice system. There is still a firm commitment to the community-based movement, but the developments cataloged here suggest that this route of reform has significant limitations. The community-based reforms have sought to identify youth amenable to treatment and to invest in individual behavioral modifications for them. The reform strategy has therefore largely left untouched policies for handling youth considered to be dangerous and in need of punitive sanctions.

The attempt to bifurcate youth, tried many times in previous policy development eras, has frequently failed because the notion of redeemable versus irredeemable individuals is largely a mythical construct and not a reality that can be objectively identified and measured. Rather, this effort reinforces a punitive ethos while excluding considerations of nonindividualized explanations and solutions for patterns of youth behavior. Carving out exceptions for the use of policies like juvenile LWOP, sex offender registries, and the death penalty do not ultimately repudiate their use and may legitimize their use on the much larger population of adult offenders. The community-based reform movement emphasizes cost savings and ignores the relationship between carceral policy and political economy, leaving it unequipped to fundamentally overturn the world's most punitive carceral responses to youth offending.

Conclusion

Bringing Public Goods Back In

Nearly a decade after the initial implementation of community-based reforms in Texas, the Council of State Governments Justice Center unveiled a comprehensive report on the reforms and celebrated the success of the changes made. In the report, Michael Thompson, director of the nonprofit, wrote, "Texas has delivered on the essential promise of its reforms. You said kids would do better closer to home, you said the state would save a lot of money, you said the state would be safer. All of those things have happened. Congratulations. You can actually provide a model for the rest of the country" (quoted in Lindell 2018). Within months of the publication of this congratulatory report, a 13-year-old boy incarcerated in Texas tied something around his neck and choked himself to the point of becoming unconscious in his prison cell. The boy was rushed to the hospital where, 12 days later, he died (Peguero 2017). The prison where this occurred, a deeply troubled state-run prison, was the same prison in Brown County whose description opened this book; it epitomizes the types of institutions that were the target of the community-based reform movement that has since been proclaimed a success. Unfortunately, far from an isolated incident, the young boy's suicide reflects the widespread continued abuse, misery, and dangers of youth incarceration that persist in Texas. For example, in 2020 a report surfaced that youth at a Dallas County facility were spending months and sometimes more than a year without going outdoors and often were confined to their rooms for 23½ hours a day (Banks 2020; Flynn 2018). While fewer youth are being sent to prisons like the one where the 13-year-old was incarcerated, the county prisons and jails that tens of thousands of youth are held in are also beset with problems of abuse and inadequate care. Meanwhile, kids still incarcerated in the remaining state-run prisons continue to suffer horrific outcomes of their incarceration.

What explains the disconnect between the congratulations showered on Texas and the appalling conditions that persist in its state and county prisons? This book has shifted the frame of analysis of juvenile justice reforms in order to look beyond some of the more myopic evaluations of success that animate the discussions of youth incarceration in the United States. If you look only at the youth being sent to state-run prisons, the enormous drop in numbers reveals a resounding success. In Texas in 2007, about 4,700 youth were sent to state-run prisons, and by 2020 about 1,000 youth were being sent to these prisons (Rangel 2012; Texas Legislative Budget Board, 2020). But, if you look at what is happening to the roughly 90% of youth who are processed in the juvenile justice system who are not sent to state-run prisons, a much more complicated picture emerges. Youth held in the expanding and privatizing county-based juvenile justice system experience problems with dangerous conditions of confinement, sparse accountability and oversight, and deep and widening inequalities in treatment and resources. Situating juvenile justice reforms within the broader historical and political developments of the United States reveals a much darker reality of the continued crisis of mass incarceration rather than a success story.

Critiques of the Community-Based Movement

This book has placed the community-based reform movement in the context of transformations in the U.S. political economy, specifically the trends of devolution, privatization, individualization of social problems, and punitiveness. All of these themes of post–New Deal American political development are tied to public-sector retrenchment and the growing political and economic inequality in the United States. Understanding this historical and material context makes clear that what many reformers champion as a major break from mass incarceration is in reality another front in the gutting of the public sector. Current juvenile justice reforms are cloaked in discourses and justifications that mask the fundamentally complementary nature of community-based reforms with the post–New Deal emergence of a bipartisan consensus of reducing public goods and expanding punitive policies. Reforms today are *part* of these larger shifts in the political economy that have defunded state institutions and provided more opportunities for expanding the private sector. This conclusion thus begins with a summary of the main conclusions drawn from the in-depth case studies of juvenile justice community-based reforms and then articulates alternatives that actually make a *break* from the political trends that drove the developments of mass incarceration.

Pitfalls of Devolution

The core goal and effect of community-based reforms is to devolve control over youth in the justice system from large state-run juvenile prisons to the local level to promote "closer to home" options. While there are certainly major problems with the high numbers of youth sent to state-run prisons and the conditions of their confinement there, a more holistic examination of the juvenile justice system shows that state-run prison incarceration rates capture the experience of a small sliver of the youth in the justice system. Most youth are handled in a variety of different ways at the county level, from private detention facilities to diversion programs and probation programs. County-based institutions and policies are being expanded under the banner of the community-based reform movement. However, these policies, such as intensive probation services, electronic monitoring, and group homes, have always been a key part of a punitive and wide-reaching juvenile justice system, not an alternative. The grant money flowing to the local level has come with few directives attached and is largely being funneled toward punitive policies and institutions. Youth held in locally run prisons are no less likely to experience abusive and dangerous conditions of confinement compared to those in state-run facilities, and there is even less oversight of these institutions. In short, the juvenile justice system is experiencing devolution, not decarceration.

Not only is devolution replicating and expanding the punitive and negative experiences of justice-involved youth at the local level, but it is bolstering a fiscal austerity approach to governance that further exacerbates these outcomes. Cost savings are often the justification and in many instances *the* motivation for devolution. While "community control" embodies a number of different policy goals, many of which are well intentioned, the turn away from centralized, federally supported social policy and the expansion of state and local control has been a primary tool for retrenching public goods and limiting spending. Devolution in the juvenile justice system has been used to circumvent the high cost of preventing the abuse of incarcerated youth in state-run prisons—high-profile abuse scandals in all three states that led to lawsuits and consent decrees precipitated the turn to cheaper solutions at the local level.

As Chapters 1 and 2 cataloged, the hollowing out of the public sector has made the turn to community solutions even more untenable. In each of the three case study states, larger political and economic trends in the form of public-sector retrenchment, privatization, and devolution have resulted in large increases in poverty and inequality. Thus, the areas of each state that have been hit the hardest by widening inequality and where the lowest income and most marginalized youth reside are the communities being asked to shoulder the responsibility of handling justice-involved youth without sufficient resources to do so. In this context, counties invest in already established traditional law-and-order institutions as the quickest and easiest solution. Additionally, devolution creates the perfect conditions for the private sector to step in and sell its services and programs to counties.

Problems with Privatization

The valorization of the community and the private sector has filled the space carved out by decades of attacks on the government and lowered expectations for what the state can and should provide for all people. The failure to appreciate the central role that government has played in improving the lives of millions of people throughout the development of the United States "fuels nostalgia for a nonexistent age of pure voluntarism and raises unrealistic expectations for the capacity of private action to ameliorate public problems" (Katz 1995, 21). Indeed, this undercounting of the role of the government is closely related to the unfounded faith in the private sector to solve a wide range of social problems, from poverty and unemployment to fighting delinquency. The pervasive promotion of private-sector solutions within the juvenile justice system today in the form of advocating for evidence-based programs (which are predominantly run, evaluated, and promoted by private actors) and public-private partnerships of all kinds is best understood in the context of trends of public-sector retrenchment and the greater concentration of wealth and political power among elites.

The increased role of the private sector in *shaping* political outcomes, as evidenced by the MacArthur and Annie E. Casey foundations' efforts to promote and disseminate the community-based reform model, is both cause and effect of the broader shifts in power away from the labor-left coalition that provided a brief but exceptional counterbalance to the conservative forces of the business community that punctuated the New Deal era. With fewer challenges being mounted by Democrats, labor, and social movements in the decades following World War II, corporate elites amassed more political and economic power. One outcome has been the massive concentration of wealth among a select few, exemplified by the growth in assets and influence of charitable foundations. The position of large foundations strengthened in the post–New Deal era, and their influence today occurs in a context in which there are even fewer popular countermobilizing forces.

As a result, policy leadership from large foundations is contributing to a crisis of civic disempowerment (Faber and McCarthy 2005). These organizations are *not* organically grounded in the communities they serve, and they actually "inhibit broad-based citizen involvement in social problem-solving" (8). Civic life in the United States is largely controlled by elites and is replicating, not challenging, the already existing inequalities in society (Eliasoph 2013). Large foundations, such as MacArthur and Annie E. Casey, are almost entirely unaccountable to anyone except their trustees (Faber and McCarthy 2005; Fleishman 2007; Reckhow 2012).[1] Scholars have pointed out that a *lack* of democratic accountability in the policymaking process contributed to the buildup of mass incarceration (Barker 2009; Miller 2008). Community-based reforms are often justified by relying on the rhetoric of community empowerment. However, while youth are supposedly brought "closer to home," there is often less democratic accountability because services are contracted out to private companies that are not transparent, lack oversight, and do not have clear channels to express grievances. The juvenile justice reforms examined in the case studies have undermined democratic responsiveness by eroding or eliminating mechanisms of oversight and accountability rather than strengthening these democratic processes.

The remarkable convergence around the community-based reform model among diverse states is largely attributed to the influence of large foundations, which is best understood as a product of these larger shifts in the political economy. The pro-privatization policy prescriptions that flow from these leading policymakers are a logical extension of this reconfiguration of American politics. Governance has shifted away from policy influenced from below and in the interest of mass constituencies and toward policy made by and for elites. In addition to the privatization of policymaking, the prisons, jails, services, and programs of the juvenile justice system are increasingly being contracted out to the private for-profit sector. Not only does the rise of privatization mark the receding role of policy formation in the interest of the public, but it also introduces actors into an institution that are a major obstacle to reforms moving forward. The privatization of the juvenile justice system entrenches interests in expansion, not retraction. The companies and private entities providing everything from the running of a prison to court-mandated anger management classes are forces that will stymie efforts at more robust decarceration in the long run. Finally, the privatization of the juvenile justice system produces the perverse outcomes of punishing youth in order to increase profits.

A look at juvenile justice system privatization reveals a fairly harrowing case study: youth being locked in cells for profit and endless services and technologies sold to "fix" youth. But the case against privatization goes even deeper by linking these developments to the broader politics they fit into. Casting youth to the fates determined by the private sector is part of building the case against *public* solutions to the complex, interrelated challenges that youth face beyond just involvement with the criminal justice system. If it was only privatization of the juvenile justice system, that would be bad enough, but the case studies here reflect a much wider change in social policy that spells even more dire consequences for youth. The community-based reform movement contributes to the government's abdication of its duty to provide for youth through education, jobs, healthcare, housing, and general social welfare.

Limitations of Individualizing Social Problems

One of the most powerful tools used to stymie demands for robust public investment in social programs is the turn to individual behavioral solutions to social problems. Placing ever more emphasis on individual responsibility and uplift while sidelining and limiting the role of the government in providing basic public services is a central part of a neoliberal turn in American governance (Brown 2003; Lafer 2004; Larner 2000; Soss, Fording, and Schram 2011; Spence 2015; Weaver 2012). The community-based reform movement bolsters the idea that youth caught up in the juvenile justice system are there because they are morally, psychologically, or intellectually inferior. The main policy prescriptions of the reforms today, as cataloged in Chapter 4, proliferate programs and services that focus on individual behavioral change, most of which are provided by the private sector. Therefore, the reforms are reinforcing rather than challenging a key political development that contributed to the rise of mass youth incarceration in the first place.

The oftentimes racist assumptions about the individual behavioral and moral deficiencies of youth have undergirded both punitive and rehabilitative approaches and contribute to justice system solutions to social problems. Many past reforms have attempted to "fix juveniles" in order to fix the system, and they have all largely failed. Even when correcting individual behavior is used to justify more treatment-oriented policies, these policies reinforce the stigmatization and dehumanization of juvenile offenders that, in turn, legitimize punishing a large number of youth. Most important, viewing the problems of the justice system as the problems of broken and damaged individuals woefully misidentifies the source of the problems in the system, which are largely political and institutional.

The many iterations of the individualization of social problems from human capital theory, culture of poverty theory, and underclass theory all have in common that they mystify the dynamics fueling inequality and social subordination (Katz 1995; Moak, 2022; A. Reed 1999; T. Reed 2020). Therefore, the turn to fixing individual behavior is problematic for what it *does* but equally for what it *doesn't do*. Blaming individuals for social problems like poverty and delinquency is degrading to them and validates the need for punitive policies. Viewing juvenile delinquency as primarily a problem caused by certain socially deviant individuals obfuscates the social policies and patterns of inequality that are the true underlying causes of most juvenile delinquency and high incarceration rates.

Persistently Punitive

The political trends of devolution, privatization, and the individualization of social problems all contribute to the rise of punitive policies. Rather than fundamentally changing the system by ending the punitive policies and abusive conditions of confinement, the community-based reforms are aimed at reducing the number of juveniles subjected to these policies. This focus affirms that when juveniles are delinquent, they *do* need to be punished, and often quite severely. The attempt to reduce delinquency as a way to solve the problems in the juvenile justice system suggests there is a rational connection between levels of youth crime and rates of youth incarceration—yet a substantial body of research suggests that the incarceration rate in the United States has a tenuous connection to crime rates (Travis, Western, and Redburn 2014, 105). This supply-side view of the source of the expansive and punitive system detracts from more effective solutions and also leaves punitive policies largely intact.

The continued use of long sentences, solitary confinement, and abusive conditions of confinement have been rationalized by the idea that the reforms have better determined that only "serious" youth offenders are given these punishments. However, evidence from the case studies suggests that youth in the adult system and state-run juvenile prisons are no more "serious" offenders than before the reforms. Poor and racial minority youth are heavily concentrated in the "worst of the worst" population, just as before the reforms. The decisions made by the U.S. Supreme Court exempting juveniles from the most punitive policies, the death penalty and life without the possibility of parole (LWOP) sentences, has been a major opening for rethinking and reshaping the treatment of youth in the justice system—a policy window that could fast be closing. However, most states have simply skirted the Court's requirements and replaced these policies with long sentences and other punitive solutions.

Trying to prevent punishment by fixing individual juveniles has been the driving force behind a juvenile justice system that has always incorporated treatment and punishment approaches to addressing delinquency. Rather than an outright repudiation of punitive policies, reforms often avoid these fraught political debates and promote prevention as a substitute for tackling the continued use of the most harmful policies. Confronting the deep-rooted assumptions about the utility of punishment and the unworthiness of those who commit serious crimes is a steep political battle that most reformers strategically avoid. However, by not looking at the harsh treatment of these offenders, which is a major driver of mass incarceration, the reform effort will continue to "nibble around the edges" while ultimately leaving the system intact (Gottschalk 2015; Pfaff 2017). This is particularly concerning because the decades-long downturn in crime rates may not last. If or when crime rates go up and the foundation of mass incarceration has largely been preserved, then we may see an overexpansion of the system again (Pfaff 2017, 181). Ultimately, as long as reform efforts stay in line with broader political developments that undermine public goods and other structural solutions to problems like delinquency, what remains on the table is punishment.

An Alternative: The Public Goods Approach to Prison Reform

There are practical ways to shift the orientation, scope, and goals of reform to press for more fundamental changes. Genuine improvements in the treatment and experience of youth will require upending deeply entrenched political commitments that buttress the current juvenile justice system. The common thread connecting devolution, privatization, the individualization of social problems, and punitiveness is that they are part of a model of governance that promotes the interests of economic elites. Therefore, what is needed is an alternative approach in which prison reforms are organized around a public goods model of governance in the interest of the majority of people in the United States.

Connecting the goals of juvenile justice reform to larger efforts to ameliorate deeper inequalities may seem unrealistic or defeating for its ambitiousness, but easier options have been tried and they have failed. There are small steps that can yield improvements that work *toward* a broader goal of tackling the complexity and depth of the issue rather than reinscribing the very political forces that created these problems in the first place. Each of the suggested political changes map out a different direction for reform efforts from the ones cataloged in this book. While they encompass long-term goals, they also include immediate steps that can be taken to reorient approaches to reform.

The Break from Devolution: The Public Goods Model

An alternative to devolution, which has largely moved the problem of abusive conditions of youth imprisonment to the local level, is to address these issues head-on through greater centralized investments and public provisions. Community-based social policy has a long history of being connected to spending less and unequally distributing resources. Rather than a retraction of the state, an alternative public goods model would entail more robust investments and a repurposing of the state. This requires shifting away from the fiscal austerity orientation of current reforms and expanding the scope of reforms to connect the injustices of the juvenile system to wider fights for greater equality.

Rejecting the Cost-Savings Goal

A key feature of an alternative approach would be to eschew the cost-savings goal of the community-based reform movement. A significant limitation of the cost-cutting arguments for prison reform is that this discourse reifies austerity and often naturalizes and accepts the size of public budgets. The emphasis on redistributing public money without changing the overall distribution of wealth is restrictive and a "missing the forest for the trees" error. The decades-long upward transfer of wealth and the hollowing out of public coffers that contribute to greater demands on the carceral state and a significantly diminished quality of life for millions should not just be put aside or accepted if genuine change is desired. Skirting these larger material distribution issues elides the reality that a major reorientation of the government will require a political struggle, one in which the economic interests of powerful elites will be challenged in the interest of the many.

In a political environment dominated by commitments to fiscal austerity and market supremacy, it is not surprising that reformers attempting to get something done fast and with as little resistance as possible will frame their case around cutting costs and acquiesce to the imperatives of austerity. However, if the goal is to have all youth well cared for, connected to their families, and supported—as the leading reform models rightfully assert—this will require significant public investments. For those within and outside of prison much *more* public spending is necessary to ensure safe and equitable outcomes for all youth.

As John Clegg and Adaner Usmani (2019) have argued, the rise of mass incarceration as an alternative to a more robust welfare state was the relatively cheaper solution to generalized insecurity and economic distress wrought by the intensification of upward wealth transfers, deindustrialization, and stagnating wages from the 1960s forward. Locking up a small percentage of youth is actually a much cheaper means of managing poverty, disorder, and delinquency than universal social provisions for all youth. For example, in California in 2018 about 46,423 youth were arrested, while about 2.5 million lived in families whose parent(s) lacked secure employment and more than 1.5 million youth lived in poverty. If the state of California is interested in improving the lives of youth rather than cutting costs through devolution, what is needed is massive investment in programs that target the economically distressed youth who are disproportionately caught up in the justice system. The challenges youth face in the justice system do not occur in isolation—they are part of broader issues related to economic and social inequality.

The United States is the wealthiest nation in the world and fully capable of robustly funding basic public goods. Other countries spend a far greater percentage of their GDP on social welfare and have greater equality, superior quality-of-life outcomes, and of course substantially lower incarceration rates (Gottschalk 2011). Redeploying public resources in the interest of the public good is "neither easy nor impossible" (Aspholm 2020, 180). The following recommendations within this framework are not simplistic fixes that can be applied in a top-down manner from state to state. Fighting for a public goods model of government will require massive grassroots organizing over a long period of time. However, there are already instances of this type of organization occurring, and being successful, despite the strong opposition to this type of politics from across the political spectrum.

The orientation of government and our expectations of it need to dramatically shift beyond just trying to allow some youth to avoid the punitive arm of the state. Rather than join a broader politics that deems public institutions a "failure" and call for introducing community-based alternatives or market-based solutions, reforms should articulate a role for the state in which it provides social protection for all people. The key question that has animated social policy in the United States is not how big or small government is, but "towards what ends and whose interest its massive institutions [will] be driven" (Cowie 2016, 207). The decades-long shift away from the policies that established an idea of collective economic security as a result of the New Deal left-labor coalition has led to deep stigmatization of the government. Generations of politicians from both political parties have largely failed to make a case for how the government can and should help people. Since "mass incarceration was a remaking of the state in the era of hegemonic market ideology," decarceration will also require a remaking of the state (Wacquant 2009, xviii).

There are a number of specific examples of how broader demands for public goods relate to prison reform. Expanding and robustly funding public housing would address the vulnerability and greater propensity for arrests of youth who are homeless or have insecure housing. Safe, stable housing is the type of "protective" factor that community-based reformers argue prevents criminal behavior, but they rarely explicitly advocate for the public investments required to provide this. Devolving the responsibility of housing to the local level and private sector has not and will not be sufficient. Similarly, providing universal healthcare has many benefits for justice-involved youth. Young people under a universal system, regardless of ability to pay, could access the healthcare system, including necessary mental health care. During and after incarceration youth would have better continuity of care and another source of stability and support in their lives. Increased funding for public schools is another important counterweight to the proliferation of punitive policies. Lowering class sizes and providing more support staff and more enriching curricular options reduce dropout and the use of punitive in-school sanctions. All of these examples of public investments that could be central pillars of juvenile justice reforms reap positive benefits in and of themselves, and they also put less demand on the carceral state.

Juvenile Justice System Investments

Improving the quality of life for youth across the board provides political space for advocating for the treatment of those in prison. Since prisons rely on relative deprivation, as long as there is inequitable and substandard public investment in housing, healthcare, and education it will be much more difficult to secure these provisions for those in prison.

Within this alternative orientation there are changes that can occur in the short and long term to ameliorate the suffering inflicted on those who come in contact with the criminal justice system. For youth currently behind bars or under correctional control, investments rather than cuts are needed to improve the conditions of their confinement and supervision. While some might find it unacceptable to continue to put more money into a system many understandably consider a failure, the on-the-ground consequences of taking this short-sighted stance is devastating for youth. Adequate oversight and resources to sufficiently train and staff the juvenile justice system is sorely lacking today, to the great detriment of thousands of young people. These chapters have cataloged the extreme as well as mundane consequences of inadequate funding of oversight, health and education services, and legal representation in the juvenile justice system. A lack of investment leads to dangerous conditions of confinement and supervision.

As long as we have youth locked up in prison, we will need to invest a considerable amount of money in ensuring that they are safe by providing robust oversight, adequate healthcare, and services necessary to support their well-being. Even if there are fewer youth in prisons, in order to ensure less abusive conditions it will likely cost *more* money than what is currently being expended on these institutions. This is why linking decarceration to cost savings is inadequate to ensuring that youth are properly cared for. All three states have justified devolution in terms of budget savings, and this has set up the reforms to fail to deliver a qualitative improvement in the treatment of youth. An alternative orientation around a commitment to spending the money to ensure no child dies while in prison or is subjected to abuse or is saddled with debt from their community supervision is needed.

Two steps that could be pursued within the public goods model are to sufficiently fund independent public oversight of prisons and to improve the pay and training of corrections and probation personnel. Each model state has balked at the expense of conducting adequate oversight of state and local juvenile lockups, which is a contributing factor in the decades-long periodic abuse scandals that arise. There have been substantial strides forward in changing some of the regulations of youth prisons. However, without proper oversight and enforcement power, these rules are rendered meaningless. Texas set up an Ombudsman Office in the wake of the 2007 abuse scandal but then failed to adequately fund it. In the wake of the "Kids for Cash" scandal, the Pennsylvania legislature turned down a proposal to invest in oversight and instead went with cheaper alternatives that left youth vulnerable to continued abuses. The notion that we can do better by youth *and* save money needs to be repudiated.

In addition to investing in proper oversight, investing in the people who take on the great responsibility of monitoring youth in prisons and on parole and probation is critical to providing better care and safety. The potential for abuse when an individual has complete authority and control over another person's life is substantial, and therefore reforms should create better channels of accountability and representation for those in prison. At the same time, the people who work for the juvenile justice system should be adequately compensated and well trained. Just as in other policy spheres, such as education, where "teacher working conditions are student learning conditions," how correctional and parole and probation officers are treated and the conditions they work under are critical to the safety and experience of youth within these institutions. A public goods model of governance would properly support the workers who have the enormous obligation to be in charge of and oversee the youth who are under correctional control (Cate 2021). This could include support for public defenders who are unevenly funded, especially in the juvenile system, to start to address the vast imbalance of support for prosecutors and public defenders (Mayeux 2020; Pfaff 2017). If reforms are oriented around promoting the best welfare for youth, no matter the cost, then it becomes clear that the people who carry out these policies—for example, being their guardians or legal representatives—need to have all the tools and resources necessary to do their best for these youths. The current reform orientation is around cost-effective interventions that rarely consider the essential role public-sector workers play in carrying out any of these programs.

Government for the public good is a framework that can produce more positive results for those seeking to reform the juvenile justice system than the current foundation-led, community-based reform movement. Linking the injustices of the juvenile system with fighting against existing social, economic, and political inequalities is necessary because if these continued and growing injustices go unchallenged, they will continue to undermine reform efforts. There are immediate incremental reforms that work toward these ends by building up expectations for the government to provide solutions to these problems rather than leaving the burden on individuals and ambiguous notions of community.

The Break from Privatization: Democratize the Reform Effort

Much of the analysis of the limitations of the community-based reform movement has cataloged the perverse outcomes of an increasingly privatized policymaking landscape and the privatization of the institutions, services, and programs within the system. In response to these negative outcomes, a key requirement of an alternative way forward is to democratize prison reform efforts. The state case studies analyzed here have suggested we should not be looking to foundations, nonprofits, or private companies to be saviors. Bringing the politics and policies of reform back into the public sphere is necessary to ensure that policy developments moving forward are capable of reflecting the needs of everyone, not just those determined by elites.

As scholars have been showing for decades, the United States has major democratic deficiencies that contribute to vast inequalities and social problems that animate many issues beyond the criminal justice system. It remains the case that "majorities of the American public actually have little influence over the policies our government adopts" (Gilens and Page 2014). A major development in post–New Deal politics has been the continued erosion of the political representation of those at the bottom of the income distribution and the rising dominance of economic elites in policymaking (Bartels 2016; Gerstle and Fraser 1990, 269). Unsurprisingly, this imbalance of power contributes to the unequal distribution of resources and the concentration of suffering among those who have no representation. Quite simply, social policies that respond to the needs of mass publics are less punitive and would better address the collective needs of vast majorities in the United States (Miller 2016, 8).

Yet, the reform landscape is dominated by elites, largely private actors, who pursue a technocratic approach to political change. While the reform rhetoric asserts that policy advocacy is done in the interest of the people harmed by the system, there is little to no effort from the major players in reforms today to actually organize broad-based constituencies and create mechanisms of accountability for representing the interests of these constituents. Other than the sprinkling of anecdotal testimonies from youth, the reform powerhouses like the MacArthur Foundation and Annie E. Casey Foundation have no democratic relationship to the youth or broader communities for whom they advocate.

There is some desire for progressive reform of the juvenile justice system, but there is little to no strategy espoused by leading reformers to upend the power imbalances at the heart of American policymaking. As the previous chapters have cataloged, the community-based reform movement has suggested that the problems of the juvenile justice system are not the result of broader political conflicts and therefore can be solved with technocratic, in-system adjustments. The limitations of this approach and the broader contextualization of the historic development of juvenile justice policy contradict this outlook and suggest that in fact meaningful improvements *will* require changes in the power dynamics of American society (Fong and Naschek 2021, 118).

An alternative approach to reform requires understanding that "ideas have to be allied with sources of political power" (Cahill 2014, 157). Ultimately, reforms are a product of the wider political environment and the power balance among various political actors. While the language and policy ideas may change over time, it remains the case that those who are most affected by the political decisions regarding juvenile justice reforms have the least say over them. The desire to truly contend with powerful forces that stymie decarceration efforts likely will not be found in the current model of elite-driven reforms. That is because these efforts will require major public investments that are at odds with prevailing commitments to austerity and the upward redistribution of wealth. Given that those who currently have the most power in designing and implementing reforms, large charitable foundations, have benefited from the status quo economic and political arrangements, it is unlikely that they will change their existing reform framework. In an alternative approach following the public goods model, the reform efforts will need to be closely related to grassroots organizing and building support and solidarity among real people around concrete objectives to address their lived concerns (Reed 1999). A rebalance of power toward the interests of majorities of people will be the necessary counterweight to excise the profit incentives currently in the justice system.

The Break from the Individualistic: Fighting for Collective Economic Security

This book has cataloged many of the negative outcomes of individualizing the problems of delinquency and youth incarceration. Not only does an individual behavioral analysis of the source and solution to these problems vastly misidentify the forces that reproduce them; it also fuels punitive solutions. Further, we are thrusting personal responsibility on youth at a time when there is more inequality, general insecurity, and limited prospects for them (Wacquant 2009, 108). Asserting that delinquent youth are caught up in the justice system because of bad values, a lack of skills, or attitudinal deficiencies not only stigmatizes these youth but also misdirects responsibility from government and society onto youth themselves (Reed 1999, 196). Therefore, an alternative vision of reform must reject all assumptions that youth caught up in the juvenile justice system are behaviorally or morally different from the rest of American society (165).

An alternative framework of reform should shift the focus off the individual characteristics of youth and onto a critical examination of social policy and the ways the government could better serve these youth. For decades now the political landscape has been dominated by ideological forces encouraging individualism at the expense of broader economic solidarity (Cowie 2016, 184). However, movements and efforts to forge economic solidarity through the organization of working-class people in the United States have been the greatest cudgels against the rightward drift in American politics that contributed to the rise of mass incarceration. Thus, an alternative path forward should assert this collective framework over the individualistic one that has animated juvenile justice reforms since the system's inception. Hitching juvenile justice reforms to the broader fights for universal provisions of housing, healthcare, and education would be part of reorienting reforms away from fixing youth to fixing the world they inhabit.

Building collective economic solidarity by organizing ordinary people is certainly a longer-term strategy for addressing these problems than top-down quick fixes, but there are numerous examples of how organizing has led to real victories for the working class. One of the best examples is the renewed wave of activism coming from public school teachers. The revitalization of the Chicago Teachers Union (CTU) is an instructive case. In 2010, the Caucus of Rank-and-File Educators took over the Chicago union through remarkable grassroots organizing and parlayed their leadership into more ground-up organizing efforts to build momentum and support for a broad antiprivatization and pro–public education platform. In two historic strike efforts in 2012 and 2019, the CTU brought together large swaths of the city in support of a vision of public education that confronted powerful elites who supported privatization.[2] The organizing effort around the strikes connected the fight for public education in the city to the effects of gaping economic inequalities in Chicago. The strikes secured immediate demands such as pay increases and money for reducing overcrowded classes and helped curtail the onslaught of school closures and layoffs. The CTU also made the case for broader public investments in housing and transportation. This broader vision built around concepts of economic and social solidarity helped organize the support for critical wins that stymied the unrelenting privatization efforts being pursued in the city.

The type of organizing and demands put forth in Chicago have inspired several other cities and unions to follow the model set by the Caucus of Rank-and-File

Educators. These public teacher movements show that bottom-up organizing is capable of challenging the entrenched interests of economic elites and can secure immediate wins and improvements to the lives of millions of people. Organizing around collective economic interests, not individual behavioral solutions, can challenge the political forces promoting privatization and public-sector retrenchment and build momentum for an encompassing public goods model of governance. Centering juvenile justice reforms on these organizing efforts, rather than leaving this effort to foundations, nonprofits, and the private sector, would be a significant reorientation of the path forward to address the problems faced by justice-involved youth.

The Break from the Punitive: "All the Above" Minus Punishment

Finally, while we need to move beyond the notion in the community-based reform movement that we have to "cure delinquency" to fix the juvenile justice system, reconfiguring how we approach crime is essential to moving away from the ineffective punitive model. Repudiating the zero-sum notion that punishment makes us safer is an important reorientation. The community-based reform movement is overly preoccupied with identifying the "right" youth to punish rather than directly challenging the utility of punishment as a public safety measure. Advocating for reductions in sentencing for serious offenders is a political challenge, and therefore it is not surprising that most reforms focus on the "low-hanging fruit" of low-level offenders. However, avoiding these more difficult debates that require deeper changes in how crime and punishment are viewed in America will prevent reforms from ever moving beyond the punitive foundations of the current system. Dramatically reducing the length of sentences youth are subjected to, ending "adult time" laws, and ending juvenile LWOP as an option are all specific policy changes that would be expressive of a fundamental shift away from punishment. These goals are within reach and are being pursued incrementally already.

The election of a number of progressive district attorneys is an example of how constituencies can be built around a specific agenda that rejects punitive law-and-order policies. Larry Krasner in Philadelphia was elected in 2017 thanks to broad organizing for a reform platform that included ending cash bail, promoting greater leniency, opposing the death penalty, and promising to take on powerful interests like the pharmaceutical companies that contribute to the opioid crisis. Despite many obstacles and persistent criticisms locally and nationally, Krasner won reelection in 2021 with a sizable majority. These efforts show that a nonpunitive agenda can be successful and lead to real changes and improvements in people's lives. While it is an uphill battle, rejecting knee-jerk punitiveness is not a political impossibility and can provide immediate improvements to those caught up in the justice system.

However, the changes progressive district attorneys can make go only so far. In conjunction with taking punitive options off the table, the benefit of a public goods alternative to the current reform approach is that it would fit with the best prescriptions for reducing violence and crime. This would not only help address the major problem of high rates of violence in the United States but would also reduce demands on punitive responses to crime. Lisa Miller (2016, xi) refers to the high rates of violence in the United States as a "state failure" and argues that elites have failed "to recognize people's lived experience and to respond with productive, inclusive, practical policy." The universality of social goods like housing, healthcare, and education would not only mitigate the causes of violence but would reduce the demands to respond punitively to it (Aspholm 2020; Miller 2016).

Punitive policies have largely gone unchallenged in the community-based reform movement because of the failure to invest in other crime prevention strategies. When the "all of the above" approach to violence that calls for investment in schools, jobs, and housing that most people support is not available, punitive policies are left as the only option on the table, and people will choose something over nothing (Forman 2017; Miller 2016). This results in the worst of both worlds: continued violence *and* locking up more and more people (Forman 2017). Gottschalk (2015) rightly asserts that prison reform should not be tethered to crime rates, which perpetuates the false belief that incarceration rates are naturally or reflexively tied to crime rates. But reducing violence, in addition to being a good in and of itself, is also a beneficial tool in curbing punitiveness. Focusing on broad public-sector investments like public housing, healthcare, education, transit, and jobs as a solution to violence would also have the benefit of building the same constituencies around the same policy goals that would also advance the interests of prison reform.

Summary

Ultimately, all of the suggested breaks from the core aspects of the community-based reforms and post–New Deal political developments can contribute to the goal of expanding public goods. There are small changes that can occur within this framework, such as improving oversight of prisons, but all of these big and small policy changes are oriented around reversing the decades of public-sector retrenchment and privatization of public institutions in an effort to bring back the notion of government for the common good. Policy changes within the juvenile justice system that aim to qualitatively improve the lives of youth will only work in the context of this much broader fight. Time and again in the developmental history of the juvenile justice system it is clear that the changes within the system are circumscribed by the larger political, social, and economic context. Even the best-intentioned efforts to make the system more equitable and safe for youth fall short in the face of shrinking public-sector spending and widening inequalities.

The notion promoted by foundations leading the community-based reform movement that we can change the juvenile justice system *without* addressing these larger issues is alluring, as simple fixes always are. However, this perspective fundamentally fails to appreciate that the juvenile justice system does not exist in isolation but is an integral part and consequence of the broader political economy. The embrace of simple fixes also relies on and facilitates the pessimism around addressing larger economic, racial, and political inequalities—suggesting that efforts to mitigate these inequities are doomed since these will never change. Nothing ensures continued and growing inequality more than the naturalization of the forces that sustain and perpetuate that inequality. Real change can happen immediately in the juvenile justice system, but this requires confronting the limitations of any reform that does not challenge the broader political forces driving economic and racial inequality. A real break from mass incarceration requires replacing devolution with robust centralized universal public goods; replacing privatization with democratic public control over policymaking, institutions, and services; replacing the individualization of social problems with a collective view of economic solidarity; and replacing punishment with meaningful safety and support.

NOTES

Introduction

1. Reports and audits found that countless youth in the Brown County state-run prison had been subjected to abuse, neglect, and severe violence while in custody (Hunter 2008).
2. Additional support for the Texas model has come from the *Washington Post* (2014), the *Wall Street Journal* (Zuckerman 2014), and a comprehensive report by the Council of State Governments (Fabelo, Arrigona, and Thompson 2015), to name a few.
3. The county now controls the facility and uses it as a regional short-term center that holds juveniles transferred from other counties. Brown County only has about one to eight juveniles housed at the county level at any given time, so the vast majority of juveniles come from other counties in the state. The number of juveniles housed in the Brown County facility has increased since the facility transfer. In 2010, the average daily population of juveniles housed in Brownwood juvenile facilities was 185. After the closure and the facility transfer, the average daily population *grew* to 252 in 2015 (Jennifer Martin, records management specialist at the Texas Juvenile Justice Department, personal communication, June 10, 2015).
4. The private company G4S (Group 4 Securicor) is the world's largest security company providing a wide range of services, such as trained security officers, facility security systems, electronic monitoring, and juvenile and adult custody facilities. The company is one of the world's largest private-sector employers (G4S USA 2015; Plimmer 2015). As of 2015, New Scotland Yard in London is investigating accusations that the company has profited from human rights abuses through its contract at Guantanamo Bay (Green 2015a). Ofsted Inspectors found that staff at a youth detention center run by G4S in Northamptonshire in England subjected youth to degrading treatment and racist comments (Green 2015b).
5. The Oaks Brownwood is a 115-bed residential unit in the facility. In 2014, employees used physical restraints on the youth in the facility 76 times, youth were put in "disciplinary seclusion assignments" on 68 occasions, and a total of 73 grievances were filed against the facility (Jennifer Martin, personal communication, April 7, 2014; Texas Juvenile Justice Department 2015).
6. Youth in county juvenile facilities in Texas are sent to solitary confinement tens of thousands of time per year (Bernier 2013).
7. *Roper v. Simmons* (2005) prohibited states from giving the death penalty to offenders under the age of 18. *Graham v. Florida* (2010) extended *Roper* and prohibited states from giving life without parole for a non-homicide offense to youth under 18. *Miller v. Alabama* (2012) prohibited *mandatory* life without parole sentencing for youth convicted of murder. *Montgomery v. Louisiana* (2016) made the ban on automatic life without parole sentences for juveniles retroactive. In 2021, the court somewhat reversed course in *Jones v. Mississippi* by interpreting that the previous decisions on life without parole do not require a court to prove a juvenile is permanently incorrigible to reimpose a life without parole sentence.

8. Scholarship on American political development takes seriously the historical construction of politics and "durable shifts in governing authority" (Orren and Skowronek 2004, 123).

Chapter 1

1. For example, the FDR administration responded to the problem of youth crime by addressing labor market deficiencies through public job creation (Edelman 2002; Katznelson 1989).
2. For example, the federal government established community action programs (CAPs) as part of the War on Poverty in the 1960s. These programs frequently channeled grassroots activism into apolitical, status quo–affirming directions. When CAPs were more confrontational, political, and radical, the federal government retracted its support (Chowkwanyun 2015).
3. For example, pointing out that poor Blacks were discriminated against and therefore did not receive adequate social welfare provisions (Nelson 2013).
4. Nixon's revenue sharing gave state and local governments more discretion in how they spent federal grant money. This strategy of devolution was taken up by Reagan and culminated in Clinton's 1996 Personal Responsibility and Work Opportunity Act, giving states and cities near total discretion over eligibility requirements.
5. The 1976 Humphrey-Hawkins Bill mandating full employment was an important political project for Democrats and was worked into the party platform, despite President Jimmy Carter's lack of enthusiasm for the proposal (Stein 2011, 149).
6. From the mid-1960s to the mid-1970s the federal government reinstated the death penalty, curtailed parole, imposed mandatory minimum sentences, and began permitting youth to be held in adult prisons. Between 1973 and 2000 the number of people in prison in the United States increased sixfold (Weaver 2007). Black civil rights actors advocated for an "all of the above" strategy to address crime by coupling "law and order" policies with proposals like John Conyers's Marshall Plan for inner cities, but ultimately they got only the punitive crime measures (Forman 2017).
7. The New Left eschewed the ideas and organization of earlier generations of Marxian radicals and championed a radical individualism in the form of decentralized, participatory communities (Isserman and Kazin 1989)
8. Importantly, both authors acknowledge that there was a diversity of ideas about how best to address issues of crime and drugs during this time, with many calling for social welfare solutions as well as punitive solutions. However, the idea that racial minorities were passive victims of calls for punitive policies denies the agency and real punitive impulses among Black leaders and political organizations expressed during these policy developments. This reflects the complexity and contradictions found in an oversimplified notion of "the Black community."
9. DAFs are investment accounts where donors can deposit money, stocks, or other assets that grow tax-free until grants are made to charity. LLCs have fewer disclosure requirements than private foundations and allow donors to combine philanthropy and political giving. Contributions to DAFs grew substantially between 2013 and 2017, from $17.24 billion to $29.23 billion.
10. This was not the preferred solution for much of organized labor, which was unsatisfied with company-funded pension and healthcare; however, postwar unions faced political conditions that seemed to offer no alternatives (Lichtenstein 1989, 142).
11. Some of the key features of the foundation-led model for education reform are charter schools, high-stakes testing, firing teachers and closing schools when performance scores are insufficient, and merit pay for teachers based on testing scores (Barkan 2011).
12. The "corporate education agenda" is comprised of major attacks on public teacher unions and promotes for-profit endeavors like virtual schooling, charter schools, and vouchers.
13. The Rockefeller Foundation launched a research series on the "urban underclass" in the late 1980s, continuing the history of foundations supporting individualized views of poverty research and influencing social scientists to do the same (Katz 1995, 60).
14. As one example, the percentage of federal spending going toward national defense steadily increased in the 1980s, while the percentage spent on social welfare dropped (Edsall 1989).

Chapter 2

1. Notably, the antitax movement supported the ascendant popularity of "law and order" policies. For an extended discussion of the relationship between the two in California, see Campbell 2016.
2. State higher education funding has steadily decline over the past four decades in California (Cook 2017).
3. The block grant gives a $117,000 per capita subsidy based on each county's share of all annual state felony juvenile adjudications and their share of the statewide at-risk youth population (California State Legislature 2007).
4. The use of lease revenue bonds in California has been a way to funnel public money toward carceral expansion without the direct involvement of voters and has effectively obscured the visibility of the state investing in these institutions (Gilmore 2007).
5. The BSCC is an independent statutory agency that provides leadership to the adult and juvenile justice systems on realignment issues and sets standards as well as administers grant funding. The board is comprised of 13 members appointed by the governor and the legislature. The BSCC reports directly to the governor, and as of 2015 the board chair was also the director of the California Department of Corrections and Rehabilitation's Department of Parole. The other members are county sheriffs, probations officers, a county supervisor, a judge, two community-based service providers, and one community member (Savage 2015).
6. This includes public and privately operated facilities, from halfway houses to detention centers, and includes low-, medium-, and high-security facilities.
7. BBRC Detention Annex (public, capacity 36, secure) opened in 2015. Lake Granbury Youth Services (private, capacity 96, secure) opened in 2014. The Center for Success and Independence Rockdale Academy (private, capacity 41, secure) opened in 2018. Gardner-Betts Juvenile Justice Center (public, capacity 120, secure) opened in 2018. Solomon Casseb Jr. Webb County Youth Village (public, capacity 72) opened in 2009.
8. Data compiled from "Allocation of State Funds to Local Communities" annual reports 2000–2014, for state grants to counties. Data on county budgets compiled from "Expenditure Survey" conducted by Texas Association of Counties for 2007–2012, retrieved through personal correspondence with survey administrator.
9. The probation funds went toward electronic monitoring, drug testing, psychological evaluations, medication management, individual and family counseling, skills training, wraparound services, and drug and alcohol counseling. Disaggregated allocations of these different programs are unavailable (Texas Juvenile Probation Commission 2010).
10. A 1993 study of the program funded by grants from the Pennsylvania Juvenile Court Judges' Commission and the Pennsylvania Commission on Crime and Delinquency showed promising outcomes. ISP juveniles had fewer arrests (50%) than parolees (74%) (Goodstein and Sontheimer 1997).
11. In 2005, the MacArthur Foundation published a report detailing the ISP in Allegheny County as an exemplary program and described it as one reason why they chose Pennsylvania as the first state to participate in the Models for Change initiative. Another ISP program in Pennsylvania carried out by Youth Advocate Programs, Inc. was described as a "highly successful model" by the U.S. Department of Justice, Office of Juvenile Justice and Delinquency Prevention (1994) and has since been endorsed by the Annie E. Casey Foundation.
12. Determined by looking at counties that have probation department websites and include electronic monitoring as a program they use (53 counties). It is possible that the other 14 use electronic monitoring but do not publicize this on their websites.
13. In 2012, the Texas Juvenile Justice Department Program and Services Registry reported there were 1,562 community-based programs in probation departments across the state (Arrigona and Gonzales 2013). This compares to 628 programs recorded in Texas Juvenile Probation Commission's annual report in 1999. Of the 1,562 programs registered in 2012, only about 30% were started before 2007 (Arrigona and Gonzales 2013). Between 1999 and 2018 the number of anger management programs in the state increased from 29 to 73, drug courts from 0 to 10, educational programs from 22 to 141, life skills from 22 to 130, programs for

parents from 0 to 63, sex offender programs from 18 to 107, substance abuse programs from 60 to 206.

14. Texas has 254 counties, more than any other U.S. state. Brown County has a population of 38,106 (as of the 2010 census). It is about 175 miles southwest of Dallas and about 140 miles northeast of Austin.
15. Named after the current Brown County judge Ray West, who was one of three members of the county commission board who voted to approve the takeover of the unit and the subsequent lease agreement with G4S (Leija 2013).
16. The Corsicana Residential Treatment Center closed in 2013 and was deeded to local officials to lease to private vendors if the facilities were used to benefit "the public interest of the state." The Sheffield Boot Camp closed in 2007 and was reopened in 2008 after Hurricane Ike hit, and the Challenge Academy operated by the Texas Military Department moved in to the facility from its Galveston location. The move was supposed to be temporary, but more than a decade later the program is still in the facility and is beset with abuse complaints and very high staff turnover (Dexheimer 2018).
17. The fate of the closed facilities has varied. One facility (Preston) was given a historical landmark, and another (Fred C. Nelles) was sold to a private developer, who razed the building to make way for commercial and residential development. Two other facilities are still in flux in terms of their sale to their home counties.
18. Two of the facilities (Karl Horton and DeWitt) that were converted for use in the adult system were renovated and turned into prison healthcare facilities. The Karl Horton prison was converted into the California Health Care Facility, costing $906 million that was allocated as part of a $7.7 billion prison construction bill signed into law in 2007, the *same year* that the juvenile reform legislation was passed. The state contracted with McCarthy Building Companies to design and construct the facility. The company has been mired in lawsuits and issues over unsafe, uninhabitable, and sometimes deadly conditions of its mental health jails. Just six months after the jail was opened in 2014 admissions were halted due to a death caused by inadequate medical responsiveness and also due to unsanitary conditions. In 2019, the facility received failing grades from the California Inspector General, and a prisoner died from an outbreak of Legionnaires' disease (*MyNewsLA* 2019; Pino 2019; Thompson 2019).
19. The Texas Public Policy Foundation (2007) celebrated the signing of Texas's major community-based reform legislation in 2007, stating that youth would no longer be sent to the state-run prison system and instead would be "punished and rehabilitated through community-based residential and day treatment programs that are more effective, less expensive, and help preserve the family unit." In 1976, the sponsor of the community-based reform bill in Pennsylvania, Republican senator Charles Dougherty, stated in his support for the legislation, "[T]he question is whether or not we are going to put emphasis on institutions that do not work or community facilities that do" (Pennsylvania State Legislature 1976). The MacArthur and Annie E. Casey community-based reform models centrally assert that youth are better served by being "closer to home" and engaged with community-based services (Models for Change 2021). Schept (2015) provides a detailed account from Illinois of the ways reformers assume the local justice system is benevolent and rehabilitative and therefore needs to be expanded.
20. Schlanger (2013) and many others have explored this phenomenon in the adult system, which underwent realignment in response to the *Brown v. Plata* case against the state-run prison system akin to the juvenile system and with many parallel outcomes (Aviram 2015, 118).
21. In 2006, a lawsuit was filed regarding the serious injury of a youth by a correctional officer in the Samuel F. Santana Challenge Boot Camp Program run by the El Paso County Juvenile Probation Department (*El Paso County v. Solarzano*, 2011).
22. In 2009, a guard from the Hays County Juvenile Detention Center was sentenced to prison for sexually abusing a female in custody (*Hays Free Press News-Dispatch*, 2011). In 2018, a woman volunteering at the Fort Bend Juvenile Detention Center was charged with the repeated sexual abuse of a juvenile in custody (McCord 2019).
23. The Youth Law Center has pursued nine different lawsuits in California since the mid-1980s just based on conditions of confinement in county institutions: *Baumgartner v. City of Long Beach* (1987), *Booraem v. Orange County* (1998), *Hollingsworth v. Orange County* (1990),

NOTES 207

Hunt v. County of Los Angeles (1986), *Jane G. v. Solano County* (1985), *Kleppe v. Superior Court of Marin County* (2010), *Robbins v. Glenn County* (1987), *Shaw v. San Francisco* (1990), *Steven v. Kern County* (1991), *Warren v. Saenz* (2001).

24. In 2014, the U.S. Department of Justice filed suit against Contra Costa County over conditions of confinement for denying special education and related services to disabled youth offenders held in solitary confinement. The lawsuit addressed the county's use of a "restrictive security program" in their 290-bed Juvenile Hall, where youth are confined in their cells for most hours of the day and are denied education services in violation of the Americans with Disabilities Act and the Individuals with Disabilities Education Act (*G.F., et al. v. Contra Costa County, et al.* 2014; Disability Rights Advocates 2019). In 2018, a lawsuit was filed against Kern County regarding its use of solitary confinement, use of pepper spray, and abusive treatment of youth with disabilities (Davis 2018; Luiz 2018). Camp Scott, operated by Los Angeles County, relies on solitary confinement for girls housed there in order to maintain order and authority (Nieto 2008).

25. Soon after proposing this bill, Yee was arrested on a number of corruption charges to which he has pled guilty, the most egregious of which was facilitating a multimillion-dollar arms deal (ironic given he was a champion of gun-control legislation) (Koseff 2015). He was indicted alongside a longtime associate of his, Raymond "Shrimp Boy" Chow, a leader of a well-known San Francisco Chinatown gang (Vives and Willon 2014).

26. Texas is also one of the 14 states that allow pepper spray in juvenile facilities.

27. In 2011, the county recorded 461 incidents involving pepper spray.

28. The East Mesa Juvenile Detention Facility, opened in 2004, is a 380-bed maximum-security facility located in a rural area of the county. Youth who can no longer be sent to the Department of Juvenile Justice or who have failed at the county probation camps are sent there. If at any stage youth are noncompliant with the programming at the facility they can have four months added to their term (San Diego County [California] District Attorney 2015).

29. In 2012, the state juvenile justice system housed about 1,000 youths per day and had about 45 pepper spray incidents per month. San Diego, in comparison, housed about 824 youths per day in 2012 and averaged 38 incidents per month.

30. Noted in the suit is the fact that 81% of youth detained in San Diego County juvenile facilities are Latino and African American, despite making up 53% of the county's total high school enrollment.

31. Estela Medina, chief probation office in Travis County and the chairwoman of the advisory council of county probation officials, who proposed the rule change, said that the new rules would not expand the use of pepper spray but would just provide guidelines for "counties that choose to use it in instances other than riots" (quoted in Grissom 2013). Her statement suggested that some counties already are violating or would violate the current restrictions.

32. There is no accessible data on the frequency with which it is used, but the *state* can also contract with local jails to house state prisoners. Counties are able to then use unoccupied beds and are reimbursed by the "Daily Jail Rate." As the California State Sheriffs' Association (2006, 5) put it, the rate is a "win/win inter-system cooperation, both state and local benefit."

33. The county does not have a competitive salary and benefits package, so many employees start at the facility but eventually transfer, leaving Lake County responsible for the expense of training new staff. Mendocino County does not have the same staff retention problems.

34. The facility is equipped with skyping, so family members can stay in touch through video conferencing.

35. In 2004, Columbia County became the first juvenile probation system to add a drug canine unit to its department (Pennsylvania Juvenile Court Judges' Commission 2004a).

36. This was despite the fact that the Evins facility was under a consent decree to improve conditions of confinement after a U.S. Department of Justice investigation was launched following a riot at the facility in 2004.

Chapter 3

1. Most of this growth was in the federal system; private prisons still comprise a minority of all prisons.

2. For example, in California, Aid to Families with Dependent Children (AFDC) funding reimbursements clearly favor private placements. Placement in county institutions is funded about 50% by state funds and 50% by the county general fund. In contrast, placement in private facilities is covered about 95% by AFDC funds (a mixture of state and federal money) and 5% from the county general fund (Shichor and Bartollas 1990, 297).
3. For example, a study of 83 public interest groups found that 30% had no members at all, only lobbyists, and of the rest, 57% had no structure for members to express their opinions (Stein 2011, 56).
4. Commonweal is sponsored by over 70 different foundations, trusts, and charities, including most notably AmazonSmile, Bank of America, California Endowment, Fidelity Charitable, Silicon Valley Community Fund, Vanguard Charitable, and Wells Fargo Charities.
5. The Texas Public Policy Foundation (2011) is a conservative, free-market think tank whose guiding principles are "individual liberty, personal responsibility, private property rights, free markets and limited government." The State Policy Network is "dedicated to advancing market-oriented public policy solutions" and is related to a variety of prominent conservative think tanks, including the Cato Institute (Fang 2013; State Policy Network 2011).
6. Founded in 1996, Texas Appleseed is a nonprofit public interest law center that is part of a national network of justice centers. The organization partners with more than 30 law firms in Texas and uses volunteer lawyers to address a number of social problems (Texas Appleseed 2014). The organization's mission is to contribute to "significant justice gains for the most vulnerable" and to promote "social and economic justice for all Texans" (Texas Appleseed 2011). In 2001, the organization worked to pass the Fair Defense Act to improve juvenile defendants' access to adequate legal representation (Texas Appleseed 2011).
7. Californians United for a Responsible Budget, comprised of inmate rights' organizations, lauded as a progressive and radically oriented organization, would likely oppose much of TPPF's broader policy positions; still, it relies on cost arguments in all its materials and campaigns (Aviram 2015, 87).
8. Between 1995 and 2017, the MacArthur Foundation made 11 grants totaling $12.9 million in support of the research network (Steinberg 2018). Research from the network was influential in the U.S. Supreme Court cases *Roper v. Simmons*, which prohibited states from giving the death penalty to offenders under the age of 18, and *Miller v. Alabama*, which prohibited states from giving a *mandatory* life without parole sentence to youth convicted of murder.
9. FreeAmerica is an initiative headed by music celebrity John Legend that partners with the philanthropic venture fund New Profit, Inc. and Bank of America to fund start-ups initiated by people who were formerly incarcerated.
10. A British charity is starting a pilot program of five YACs in England and Wales (Requarth 2017).
11. While there are relatively fewer private juvenile prisons in California, this point is not meant to understate the role of private prison companies in the state. California gets the greatest amount of lobbyist contributions from CCA of any state in the country (Aviram 2015, 105). In 2013, Governor Brown announced he would invest $315 million in private prisons as an answer to the crisis of prison overcrowding (165).
12. The capacity for the facilities is available on Abraxas's website for 7 of the 10 facilities: Abraxas I (Marienville, PA): 266 secure beds; Abraxas Academy (Morgantown, PA): 148 secure beds; Abraxas Youth Center (South Mountain, PA): 72 secure beds; Harrisburg Abraxas Student Academy (Harrisburg, PA): 33-person enrollment; Leadership Development Program (South Mountain, PA): 128 secure beds; Lehigh Valley Community Programs (Allentown, PA): capacity unavailable; Non-Residential Treatment (Harrisburg, PA): capacity unavailable; Open Residential Firesetting and Sexual Behavior Treatment Program (South Mountain, PA): capacity unavailable; WorkBridge (Pittsburgh, PA): nonresidential 800-person program; Philadelphia Community Based Programs: nonresidential 71-person program. Abraxas provides a variety of residential, community-based, alternative education, detention, and shelter services (Abraxas Academy 2016).
13. The GEO Group, Inc. (2016) facility in Berks County has a capacity of 148 beds located in a large compound in the middle of undeveloped land about five miles outside of Morgantown, Pennsylvania, a small town with a population of just 826 (as of the 2010 Census). Abraxas I has 266 secure beds and is located in Marienville, Pennsylvania, a town of just 3,137

residents in northeastern Pennsylvania, two hours from Pittsburgh. The implementation of community-based reforms coincided with for-profit and nonprofit takeovers of facilities, and their reach has grown ever since.

14. One Secure Care Program, four Male Residential Programs, two Male Special Needs Residential Programs (one for sexual behavior and the other for mental health), one Female Residential Program, two Neighborhood Reporting Centers, and one Shelter Care Program.
15. ARC also runs several evening reporting centers, where youth are placed after being released from a detention center. Juveniles typically get 90 to 120 days of treatment. If they succeed in the treatment program they get in-home probation, where they are placed on electronic monitoring supervision (Pennsylvania Juvenile Court Judges' Commission 2010c).
16. For example, in 2015 the MacArthur Foundation awarded Harris County $2 million as the winner of its Safety and Justice Challenge; over 200 counties applied for the grant (Hasan 2015). Shortly after receiving the grant, the county shipped 133 inmates to private prisons in two other Texas counties (Barned-Smith 2016).
17. Democratic senator Juan "Chuy" Hinojosa and Republican representative Jerry Madden partnered to sponsor the 2007 legislation. Senate Bill 653 in 2011 was sponsored by Madden and Democratic senator John Whitmire. Senate Bill 1630 in 2015 was sponsored by Whitmire (D) and Republican representative Lyle Larson.
18. The company places a strong emphasis on cognitive behavior therapy and can provide isolated confinement conditions for juveniles (Cornerstone Programs 2014). The Cornerstone Programs closed one of its facilities in Montana after state officials found the company had failed to report child abuse and had neglected the juveniles housed there (*Plainview (TX) Daily Herald* 2007).
19. Lake Granbury Youth Services and the Center for Success and Independence Rockdale Academy are both new private facilities constructed after the community-based reforms. A jail counselor at the Lake Granbury Youth Services prison was charged with "violating the civil rights of a person in custody, and indecency with a child by sexual contact" in 2016 (Ng 2016).
20. The Commission, however, did endorse the Annie E. Casey Foundation's JDAI model to use risk-assessment tools for determining juvenile placement decisions (Interbranch Commission on Juvenile Justice 2010, 54).
21. The school is a privately run nonprofit that charges a hefty tuition, attracting more wealthy families whose sons are caught up with the law. The students at Glen Mills are sent from dozens of different Pennsylvania counties, from out of state and even from out of country, to take advantage of its supposed superior treatment and prestigious athletics program. About 40% of the students are from Philadelphia County. The school is about an hour drive outside of Philadelphia.
22. For example, in 2016, only 5.5% of the youth in this category went to foster homes.
23. "Other" includes admissions to secure facilities, drug and alcohol, independent living, and other placements.
24. Many of the major reform players in the state signed on in support of the Youth Reinvestment Fund, including Center on Juvenile and Criminal Justice, the Children's Defense Fund, the Ella Baker Foundation, National Council on Crime and Delinquency, PolicyLink, the W. Haywood Burns Institute, Los Angeles mayor Eric Garcetti, and a number of county public defender organizations.
25. Coded from list available at http://www.ojjdp.gov/mpg/Program.
26. Determination of nonprofit versus for-profit status was made through personal email correspondence with representatives from the programs.
27. Data for "competency development" program participation is available only from 2004 to 2013. Likely the number of juveniles and percentage of juveniles participating in these programs grew substantially between 1995 and 2004.
28. Electronic monitoring has grown by at least 140% broadly for all offenders, including adults and those held in immigration detention centers (Coen et al. 2017).
29. Some of the companies that sell electronic monitoring devices are SuperCom, USA Technologies, Sentinel Offender Services, Attenti, BI Incorporated (the sole provider for ICE), Libre, and Satellite Tracing of People (Electronic Frontier Foundation n.d.).

30. The screening tool was developed with a William T. Grant Foundation grant.
31. The specific tool from the company that most counties are purchasing is PACT (Positive Achievement Change Tool).
32. Assessments.com has seen large growth in its revenue in the past few years. In the third quarter of 2019, its revenue was $9.4 million, up from $6 million in the first quarter of 2018 (Crunchbase 2019).
33. In the same year, Yolo County contracted with Tyler for all of the aspects of their Superior Court, which includes the juvenile division (Business Wire 2019b).
34. For example, in 2016 public defenders joined a lawsuit accusing the company of errors that led to extended jail stays and false arrests in the Alameda County adult probation system (Emslie 2017). In 2017, a federal lawsuit was filed against the company in Shelby County, Tennessee, over defendants being held after posting bond and after having charges dismissed (*Cortez et al. v. Oldham* 2018).

Chapter 4

1. A 2012 editorial in the *New York Times* asserted, "California did it [juvenile justice reform] the right way: providing generous financing to the counties for therapeutically based juvenile offender programs."
2. In 1942, two young men at the Whittier and Preston state-run reform schools committed suicide. Whittier State School closed in 2005, and the Preston School of Industry remains open today.
3. One particularly notable case was the Sleepy Lagoon trial in 1942, when 17 boys were convicted of murdering Jose Diaz. These boys were convicted of a crime they did not commit, *and* they were identified as biologically criminal. Expert witnesses at the trial testified that boys' Indian or Aztec heritage predisposed them to violence (Chávez-García 2012, 2).
4. For an extended account of the passage of TSYDC legislation, see Bush (2010). While large state institutions were growing in disfavor, the legislation also came at a time when there was a great deal of concern about juvenile crime nationally, second only to "Communist subversion" for what Americans listed as the most pressing public concerns in the 1950s.
5. Houston was one of 10 cities to receive federal funds appropriated under the Juvenile Delinquency and Youth Offenses Control Act of 1961, administered by a committee appointed by President Kennedy (Bush 2010, 138). Lloyd Ohlin was the assistant director of the committee, and the allocations were to help state and local communities prevent and control delinquency (Binder and Polan 1991, 250).
6. Alicia Morales was the lead plaintiff in a class action lawsuit filed in 1971 against Dr. James Turman, executive director of TYC, over the routine denial of court hearings for juveniles and, once incarcerated, abusive conditions of confinement for youth.
7. From 1988 to 2013 California enacted 200 new pieces of legislation that increased punishment for criminal offenders (Kwon 2013, 40). Proposition 8, the Victims' Bill of Rights, passed in 1981. In 1987 a database of gang suspects, CalGang, was established, and in 1988 California's Street Terrorism Enforcement and Prevention Act passed. In 1990 the state passed Proposition 115 establishing life without the possibility of parole for juveniles. And at this time the state launched the largest prison-building project in the history of the world. A 2000 ballot initiative, Proposition 21, the Gang Violence and Juvenile Crime Prevention Act, passed and made significant changes to the juvenile justice system. The Act expanded the circumstances in which juveniles could be charged as adults and sentenced to adult prisons, expanded eligibility for the death penalty and life without parole sentences, and expanded the three-strikes law. The Act also prohibited sealing juvenile records in a variety of instances, rejected rehabilitation, promoted zero tolerance policies for gang crimes, instituted gang enhancement measures to increase sentences, lowered criminal responsibility for a number of charges to 14 years of age, and increased detentions before hearings. The California District Attorney Association as well as corporate donors and an army of petitioners drafted the proposition and supported its passage (Raymond 2000, 311).
8. In 1995, the state established seven levels of sanctions that are incrementally more severe (based on the severity of the offense and a juvenile's prior history) as a guideline for juvenile

probation departments and added 11 offenses eligible for a determinate sentence (Fabelo 1999). In 1996, the legislature eroded protections for the confidentiality of juveniles, allowed the creation of "gang books" (catalogs of gang members and related information to help criminal investigations), instituted measures of parental accountability (parents fined for not appearing in court), expanded intermediate sanction facilities like boot camps, expanded contracts with private operators of these facilities, and lowered the minimum age of waiver to adult court to 14 (Johnson 1998, 2–13).

9. Policies enacted during this year made sentencing juveniles to life without parole easier and increased the number of offenses in which juveniles would be automatically tried as adults. During the session, the legislature created the Pennsylvania Office of the Victim Advocate and the Office of Safe Schools within the Pennsylvania Department of Education.
10. For comparison, in the same year $14 million went toward intensive probation supervision.
11. The major programs in this field are Reasoning and Rehabilitation, Aggression Replacement Training, and Thinking for a Change.
12. Calculated from the appendices of the 2010 Annual Report to the Governor and Texas Legislative Budget Board, "Juvenile Probation Appropriations, Riders and Special Diversion Programs," https://www2.tjjd.texas.gov/publications/reports/RPTOTH201202.pdf.
13. The website is http://www.whytry.org/. The program is in over 10,000 schools worldwide.
14. Lafer (2004) work also points out that "job training" under Temporary Assistance for Needy Families came in the form of "self-esteem" training.
15. The MacArthur Foundation (2016a) provided $536,000 for the program between 2002 and 2014.
16. Similarly, in 2016 the Annie E. Casey Foundation launched an initiative called Generation Work that employs a "demand-driven" approach to improving youth employment—meaning they foster relationships with employers to determine their hiring needs, training requirements, and what "work-based learning" opportunities they can provide. Philadelphia was chosen as one of five cities to partner with to launch the initiative (Angwin et al. 2016).
17. The MacArthur Foundation published outcome data for the Philadelphia Reintegration Initiative from 2008 that showed 31% of youth in the program received a high school diploma or GED, 84% enrolled in school or career training upon discharge from the program, and 37% were employed at some point during the reintegration process (*Juvenile Justice Information Exchange* 2016). The Stoneleigh Foundation has similarly limited data on the PACTA program for 2009–2010. The Foundation reports that about 25% of students discharged from PACTA left with a ServSafe, OSHA-10, or Microsoft Certification, and about 50% of discharged students had authentic, paid work experience from their time in the program (Stoneleigh Foundation 2013a).
18. In Pennsylvania, California, and Texas about 30% or more of children (ages 0–18) live in families in which their parents lack stable, full-time jobs (Annie E. Casey Foundation 2020a).
19. Based on three-year rearrest rates for juveniles starting a program in 2007, electronic monitoring and boot camps have the highest rates of recidivism (71% and 66%, respectively). Juveniles in "life skills" have a lower recidivism rate than these programs, but it is still very high, about 58%. The following are the recidivism rearrest rates for different types of programs: anger management (57%), counseling (63%), educational (64%), family preservation (65%), mental health (65%), substance abuse prevention/intervention (63%) (Texas Legislative Budget Board 2013).
20. Corbett's initiative recommended expanding diversionary court and intermediate punishment programs and combining treatment with incarceration. The other two pillars of the initiative were to invest in risk-assessment measures and job training for juvenile offenders.
21. The reliability of the tools can vary widely depending on the complexity of the tool and the amount of training and funding there is for implementing the assessment.
22. Reed (1999) astutely critiqued a similar process in the "underclass theory." By using a snapshot of an incident in an individual's life (for example, their use of drugs), this framework imputes a static behavioral evaluation of an individual even though a particular incident might be transitory and say little about the behavior of the youth (185).

23. In California, many counties purchase a tool from Assessments.com called Positive Achievement Change Tool, which similarly measures individual characteristics of a youth along with variables about the stability of their family.
24. For example, if a youth is homeless, this is a risk factor in need of mitigation, not necessarily the problem that can or needs to be solved.
25. Programs that provide self-evaluations are Big Brothers/Big Sisters, Nurse-Family Partnership, Olweus Bullying Prevention, Positive Action, The Incredible Years, Project towards No Drug Abuse. Programs evaluated by the Blueprints project are LifeSkills, PATHS, Strong African American Families Program.
26. P.A.C.E. stands for Proper Self-image, Academics, Character Development and Employment prep. In 2012, the GEO Group Foundation (the second largest private prison operator in the United States) donated $10,000 to P.A.C.E. Youth Programs, Inc. (Hall 2012). P.A.C.E. has also received funding from Wells Fargo and Exxon/Mobil (LinkedIn 2021).
27. Senate Bill 103 stipulated that the juvenile system develop a comprehensive assessment process when juveniles are admitted to TYC (now Texas Juvenile Justice Department).
28. For example, CoNEXTions contracts with Cognitive Life Skills, Thinking for a Change, Aggression Replacement Training, WhyTry, Seeking Safety, Functional Family Therapy, and Parenting with Love and Limits.

Chapter 5

1. States can still choose to sentence a juvenile to a LWOP sentence, but the state is prohibited from making this mandatory for all homicides.
2. This is in part due to the influence of the "superpredator" rhetoric undergirding the 1990s "get tough" laws, a discourse employed by Lynne Abraham, who was Philadelphia's district attorney from 1991 to 2010.
3. Juveniles convicted of first-degree murder who are under 15 years of age receive a mandatory minimum sentence of 25 years. Juveniles between 15 and 17 receive a mandatory minimum sentence of 35 years. For second-degree murder (killing in the course of a felony, such as robbery), the state set a mandatory minimum sentence of 20 years for those under the age of 15 and a 30-year sentence for those between 15 and 17.
4. The main objection in the state senate to the bill was that the legislation had circumvented the Committee on the Judiciary. Senator Mary Jo White (Republican) accused the sponsors of the bill of avoiding the Committee because it "has expressed an extreme displeasure with mandatory minimum sentences" (Pennsylvania State Legislature 2012b). But in the end the Senate supported the bill 37–12. (Six Republicans and 6 Democrats voted against the bill.)
5. As of 2012, there were 310 prisoners in California serving LWOP sentences for a crime they committed when they were younger than 18 (Gerber 2015). Nationwide there are about 2,500 juvenile lifers. California's juvenile lifer population is about 12.4% of all youth serving LWOP sentences in the United States.
6. Some notable supporters of the legislation were Human Rights Watch, ACLU, W. Haywood Burns Institute, Taxpayers for Improving Public Safety, Grover Norquist, Pat Nolan, and Newt Gingrich.
7. In the first year the bill was in effect, there were 490 parole hearings thanks to the legislation, and 155 individuals were approved for release (Pitre 2015).
8. The law does not apply to those who were older than 18 at the time of the crime, were sentenced to LWOP for a crime in which the defendant tortured their victim, were sentenced to LWOP for a crime in which the victim was a public safety official, or have already been in custody more than 25 years (Fair Sentencing for Youth 2016).
9. Texas and Nebraska set the minimum sentence at 40 years. Pennsylvania, Louisiana, and Florida (which account for 40% of the total population of juveniles serving LWOP in the United States) set the minimum at 35 years. Six other states set the minimum at 25 years (Rovner 2014).
10. Youth who are certified as adults are exempt from the Juvenile Justice and Delinquency Prevention Act of 1974's requirement that youth be "sight and sound separated" from adults. However, the majority of adult jails in Texas treat certified juveniles as youth and house them

in single cells based on this status. In a survey, 11 jails reported they commingle certified juveniles with adults. Even in the jails that separated juveniles from adults, many were not making efforts to prevent any contact with adults in non-housing contexts (Deitch, Galbraith, and Pollock 2012). In a survey of 41 jails in Texas 25 of them reported giving youth less than one hour of out-of-cell time per day. The average length of stay in county jails for adult-certified youth is six months to longer than one year (xi).

11. This has reduced the number of youth with an adult sentence who are sent to serve their time in juvenile facilities. As a result of the 1996 legal change, the number of youth convicted of an adult sentence sent to state-run juvenile prisons fell from 811 in 1995 to 198 in 1997. In 1990, 992 youth were committed to the California Department of Justice with an adult sentence; in 2003, 54 youth; and in 2005, 176 youth (Jannetta and Lin 2007).

12. While in 2013 only 0.65% of all arrested juveniles were sent to adult courts, this was three times greater than the percentage (0.20%) sent to adult prisons in 2002.

13. The breakdown of arrest offenses over the past decade is consistently at about 30% for felony charges, 55% for misdemeanors, and 15% for status offenses. Calculated from State of California Department of Justice statistical reports, oag.ca.gov/cjsc/pubs#juvenileJustice.

14. Youth can also end up in the adult court through mandatory transfers based on the seriousness of the crime or through judicial hearings to determine if they should be tried as a juvenile or adult.

15. Truancy charges can be filed in juvenile court as a "Conduct in Need of Supervision" (CINS) offense or in adult criminal courts as "Failure to Attend School" (FTAS), a Class C misdemeanor offense. In 2013, 1,000 truancy cases were filed in juvenile courts as a CINS offense and 115,000 cases were filed in the adult criminal court as an FTAS offense. Parents can also be charged with a Class C misdemeanor offense, "Parent Contributing to Nonattendance," in addition to or in lieu of a student's truancy charge.

16. As Wacquant (2009, 31) argues, the treatment of the sex offender builds on the "career recidivist" typology first introduced by Cesare Lombroso in 1884, who described the "career recidivist" as having distinct psychophysiological and anthropometric characteristics.

17. Registries are often unhelpful to law enforcement because they cast a wide and undifferentiated net, making it difficult to monitor large numbers of people without a sense of who is most dangerous. Research also shows that people who commit sex offenses as children are among those least likely to offend again. Those on the registry often experience serious psychological harm, high suicide rates, and harassment and physical violence. They can face serious challenges in finding employment, getting an education, and accessing housing. For more on the negative effects of registries on juveniles, see Human Rights Watch (2013).

18. Annie E. Casey Foundation was one of several funders of a 2016 study that concluded that sex offender registries are harmful to juveniles. In 2014, the MacArthur Foundation issued a report listing "registries for youth who commit sex offenses" as one of five practices in the juvenile justice system that are "incompatible with healthy adolescent development" (Chambers and Balck 2014). However, there is no mention of policies related to sex offenses in either of the core reform models (Models for Change and JDAI).

19. For example, the MacArthur policy brief on reforming sex offender registries is titled "Because Kids Are Different" (Chambers and Balck 2014).

20. This includes rape, involuntary deviate sexual intercourse, sexual assault, aggravated indecent assault, indecent assault, and incest. A mental abnormality is defined as "a congenital or acquired condition of a person affecting the person's emotional or volitional capacity" (Lawrence and Barnes 2014).

21. As of 2016, 13 states allow civil commitment in sexually violent predator programs for people who committed their crimes as juveniles (Steptoe and Goldet 2016). About 5,400 people in 20 states are being held indefinitely in civil commitment programs for sex offenses (Steptoe and Goldet 2016). In 2004, the state passed a bill requiring youth convicted of a sex offense to have a DNA sample drawn and submitted to the DNA Detection Fund. The cost of the DNA sample is $250 and is added to the other costs imposed on delinquent offenders (Pennsylvania Juvenile Court Judges' Commission 2005a).

22. Of the five other individuals who have left the program, three were transferred to the civil side of Torrance State Hospital, one was reincarcerated, and one passed away at the facility due to "an unexpected illness" (Lawrence and Barnes 2014).
23. The data from Juvenile Court Judges' Commission does not specify the year of commitment for the youth, so it is not possible to calculate the average length of commitment for the 59 residents of the program or for the 9 who were discharged or died.
24. The Act also expanded the circumstances in which juveniles could be charged as adults and sentenced to adult prisons, expanded the death penalty and LWOP sentences, expanded the three-strikes law, prohibited sealing juvenile records in a variety of instances, rejected rehabilitation, lowered criminal responsibility for a number of charges to 14 years of age, and increased detentions before hearings. The California District Attorney Association as well as corporate donors and an army of petitioners drafted the proposition and supported its passage (Raymond 2000, 311).
25. In 2010, of all 235,579 gang members (youth and adult) in the CalGang database, 66% were Hispanic, 19.6% Black, 7.8% white, 2.6% Asian, 0.5% Pacific Islander, and 2.8% undesignated race (Harris 2010).
26. For example, in Berks County, Pennsylvania, a DMC demonstration site has invested in diversity training where law enforcement participate in "cultural competency training" (Griffin 2008, 5). Many community-based programs throughout the state are considered part of the DMC effort, such as the Positive Choice program, which provides minority youths with tutoring and special classes (Clouser 1994). Youth are taught how to "analyze the alternative choices in everyday situations, to make the 'positive choice' for their future, and to accept responsibility for the consequences of the choices they make" (3).
27. In 2012, Hispanic and Black youth made up 58% of youth age 10 to 16 in Texas and 79% of the youth sent to state-run facilities. This is about the same disparity as before the reforms. In 2005, Hispanics and Blacks made up 55% of youth age 10 to 16, but 75% of the youth sent to state-run facilities.
28. Data was collected on 2,016 juvenile delinquency cases from 14 Pennsylvania counties in 1989.
29. Also, in Texas recidivism rates have not budged; they remain the same for youth leaving both state-run facilities and local juvenile probation programs from before and after the implementation of the 2007 reforms.
30. The last annual report available for the state that measures arrest rates is from 2016.
31. For example, studies on lead exposure of children are often referenced (Drum 2013), but this explanation has been criticized by criminologists (Lauritsen, Rezey, and Heimer 2016).
32. In "wardship" a minor is declared a "ward of the court" and placed under the court's strict supervision.
33. Studies on the effect of prison isolation find that the conditions of solitary have serious psychological consequences, such as insomnia, depression, self-mutilation, suicidal ideation and behavior, and hallucinations (American Civil Liberties Union 2014; Gately 2014; Haney 2003; Human Rights Watch 2012).
34. There is no public record of a connection between the solitary confinement program in Texas and the Phoenix program in Vietnam, the CIA's systematic torture and assassination program aimed at the National Liberation Front.
35. Despite the misnomer, McLennan County Juvenile Correctional Facility is a state-run facility.
36. Mart is in central Texas, 20 miles west of Waco. According to the 2010 census, its population was 2,426.

Conclusion

1. In 2002 large foundations held $429 billion in assets (Faber and McCarthy 2005, 4).
2. In 2019, over 30,000 teachers, support staff, parents, students, and community members flooded the streets of Chicago in support of this broad agenda (Sharkey 2019).

REFERENCES

Abraxas Academy. 2016. "Abraxas Academy: Secure Treatment Program." http://www.abraxasyfs.com/facilities/academy/pdf/AA_Brochure.pdf.
Ajmani, N., & E. Webster. 2016. "Failure after Farrell: Violence and Inadequate Mental Health Care in California's Division of Juvenile Justice." *Center on Juvenile and Criminal Justice*. http://www.cjcj.org/uploads/cjcj/documents/failure_after_farrell_djj.pdf.
Akard, P. J. 1992. "Corporate Mobilization and Political Power: The Transformation of U.S. Economic Policy in the 1970s." *American Sociological Review* 57(5): 597–615.
Aldrich, S. 2017. "Beaumont Dream Center Hoping to Move into Former Al Price Youth Facility." *12News*, July 31.
Alexander, M. 2010. *The New Jim Crow: Mass Incarceration in the Age of Colorblindness*. New York: New Press.
Alfonseca, K. 2019. "California's Juvenile Justice System Had 16 Years to Fix Its Abuse Problems. It Didn't." *The Huffpost*, February 19. https://www.huffpost.com/entry/california-juvenile-justice-abuse-harassment_n_5c51cf59e4b00906b26fcc11.
Alternative Rehabilitation Communities. 2016a. "About Us." http://www.arcfamily.com/about/about-us/.
Alternative Rehabilitation Communities. 2016b. "Success Stories." http://www.arcfamily.com/success-stories/.
American Civil Liberties Union. 2014. "Alone and Afraid: Children Held in Solitary Confinement and Isolation in Juvenile Detention and Correctional Facilities." https://www.aclu.org/files/assets/Alone%20and%20Afraid%20 COMPLETE%20FINAL.pdf.
American Federation of Teachers. 2018. "A Decade of Neglect: Public Education Funding in the Aftermath of the Great Recession." https://www.aft.org/sites/default/files/decade-of-neglect-2018.pdf.
AngelList. 2015. "Assessments.com." https://angel.co/assessments-com.
Angwin, J., J. Larson, S. Mattu, and L. Kirchner. 2016. "Machine Bias: There's Software Used across the Country to Predict Future Criminals. And It's Biased against Blacks. ProPublica, May 23. https://www.propublica.org/article/machine-bias-risk-assessments-in-criminal-sentencing.
Annie E. Casey Foundation. 2013. "Reducing Youth Incarceration in the United States." Data Snapshot: Kids Count. http://www.aecf.org/ resources/reducing-youth-incarceration-in-the-united-states/.
Annie E. Casey Foundation. 2014. "Juvenile Detention Alternatives Initiative." http://www.aecf.org/work/juvenile-justice/jdai/.

Annie E. Casey Foundation. 2018. "Court Fees and Fines Are Hurting Low-Income Families in Alabama." https://www.aecf.org/blog/court-fees-and-fines-are-hurting-low-income-families-in-alabama/.

Annie E. Casey Foundation. 2020a. "Children Whose Parents Lack Secure Employment in Texas." Data set. Kids Count Data Center. https://datacenter.kidscount.org/data/tables/5043-children-whose-parents-lack-secure-employment?loc=45&loct=2#detailed/2/6,40,45/false/37,871,870,573,869,36,868,867,133,38/any/11452,11453.

Annie E. Casey Foundation. 2020b. "Persons 18 to 24 in Poverty in Texas." Data set. Kids Count Data Center. https://datacenter.kidscount.org/data/tables/51-persons-18-to-24-in-poverty?loc=45&loct=2#detailed/2/6,40,45/false/1729,37,871,870,573,869,36,868,867,133/any/337,338.

Arena, J. 2012. *Driven from New Orleans: How Nonprofits Betray Public Housing and Promote Privatization.* Minneapolis: University of Minnesota Press.

Armstrong, S. 2002. "Punishing Not-for-Profit: Implications of Nonprofit Privatization in Juvenile Punishment." *Punishment & Society* 4(3): 345–368.

Arnove, R. F. 1980. *Philanthropy and Cultural Imperialism: The Foundations at Home and Abroad.* Bloomington: Indiana University Press.

Arrigona, N., & J. Gonzales. 2013. "Community-Based Program Evaluation Series: Overview of Community-Based Juvenile Probation Programs." Report. Austin TX: Texas Juvenile Justice Department.

Aviram, H. 2015. *Cheap on Crime: Recession-Era Politics and the Transformation of American Punishment.* Berkeley: University of California Press.

Aryna, N., E. Lotke, L. Ryan, M. Schindler, D. Shoenberg, and M. Soler. 2005. "Keystones for Reform: Promising Juvenile Justice Policies and Practices in Pennsylvania." MacArthur Foundation: Models for Change, October. http://www.modelsforchange.net/publications/151.

Aspholm, R. 2020. *Views from the Streets: The Transformation of Gangs and Violence on Chicago's South Side.* New York: Columbia University Press.

Austin Chronicle. 1998. "Naked City: Off the Desk." August 7. https://www.austinchronicle.com/news/1998-08-07/523735/.

Austin, J., K. D. Johnson, and M. Gregoriou. 2000. "Juvenile in Adult Prisons and Jails: A National Assessment." Bureau of Justice Assistance. https://www.ncjrs.gov/pdffiles1/bja/182503.pdf.

Austin, J., and B. Krisberg. 1981. "NCCD Research Review: Wider, Stronger, and Different Nets: The Dialectics of Criminal Justice Reform." *Journal of Research in Crime and Delinquency* 18(1): 165–196.

Baird, C., T. Healy, K. Johnson, A. Bogie, E. W. Dankert, and C. Scharenroch. 2013. "A Comparison of Risk Assessment Instrument in Juvenile Justice." National Council on Crime and Delinquency. http://nccdglobal.org/sites/default/files/publication_pdf/nccd_fire_report.pdf.

Bakal, Y. 1998. "Reflections: A Quarter Century of Reform in Massachusetts Youth Corrections." *Crime and Delinquency* 44: 110–116.

Ball, W. D. 2011. "Tough on Crime (on the State's Dime): How Violent Crime Does Not Drive California Counties' Incarceration Rates and Why It Should." *Georgia State Law Review* 28: 987.

Banks, G. 2020. "Reports: Children Are in 23½ Hour-a-Day Lockup at Harris County Juvenile Facility amid COVID-19." *Houston Chronicle*, April 8. https://www.houstonchronicle.com/news/houston-texas/houston/article/Reports-Children-are-in-23-hour-a-day-lockup-15187249.php.

Barajas, M. 2013. "In Texas, Juvenile Sex Offenders Get Virtual Life Sentence." *San Antonio Current,* May 7. https://www.sacurrent.com/sanantonio/in-texas-juvenile-sex-offenders-get-virtual-life-sentence/Content?oid=2246573.

Barkan, J. 2011. "Got Dough? How Billionaires Rule Our Schools." *Dissent Magazine*, Winter. https://www.dissentmagazine.org/article/got-dough-how-billionaires-rule-our-schools.

Barker, V. 2009. *The Politics of Imprisonment: How the Democratic Process Shapes the Way America Punishes Offenders*. Oxford: Oxford University Press.

Barlow, J. 2019. "Study Finds Parole 'A Roll of the Dice' for Those Convicted as Teens." *University of Oregon: Around the O*. https://around.uoregon.edu/content/study-finds-parole-roll-dice-those-convicted-teens.

Barmann, J. 2019. "No One Knows Why, but Juvenile Crime Has Gone Way Down in California." *SFist*. https://sfist.com/2019/03/21/no-one-knows-why-but-juvenile-crime-has-gone-way-down-in-california/.

Barned-Smith, S. J. 2016. "Jail Nears Capacity, Ships 133 Inmates to Private Facilities." *Houston Chronicle*, April 15. http://www.chron.com/news/houston-texas/article/As-jail-hits-capacity-county-ships-133-inmates-7251276.php.

Bartels, L. M. 2016. *Unequal Democracy: The Political Economy of the New Gilded Age*. Princeton, NJ: Princeton University Press.

Bateman, T. 2011. "'We Now Breach More Kids in a Week Than We Used to in a Whole Year': The Punitive Turn, Enforcement and Custody." *Youth Justice* 11(2): 115–133.

Baumgartner v. City of Long Beach (Ca. 1987). https://www.ylc.org/wp-content/uploads/2018/11/baumgartnercomplaint1stamended.pdf.

Beatty, D. 2002. "An Assessment of Texas Juvenile Intensive Supervision Programs." Applied Research Projects, Texas State University–San Marcos. https://digital.library.txstate.edu/handle/10877/3673.

Beckett, K., and N. Murakawa. 2012. "Mapping the Shadow Carceral State: Toward an Institutionally Capacious Approach to Punishment." *Theoretical Criminology* 16(2): 221–244.

Beckett, K. 1997. *Making Crime Pay: Law and Order in Contemporary American Politics*. New York: Oxford University Press.

Beitsch, R. 2015. "States Slowly Scale Back Juvenile Sex Offender Registries." Pew Charitable Trusts, November 19. https://www.pewtrusts.org/en/research-and-analysis/blogs/stateline/2015/11/19/states-slowly-scale-back-juvenile-sex-offender-registries.

Bell, B. 2012. "'Fix It': How Jay Kimbrough Became Rick Perry's Troubleshooter." *Austin Statesman*, August 19.

Bell, M. C. 2019. "The Community in Criminal Justice: Subordination, Consumption, Resistance, and Transformation." *Du Bois Review: Social Science Research on Race* 16(1): 197–220.

Bennett, P. M., and V. Schiraldi. 2018. "LA Probation Governance Study." Los Angeles County Executive's Office. http://file.lacounty.gov/SDSInter/probation/1033765_LAPGS_FinalMergedReport_20180206.pdf.

Berman, E. H. 1983. *The Influence of the Carnegie, Ford, and Rockefeller Foundations on American Foreign Policy: The Ideology of Philanthropy*. Albany, NY: SUNY Press.

Bernard, T. J. 1992. *The Cycle of Juvenile Justice*. Oxford: Oxford University Press.

Bernier, N. 2013. "Texas Youth Placed in Solitary Confinement More Than 36,000 Times Last Year." KUT Radio, Austin, April 22. https://www.kut.org/post/texas-youth-placed-solitary-confinement-more-36000-times-last-year.

Bernstein, N. 2015. *Burning Down the House: The End of Juvenile Prison*. New York: New Press.

Bertram, E. 2015. *The Workfare State: Public Assistance Politics from the New Deal to the New Democrats*. Philadelphia: University of Pennsylvania Press.

Binder, A., and S. L. Polan. 1991. "The Kennedy-Johnson Years, Social Theory, and Federal Policy in the Control of Juvenile Delinquency." *Crime & Delinquency* 37(2): 242–261.

Blakinger, K. 2019. "'This Place Is a Jungle': Texas Youth Prisons Still Beset by Gangs, Violence, Abuse." *Houston Chronicle*. December 30, 2019.

Block, K. J., and D. C. Hale. 1991. "Turf Wars in Progressive Era Juvenile Justice: The Relationship of Private and Public Child Care Agencies." *Crime & Delinquency* 37(2): 225–241.

Blueprints for Healthy Youth Development. 2016a. "Promoting Alternative Thinking Strategies (PATHS)." http://www.blueprintsprograms.com/evaluation-abstract/promoting-alternative-thinking-strategies-paths.

Blueprints for Healthy Youth Development. 2016b. "Strong African American Families Program." http://www.blueprintsprograms.com/evaluation-abstract/strong-african-american-families-program.

Blueprints for Violence Prevention. 2016. "LifeSkills Training Program and Positive Educational Outcomes." http://www.colorado.edu/cspv/blueprints/lst-grant/forms/Application/LST EducationalOutcomes.pdf. Bonk, C. 2020. "Inside the Alleged Abuse of At-Risk Youth in PA Treatment Centers." Public Opinion Online, April 30. https://www.publicopiniononline.com/in-depth/news/local/2020/04/30/pennsylvania-youth-treatment-centers-have-been-accused-abusing-kids-south-mountain/4084874002/.

Booraem v. Orange County (Ca. 1998). ylc.org/wp content/uploads/2018/11/booraemsettlement.pdf.

Bosworth, M. 2007. "Creating the Responsible Prisoner Federal Admission and Orientation Packs." *Punishment & Society* 9(1): 67–85.

Bowman, T. 2003. "Judge Warns Child Rapist 'a High Risk to Re-Offend.'" *Patriot-News* (Harrisburg, PA), February 4.

Breen, J. S. 2011. "Capitalizing Labor: What Work Is Worth and Why, from the New Deal to the New Economy." PhD dissertation, University of Pennsylvania. https://repository.upenn.edu/dissertations/AAI3462187/.

Brinkley, A. 1996. *The End of Reform: New Deal Liberalism in Recession and War*. New York: Vintage.

Brown, W. 2003. "Neo-liberalism and the End of Liberal Democracy." *Theory & Event* 7(1).

Bundy, T. 2014. "Solitary Confinement, Even for Youth." *San Diego Union-Tribune*, April 17. http://www.sandiegouniontribune.com/news/2014/apr/17/cir-youth-solitary-confinement/.

Burke, B., and M. Simpson. (2015). "A Solitary Failure: The Waste, Cost and Harm of Solitary Confinement in Texas." American Civil Liberties Union. file:///Users/sarahcate/Downloads/SolitaryReport_2015%20(2).pdf.

Burrell, S. 2014. "The Legislature's Role in Juvenile Justice Reform: A California Example." National Council on Crime & Delinquency. http://nccdglo bal.org/blog/the-legislature-s-role-in-juvenile-justice-reform-a-california-example.

Bush, W. S. 2004. "Representing the Juvenile Delinquent: Reform, Social Science, and Teenage Troubles in Postwar Texas." PhD dissertation. Texas A&M University-San Antonio.

Bush, W. S. 2010. *Who Gets a Childhood? Race and Juvenile Justice in Twentieth-Century Texas*. Athens: University of Georgia Press.

Business Wire. (2019a). "Alameda County, California Expands Relationship with Tyler Technologies." August 13. https://www.businesswire.com/news/home/20190813005039/en/Alameda-County-California-Expands-Relationship-Tyler-Technologies.

Business Wire. 2019b. "Yolo County, California, Selects Courts and Justice Solutions from Tyler Technologies." *Yahoo! Finance*. https://finance.yahoo.com/news/yolo-county-california-selects-courts-131700235.html.

Butts, J., and D. Evans. (2011). "Resolution, Reinvestment and Realignment: Three Strategies for Changing Juvenile Justice." John Jay College of Criminal Justice. http://www.jjay.cuny.edu/4851.php.

Cahill, D. 2014. *The End of Laissez-Faire? On the Durability of Embedded Neoliberalism*. Cheltenham: Edward Elgar.

California Board of State and Community Corrections. 2014. "Youthful Offender Block Grant 2013–14: Planned Programs and Expenditures." http://www.bscc.ca. gov/downloads/YOBG_Program_Descriptions_for_Posting_on_the_Web_7_18_2013.pdf.

California Board of State and Community Corrections. 2015. "Youthful Offender Block Grant 2015–16: Planned Programs and Expenditures." http://www.bscc.ca.gov/ downloads/201516%20YOBG%20Program%20Descriptions.pdf.

REFERENCES

California Board of State and Community Corrections. 2018. "Juvenile Justice Crime Prevention Act and Youthful Offender Block Grant: JJCPA-YOBG County Expenditure and Data Reports." March. http://www.bscc.ca.gov/wp-content/uploads/2018-JJCPA-YOBG-Leg-Report-FINAL-3.9.18.pdf.

California Budget and Policy Center. 2020. "High-Income Households and Corporations Benefit the Most from California's Tax Breaks." https://calbudgetcenter.org/wp-content/uploads/2020/01/CA_Budget_Center_tax-expenditures-2020.pdf.

California Department of Corrections and Rehabilitation. 2019. *California Code of Regulations.* https://www.cdcr.ca.gov/juvenile-justice/wp-content/uploads/sites/168/2019/07/Adopted-Regulation-YAP-Pilot-18-001remediated.pdf.

California Department of Justice. 2021. "Frequently Asked Questions: California Tiered Sex Offender Registration (Senate Bill 384) for Registrants." https://oag.ca.gov/sites/all/files/agweb/pdfs/csor/registrant-faqs.pdf.

California Division of Juvenile Justice. 2021. "Our Mission." https://www.cdcr.ca.gov/juvenile-justice/mission-statement/.

California Legislative Analyst's Office. 2004. "Proposition 1A: Local Government Finance." http://www.lao.ca.gov/ballot/2004/1A_11_2004.htm.

California Rural Legal Assistance. 2011. "Pepper Spray." http://www.crla.org/pepper-spray.

California State Auditor. 2016. "The CalGang Criminal Intelligence System." https://www.auditor.ca.gov/pdfs/reports/2015-130.pdf.

California State Legislature. 2007. Senate Bill 81. http://www.cdcan.us/budget/2007-2008/SB%2081%20Senate%20Bill%20-%20AMENDED.htm.

California State Legislature. 2014. Senate Bill 260. http://leginfo.legislature.ca.gov/faces/billNavClient.xhtml?bill_id=201320140SB260.

California State Sheriffs' Association. 2006. "Do the Crime, Do the Time? Maybe Not, in California: Jail Cell Shortage Is Upsetting the Balance." https://www.calsheriffs.org/attachments/094_DotheCrimeDotheTimeMaybeNotInCaliforniaJune2006.pdf.

California Superior Court, San Francisco County. 2019. "Young Adult Court." https://www.sfsuperiorcourt.org/divisions/collaborative/yac.

Call, J. 2020. "Struggling to Make Ends Meet: Food Insecurity in CA." California Food Policy Advocates. https://cfpa.net/GeneralNutrition/CFPAPublications/FoodInsecurity-Factsheet-2019.pdf.

Callahan, D. 2018. *The Givers: Money, Power, and Philanthropy in a New Gilded Age.* New York: Vintage Books.

Campbell, M. C. 2016. "Are All Politics Local? A Case Study of Local Conditions in a Period of 'Law and Order' Politics." *Annals of the American Academy of Political and Social Science* 664(1): 43–61.

Capps, R., N. Pindus, K. Snyder, and J. L. Leos. 2001. "Assessing the New Federalism: Recent Changes in Texas Welfare and Work, Child Care and Child Welfare Systems." Urban Institute. https://www.urban.org/sites/default/files/publication/61146/310182-Recent-Changes-in-Texas-Welfare-and-Work-Child-Care-and-Child-Welfare-Systems.PDF.

Carreon, J., E. A. Henneke, and J. J. Kreager. 2015. "Unfinished Business: Deepening the Gains in Texas Juvenile Justice Reform." Texas Criminal Justice Coalition. https://www.texascjc.org/system/files/publications/TCJC%20Unfinished%20Business%20Policy%20Paper%202015.pdf.

Carson, E. A. 2014. "Imprisonment Rate of Sentenced Prisoners under the Jurisdiction of State or Federal Correctional Authorities." Bureau of Justice Statistics. http://www.bjs.gov/index.cfm?ty=nps.

Castro, E. D., and D. Lavine. 2013. "How Texas Spends Its Money. How Texas Gets Its Money. Why It Doesn't Add Up." *San Antonio Report,* February 27. https://sanantonioreport.org/how-texas-spends-its-money-how-texas-gets-its-money-why-it-doesnt-add-up.

REFERENCES

Cate, S. D. 2021. "The Mississippi Model: Dangers of Prison Reform in the Context of Fiscal Austerity." *Punishment & Society* 24(4): 715–741. https://doi.org/10.1177/1462474521 1006176.

Cavadino, M., and J. Dignan. 2006. *Penal Systems: A Comparative Approach*. London: Sage.

CDCR Today (Blog). 2011. "State Corrections Officials Join Stanislaus County in Breaking Ground for Juvenile Detention Facility." October 18. http://cdcrtoday.blogspot.com/2011/10/state-corrections-officials-join_18.html.

Center for Juvenile Justice Training & Research. 2002. "Pennsylvania Juvenile Court Dispositions 2002." https://www.jcjc.pa.gov/Research-Statistics/Disposition%20Reports/2002%20Pennsylvania%20Juvenile%20Court%20Disposition%20Report-Part1.pdf.

Cervantes, B. 2012. "Detention Center Expansion Aims to Ease Overcrowding." *Amarillo (TX) Globe-News*, February 8.

Chambers, B., and A. Balck. 2014. "Because Kids Are Different: Five Opportunities for Reforming the Juvenile Justice System." MacArthur Foundation. http://www.modelsforchange.net/publications/718.

Change Happens. 2022. "Mission Statement." https://www.changehappenstx.org/

Chávez, S. M. 2017. "Behind Oklahoma, Texas Has Made Deepest Cuts to State Education Funding in Past Decade." KERA News, November 30. https://www.keranews.org/post/behind-oklahoma-texas-has-made-deepest-cuts-state-education-funding-past-decade.

Chávez-García, M. 2012. *States of Delinquency: Race and Science in the Making of California's Juvenile Justice System*. Berkeley: University of California Press.

Chen, A. S. 2009. *The Fifth Freedom: Jobs, Politics, and Civil Rights in the United States, 1941–1972*. Princeton, NJ: Princeton University Press.

Chief Probation Officers of California. 2018. "Governor Brown Signs Transitional Age Youth Pilot Program Legislation Relying on Mounting Brain Research of Treatment Options for Youthful Offenders Age 18–21." October 3. https://www.cpoc.org/post/governor-brown-signs-transitional-age-youth-pilot-program-legislation-relying-mounting-brain.

Chowkwanyun, M. (2015). "Grassroots Isn't Always the Best: Community Development and Its Woes." *Boston Review*. http://bostonreview.net/books-ideas/merlin-chowkwanyun-daniel-immerwahr-thinking-small.

Chuck, E. 2019. "12-Year-Old Charged with Capital Murder Spotlights Justice System Ill-Equipped for Juveniles." NBC News, January 25. https://www.nbcnews.com/news/us-news/12-year-old-charged-capital-murder-spotlights-justice-system-ill-n962886.

City of Philadelphia. 2022. "E^3 Services." https://www.phila.gov/programs/e3-services/.

Clarke, M. 2012. "Texas Teenager Killed at Private Juvenile Detention Center." *Prison Legal News*, August 15. https://www.prisonlegalnews.org/news/2012/aug/15/texas-teenager-killed-at-private-juvenile-detention-center/.

Clarke, M. 2014. "Despite Reforms, Juvenile Offenders in Texas Remain Endangered." *Prison Legal News*. June 5.

Clarke, P., D. L. Meyer, B. Warner. 2009. "Juvenile Justice Operational Master Plan: Blueprint for an Outcome Oriented Juvenile Justice System." California State Commission on Juvenile Justice. http://www.cdcr.ca.gov/reports_research/docs/JJOMP_Final_Report.pdf.

Clear, T. R. 2010. "Policy and Evidence: The Challenge to the American Society of Criminology: 2009 Presidential Address to the American Society of Criminology." *Criminology* 48(1): 1–25.

Clear, T. R., and D. Schrantz. 2011. "Strategies for Reducing Prison Populations." *Prison Journal* 91(3 Supplement): 138S–159S.

Clegg, J., and A. Usmani. (2019). "The Economic Origins of Mass Incarceration." *Catalyst Journal*, December. https://catalyst-journal.com/2019/12/the-economic-origins-of-mass-incarceration.

Clouser, M. 1994. "Reducing Minority Youth Over-Representation." In *Pennsylvania Progress*, vol. 1, issue 1. Pittsburgh, PA: National Center for Juvenile Justice.

Cloward, R. A. and L. E. Ohlin. 1960. *Delinquency and Opportunity: A Study of Delinquent Gangs.* New York: Routledge.

Coen, R., C. Tung, C. Koningisor, and C. Crump. 2017. "Electronic Monitoring of Youth in the California Juvenile Justice System." University of California Berkley Law. https://www.law.berkeley.edu/wp-content/uploads/2017/04/Report_Final_Electronic_Monitoring.pdf.

Cohen, D. M. 2014. "Juvenile Justice System Primed for Private Sector Partnership." Texas Public Policy Foundation. http://www.texas policy.com/center/ effective-justice/opinions/juvenile-justice-system-primed-private-sector-partnership.

Cohen, M. 2020. "Can Fourteen- and Fifteen-Year-Olds Be Transferred to Adult Court in California? A Conceptual Roadmap to the Senate Bill 1391 Litigation." *UCLA Law Review Discourse* 67 (January 25): 199–200.

Cohen, S. 2007. "Rethinking Juvenile Justice System." *Fort Worth Star-Telegram*, December 2.

Cohn, G. 2014. "Creative Destruction at a California Juvenile Lockup." *Juvenile Justice Information Exchange*, May 21. http://jjie.org/creative-destruction-at-a-calif-juvenile-lockup/.

Collier, R. B., and D. Collier. 1991. *Shaping the Political Arena: Critical Junctures, the Labor Movement, and Regime Dynamics in Latin America.* Princeton, NJ: Princeton University Press.

Commonweal. 2014. "Our Role." https://www.comjj.org/realignment/our-role/.

Commonweal. 2015. "California Budget Report: Governor Signs On-Time California Budget." http://www.comjj.org/updates/budget/.

Cook, K. 2017. "Higher Education Funding in California." Public Policy Institute of California. https://www.ppic.org/wp-content/uploads/content/pubs/jtf/JTF_HigherEducationFundingJTF.pdf.

Copelin, L. 2007a. "Agency Overhaul Moves Forward." *Austin American-Statesman*, April 12.

Copelin, L. 2007b. "House Panel Approves Cleanup Plan." *Austin American-Statesman*, May 4.

Cornerstone Programs. 2014. About Us. http://www.cornerstonepro grams.com/index.php/about-us.

CorrectionalOfficerEDU. 2016. "Corrections Officers Salaries." http://www.correctionalofficer edu.org/salaries/.

Cortez et al. *v.* Oldham, 346 F. Supp. 3d 1141 (W.D. Tenn. 2018).

Council of Juvenile Correctional Administrators. 2011. "Issue Brief: Pepper Spray in Juvenile Facilities." http://cjca.net/attachments/article/172/CJCA. Issue.Brief.OCSpray.pdf.

Cowie, J. 2016. *The Great Exception.* Princeton, NJ: Princeton University Press.

Crawford, A. 1999. "Questioning Appeals to Community within Crime Prevention and Control." *European Journal on Criminal Policy and Research* 7(4): 509–530.

Crunchbase. 2019. "Assessments.com." https://www.crunchbase.com/organization/assessments-com.

Curran, D. J. 1988. "Destructuring, Privatization, and the Promise of Juvenile Diversion: Compromising Community-Based Corrections." *Crime & Delinquency* 34(4): 363–378.

Dagan, D., and S. M. Teles. 2016. *Prison Break: Why Conservatives Turned against Mass Incarceration.* New York, NY: Oxford University Press.

Dallas Morning News. 2007. "A Fix Closer to Home: Wiser Spending Can Help TYC Get House in Order." Editorial. November 11.

Daly, L. 2011. "Juvenile Justice Agencies: Summary of Sunset Legislation—82nd Legislature." Sunset Advisory Commission. https://www.sunset.texas.gov/public/uploads/files/reports/Youth%20Commission_Juvenile%20Probation_Ombudsman%20SOL%202011%2082%20leg.pdf.

Davis, A., A. Irvine, and J. Ziedenberg. 2014. "Examining the Role of States in Monitoring Conditions and Outcomes for Youth." National Council on Crime & Delinquency. http://nccdglobal.org/sites/default/files/publication_pdf/oversight-info-sheet.pdf.

Davis, C. 2018. "Calif. Juvenile Detention Center Uses Excessive Force, Class Action Says." Top Class Actions: Connecting Consumers to Settlements, Lawsuits and Attorneys. https://topc

lassactions.com/lawsuit-settlements/lawsuit-news/836468-calif-juvenile-detention-center-uses-excessive-force-class-action-says.

Dawood, N. 2009. "Juvenile Justice at a Crossroads: The Future of Senate Bill 81 in California." *Prison Law Office.* https://www.ojp.gov/ncjrs/virtual-library/abstracts/juvenile-justice-crossroads-future-senate-bill-81-california.

Death Penalty Information Center. 2015. "Juvenile Offenders Who Were on Death Row." http://www.deathpenaltyinfo.org/juvenile-offenders-who-were-death-row.

Dees, J. G., and B. B. Anderson. 2003. "Sector-Bending: Blurring Lines between Nonprofit and For-Profit." *Society* 40(4): 16–27.

Deitch, M., A. Barstow, L. Lukens, and R. Reyna. 2009. *From Time Out to Hard Time: Young Children in the Adult Criminal Justice System.* Austin: University of Texas at Austin, LBJ School of Public Affairs.

Deitch, M., A. L. Galbraith, and J. Pollock. 2012. *Conditions for Certified Juveniles in Texas County Jails.* Austin: University of Texas at Austin, LBJ School of Public Affairs.

Deitch, M., A. Madore, K. Vickery, and A. Welch. 2013. "Understanding and Addressing Youth Violence in the Texas Juvenile Justice Department: Report to the Office of the Independent Ombudsman." Austin, TX: Lyndon B. Johnson School of Public Affairs.

Denton County, Texas. 2014a. "Juvenile Anger Management, Parenting Classes, and Truancy." http://www.orgsites.com/tx/dentoncounty/_pgg8.php3.

Denton County, Texas. 2014b. "Juvenile Probation: Post Adjudication." http://dentoncounty.com/Departments/Probation/Juvenile-Probation/Juvenile-Post-Adjudication.aspx.

Deutsch, A. 1950. *Our Rejected Children.* Boston: Little, Brown.

Dexheimer, E. 2018. "Miles from Anywhere, Texas Military School Faces Closure." *The Austin American–Statesman,* May 30.

DiMaggio, P. J., H. K. Anheier. 1990. "The Sociology of Nonprofit Organizations and Sectors." *Annual Review of Sociology* 16: 137–159.

Disability Rights Advocates. 2019. "G.F. et al. v. Contra Costa County et al." https://dralegal.org/case/g-f-et-al-v-contra-costa-county-et-al/#files.

Disability Rights California. 2016. "Report on Inspection of the San Diego Juvenile Detention Facilities." February 23. https://www.disabilityrightsca.org/system/files?file=file-attachments/703001.pdf. Doerr, D. 2008. "Local Officials Dismiss Talk of Abolishing TYC." *Waco (TX) Tribune-Herald,* April 13.

Domback, D., B. Lawrence. 2018. "Demystifying Act 21 of 2003 and the Sexual Responsibility and Treatment Program." Pennsylvania Department of Human Services. https://www.jcjc.pa.gov/Program-Areas/AnnualConference/Documents/2018%20Conference%20Documents/Demystifying%20Act%2021%20and%20the%20Sexual%20Responsibility%20and%20Treatment%20Program.pdf.

Domhoff, G. W. 2009. "The Power Elite and Their Challengers: The Role of Nonprofits in American Social Conflict." *American Behavioral Scientist* 52(7): 955–973.

Domhoff, G. W. 2017. *The Power Elite and the State: How Policy Is Made in America.* New York, NY: Routledge.

Dowie, M. 2001. *American Foundations: An Investigative History.* Cambridge, MA: MIT Press.

Drum, K. 2013. "Lead: America's Real Criminal Element: The Hidden Villain behind Violent Crime, Lower IQs, and Even the ADHD Epidemic.: *Mother Jones,* February. https://www.motherjones.com/environment/2016/02/lead-exposure-gasoline-crime-increase-children-health/.

Durand, M. 2012a. "County Analyzes State Budget Hit." *San Mateo (CA) Daily Journal,* January 25.

Durand, M. 2012b. "County Assessing State Budget Hit." *San Mateo (CA) Daily Journal,* July 6.

Dzur, A. W. 2011. "Restorative Justice and Democracy: Fostering Public Accountability for Criminal Justice." *Contemporary Justice Review* 14(4): 367–381.

Eason, J. M. 2017. *Big House on the Prairie: Rise of the Rural Ghetto and Prison Proliferation.* Chicago: University of Chicago Press.

Ecenbarger, W. 2012. *Kids for Cash: Two Judges, Thousands of Children and a $2.6 Million Kickback Scheme*. New York: New Press.
Edelman, P. 2002. "American Government and the Politics of Youth." In *A Century of Juvenile Justice*, ed. D. S. Taenehaus, M. K. Rosenheim, F. E. Zimring, and B. Dohrn, 315–316. Chicago: University of Chicago Press.
Edsall, T. B. 1989. "The Changing Shape of Power: A Realignment in Public Policy." In *The Rise and Fall of the New Deal Order, 1930–1980*, ed. G. Gerstle and S. Fraser, 269–293. Princeton, NJ: Princeton University Press.
El Paso County v. Solorzano, 351 S.W.3d 577 (Tex. App. 2011). https://caselaw.findlaw.com/tx-court-of-appeals/1580757.html.
Electronic Frontier Foundation. n.d. "Street-Level Surveillance: Electronic Monitoring." https://www.eff.org/pages/electronic-monitoring.
Eliasoph, N. 2013. *The Politics of Volunteering*. Malden, MA: Polity Press.
Emison, C. 2011. "Changing Approach: TYC Could Be Dismantled for New Agency." *Abilene (TX) Reporter-News*, April 10.
Emslie, A. 2017. "Alameda County Court Dispute with Software Vendor Escalates, Could Spark Litigation." KQED, February 7. https://www.kqed.org/news/11305903/alameda-county-court-dispute-with-software-vendor-escalates-could-spark-litigation.
EPISCenter. 2014. "Multisystemic Therapy in Pennsylvania: Three Years of Data, Fiscal Years 2012–2014." http://www.episcenter.psu.edu/sites/default/ files/ebp/MST-Three-Year-Report-FINAL.pdf.
Every Texan. 2020a. "Jobs and Financial Security; Fair Wages and Savings." https://everytexan.org/our-work/policy-areas/jobs-financial-security/fair-wages/.
Every Texan. 2020b. "Policy Areas: Budget and Taxes: Property Taxes." https://everytexan.org/our-work/policy-areas/budget-taxes/where-money-comes-from/property-taxes/.
Ewing, M. 2017. "Philly's Gang Violence Strategy Doesn't Work. Here's Why." *The Appeal*, December 21. https://theappeal.org/former-lead-social-worker-says-philly-violence-reduction-strategy-fails-to-deliver-on-promises-a2b8a95df8af/.
Fabelo, T. 1999. "Monitoring the Use of Progressive Sanction Guidelines." *Criminal Justice Policy Council*. http://www.lbb.state.tx.us/Public_Safety_ Criminal_Justice/Reports/psanctmonitoring.pdf.
Fabelo, T., N. Arrigona, and M. D. Thompson. 2015. "Closer to Home: An Analysis of the State and Local Impact of the Texas Juvenile Justice Reforms." Council of State Governments. http://csgjusticecenter.org/wp-content/uploads/2015/01/texas-JJ-reform-closer-to-home.pdf.
Faber, D., and D. McCarthy. 2005. *Foundations for Social Change: Critical Perspectives on Philanthropy and Popular Movements*. Lanham, MD: Rowman & Littlefield.
Fagan, J., and F. E. Zimring, eds. 2000. *The Changing Borders of Juvenile Justice: Transfer of Adolescents to the Criminal Court*. Chicago: University of Chicago Press.
Fair Punishment Project. 2016. "Juvenile Life without Parole in Philadelphia: A Time for Hope?" Philips Black Project. http://fairpunishment.org/wp-content/uploads/2016/03/FPP_JLWOP_philadelphia_r601.pdf.
Fair Sentencing for Youth. 2016. "Senate Bill 9: California Fair Sentencing for Youth." http://fairsentencingforyouth.org/legislation/senate-bill-9-california-fair-sentencing-for-youth/.
Farivar, C. 2016. Lawyers: New Court Software Is So Awful It's Getting People Wrongly Arrested." *ARS Technica*. https://arstechnica.com/tech-policy/2016/12/court-software-glitches-result-in-erroneous-arrests-defense-lawyers-say/.
Farrell v. Beard, No. RG 03079344 (Cal. Super. Ct., Alameda Cnty. July 28, 2014).
Featherstone, L., D. Henwood, and C. Parenti. 2004. "'Action Will Be Taken': Left Anti-Intellectualism and Its Discontents." *Radical Society*, debut issue. https://www.leftbusinessobserver.com/Action.html.
Feeley, M. 2002. "Entrepreneurs of Punishment: The Legacy of Privatization." *Punishment & Society* 4(3): 321–344.

Feld, B. C. 1991. "Justice by Geography: Urban, Suburban, and Rural Variations in Juvenile Justice Administration." *Journal of Criminal Law & Criminology* 82: 156–210.

Feld, B. C. 1999. *Bad Kids: Race and the Transformation of the Juvenile Court*. New York, NY: Oxford University Press.

Feld, B. C. 2013. "Youth Discount: Old Enough to Do the Crime, Too Young to Do the Time." *Ohio State Journal of Criminal Law* 11: 107–148.

Feld, B. C., and S. Schaefer. 2010. "The Right to Counsel in Juvenile Court: Law Reform to Deliver Legal Services and Reduce Justice by Geography." *Criminology & Public Policy* 9(2): 327–356.

Ferdik, F. V., and H. P. Smith. 2017. *Correctional Officer Safety and Wellness Literature Synthesis*. Washington, DC: U.S. Department of Justice, National Institute of Justice.

Ferguson, J. W. 2012. "Decision on Juvenile Sentences Stirs Questions in Texas." *Texas Tribune*, June 26.

Ferguson, T. 1989. "Industrial Conflict and the Coming of the New Deal: The Triumph of Multinational Liberalism in America." In *The Rise and Fall of the New Deal Order, 1930–1980*, ed. G. Gerstle and S. Fraser, 3–31. Princeton, NJ: Princeton University Press.

Feuer, Mike. n.d. "Los Angeles City Attorney's Gang Unit." https://www.lacityattorney.org/gang-division. Flamm, M. 2005. *The Crisis of Liberalism: Street Crime, Civil Unrest and the Crisis of Liberalism in the 1960s*. New York: Columbia University Press.

Fleishman, J. 2007. *The Foundation: A Great American Secret. How Private Wealth Is Changing the World*. New York: PublicAffairs.

Fleury, J. B. 2019. "Social Scientists on Crime after World War II." SSRN, December 10. https://ssrn.com/abstract=3313388.

Flynn, M. 2018. "Harris County Jails Hundreds of Juveniles Each Year for Minor Probation Violations." *Houston Chronicle*. January 31.

Fong, B. Y., and M. Naschek. 2021. "NGOism: The Politics of the Third Sector." *Catalyst* 5(1). https://catalyst-journal.com/2021/05/ngoism-the-politics-of-the-third-sector.

Forman, J., Jr. 2017. *Locking Up Our Own: Crime and Punishment in Black America*. New York: Farrar, Straus, and Giroux.

Fortner, M. J. 2015. *Black Silent Majority: The Rockefeller Drug Laws and the Politics of Punishment*. Cambridge, MA: Harvard University Press.

Frederick, H. 2017. "Problems at Pittsburgh's Shuman Juvenile Detention Center Reflect Larger Issues in the Integrity of the Juvenile-Justice System." *Pittsburgh City Paper*, December 6. https://www.pghcitypaper.com/pittsburgh/problems-at-pittsburghs-shuman-juvenile-detention-center-reflect-larger-issues-in-the-integrity-of-the-juvenile-justice-system/Content?oid=5655695.

Fritsch, E. J., and C. Hemmens. 1995. "An Assessment of Legislative Approaches to the Problem of Serious Juvenile Crime: A Case Study of Texas 1973–1995." *American Journal of Criminal Law* 23: 563–610.

G.F., et al. v. Contra Costa County, et al. C13-3667 (2014).

G4S USA. 2015. "Who We Are." http://www.g4s.us/en-US/Who%20we%20are/.

Garcia-Leys, S., and N. Brown. 2019. "Analysis of the Attorney General's Annual Report on CalGang For 2018." Urban Peace Institute. https://www.courthousenews.com/wp-content/uploads/2019/09/CalGang.pdf.

Garland, D. 2001. *The Culture of Control: Crime and Social Order in Contemporary Society*. Chicago: University of Chicago Press.

Gartner, L. 2019. "At Glen Mills Schools, Boys Are Beaten, Then Silenced." *Philadelphia Inquirer*, March 28. https://www.inquirer.com/crime/a/glen-mills-schools-pa-abuse-juvenile-investigation-20190220.html.

Gately, G. 2014. "Juvenile Solitary Confinement: Modern-Day 'Torture' in the U.S." *Juvenile Justice Information Exchange*, March 5. http://jjie.org/juvenile-solitary-confinement-modern-day-torture-in-the-u-s/.

Gearan, A., and A. Phillip. 2016. "Clinton Regrets 1996 Remark on 'Super-Predators' after Encounter with Activist." Washington Post, February 25. Retrieved from: https://www.was

hingtonpost.com/news/post-politics/wp/2016/02/25/clinton-heckled-by-black-lives-matter-activist/.

GEO Group, Inc. 2014. "The Leader in Alternatives to Detention Proven to Reduce Recidivism." http://geogroup.com/reentry_services.

GEO Group, Inc. 2016. "Abraxas." https://www.hrapply.com/gginc/AppJob View.jsp?link=58048&page=AppJobList.jsp.

George, C. 2016. "Proposed Southlawn Gang Injunction Protested at Meeting." *Chron*, February 25. https://www.chron.com/news/houston-texas/houston/article/Proposed-Southlawn-gang-injunction-protested-at-6855395.php.

Gerber, M. 2015. "California Inmate's Parole Reflects Rethinking of Life Terms for Youths." *Los Angeles Times*, March 24. http://www.latimes.com /local/crime/la-me-juvenile-lwop-20150325-story.html.

Gerstle, G., and S. Fraser, eds. 1990. *The Rise and Fall of the New Deal Order, 1930–1980*. Princeton, NJ: Princeton University Press.

Gibson, C., and D. M. Vandiver. 2008. *Juvenile Sex Offenders: What the Public Needs to Know*. Westport, CT: Greenwood.

Gilens, M., and B. I. Page. 2014. *Testing Theories of American Politics: Elites, Interest Groups, and Average Citizens*. Cambridge: Cambridge University Press.

Gillstrom, H. 2016. "Clinton's 'Superpredators' Comment Most Damaging by Either Candidate." *The Hill*, September 30. https://thehill.com/blogs/pundits-blog/crime/298693-hillary-clintons-superpredators-still-the-most-damaging-insult-by.

Gilmore, R. W. 2007. *Golden Gulag: Prisons, Surplus, Crisis, and Opposition in Globalizing California*. Berkeley: University of California Press.

Giridharadas, A. 2018. *Winners Take All: The Elite Charade of Changing the World*. New York: Knopf.

Goldeen, J. 2019. "In Visit to O. H. Close, Governor Calls Importance of Prison Training Program 'Basic.'" *Recordnet.com*. https://www.recordnet.com/news/20190127/in-visit-to-oh-close-governor-calls-importance-of-prison-training-program-basic.

Goodman, P., J. Page, and M. Phelps. 2017. *Breaking the Pendulum: The Long Struggle over Criminal Justice*. New York, NY: Oxford University Press.

Goodstein, L., and H. Sontheimer. 1997. "The Implementation of an Intensive Aftercare Program for Serious Juvenile Offenders: A Case Study." *Criminal Justice and Behavior* 24(3): 332–359.

Goss, S. (2006). "Pennsylvania Juvenile Justice Newsletter." *Pennsylvania Juvenile Court Judges' Commission*. jcjc.pa.gov/Publications/Newsletters/2006/October.pdf.

Gotsch, K., and V. Basti. 2018. "Capitalizing on Mass Incarceration: U.S. Growth in Private Prisons." The Sentencing Project, August 2. https://www.sentencingproject.org/publications/capitalizing-on-mass-incarceration-u-s-growth-in-private-prisons/.

Gottschalk, M. 2000. *The Shadow Welfare State: Labor, Business, and the Politics of Health Care in the United States*. Ithaca, NY: Cornell University Press.

Gottschalk, M. 2006. *The Prison and the Gallows: The Politics of Mass Incarceration in America*. Cambridge: Cambridge University Press.

Gottschalk, M. 2011. "The Past, Present, and Future of Mass Incarceration in the United States." *Criminology & Public Policy* 10(3): 483–504.

Gottschalk, M. 2015. *Caught: The Prison State and the Lockdown of American Politics*. Princeton, NJ: Princeton University Press.

Gottschalk, M. 2020. "Caught in the Countryside: Race, Class, and Punishment in Rural America." *Rethinking Class and Social Difference, Political Power and Social Theory* 37: 25–52.

Graham v. Florida, 560 U.S. 48 (2010). https://www.oyez.org/cases/2009/08-7412.

Graham, L. 2010. "McReynolds: Prison Cuts 'Could Have Rippling Effects' across Texas." *Lufkin (TX) Daily News*, February 20.

Granite Public Affairs. n.d. "Juvenile Justice Reform: Improving Public Safety and Youth Outcomes within Available Revenue." https://www.texasappleseed.org/sites/default/files/48-JJReformpage.pdf.

Grasso, A. 2017. "Broken beyond Repair: Rehabilitative Penology and American Political Development." *Political Research Quarterly* 70(2): 394–407.

Gray, G. C. 2009. "The Responsibilization Strategy of Health and Safety Neo-liberalism and the Reconfiguration of Individual Responsibility for Risk." *British Journal of Criminology* 49(3): 326–342.

Green, C. 2015a. "Activists Report Security Company G4S to Police over Its 'Illegal' Work at Guantanamo Bay." *The Independent*, January 12. http://www.independent.co.uk/news/uk/crime/exclusive-activists-report-g4s-to-police-over-itsillegal-work-at-guantanamo-bay-9971328.html.

Green, C. 2015b. "Rainsbrook G4S Youth Prison Slammed by Ofsted Report as Children Suffer 'Racist,' 'Degrading' Abuse from Guards High on Drugs." *The Independent*, May 20. http://www.independent.co.uk/news/uk/home-news/rainsbrook-g4s-youth-prison-slammed-by-ofsted-report-as-children-suffer-racist-degrading-abuse-from-guards-high-on-drugs-10263121.html.

Greenblatt, A. 2019. *Trends in Philanthropy*. CQ Researcher. https://library.cqpress.com/cqresearcher/document.php?id=cqresrre2019030800

Greenwood, P. W., A. J. Lipson, A. Abrahamse, and F. Zimring. 1983. "Youth Crime and Juvenile Justice in California: A Report to the Legislature." RAND Corporation. http://www.rand.org/content/dam/rand/pubs/reports/2007/R3016.pdf.

Griffin, P. 2003. "Following the Money." In *Pennsylvania Progress*, vol. 10, no. 1, 1–10. Pittsburgh, PA: National Center for Juvenile Justice.

Griffin, P. 2008. "Doing Something about DMC." In *Pennsylvania Progress*, 1–8. Pittsburgh, PA: National Center for Juvenile Justice. http://www.ncjj.org/PDF/PA_Progress/PAProgress_dmc_2008.pdf

Griffin, P., and M. Hunninen. 2008. "Preparing Youth for Productive Futures." In *Pennsylvania Progress*, 1–12. Pittsburgh, PA: National Center for Juvenile Justice. https://www.modelsforchange.net/publications/202/Pennsylvania_Progress_Preparing_Youth_for_Productive_Futures.pdf

Griffith, J., S. Jirard, and M. Ricketts. 2012. *Pennsylvania Juvenile Justice Disproportionate Minority Contact (DMC) Monitoring, Reduction, and Prevention Efforts*. Shippensburg, PA: Center for Juvenile Justice Training and Research, Juvenile Court Judges' Commission.

Grissom, B. 2012a. "Phoenix Program Aims to Transform Troubled Youths. *Texas Tribune*, September 2.

Grissom, B. 2012b. "Report: Local Youth Programs Need More Funds, Oversight." *Texas Tribune*, October 17. http://www.texastribune.org/2012/10/17/report-local-youth-programs-need-more-funds-oversi/.

Grissom, B. 2013. "Proposed Rules Could Increase Use of Pepper Spray on Youths." *Texas Tribune*, October 31. https://www.texastribune.org/2013/10/31/proposed-rules-would-allow-increased-use-pepper-sp/.

Grissom, B. 2016. "Sexual Abuse Allegations, Suicide Attempts Follow Jump in Juvenile Offender Population. *Dallas Morning News*, October 28. https://www.dallasnews.com/news/texas/2016/10/28/sexual-abuse-allegations-suicide-attempts-follow-jump-in-juvenile-offender-population/.

Grissom, B., and R. Aaronson. 2012. "Despite Reform, Violence Rises among Youths at Juvenile Lockups." *Texas Tribune*, February 12. https://flatpage-archive.texastribune.org/library/data/tjjd-youth-violence-up/.

Grissom, B., and S. Ambrose. 2017a. "Four Officers Facing Prison Time in Sexual Misconduct Scandal at State Youth Lockup." *Dallas Morning News*, November 7. https://www.dallasnews.com/news/politics/2017/11/07/four-officers-facing-prison-time-in-sexual-misconduct-scandal-at-state-youth-lockup/.

Grissom, B., and S. Ambrose. 2017b. "Fights, Sex, Drugs: Texas Juvenile Lockup on the Verge of Crisis, Reports Show." *Dallas Morning News*, November 16. https://www.dallasnews.com/

news/investigations/2017/11/17/fights-sex-drugs-texas-juvenile-lockup-on-the-verge-of-crisis-reports-show/.
Grissom, B., and J. Serrano. 2013. "House OKs Life with Parole for Juvenile Murderers." *Texas Tribune*, July 11. https://www.texastribune.org/2013/07/11/senate-approves-key-special-session-measures/.
Guckenburg, S., A. Stern, H. Sutherland, G. Lopez, and A. Petrosino. 2019. *Juvenile Detention Alternatives Initiative Scale-Up: Study of Four States*. San Francisco, CA: WestEd. https://www.wested.org/resources/juvenile-detention-alternatives-initiative-scale-up-study-of-four-states/.
GuideStar. 2016. "Alternative Rehabilitation Communities, Inc." http://www.guidestar.org/View Pdf.aspx?PdfSource=0&ein=25-1291039.
GuideStar. 2021. "P.A.C.E. Youth Programs Inc." https://www.guidestar.org/profile/86-1095495.
Hacker, J. S. 2002. *The Divided Welfare State: The Battle over Public and Private Social Benefits in the United States*. Cambridge: Cambridge University Press.
Hacker, J. S. 2004. "Privatizing Risk without Privatizing the Welfare State: The Hidden Politics of Social Policy Retrenchment in the United States." *American Political Science Review* 98(2): 243–260.
Hager, E. 2015. "Our Prisons in Black and White." *Marshall Project*, November 18.
Hall, B. 2012. "Creating Possibilities Today for New Tomorrows." Paceyouth.org. http://www.paceyouth.org/pdf/GEO-Care-Foundation-2013.pdf.
Hambright, B. 2012. "New Law Gives Lancaster County Judges Discretion in Sentencing Juvenile Killers." *LancasterOnline*, November 4. http://lancasteronline.com/news/new-law-gives-lancaster-county-judges-discretion-in-sentencing-juvenile/article_8de7d9c9-26d3-5031-a0e5-1acd0e6ac6b7.html.
Hammack, D. C., ed. 1998. *Making the Nonprofit Sector in the United States: A Reader*. Bloomington: Indiana University Press.
Haney, C. 2003. "Mental Health Issues in Long-Term Solitary and 'Supermax' Confinement." *Crime & Delinquency* 49(1): 124–156.
Harcourt, B. E. 2015. "Risk as a Proxy for Race: The Dangers of Risk Assessment." *Federal Sentencing Reporter* 27(4): 237–243.
Harris, K. D. 2010. "Organized Crime in California." California Department of Justice. http://oag.ca.gov/sites/all/files/agweb/pdfs/publications/org_crime2010.pdf.
Hasan, S. 2015. "Harris County Wins MacArthur Foundation's Criminal Justice Challenge." *Houston Public Media*, May 27. http://www.houstonpublicmedia.org/articles/news/2015/05/27/60627/harris-county-wins-macarthur-foundations-criminal-justice-challenge/.
Hays Free Press News-Dispatch (Kyle, TX). 2011. "Former Guard Gets Eight Years for Juvenile Detention Center Abuse." April 13. https://haysfreepress.com/2011/04/13/former-guard-gets-eight-years-for-juvenile-detention-center-abuse/.
HealthRIGHT 360. 2022. "Stand Tall." https://www.healthright360.org/program/stand-tall.
Hennigan, K., K. Kolnick, J. Poplawski, A. Andrews, N. Ball, C. Cheng, and J. Payne. 2007. "Juvenile Justice Data Project: Phase 1." University of California Center for Research on Crime. http://www.cdcr.ca.gov/Reports_Research/docs/JJDPSurveyFinalReport.pdf.
Hernandez, E. 2007a. "House Passes TYC Overhaul." *Brownsville (TX) Herald*, May 8.
Hernandez, E. 2007b. "Lawmakers Want New TYC Ombudsman to Visit Facilities Often." *Brownsville (TX) Herald*, June 29.
Hernandez, E. 2007c. "TYC Overhaul Bill Clears Committee." *The Monitor (McAllen, TX)*. April 11.
Hertel-Fernandez, A. 2019. *State Capture: How Conservative Activists, Big Businesses, and Wealthy Donors Reshaped American States—and the Nation*. New York, NY: Oxford University Press.
Herz, D. C., K. Chan, S. K. Lee, M. N. Ross, J. McCroskey, M. Newell, and C. Fraser. 2015. "The Los Angeles County Juvenile Probation Outcomes Study." Advancement Project. https://file.lacounty.gov/SDSInter/bos/supdocs/92794.pdf.

Himmelstein, D. U., and S. Woolhandler. 2008. "Privatization in a Publicly Funded Health Care System: The U.S. Experience." *International Journal of Health Services: Planning, Administration, Evaluation* 38(3): 407–419. https://doi.org/10.2190/HS.38.3.a.

Hinton, E. 2016. *From the War on Poverty to the War on Crime: The Making of Mass Incarceration in America*. Cambridge, MA: Harvard University Press.

Hockenberry, S., M. Sickmund, and A. Sladky. 2015. "Juvenile Residential Facility Census, 2012: Selected Findings." U.S. Office of Juvenile Justice and Delinquency Prevention. http://www.ojjdp.gov/pubs/247207.pdf.

Hollingsworth v. Orange County (Ca. 1990). https://caselaw.findlaw.com/ca-court-of-appeal/1845449.html.

Hudson, N. 2013. "Senator Jose Rodriguez: Senate Bill 2 'Likely Unconstitutional.'" *Burnt Orange Report*. July 15.

Human Rights Watch. 2012. "Growing Up Locked Down: Youth in Solitary Confinement in Jails and Prisons across the United States." http://www.hrw.org/sites/default/files/reports/us1012ForUpload.pdf.

Human Rights Watch. 2013. "Raised on the Registry: The Irreparable Harm of Placing Children on Sex Offender Registries in the U.S." https://www.hrw.org/report/2013/05/01/raised-registry/irreparable-harm-placing-children-sex-offender-registries-us#.

Hunt v. County of Los Angeles (Ca. 1986). https://caselaw.findlaw.com/ca-court-of-appeal/1772100.html.

Hunt, D. 2011. "Tarrant Juvenile Justice Officials Wary about New Combined State Agency." *Fort Worth Star-Telegram*, December 5.

Hunter, G. 2008. "Scandal Rocks Texas Youth Commission; Youths Molested by School Supervisors." *Prison Legal News*, February 15. https://www.prisonlegalnews.org/news/2008/feb/15/scandal-rocks-texas-youth-commission-youths-molested-by-school-supervisors/.

Immerwahr, D. 2015. *Thinking Small: The United States and the Lure of Community Development*. Cambridge, MA: Harvard University Press.

Independent Ombudsman for the Texas Juvenile Justice Department. 2013. "Phoenix Program Special Report." https://www.documentcloud.org/documents/813666-texas-juvenile-justice-department-special-report.html.

Institute on Money in State Politics. 2006. "Policy Lockdown: Prison Interests Court Political Players." http://www.privateci.org/private_pics/follow.pdf.

Interbranch Commission on Juvenile Justice. 2010. "Final Report on Implementation on Recommendations of the Interbranch Commission on Juvenile Justice." http://www.pacourts.us/news-and-statistics/archived-resources/interbranch-commission-on-juvenile-justice.

Isserman, M., and M. Kazin. 1989. "The Failure and Success of the New Radicalism." In *The Rise and Fall of the New Deal Order, 1930–1980*, ed. G. Gerstle and S. Fraser, 212–242. Princeton, NJ: Princeton University Press.

Jails to Jobs. 2021. "Jails to Jobs: Transforming Youth Transforming Justice." https://www.jailtojobs.com.

Jane G. v. Solano County (Ca. 1985). https://www.ylc.org/wp-content/uploads/2018/11/JaneGsettlement.pdf.

Jannetta, J., and J. Lin. 2007. "The Role of the DJJ in the California Juvenile Justice System." UC Irvine Center for Evidence-Based Corrections. http://ucicorrections.seweb.uci.edu/files/2013/06/The-Role-of-the-DJJ-in-the-CA-Juvenile-Justice-System1.pdf.

Jenkins, J. C. 1986. *Foundation Funding of Progressive Social Movements*. The Grant Seekers Guide. Mt. Kisco, NY: Moyer Bell Lyt.

Jenkins, J. C., J. T. Carmichael, R. J. Brulle, and H. Boughton. 2017. "Foundation Funding of the Environmental Movement." *American Behavioral Scientist* 61(13): 1640–1657. https://doi.org/10.1177/0002764217744839.

Johnson, C. 2017. "The Panthers Can't Save Us Now." *Catalyst*, November. https://catalyst-journal.com/2017/11/panthers-cant-save-us-cedric-johnson.

Johnson, C. 2019. "What Black Life Actually Looks Like." *Jacobin Magazine*, April. https://jacobinmag.com/2019/04/racism-black-lives-matter-inequality.

Johnson, C. 2022. *The Panthers Can't Save Us Now: Debating Left Politics and Black Lives Matter.* Brooklyn, NY: Verso Books.

Johnson, K., and E. Surtees. 2021. *DOJ Opens Statewide Investigation into Abuse of Youth in Texas' Juvenile Facilities.* Austin, TX: Texas Appleseed. https://www.texasappleseed.org/press-releases/doj-opens-statewide-investigation-abuse-youth-texas%E2%80%99-juvenile-facilities.

Johnson, K. D. (2010). "Certifications in Texas: A General Overview." Nuts and Bolts of Juvenile Law: Austin, TX. http://www.juvenilelaw.org/Articles/ 2010/NB/Johnson.pdf.

Johnson, M. 1998. "Texas Revised Juvenile Justice and Education Codes: Not All Change Is Good." *Journal of Juvenile Law* 19(1): 1–45.

Johnson, N., P. Oliff, and E. William. 2011. "An Update on State Budget Cuts: At Least 46 States Have Imposed Cuts That Hurt Vulnerable Residents and the Economy." Center on Budget and Policy Priorities. https://www.cbpp.org/sites/default/files/atoms/files/3-13-08sfp.pdf.

Joint Venture Program. 2021. "Free Venture Program." June 16. https://jointventureprogram.calpia.ca.gov/free-venture-program/.

Jones v. Mississippi, 593 U.S. 2021. https://www.oyez.org/cases/2020/18-1259.

Jordan, H. 2015. "Beyond Zero Tolerance: Discipline and Policing in Pennsylvania Public Schools." American Civil Liberties Union of Pennsylvania. https://www.aclupa.org/files/5714/2436/0535/2-16-2015_FINAL_64204_ACLU_ONLINE.pdf.

Joseph, G. 2016. "The Private Prison Industry's New Criminal Justice Ventures." *Bloomberg CityLab*, September 14. https://www.bloomberg.com/news/articles/2016-09-14/private-prison-industry-invests-in-for-profit-criminal-justice-companies.

Juvenile Justice Information Exchange. 2016. "Re-Entry Reform Trends." http://jjie.org/hub/reentry/reform-trends.

Kaplan, J. 2020. "Corporations Pay Far Less of Their California Income in State Taxes Than a Generation Ago—Even amid COVID-19." California Budget & Policy Center. https://calbudgetcenter.org/resources/corporations-pay-far-less-of-their-income-in-state-taxes/.

Katy (TX) News. 2019. "Staff Shortages, Violent Offenders Impacting Juvenile Justice Facilities." March 13. https://thekatynews.com/2019/03/13/staff-shortages-violent-offenders-impacting-juvenile-justice-facilities/.

Katz, M. B. 1989. *The Undeserving Poor: America's Enduring Confrontation with Poverty.* New York, NY: Oxford University Press.

Katz, M. B. 1995. *Improving Poor People.* Princeton, NJ: Princeton University Press.

Katz, M. B. 2002. *The Price of Citizenship: Redefining the American Welfare State.* New York, NY: Macmillan.

Katznelson, I. 1989. "Was the Great Society a Lost Opportunity?" In *The Rise and Fall of the New Deal Order, 1930–1980,* ed. G. Gerstle and S. Fraser, 185–211. Princeton, NJ: Princeton University Press.

Keller, B. (2015). "Prison Revolt." *The New Yorker*, June 29. https://www.newyorker.com/magazine/2015/06/29/prison-revolt.

Kemerer, F. 2008. *William Wayne Justice: A Judicial Biography.* Austin: University of Texas Press.

Kempf, K. L. 1992. "The Role of Race in Juvenile Justice Processing in Pennsylvania." Prepared for The Center for Juvenile Justice Training and Research, Shippensburg University, Shippensburg, PA.

Kerstein, R. J., and D. R. Judd. 1980. "Achieving Less Influence with More Democracy: The Permanent Legacy of the War on Poverty." *Social Science Quarterly* 61(2): 208–220.

Kettl, D. F. 2000. "The Transformation of Governance: Globalization, Devolution, and the Role of Government." *Public Administration Review* 60(6): 488–497.

King, R. D. 1999. "The Rise and Rise of Supermax: An American Solution in Search of a Problem?" *Punishment & Society* 1(2): 163–186.

Kirk, S. 2012. "Brown County Could Obtain Closed Juvenile Facility at No Cost from State." *Abilene (TX) Reporter-News*. http://www.reporternews.com/news/ big-country/brown-county-could-obtain-close-juvenile-at-no.

Klein, M. W. 1979. "Deinstitutionalization and Diversion of Juvenile Offenders: A Litany of Impediments." *Crime and Justice*, 1: 145–201.

Kleppe v. Superior Court of Marin County (Ca. 2010). https://www.ylc.org/lawsuit-filed-to-stop-marin-juvenile-court-hearings-by-videoconference/.

Kofman, A. 2019. "Digital Jail: How Electronic Monitoring Drives Defendants into Debt." ProPublica, July 3. https://www.propublica.org/article/digital-jail-how-electronic-monitoring-drives-defendants-into-debt.

Kohl-Arenas, E. 2015. *The Self-Help Myth: How Philanthropy Fails to Alleviate Poverty*. Berkeley: University of California Press.

Kohler, S. 2007. "Bedford-Stuyvesant and the Rise of the Community Development Corporation." In *Casebook for the Foundation: A Great American Secret*, ed. Joel L. Fleishman, Scott Kohler, and Steven Schindler, 94–99. New York: Public Affairs.

Koseff, A. 2015. "Former State Sen. Leland Yee Pleads Guilty to Corruption Charge." *Sacramento Bee*, July 1.

Krisberg, B. (2011). "The Long and Winding Road: Juvenile Corrections Reform in California." Report. Chief Justice Earl Warren Institute on Law and Social Policy, Berkeley.

Krisberg, B., P. Litsky, and I. Schwartz. 1984. "Youth in Confinement: Justice by Geography." *Journal of Research in Crime and Delinquency* 21(2): 153–181.

Krisberg, B., I. M. Schwartz, P. Litsky, and J. Austin. 1986. "The Watershed of Juvenile Justice Reform." *Crime & Delinquency* 32(1): 5–38.

Kwon, S. A. 2013. *Uncivil Youth: Race, Activism, and Affirmative Governmentality*. Durham, NC: Duke University Press.

Lafer, G. 2004. *The Job Training Charade*. Ithaca, NY: Cornell University Press.

Lafer, G. 2017. *The One Percent Solution: How Corporations Are Remaking America One State at a Time*. Ithaca, NY: Cornell University Press.

Lafferty, S., S. Ochoa, F. Nominati, and S. Burrell. 2017. "The Changing Landscape of Juvenile Transfer in the Wake of Proposition 57." PowerPoint slides. Beyond the Bench 24: Uniting for a Better Future, December 20. https://www.courts.ca.gov/documents/BTB24-5H-00PPT.pdf.

Lagos, M. 2012. "Brown Pushes $1 Billion in Cuts." *San Francisco Chronicle*, January 15.

Lahey, J. 2016. "The Steep Cost of Keeping Juveniles in Adult Prisons." *The Atlantic*, January 8. http://www.theatlantic.com/education/archive/2016/01/the-cost-of-keeping-juveniles-in-adult-prisons/423201/.

Lancaster, R. N. 2011. *Sex Panic and the Punitive State*. Berkeley: University of California Press.

Lancaster County, Pennsylvania. n.d. "Youth Intervention Center." https://www.co.lancaster.pa.us/165/Youth-Intervention-Center.

LancasterOnline Editorial Board. 2020. "County and State Need to Act to Ensure Safety of Children at Youth Intervention Center." February 16. https://lancasteronline.com/opinion/editorials/county-and-state-need-to-act-to-ensure-safety-of-children-at-youth-intervention-center/article_dd798ec4-4f7e-11ea-b190-3b91101e6776.html.

Larner, W. 2000. "Neo-liberalism: Policy, Ideology, Governmentality." *Studies in Political Economy* 63(1): 5–25.

The Last Mile: Paving the Road to Success. 2019. "About." https://thelastmile.org/about/.

Lauritsen, J. L., M. L. Rezey, and K. Heimer. 2016. "When Choice of Data Matters: Analyses of U.S. Crime Trends, 1973–2012." *Journal of Quantitative Criminology* 32(3): 335–355.

Lawrence, B., S. Barnes. 2014. "PA Sexual Responsibility and Treatment Program 10 Years in Review." Presentation. Juvenile Court Judges' Commission. http://www.jcjc.pa.gov/Program-Areas/AnnualConference/Documents/2014%20Conference%20Documents/ACT%2021.pdf.

Le, M. 2019. "Pennsylvania Harming Kids by Sending Them to Adult Prisons." *LehighValleyLive*, October 16. https://www.lehighvalleylive.com/opinion/2019/10/pennsylvania-harming-kids-by-sending-them-to-adult-prisons-opinion.html.
League of Women Voters of California. 2016. "Bill Status Report for 2007–2008 Legislative Session." http://archive.lwvc.org/lwvc/action/bsr/bsr_07oct.html.
Lee, F. 2013. *The Machine: A Field Guide to the Resurgent Right*. New York: The New Press.
Lee, R. C. 2009. "Breaking Cycle Of Youth Crime Area Counties To Focus On Mental Health Disorders." *Houston Chronicle*, November 28.
Leija, A. 2013. "G4S Lease Approved for Juvenile Justice Center." *Brownwood (TX) Bulletin*, March 12.
Lemert, E. M. 1970. *Social Action and Legal Change: Revolution within the Juvenile Court*. Chicago: Aldine.
Lena Pope. 2022. "Glossary." https://lenapope.org/glossary/.
Leon, C. S. 2011. *Sex Fiends, Perverts, and Pedophiles: Understanding Sex Crime Policy in America*. New York: New York University Press.
Leopold, L. 2015. *Runaway Inequality: An Activist's Guide to Economic Justice*. New York, NY: Labor Institute Press.
Lerman, P. 1984. "Child Welfare, the Private Sector, and Community-based Corrections." *Crime & Delinquency* 30(1): 5–38.
Levin, M. 2014. "The True Cost of Juvenile Incarceration." Texas Public Policy Foundation. http://www.texaspolicy.com/press_release/detail/the-true-cost-of-juvenile-incarceration.
Levin, M., and J. Moll. 2011. "Comprehensive Juvenile Justice Reform: Cutting Costs, Saving Lives." *The Texas Model: A Texas Public Policy Foundation Publication*, September. http://rightoncrime.com/wp-content/uploads/2011/09/Texas-Model-Juvenile.pdf.
Levin, S. 2015. "California Senate Passes Bill to Limit Youth Solitary Confinement." *East Bay Express* (Oakland, CA), June 3. http://m.eastbayexpress.com/ SevenDays/archives/2015/06/03/california-senate-passes-bill-to-limit-youth-solitary-confinement.
Levine, J. R. 2016. "The Privatization of Political Representation: Community-based Organizations as Nonelected Neighborhood Representatives." *American Sociological Review* 81(6): 1251–1275.
Lichtenstein, N. 1989. "From Corporatism to Collective Bargaining: Organized Labor and the Eclipse of Social Democracy in the Postwar Era." In *The Rise and Fall of the New Deal Order, 1930–1980*, ed. G. Gerstle and S. Fraser, 122–152. Princeton, NJ: Princeton University Press.
Lieberman, R. C. 1998. *Shifting the Color Line: Race and the American Welfare State*. Cambridge, Massachusetts: John Wiley & Sons.
Lindell, C. 2018. "Study Praises Texas Juvenile-Justice Reforms." *Statesmen News Network*, September 25. https://www.statesman.com/NEWS/20160924/Study-praises-Texas-juvenile-justice-reforms.
LinkedIn. 2021. "Pace Youth Programs Inc., Profile." https://www.linkedin.com/company/pace-youth-programs-inc.
Los Angeles Daily News. 2018. "Malibu's Camp Kilpatrick Was Supposed to Be the Face of Reform for L.A. County's Probation Department. But Watchdogs Are Sounding Alarm." September 23. https://www.dailynews.com/2018/09/23/malibus-camp-kilpatrick-was-supposed-to-be-the-face-of-reform-for-l-a-countys-probation-department-but-watchdogs-are-sounding-alarm/.
Los Angeles Police Department. n.d. "LAPD Online." https://www.lapdonline.org/.
Loudenback, J. 2016. "Buoyed by L.A.'s Rejection of Juvenile Solitary Confinement, Advocates Eye Elusive Sacramento Win." *Chronicle of Social Change: Children and Youth, Front and Center*. https://chronicleofsocialchange.org/justice/juvenile-justice-2/buoyed-l-s-reject ion-juvenile-solitary-confinement-advocates-eye-elusive-sacramento-win/18251.
Loudenback, J. 2019. "A Governor Considers Reforms, Violence Rising at California's Juvenile Justice Facilities." *Chronicle of Social Change: Children and Youth, Front and Center*. https://

chronicleofsocialchange.org/news-2/as-governor-considers-reforms-violence-rising-at-cali fornias-juvenile-justice-facilities/33945.

Lowi, T. J. 1998. "Think Globally, Lose Locally." *Boston Review*. http://boston review.net/archives/BR23.2/lowi.html.

Lozano, A. V. 2019. "$10M Lawsuit Filed against Glen Mills Schools for 'Cruel and Unusual Punishment.'" NBC Philadelphia, April 11. https://www.nbcphiladelphia.com/news/local/State-Revokes-Glen-Mills-Schools-Investigation-Abuse-Probes-508433491.html.

Lucken, K. 1997. "Privatizing Discretion: 'Rehabilitating' Treatment in Community Corrections." *Crime & Delinquency* 43(3): 243–259.

Luiz, J. 2018. "Lawsuit, Report Allege Kern County's Mistreatment of Disabled Youth." *Bakersfield Californian*, February 23. https://www.bakersfield.com/news/lawsuit-report-allege-kern-county-s-mistreatment-of-disabled-youth/article_0b42469a-1834-11e8-bddb-7766b3011be9.html.

Lundahl, B. W., C. Kunz, C. Brownell, N. Harris, and R. Van Vleet. 2009. "Prison Privatization: A Meta-Analysis of Cost and Quality of Confinement Indicators." *Research on Social Work Practice* 19(4): 383–394.

Lynch, M. 2000. "Rehabilitation as Rhetoric: The Ideal of Reformation in Contemporary Parole Discourse and Practices." *Punishment & Society* 2(1): 40–65.

Lynch, M. P. (2010). *Sunbelt Justice: Arizona and the Transformation of American Punishment*. Stanford, CA: Stanford Law Books.

Lyons, W. 1999. *The Politics of Community Policing: Rearranging the Power to Punish*. Ann Arbor: University of Michigan Press.

Maass, D. 2012. "461 Pepper Spray Incidents Documents in Juvenile Detention Last Year." *San Diego City Beat*, May 2. http://sdcitybeat.com/article-10480-461-pepper-spray-incidents-documented-in-sd-juvenile-detention-last-year.html.

Macallair, D. 2003. "The San Francisco Industrial School and the Origins of Juvenile Justice in California: A Glance at the Great Reformation." *UC Davis Journal of Juvenile Law & Policy* 7(1): 1–60.

Macallair, D. 2007. "California Juvenile Justice Reform and SB 81: Testimony of Daniel Macallair." *Center on Juvenile and Criminal Justice*. 1–5. https://lhc.ca.gov/sites/lhc.ca.gov/files/Reports/192/WrittenTestimony/MacallairNov2007.pdf.

Macallair, D., M. Males, D. M. Enty, and N. Vinakor. 2011. "Renewing Juvenile Justice." *Sierra Health Foundation*. 1–68. https://www.shfcenter.org/wp-content/uploads/2022/03/SHF_RJJ_Report_Final.pdf.

Macallair, D., M. Males, and C. McCracken. 2009. "Closing California's Division of Juvenile Facilities: An Analysis of County Institutional Capacity." *Center on Juvenile and Criminal Justice*. 1–25. https://www.ojp.gov/ncjrs/virtual-library/abstracts/closing-californias-division-juvenile-facilities-analysis-county

MacArthur Foundation. 2016a. "Grantee Profile: Philadelphia Department of Human Services." https://www.macfound.org/grantees/1351/.

MacArthur Foundation. 2016b. "The MacArthur Foundation Research Network on Law and Neuroscience." http://www.lawneuro.org/index.php.

MacArthur Foundation. 2019. "Grant Search: City of Philadelphia." https://www.macfound.org/grantees/7051/.

Maciag, M. 2013. "Youth Unemployment Reached Record Highs: What Can Officials Do about It?" *Governing the States and Localities*, April 29. http://www.governing.com/blogs/by-the-numbers/youth-unemployment-rate-by-state.html.

Mack, L. 2018. "Electronic Monitoring Hurts Kids and Their Communities." *Juvenile Justice Information Exchange*, October 24. https://jjie.org/2018/10/24/electronic-monitoring-hurts-kids-and-their-communities/.

Males, M. 2019. "Fewer California Youths Are Getting Arrested, but Consequences Are More Serious." *GV Wire*, March 26. https://gvwire.com/2019/03/26/fewer-california-youths-are-getting-arrested-but-consequences-are-more-serious-for-those-arrested/.

Maloney, D., D. Romig, and T. Armstrong. 1988. "The Balanced Approach to Juvenile Probation." *Juvenile and Family Court Journal* 39(3): 1–4.

Matsuda, K. N., J. Hess, and S. F. Turner. 2020. "Division of Juvenile Justice: Treatment Model Process Evaluation." University of California, Irvine, May 15. https://cpb-us-e2.wpmucdn.com/sites.uci.edu/dist/0/1149/files/2020/07/DJJ-Treatment-Model-Process-Evaluation-FINAL.pdf.

Mayeux, S. 2020. *Free Justice: A History of the Public Defender in Twentieth Century America.* Chapel Hill, NC: UNC Press.

McCord, C. 2019. "Woman Sued, Accused of Sexually Abusing Juvenile Detention Detainee 300+ Times." *Click2Houston*, February 10. https://www.click2houston.com/news/2019/02/10/woman-sued-accused-of-sexually-abusing-juvenile-detention-detainee-300-times/.

McCullough, J. 2018. "Texas Rangers Arrest Four Amid Investigation of Abuse at State-run Juvenile Lockups." *The Texas Tribune*, February 1.

McCullough, J. 2019. "Texas Senator Proposes Moving All Youth in State Lockups to Shuttered Adult Jail." *Texas Tribune*, March 12. https://www.texastribune.org/2019/03/12/john-whitmire-juvenile-justice-lockup-adult-jail/.

McDonald, D. C. 1994. "Public Imprisonment by Private Means: The Re-emergence of Private Prisons and Jails in the United States, the United Kingdom, and Australia." *British Journal of Criminology* 34: 29–48.

McGaughy, L. 2019. "After Years of Scandal, Texas' Juvenile Justice Agency Sets New Goals to Rehabilitate Teen Lawbreakers." *Dallas Morning News*, June 1. https://www.dallasnews.com/news/politics/2018/06/01/after-years-of-scandal-texas-juvenile-justice-agency-sets-new-goals-to-rehabilitate-teen-lawbreakers/.

McKim, A. 2014. "Roxanne's Dress: Governing Gender and Marginality through Addiction Treatment." *Signs: Journal of Women in Culture and Society* 39(2): 433–458.

Mears, D. 2000. "Assessing the Effectiveness of Juvenile Justice Reforms: A Closer Look at the Criteria and the Impacts on Diverse Stakeholders." *Law & Policy* 22(2): 175–202.

Melamed, S. 2016a. "After 43 Years for a Purse-Snatching Gone Wrong, a Juvenile Lifer's Chance at Freedom." *Philly.com*, March 29. http://articles.philly.com/2016-03-29/news/71877115_1_life-sentence-only-sentence-parole.

Melamed, S. 2016b. "Juvenile Lifers Will Get New Sentences, but What Law Applies?" *Philly.com*, March 12. http://articles.philly.com/2016-03-12/news/71420922_1_new-sentences-life-sentences-qu-eed-batts.

Melamed, S. 2018. "Why Are Juvenile Lifers from Philly Getting Radically Different Sentences from Those in the Rest of Pennsylvania?" *Philadelphia Inquirer*. July 10. https://www.inquirer.com/philly/news/philly-bucks-county-pennsylvania-juvenile-lifers-jlwop-juvenile-law-center-life-without-parole-20180710.html.

Melton, G. B., and P. M. Pagliocca. 1992. "Treatment in the Juvenile Justice System: Directions for Policy and Practice." In *Responding to the mental health needs of youth in the juvenile justice system*, ed. J. J. Cocozza, 107–129. Seattle, WA: The National Coalition for the Mentally Ill in the Criminal Justice System.

Mendel, R. A. 2000. *Less Hype, More Help: Reducing Juvenile Crime, What Works and What Doesn't.* Collingdale, PA: Diane Publishing.

Mendel, R. A. 2010. "The Missouri Model: Reinventing the Practice of Rehabilitating Youthful Offenders." Annie E. Casey Foundation. https://www.aecf.org/blog/the-missouri-model-worthwhile-reform-benefits-youth-states.

Meronek, T. 2013. "The Fight against Putting Teens in Solitary." *East Bay Express* (Oakland, CA), August 21.

Metro Community Ministries, Inc. 2022. "Our Programs." https://mcmserves.org/our-programs/.

Mettler, S. 1998. *Dividing Citizens: Gender and Federalism in New Deal Public Policy.* Ithaca, NY: Cornell University Press.

Michaels, W. B., and A. Reed Jr. 2020. "The Trouble with Disparity." NonSite. https://nonsite.org/the-trouble-with-disparity/.

Michels, P. 2013. "Guards Joined in Fights at Specialized Juvenile Lockup." *Texas Observer*, November 1.

Middlemass, K. 2017. *Convicted and Condemned: The Politics and Policies of Prisoner Reentry*. New York: New York University Press.

Mihalic, S., and D. Elliott, D. 2015. "Evidence-Based Programs Registry: Blueprints for Healthy Youth Development." *Evaluation and Program Planning* 48: 124–131.

Miller v. Alabama, 567 U.S. 2012. https://www.oyez.org/cases/2011/10-9646.

Miller, L. 2008. *The Perils of Federalism: Race, Poverty, and the Politics of Crime Control*. Oxford: Oxford University Press.

Miller, L. 2014. "Making the State Pay: Race, Violence and the Politicization of Crime in Cross-National Perspective." Paper presented at American Political Science Association Annual Meeting, Politics after the Digital Revolution, Washington D.C.

Miller, L. 2016. *The Myth of Mob Rule: Violent Crime and Democratic Politics*. New York, NY: Oxford University Press.

Miller, R. J. 2014. "Devolving the Carceral State: Race, Prisoner Reentry, and the Micro-politics of Urban Poverty Management." *Punishment & Society* 16(3): 305–335.

Miller, M. 2012. "Dauphin County Commissioners Eye Leasing Schaffner Youth Center to Nonprofit." *PennLive*, September 19. http://www.pennlive.com/midstate/index.ssf/2012/09/dauphin_county_commissioners_e_1.html.

Mitman, H. 2016. "Report Asks Philly to Seek 'New Approach' for Juveniles Sentenced to Life without Parole." *Philly Voice*, April 1. http://www.phillyvoice.com/report-seeks-philly-seek-new-approach-juveniles-sentenced-life-without-parole/.

Moak, D. S. 2016. "Supply-Side Education: Race, Inequality, and the Rise of the Punitive Education State." PhD dissertation, University of Pennsylvania.

Moak, D. S. 2022. *From the New Deal to the War on Schools: Race, Inequality, and the Rise of the Punitive Education State*. Chapel Hill: University of North Carolina Press.

Moak, D. S., and S. D. Cate. 2022. "The Political Development of Schools as Cause and Solution to Delinquency." *Journal of Policy History* 34(2): 180–212.

Models for Change. 2021. "Community-Based Alternatives: Local Alternatives to Formal Processing and Incarceration." http://modelsforchange.net/reform-areas/community-based-alternatives/index.html.

Moll, J. 2011. "A Fresh Start for Juvenile Justice." *Odessa (TX) American*, December 7.

Moore, C. 2017. "Former Al Price Facility May Not Be Empty Much Longer." *The Port Arthur News*, January 23.

Montgomery v. Louisiana, 577 U.S. 2016. https://www.oyez.org/cases/2015/14-280.

Morales v. Turman, 430 U.S. 322 1977. https://supreme.justia.com/cases/federal/us/430/322/.

Morgan, K. J., and A. L. Campbell. 2011. *The Delegated Welfare State: Medicare, Markets, and the Governance of Social Policy*. New York, NY: Oxford University Press.

Morris, A. 2004. "The Voluntary Sector's War on Poverty." *Journal of Policy History* 16(4): 275–305.

Moyers & Company. (2014). "Public Schools for Sale?" March 28. https://billmoyers.com/episode/public-schools-for-sale/.

M.S.T. Services. n.d. "MST Services: Multisystemic Therapy for Juveniles." http://www.mstservices.com/.

Multi-Health Systems Inc. n.d. "Helping You Help Others." https://mhs.com/about-mhs/.

Multisystemic Therapy. 2015. "MST Treatment Model." http://mstservices.com/what-is-mst/treatment-model.

Multisystemic Therapy Services. 2007. "MST Services." https://www.mstservices.com/.

Muncie, J. 2005. "The Globalization of Crime Control—The Case of Youth and Juvenile Justice: Neo-liberalism, Policy Convergence and International Conventions." *Theoretical Criminology* 9(1): 35–64.

REFERENCES

Munger, C., L. Zhang, and K. Liao. 2018. "What SB-384 Means for California's Sex Offenders." *Medium*, March 9. https://medium.com/@laurazhang/what-sb-384-means-for-californias-sex-offenders-29a988001cfd.

Muñiz, A. 2015. *Police, Power, and the Production of Racial Boundaries: Critical Issues in Crime and Society.* New Brunswick, NJ: Rutgers University Press.

Murakawa, N. 2014. *The First Civil Right: How Liberals Built Prison America.* New York: Oxford University Press.

Murphy, B. 2007. "Plan to Thin Out TYC Lockups Blasted." *Houston Chronicle*, May 10.

MyNewsLA. 2019. "Criminal Justice Advocates Push County Official to Cancel Jails Contract." August 6. https://mynewsla.com/crime/2019/08/06/criminal-justice-advocates-push-county-officials-to-cancel-jails-contract/.

Nash, S. 2011. "County May Request Ron Jackson's Unit 2." *Brownwood (TX) Bulletin*, December 31.

Nash, S. 2012. "West: Ron Jackson Unit 2 Is Going to Brown County." *Brownwood (TX) Bulletin*, January 20.

Nash, S. 2014. "G4S Youth Services Facility Finding Home in Brownwood." *Brownwood (TX) Bulletin*, January 1. http://www.brownwoodtx.com/news/community/article_d63db500-7342-11e3-a2d1-001a4bcf887a.html.

Nathan, R. P., and T. L. Gais. 1999. *Implementing the Personal Responsibility Act of 1996: A First Look.* Albany, NY: SUNY Press.

National Alliance on Mental Illness. 2011. "State Mental Health Cuts: The Continuing Crisis." http://www.nami.org/Template.cfm?Section=state_budget_cuts_report.

National Center for Juvenile Justice. 2021. "Easy Access to the Census of Juveniles in Residential Placement: 1997–2019. https://www.ojjdp.gov/ojstatbb/ezacjrp/.

National Institute of Justice. 2011. "Program Profile: Project Towards No Drug Abuse." https://crimesolutions.ojp.gov/ratedprograms/73#pd.

National Juvenile Justice Network. 2015. "Policy Platform: Confining Youth for Profit." https://www.njjn.org/our-work/confining-youth-for-profit—policy-platform.

National Youth Screening & Assessment Project. 2009. "Youth Level of Service/Case Management Inventory (YLS/CMI) in PA." PowerPoint presentation. https://www.umassmed.edu/globalassets/center-for-mental-health-services-research/documents/products-publications/presentations/juvenile-justice/youth.pdf.

National Youth Screening & Assessment Partners. 2021. "Massachusetts Youth Screening Instrument- Second Version (MAYSI-2)." http://nysap.us/maysi2/index.html.

Navarro, V. 2010. "Consequences of the Privatized Funding of Medical Care and of the Privatized Electoral Process." *American Journal of Public Health* 100(3): 399–402. https://doi.org/10.2105/AJPH.2009.187633.

Neill, K. A., J. E. W. Yusuf, and J. C. Morris. 2014. "Explaining Dimensions of State-Level Punitiveness in the United States: The Roles of Social, Economic, and Cultural Factors." *Criminal Justice Policy Review* 26(8): 751–772.

Nellis, M., K. Beyens, and D. Kaminski, eds. 2013. *Electronically Monitored Punishment: International and Critical Perspectives.* New York, NY: Willan.

Nelson, A. 2013. *Body and Soul: The Black Panther Party and the Fight against Medical Discrimination.* Minneapolis: University of Minnesota Press.

New York Times. 2011. "Texas's Progress on Juvenile Justice." Editorial. July 9.

New York Times. 2012. "Some Good News from California's Justice System." Editorial. January 15.

New York Times. 2015. "The Texas Way on Juvenile Justice." Editorial. February 6.

Newell, M., and J. Leap. 2013. "Reforming the Nation's Largest Juvenile Justice System." Children's Defense Fund, California. https://staging.childrensdefense.org/wp-content/uploads/2018/06/reforming-the-nations.pdf.

Nielsen, J. 2011a. "Governor's Early Release Plan an Injustice for California." *Red Bluff (CA) Daily News.*

REFERENCES

Nielsen, J. 2011b. "Realignment Dumps State's Responsibility on Local Governments." *Sacramento Bee*.

Nieto, M. 2008. "County Probation Camps and Ranches for Juvenile Offenders." California Research Bureau. https://www.worldcat.org/title/277240100.

Ng, A. 2016. "Texas Juvenile Jail Counselor Had Dirty Dates with Teen Inmate, Sent Boy Nude Photos and Love Texts." *New York* Daily News, January 5. https://www.nydailynews.com/news/crime/tx-juvenile-jail-counselor-dirty-relationship-teen-article-1.2486655.

Nonprofit Metrics, LLC. 2022. "Incarcerated Men Putting Away Childish Things." https://www.causeiq.com/organizations/project-impact-incarcerated-men-putting-away-child,943402534/.

Norman, M. 2013. "Juvenile Detention Not the Way It's Done." *Keller (TX) Citizen*, December 21.

NPR. 2014. "State-by-State Court Fees." May 19. https://www.npr.org/2014/05/19/312455680/state-by-state-court-fees.

NPR Staff. 2014. "'Kids for Cash' Captures a Juvenile Justice Scandal from Two Sides." March 8. https://www.npr.org/2014/03/08/287286626/kids-for-cash-captures-a-juvenile-justice-scandal-from-two-sides.

Nurse, A. M., J. Sankofa, A. Cox, J. Fader, M. Inderbitzin, and L. Abrams. 2018. "Juvenile Corrections in the Era of Reform: A Meta-Synthesis of Qualitative Studies." *International Journal of Offender Therapy and Comparative Criminology* 62(7): 1763–1786. https://openworks.wooster.edu/facpub/281/.

O'Connor, A. 2001. *Poverty Knowledge: Social Science, Social Policy, and the Poor in Twentieth-Century US History*. Princeton, NJ: Princeton University Press.

O'Connor, A. 2007. *Social Science for What? Philanthropy and the Social Question in a World Turned Right-Side Up*. New York, NY: Russell Sage Foundation.

Orren, K., and S. Skowronek. 2004. *The Search for American Political Development*. Cambridge: Cambridge University Press.

Office of Juvenile Justice and Delinquency Prevention. 2022. "Project M2 – Mobilizing Mentors." https://ojjdp.ojp.gov/funding/awards/2008-ju-fx-0022.

Osborn, C. 2014. "Lawsuit: Bartlett State Jail Allowed Assault, Hazing." *Austin American-Statesman*, September 6.

Owler. 2021. "Multi-Health Systems, Competitors, Revenue, and Number of Employees." https://www.owler.com/company/mhs.

Page, J. 2011. *The Toughest Beat: Politics, Punishment, and the Prison Officers' Union in California*. Oxford: Oxford University Press.

Palmer, C. 2018. "Report: PA DHS Failing Vulnerable Children Due to Lack of Oversight at Placement Facilities." *Philadelphia Inquirer*, December 13. https://www.inquirer.com/news/report-pennsylvania-juvenile-abuse-dhs-glen-mills-wordsworth-philadelphia-20181213.html.

Palomino, J., and J. Tucker. 2019. "Vanishing Violence." *San Francisco Chronicle*. March 21. https://projects.sfchronicle.com/2019/vanishing-violence/.

Parental Survival Skills. 2022. "About Us." http://nevertheless-psst.blogspot.com/.

Parker, C. S., and M. A. Barreto. 2014. *Change They Can't Believe In: The Tea Party and Reactionary Politics in America*. Princeton, NJ: Princeton University Press.

Paterson, C. 2013. "Commercial Crime Control and the Development of Electronically Monitored Punishment: A Global Perspective." In *Electronically Monitored Punishment: International and Critical Perspectives*, ed. M. Nellis, K. Beyens, and D. Kaminski, 211–228. New York, NY: Willan.

Payne, B. K., and R. R. Gainey. 1998. "A Qualitative Assessment of the Pains Experienced on Electronic Monitoring." *International Journal of Offender Therapy and Comparative Criminology* 42(2): 149–163.

Peguero, J. 2017. "Teen's Death at Brownwood Juvenile Detention Center Prompts Investigation," KTX, June 7. https://ktxs.com/archive/teens-death-at-brownwood-juvenile-detention-center-prompts-investigation.

Pennsylvania Budget and Policy Center. 2007. "Understanding Welfare Spending in Pennsylvania." http://www.pennbpc.org/pdf/PBPCUnderStdWelfare.pdf.

Pennsylvania Commission on Crime and Delinquency. 2012. "Pennsylvania's Juvenile Justice System Enhancement Strategy." http://www.pccd.pa.gov/Juv enileJustice/Documents/JJSES%20Monograph%20Final%20version%20press%20ready%2005%2025%2012.pdf.

Pennsylvania Commission on Crime and Delinquency. 2021. "Juvenile Justice and Delinquency Prevention." https://www.pccd.pa.gov/Juvenile-Justice/Pages/default.aspx.

Pennsylvania DMC Youth/Law Enforcement Corporation. n.d. "The DMC Corporation."

Pennsylvania Juvenile Court Judges' Commission. 1999. "March 1999 Newsletter." *Pennsylvania Juvenile Justice* 8(3). https://www.jcjc.pa.gov/Publications/Newsletters/1999/March.pdf.

Pennsylvania Juvenile Court Judges' Commission. 2004a. "January 2004 Newsletter." *Pennsylvania Juvenile Justice* 12(1). https://www.jcjc.pa.gov/Publications/Newsletters/2004/January.pdf.

Pennsylvania Juvenile Court Judges' Commission. 2004b. "June 2004 Newsletter." *Pennsylvania Juvenile Justice* 12 (6). https://www.jcjc.pa.gov/Publications/Newsletters/2004/June.pdf.

Pennsylvania Juvenile Court Judges' Commission. 2004c. "Pennsylvania Juvenile Justice Newsletter." https://www.jcjc.pa.gov/Publications/Newsletters/2004/March.pdf.

Pennsylvania Juvenile Court Judges' Commission. 2005a. "January 2005 Newsletter." *Pennsylvania Juvenile Justice* 13(1). https://www.jcjc.pa.gov/Publications/Newsletters/2005/January.pdf.

Pennsylvania Juvenile Court Judges' Commission. 2005b. "Juvenile Justice in Pennsylvania." http://www.centerschool.org/restitution/ pdf/JuvenileJusticeInPA.pdf.

Pennsylvania Juvenile Court Judges' Commission. 2008. "April 2008 Newsletter." *Pennsylvania Juvenile Justice* 16(4). http://www.jcjc.pa.gov/ Publications/Newsletters/2008/April.pdf.

Pennsylvania Juvenile Court Judges' Commission. 2010a. "April 2010 Newsletter." *Pennsylvania Juvenile Justice* 18(4). http://www.jcjc. pa.gov/Publications/Newsletters/2010/April.pdf.

Pennsylvania Juvenile Court Judges' Commission. 2010b. "December 2010 Newsletter." *Pennsylvania Juvenile Justice* 18(12). http://www.jcjc.pa.gov/ Publications/Newsletters/2010/December.pdf.

Pennsylvania Juvenile Court Judges' Commission. 2010c. "March 2010 Newsletter." *Pennsylvania Juvenile Justice* 18(3). http://www.jcjc.pa.gov/ Publications/Newsletters/2010/March.pdf.

Pennsylvania Juvenile Court Judges' Commission. 2013. "Juvenile Justice Outcome Measures." http://www.jcjc.pa.gov/Publications/Documents/ 2013%20Pennsylvania%20Juvenile%20Justice%20Outcome%20Measures%20Report.pdf.

Pennsylvania Juvenile Court Judges' Commission. 2015. "January 2015 Newsletter." *Pennsylvania Juvenile Justice* 26(1). http://www.jcjc.pa.gov/ Publications/Newsletters/2015/January.pdf.

Pennsylvania Juvenile Court Judges' Commission. 2019. "2019 Juvenile Court Annual Report." PowerPoint slides. https://www.jcjc.pa.gov/Research-Statistics/Disposition%20Reports/2019%20Juvenile%20Court%20Annual%20Report.pdf.

Pennsylvania Office of Attorney General Josh Shapiro. (2021). "Open Data: UCR." https://www.attorneygeneral.gov/open-data-urc-arrests-age/.

Pennsylvania Office of the Governor. 2013. "Governor Corbett Invests $10 Million for At-Risk Youth and Juvenile Offenders." *Cision PR Newswire*. https://www.prnewswire.com/news-releases/governor-corbett-invests-10-million-for-at-risk-youth-and-juvenile-offenders-186952501.html.

Pennsylvania State Legislature. 1976. "Senate Bill 852." http://www.legis.state .pa.us/cfdocs/billInfo/bill_history.cfm?syear=1975&sind=0&body=S&type=B&bn=852.

Pennsylvania State Legislature. 2002. "Act 215." http://www.legis.state.pa. us/cfdocs/legis/li/uconsCheck.cfm?yr=2002&sessInd=0&act=215.

Pennsylvania State Legislature. 2003. "Act 21." http://www.legis.state.pa.us/WU01/LI/HJ /2003/0/20030716.pdf.

Pennsylvania State Legislature. 2012a. "Act 204." http://www.legis.state.pa.us /cfdocs/legis/li/uconsCheck.cfm?yr=2012&sessInd=0&act=204.

Pennsylvania State Legislature. 2012b. "SB 850." http://www.legis.state.pa.us/ cfdocs/billInfo/bill_history.cfm?syear=2011&sind=0&body=S&type=B&bn=850.

Perkinson, R. 2010. *Texas Tough: The Rise of America's Prison Empire*. New York: Metropolitan Books.

Petek, G. 2019. *Reorganization of the Division of Juvenile Justice, The Legislative Analyst's Office*. Retrieved from https://lao.ca.gov/reports/2019/3998/juvenile-justice-041019.pdf.

Petersilia, J. 2016. "Realigning Corrections, California Style." *Annals of the American Academy of Political and Social Science* 664(1): 8–13.

Pfaff, J. F. 2017. *Locked In: The True Causes of Mass Incarceration and How to Achieve Real Reform*. New York, NY: Basic Books.

Pfaff, J. F., and J. A. Butts. 2019. "It's about Quality: Private Confinement Facilities in Juvenile Justice." *Criminology & Public Policy* 18(2): 361–378.

Phelps, M. S. 2011. "Rehabilitation in the Punitive Era: The Gap between Rhetoric and Reality in US Prison Programs." *Law & Society Review* 45(1): 33–68.

Phelps, M. S. 2017. "Mass Probation: Toward a More Robust Theory of State Variation in Punishment." *Punishment & Society* 19(1): 53–73.

Pierson, P. 1994. *Dismantling the Welfare State? Reagan, Thatcher and the Politics of Retrenchment*. Cambridge: Cambridge University Press.

Pierson, P. 2000. "Increasing Returns, Path Dependence, and the Study of Politics." *American Political Science Review* 94(2): 251–267.

Pierson, P., and T. Skocpol. 2002. "Historical Institutionalism in Contemporary Political Science." *Political Science: The State of the Discipline* 3: 693–721.

Pierson, P., and T. Skocpol, T. 2007. *The Transformation of American Politics: Activist Government and the Rise of Conservatism*. Princeton, NJ: Princeton University Press.

Pilnik, L., R. G. Schwartz, K. Lindell, J. Feierman, and C. Sorenson. 2019. "Transforming Justice: Bringing Pennsylvania's Young People Safely Home from Juvenile Justice Placements." Juvenile Law Center. https://jlc.org/sites/default/files/attachments/2019-10/Transforming_Justice_final.pdf.

Pino, F. A. 2019. "Los Angeles County Votes to Stop Construction of New Jail-Like Facility, Adding Momentum to National Abolition Movement." *The Intercept*, August 22. https://theintercept.com/2019/08/22/los-angeles-county-mental-health-facility-abolition/.

Pitre, A. 2015. "California Measure Is Step toward True Justice." *Juvenile Justice Information Exchange*, June 5.

Plainview (TX) Daily Herald. 2007. "TYC Contractors Faced Closures, Lawsuits in Other States." July 29.

Platt, A. M. 1977. *The Child Savers: The Invention of Delinquency*. Chicago: University of Chicago Press.

Plimmer, G. 2015. "G4S Dogged by Scandal Provisions As It Returns to Profit." *Financial Times*, March 10. http://www.ft.com/cms/s/0/c2c877b6-c6fd-11e4-8e1f-00144feab7de.html#axzz3ek9fYhdj.

Polsky, A. J. 1993. *The Rise of the Therapeutic State*. Princeton, NJ: Princeton University Press.

Project Towards No Drug Abuse. 2016. "Publications." *University of Southern California Institute for Prevention Research*. http://tnd.usc.edu/ publications.php.

Puzzanchera, C., and W. Kang. 2014. "Easy Access to FBI Arrest Statistics 1994–2012." OJJDP. http://www.ojjdp.gov/ojstatbb/ezaucr/.

Quality Counts. 2019. "Map: How Much Money Each State Spends per Student." *Education Week*, June 4. https://www.edweek.org/ew/collections/quality-counts-2019-state-finance/map-per-pupil-spending-state-by-state.html.

Queally, J. 2020. "On First Day as L.A. County D.A., George Gascón Eliminates Bail, Remakes Sentencing Rules." *Los Angeles Times*, December 7. https://www.latimes.com/california/story/2020-12-07/in-first-day-on-job-gascon-remakes-bail-sentencing-rules.

Quinney, R. 1973. *Critique of Legal Order: Crime Control in Capitalist Society*. Boston: Little, Brown.

Quirino, B. 2015. "Juvenile Hall to Close." *Lake County (CA) Record-Bee*, October 8. http://www.record-bee.com/article/NQ/20151008/NEWS/151009866.

Ramsey, R. 2018. "Analysis: Texas' School Finance Problem in One Pesky Chart." *Texas Tribune*, October 10. https://www.texastribune.org/2018/10/10/analysis-texas-school-finance-bud get-lbb/.
Rangel, E. 2012. "Juvenile Justice: State Sees Decrease in Incarcerated Youth." *Amarillo (TX) Globe-News*, December 28.
Ravitch, D. 2014. *Reign of Error: The Hoax of the Privatization Movement and the Danger to America's Public Schools*. New York: Vintage.
Raymond, S. 2000. "From Playpens to Prisons: What the Gang Violence and Juvenile Crime Prevention Act of 1998 Does to California's Juvenile Justice System and Reasons to Repeal It." *Golden Gate Law Review* 30(2): 233–284.
Reckhow, S. 2012. *Follow the Money: How Foundation Dollars Change Public School Politics*. Oxford: Oxford University Press.
Reed, A., Jr. 1999. *Stirrings in the Jug: Black Politics in the Post-Segregation Era*. Minneapolis: University of Minnesota Press.
Reed, A., Jr. 2000. *Class Notes: Posing as Politics and Other Thoughts on the American Scene*. New York: New Press.
Reed, A., Jr., and M. Chowkwanyun. 2012. "Race, Class, Crisis: The Discourse of Racial Disparity and Its Analytical Discontents." *Socialist Register* 48: 149–175.
Reed, T. F. 2020. *Toward Freedom: The Case against Race Reductionism*. Brooklyn, NY: Verso Books.
Reich, R. 2018. *Just Giving: Why Philanthropy Is Failing Democracy and How It Can Do Better*. Princeton, NJ: Princeton University Press.
Reinlie, L. 2008. "Lax Oversight Plagues Private Prisons in Texas." Texans for Public Justice and Grassroots Leadership. http://www.privateci.org/ private_pics/Watch_Your_Assets_ Grassroots_Leadership_report_on_Private_Prisons_in_TX_2008.pdf.
Reiter, K. A. 2012. "Parole, Snitch, or Die: California's Supermax Prisons and Prisoners, 1997–2007." *Punishment & Society* 14(5): 530–563.
Renzema, M. 2013. "Evaluative Research on Electronic Monitoring." In *Electronically Monitored Punishment: International and Critical Perspectives*, ed. M. Nellis, K. Beyens, and D. Kaminski. Willan, 247–272. New York, NY.
Requarth, T. 2017. "A California Court for Young Adults Calls on Science." *New York Times*, April 17. https://www.nytimes.com/2017/04/17/health/young-adult-court-san-francisco-cal ifornia-neuroscience.html.
ReWired For Change [@ReWired4Change]. 2010. https://twitter.com/rewired4change?lang=en.
Rhodes, L. A. 2004. *Total Confinement: Madness and Reason in the Maximum Security Prison*. Berkeley: University of California Press.
Ridolfi, L. W., M. Washburn, and F. Guzman. 2017. "Youth Prosecuted as Adults in California; Addressing Racial, Ethnic, and Geographic Disparities after the Repeal of Direct File." Youth Law. http://www.cjcj.org/uploads/cjcj/documents/youth_prosecuted_as_adults_in_cal ifornia.pdf.
Rigby, M. 2008. "Texas Youth Commission Wants Increased Pepper Spray Use Despite Settlement." *Prison Legal News*, May 15. https://www.prisonlegalnews.org/news/2008/may/15/texas-youth-commission-wants-increased-pepper-spray-use-despite-settlement/.
Robbins v. Glenn County (Ca. 1987). https://www.ylc.org/wp-content/uploads/2018/11/rob binsconsent.pdf.
Roberts, A. R. 2004. *Juvenile Justice Sourcebook: Past, Present, and Future*. New York, NY: Oxford University Press.
Rodgers, D. T. 2012. *Age of Fracture*. Cambridge, MA: Belknap Press of Harvard University Press.
Roelofs, J. 2003. *Foundations and Public Policy: The Mask of Pluralism*. Albany, NY: SUNY Press.
Roelofs, J. 2007. "Foundations and Collaboration." *Critical Sociology* 33(3): 479–504.
Romer, P. A. 2008. "Mentally Ill Don't Belong in Jailhouse." *Temple (TX) Daily Telegram*. July 27. http://www.tdtnews.com/archive/article_be1c1cb6-df63-58a3-8fdc-9348c0383d75.html.
Roper v. Simmons, 543 U.S. 551 2005. https://www.oyez.org/cases/2004/03-633.

Rovner, J. 2014. "Slow to Act: State Responses to 2012 Supreme Court Mandate on Life without Parole." The Sentencing Project. http://sentencingproject.org/doc/publications/jj_State_Responses_to_Miller.pdf.

Rubin, A. T. 2016. "Penal Change as Penal Layering: A Case Study of Proto-Prison Adoption and Capital Punishment Reduction, 1785–1822." *Punishment & Society* 18(4): 420–441.

Rusche, G., and O. Kirchheimer. 1968. *Punishment and Social Structure*. New York: Russell & Russell.

Sagona, N. 2014. "Camp Kilpatrick: The New LA Model." *Malibu Times*, February 19. http://www.malibutimes.com/news/article_fad04280-9975-11e3-bbbb-001a4bcf887a.html.

San Diego County (California) District Attorney. 2015. "Navigating the Juvenile Court System." http://www.sdcda.org/prosecuting/juvenile/navigating-juvenile-court-system.html.

Sanchez, Cyn Yamachiro, Shiela Balkan, Jose Osuna, Mack Jenkins, and Saul Sarabia. 2019. "Summary Report of the Los Angeles County Probation Systemic Reform Plan." Los Angeles County Probation Reform and Implementation Team. http://prit.lacounty.gov/LinkClick.aspx?fileticket=BmWgSiQvaVQ%3d&portalid=37.

Sandberg, L. 2008. "Watchdog: Texas Holds Young Offenders in Solitary for Weeks." *Houston Chronicle*. January 16. http://www.chron.com/news/houston-texas/article/Watchdog-Texas-holds-young-offenders-in-solitary-1647523.php.

Savage, Q. 2015. "Shutting Down the Board of State and Community Corrections." Community Alliance, August 1. http://fresnoalliance.com/wordpress/?p=11177.

Sawyer, W. 2019. *Youth Confinement: The Whole Pie 2019*. Northampton, MA: Prison Policy Initiative. https://www.prisonpolicy.org/reports/youth2019.html.

Scheingold, S. A. 1991. *The Politics of Street Crime: Criminal Process and Cultural Obsession*. Philadelphia: Temple University Press.

Schept, J. 2015. *Progressive Punishment: Job Loss, Jail Growth, and the Neoliberal Logic of Carceral Expansion*. New York: New York University Press.

Schill, R. 2011. "Texas under Rick Perry Makes Strides in Juvenile Justice Reform." *Juvenile Justice Information Exchange*, August 29.

Schlanger, M. 2013. "Plata v. Brown and Realignment: Jails, Prisons, Courts, and Politics." *Harvard Civil Rights-Civil Liberties Law Review* 48(1): 165–215.

Schmitt, E. R. 2010. *President of the Other America: Robert Kennedy and the Politics of Poverty*. Amherst: University of Massachusetts Press.

Schneider, S. 2007. *Crime Prevention: Theory and Practice*. Boca Raton, FL: CRC Press.

Schoenfeld, H. 2018. *Building the Prison State: Race and the Politics of Mass Incarceration*. Chicago: University of Chicago Press.

Schur, E. M. 1973. *Radical Nonintervention: Rethinking the Delinquency Problem*. Englewood Cliffs, NJ: Prentice-Hall.

Schwartz, I. M., and W. H. Barton, eds. 1994. *Reforming Juvenile Detention: No More Hidden Closets*. Columbus: Ohio State University Press.

Schwartz, R. G. 2013. "Pennsylvania and MacArthur's Models for Change: The Story of a Successful Public-Private Partnership." Juvenile Law Center and The MacArthur Foundation. http://jlc.org/sites/default/files/publication_pdfs/Pennsylvania%20and%20MacArthur's%20Models%20for%20Change%20-%20Story%20of%20a%20Successful%20Partnership.pdf.

Skocpol, T. 2016. "Why Political Scientists Should Study Organized Philanthropy." *PS-Political Science & Politics* 49(3): 433–436.

Scull, A. T. 1984. *Decarceration: Community Treatment and the Deviant: A Radical View*. New Brunswick, NJ: Rutgers University Press.

Seeds, C. 2017. "Bifurcation Nation: American Penal Policy in Late Mass Incarceration." *Punishment & Society* 19(5): 590–610. https://doi.org/10.1177/1462474516673822.

Segal, S. P., and U. Aviram. 1978. *The Mentally Ill in Community-Based Sheltered Care: A Study of Community Care and Social Integration*. New York: Wiley-Interscience.

Seibert, T. 2017. "Charges, Denials of Corruption in Brown County, but No Investigation." *Texas Monitor*, December 25. https://texasmonitor.org/ray-west-corruption-brown-county-investigation/.

Sentencing Project. 2013. "Interactive Map." http://www.sentencingproj ect.org/map/map.cfm.

Sexton, T. L., and J. F. Alexander. 2000. "Functional Family Therapy." *Office of Juvenile Justice and Delinquency Prevention.* https://www.ncjrs.gov/pdffiles1/ ojjdp/184743.pdf.

Shalev, S. 2013. *Supermax: Controlling Risk through Solitary Confinement*. New York, NY: Willan.

Sharkey, J. 2019. "President's Letter: Not a Moment, but a Movement." *Chicago Union Teacher*, November. https://www.ctulocal1.org/chicago-union-teacher/2019/11/not-a-moment-but-a-movement/.

Shaw v. San Francisco (Ca. 1990). https://casetext.com/case/shaw-v-san-francisco.

Shichor, D., and C. Bartollas. 1990. "Private and Public Juvenile Placements: Is There a Difference?" *Crime & Delinquency* 36(2): 286–299.

Sickmund, M., and C. Puzzanchera. 2014. "Juvenile Offenders and Victims: 2014 National Report." *National Center for Juvenile Justice.*

Simon, J. 1993. *Poor Discipline*. Chicago: University of Chicago Press.

Simon, J. 2009. *Governing through Crime: How the War on Crime Transformed American Democracy and Created a Culture of Fear.* New York, NY: Oxford University Press.

Skeem, J. L., P. J. Kennealy, J. R. Tatar, II, I. R. Hernandez, and F. A. Keith. 2017. "How Well Do Juvenile Risk Assessments Measure Factors to Target in Treatment? Examining Construct Validity." *Psychological Assessment* 29(6): 679–691. https://doi.org/10.1037/pas0000409.

Skiba, R. J., and K. Knesting. 2002. "Zero Tolerance, Zero Evidence: An Analysis of School Disciplinary Practice." In *Zero Tolerance: Can Suspension and Expulsion Keep School Safe?*, ed. R. J. Skiba and G. G. Noam, 17–43. San Francisco, CA: Jossey-Bass/Wiley.

Smith, P. H. 2012. *Racial Democracy and the Black Metropolis: Housing Policy in Postwar Chicago.* Minneapolis: University of Minnesota Press.

Smith, R. L. 1972. "A Quiet Revolution: Probation Subsidy." Office of Juvenile Delinquency and Youth Development. DHEW publication no. (SRS) 72-26011: United States Department of Health, Education and Welfare.

Smith, R. M. 2014. "Ideas and the Spiral of Politics: The Place of American Political Thought in American Political Development." *American Political Thought* 3(1): 126–136. https://doi.org/10.1086/675651.

Smith, S. R., and M. Lipsky. 1993. *Nonprofits for Hire: The Welfare State in the Age of Contracting.* Cambridge, MA: Harvard University Press.

Social and Environmental Entrepreneurs. 2021. "Our Board." https://saveourplanet.org/about-see/our-team/our-board/.

Soss, J., R. C. Fording, and S. F. Schram. 2008. "The Color of Devolution: Race, Federalism, and the Politics of Social Control." *American Journal of Political Science* 52(3): 536–553.

Soss, J., R. C. Fording, and S. F. Schram. 2011. *Disciplining the Poor: Neoliberal Paternalism and the Persistent Power of Race.* Chicago: University of Chicago Press.

Spence, L. K. 2015. *Knocking the Hustle: Against the Neoliberal Turn in Black Politics.* Brooklyn, NY: Punctum Books.

Staklis, S., and S. Klein. 2010. "Technical Skill Attainment and Post-Program Outcomes: An Analysis of Pennsylvania Secondary Career and Technical Education Graduates." *National Research Center for Career and Technical Education.* Louisville, Kentucky. 37 pages. https://www.voced.edu.au/content/ngv%3A45482

State Policy Network. 2011. "History." http://www.spn.org/.

Stein, J. 2011. *Pivotal Decade: How the United States Traded Factories for Finance in the Seventies.* New Haven, CT: Yale University Press.

Steinberg, L. 2018. "Understanding Adolescent Development, Reforming Juvenile Justice." MacArthur Foundation. https://www.macfound.org/press/40-years-40-stories/research-network-adolescent-development-and-juvenile-justice/.

Steptoe, G., and A. Goldet. 2016. "Why Some Young Sex Offenders Are Held Indefinitely." Marshall Project, January 27. https://www.themarshallproject.org/ 2016/01/27/why-some-young-sex-offenders-are-held-indefinitely#.Y5L3ovyj5.

Steven v. Kern County (Ca. 1991). https://caselaw.findlaw.com/ca-supreme-court/1554011.html.

Stiles, M. 2019. "Danger and Dysfunction in L.A. County Juvenile Halls; Youth Rehabilitation Facilities Are So Marred by Tension and 'Chaos' That Some Staffers Fear Reporting for Work." *Los Angeles Times*, May 19. https://enewspaper.latimes.com/infinity/article_share.aspx?guid=62805e33-b182-4944-bee1-9f40fc94f9e7.

Stillman, S. 2014. "Get out of Jail, Inc.: Does the Alternatives-to-Incarceration Industry Profit from Injustice?" *The New Yorker*, June 16. https://www.newyorker.com/magazine/2014/06/23/get-out-of-jail-inc.

Stoneleigh Foundation. 2013a. "The Pennsylvania Academic and Career/Technical Training Alliance." http://stoneleighfoundation.org/sites/default/files/ Moving%20the%20Dial%20-%20Candace%20Putter.pdf.

Stoneleigh Foundation. 2013b. "Pennsylvania Academic and Career/Technical Training (PACTT) Project." http://stoneleighfoundation.org/content/ pennsylvania-academic-and-careertechnical-training-pactt-project.

Students Against Destructive Decisions. 2022. "About Us." https://www.sadd.org/aboutus.

Stuntz, W. J. 2011. *The Collapse of American Criminal Justice*. Cambridge, MA: Harvard University Press.

Sunset Advisory Commission. 2009. Final Report. http://www.sunset.state.tx.us/81.htm.

Sutton, J. R. 1988. *Stubborn Children: Controlling Delinquency in the United States, 1640–1981*. Berkeley: University of California Press.

Swanson, D. J. 2007. "Youth Jail Sex Abuse Reported." *Dallas Morning News*, February 18.

Terruso, J., and C. Palmer. 2018. "Two Years after Wordsworth Teen's Death, More Details Released but No Charges." *Philadelphia Inquirer*, December 20. https://www.inquirer.com/news/wordsworth-philadelphia-david-hess-death-dhs-report-charges-20181220.html.

Texas Appleseed. 2011. "Sowing the Seeds of Justice." http://www.texasappleseed.net/.

Texas Appleseed. 2014. "Pro Bono Partners." http://www.texasappleseed.net/index.php?option=com_content&view=article&id=28&Itemid=288.

Texas Appleseed. 2015. "Class, Not Court: Reconsidering Texas' Criminalization of Truancy." http://www.texasappleseed.net/index.php?option=com_docman&task=doc_download&gid=1208&Itemid=.

Texas Appleseed. 2021. "Institutional Donors." https://www.texasappleseed.org/institutional-donors.

Texas Association of Counties. 2012. "County Expenditures Survey 2011: The County Information Project." https://www.county.org/about-texas-counties/county-data/Documents/Expenditures-2011-Final.pdf.

Texas Center for Justice and Equity. 2021. "Publications Library." https://texascje.org/library?field_policy_areas_tid=2&field_publication_type_value=All&sort_by=field_publication_date_value&sort_order=ASC&field_policy_areas_target_id=All&page=5.

Texas Comptroller of Public Accounts. 2019. "Sources of Revenue: A History of State Taxes and Fees 1972–2018." https://comptroller.texas.gov/transparency/revenue/docs/96-1774.pdf.

Texas Criminal Justice Coalition. 2012. "Community Solutions for Youth in Trouble." http://www.texascjc.org/community-solutions-youth.

Texas Department of Public Safety. 2019. "TXGANG Index: Operating Policies and Procedures." https://www.dps.texas.gov/txgangs/gangOPP.pdf.

Texas House of Representatives. 2007. "February 26th Corrections, 10:10am. 80th Session Committee Broadcast Archives." http://www.house.state.tx.us/video-audio/committee-broadcasts/80/.

REFERENCES

Texas Juvenile Justice Department. 2012a. "Comprehensive Report: Youth Reentry and Reintegration." https://www.tjjd.texas.gov/publications/reports/2012Reentry ReintegrationReport.pdf.

Texas Juvenile Justice Department. 2012b. "Juvenile Recidivism Trends. Data Coordinators Conference: Regional Training." http://www.tjjd.texas.gov/statistics/ 2012DataCoordConf/Recidivism%20Trends.pdf.

Texas Juvenile Justice Department. 2013. "CoNEXTions." http://www.tjjd.texas.gov/programs/conextions.aspx.

Texas Juvenile Justice Department. 2014a. "Allocation of State Funds to Local Communities." http://www.tjjd.texas.gov/publications/other/searchcontracts.aspx.

Texas Juvenile Justice Department. 2014b. "Texas Juvenile Justice Department Statistical Report Calendar Years 1992–2012." http://www.tjjd.texas.gov/publications/default.aspx.

Texas Juvenile Justice Department. 2015. "Registered Juvenile Facilities in Texas." http://www.tjjd.texas.gov/publications/other/facilityinfo.aspx?ID=dBbw2leV0nhYaDg5vYkCIxVim/ZWXA3rIc1PRUBbnJITFC1jevmItg==.

Texas Juvenile Justice Department. 2017a. "Workforce Development." https://www2.tjjd.texas.gov/programs/workforce/pie.aspx.

Texas Juvenile Justice Department. 2017b. "CoNEXTions." https://www2.tjjd.texas.gov/programs/conextions.aspx.

Texas Juvenile Justice Department. 2021a. "Operating Budget." https://www.tjjd.texas.gov/index.php/doc-library/category/613-operating-budget.

Texas Juvenile Justice Department. 2021b. "Quarterly Reports." https://www.tjjd.texas.gov/index.php/doc-library/category/283-quarterly-reports.

Texas Juvenile Probation Commission 2010. "Annual Report to the Governor and Legislative Budget Board: Juvenile Probation Appropriations, Riders and Special Diversion Programs." https://www2.tjjd.texas.gov/publications/reports/RPTOTH201202.pdf.

Texas Legislative Budget Board. 2013. "Statewide Criminal Justice Recidivism and Revocation Rates." http://www.lbb.state.tx.us/Public_Safety_Criminal_Justice/RecRev_Rates/Statewide%20Criminal%20Justice%20Recidivism%20and%20Revocation%20Rates2012.pdf.

Texas Legislative Budget Board. 2019. "Adult and Juvenile Correctional Populations Projections: Fiscal Years 2019 to 2024." January. https://www.lbb.state.tx.us/Documents/Publications/Policy_Report/4910_Correctional_Population_Projections_Jan_2019.pdf.

Texas Legislative Budget Board. 2020. "Adult and Juvenile Correctional Population Projects: Fiscal Years 2020 to 2025." Staff to the 86th Texas Legislature. https://www.lbb.state.tx.us/Documents/Publications/Policy_Report/5939_Population_Projections_June_2020.pdf.

Texas Public Policy Foundation. 2007. "Governor Perry Signs TYC Reform Bill." June 8. https://www.texaspolicy.com/governor-perry-signs-tyc-reform-bill/.

Texas Public Policy Foundation. 2011. "About." http://www.texaspolicy.com/.

Texas State Auditor. 2020. "An Annual Report on Classified Employee Turnover for Fiscal Year 2020." https://sao.texas.gov/SAOReports/ReportNumber?id=21-703.

Texas State Employees Union. 2021. "TJJD Budget Requests Calls for Pay Raises, Increased Staffing." https://cwa-tseu.org/tjjd-budget-request-calls-for-pay-raises-increased-staffing/.

Texas State Legislature. 2007. "Senate Bill 103." http://www.legis.state.tx.us/billlookup/Text.aspx?LegSess=80R&Bill=SB103.

Texas State Legislature. 2011. "Senate Bill 653." http://www.capitol.state.tx.us/tlodocs/82R/billtext/pdf/SB00653F.pdf.

Texas State Teachers Association. 2018. "TSTA: Teachers Taking Extra Jobs and Subsidizing Under-Funded Education Budget." *TSTA News*, August 6. https://tsta.org/sites/default/files/20180806survey.pdf.

Texas Youth Commission. 2009. "Brief History of the Texas Youth Commission: From the Roots of Texas Juvenile Justice through the Present." http://www.lb5.uscourts.gov/ArchivedURLs/Files/08-70042(1).pdf.

Therolf, G. 2015. "Advocates Seek to End Solitary Confinement Options for Young Offenders." *Los Angeles Times*, May 28. http://www.latimes.com/local/crime/la-me-solitary-juvenile-20150528-story.html.

Thompson, D. 2013. "Juvenile Justice: California Locking Up Far Fewer Young People." Associated Press, June 17. http://bakersfieldnow.com/news/local/juvenile-justice-california-locking-up-far-fewer-young-people.

Thompson, D. 2018. "California Weighs Limits to Pepper Spray in Juvenile Jails." AP News. https://www.apnews.com/ad0613ffdce0482e805b65275ff41d94.

Thompson, D. 2019. "Inspectors Slam Stockton Prison Medical Facility." Recordnet. https://www.recordnet.com/news/20190425/inspectors-slam-stockton-prison-medical-facility.

Thompson, D. 2020. "Governor Newsom Wants to Shrink California Prisons as a Part of Budget Cuts." KRCR, May 16. https://krcrtv.com/news/local/governor-newsom-wants-to-shrink-california-prisons-as-a-part-of-budget-cuts.

Thompson, H. A. 2011a. "Downsizing the Carceral State: The Policy Implications of Prison Guard Unions." *Criminology and Public Policy* 10(3): 771–779.

Thompson, H. A. 2011b. "Rethinking Working Class Struggle through the Lens of the Carceral State: Toward a Labor History of Inmates and Guards." *Labor: Studies in Working-Class History of the Americas* 8(3): 15–45.

3 CBS Philly. 2019. "State Orders Emergency Removal of All Children Remaining at Glen Mills School Following Abuse Allegations." March 25. https://philadelphia.cbslocal.com/2019/03/25/glen-mills-school-emergency-removal-order-abuse-allegations/.

Tofte, S., and J. Fellner. (2007). "No Easy Answers: Sex Offender Laws in the U.S." *Human Rights Watch* 19(4): 1–146. https://www.hrw.org/report/2007/09/11/no-easy-answers/sex-offender-laws-us.

Tonry, M. H. 2011. *Punishing Race: A Continuing American Dilemma*. New York, NY: Oxford University Press.

Torbet, P., H. Hurst Jr., and M. Soler, M. 2006. "Guidelines for Collecting and Recording the Race and Ethnicity of Juveniles in Conjunction with Juvenile Delinquency Disposition Reporting to the Juvenile Court Judges' Commission." National Center for Juvenile Justice. https://www.ojp.gov/ncjrs/virtual-library/abstracts/guidelines-collecting-and-recording-race-and-ethnicity-juveniles.

Travis, J., B. Western, and S. Redburn, eds. 2014. *The Growth of Incarceration in the United States: Exploring Causes and Consequences*. Washington, D.C.: National Academies Press.

Trimble, M. 2019. "How Alameda County, CA, Connects Justice Partners with Odyssey." Tyler Technologies. https://www.tylertech.com/resources/blog-articles/how-alameda-county-ca-connects-justice-partners-with-odyssey.

Ura, A. 2017. "How Texas Killed Welfare: 'We Spend Our Dollar on Anything but Poor Families.'" *The Guardian*, November 30. https://www.theguardian.com/us-news/2017/nov/30/texas-welfare-spending-poor-families.

U.S. Department of Justice. 2008. "Los Angeles County Juvenile Probation Camps, Juvenile Justice Docket." http://www.justice.gov/crt/about/spl/casesummaries.php#lacamps-summ.

U.S. Department of Justice, Office of Juvenile Justice and Delinquency Prevention. 1994. "Juvenile Intensive Supervision: Planning Guide, Program Summary." https://www.google.com/books/edition/Juvenile_Intensive_Supervision/bOj7Da-1NWQC?hl=en&gbpv=0.

U.S. Department of Justice, Office of Juvenile Justice and Delinquency Prevention. 2009. "Juvenile Suicide in Confinement: A National Survey." https://www.ncjrs.gov/pdffiles1/ojjdp/213691.pdf.

U.S. Department of Justice, Office of Juvenile Justice and Delinquency Prevention. 2013. "Statistical Briefing Book: Juveniles in Corrections." http://www.ojjdp.gov/ojstatbb/corrections/qa08201.asp?qaDate=2013.

Valentino, S., and M. Wheeler. 2013. "Big Brothers Big Sisters Report to America: Positive Outcomes for a Positive Future." *Big Brothers Big Sisters of America*. http://www.bbbs.

org/atf/cf/%7B8778D05C-7CCB-4DEE-9D6E-70F27C016CC9%7D/20130425_BB BSA_YOS2013.pdf.

Vincent, G. M. 2012. "Risk Assessment in Juvenile Justice: A Guidebook for Implementation." Implementation Science and Practice Advances Research Center Publications. https://escholarship.umassmed.edu/psych_cmhsr/573.

Vives, R., and P. Willon. 2014. "Sen. Leland Yee, S.F. Chinatown Figure Arrested in Corruption Raids." *Los Angeles Times*, March 26.

Wacquant, L. 2006. "The Scholarly Myths of the New Law and Order Doxa." *Socialist Register* 2006: 93–115.

Wacquant, L. 2009. *Punishing the Poor: The Neoliberal Government of Social Insecurity*. Durham, NC: Duke University Press.

Wadsworth, J. 2019. "Traffic Court's Ticketing Glitch Is Latest in Long line of Missteps Linked to Tyler Technologies." *San Jose Inside*, March 20. https://www.sanjoseinside.com/2019/03/20/traffic-courts-ticketing-glitch-is-latest-in-long-line-of-missteps-linked-to-tyler-technologies/.

Ward, D. A., and T. G. Werlich. 2004. "Alcatraz and Marion Evaluating Super-Maximum Custody." *Punishment & Society* 5(1): 53–75.

Ward, G. K. 2012. *The Black Child-Savers; Racial Democracy and Juvenile Justice*. Chicago: University of Chicago Press.

Ward, M. 2007a. "Agency Culture Resists Change." *Austin American Statesman*, May 6.

Ward, M. 2007b. "State Youth Agency Fixes Could Cost $100 Million." *Austin American-Statesman*, April 5.

Ward, M. 2012. "Texas confronts broken juvenile justice system, again." *Austin American-Statesman*, September 1.

Ward, M. 2017. "Incarcerated Texas Juvenile: 'This Place Is Hurting Me More Than Helping Me.'" *Houston Chronicle*, December 23. https://www.houstonchronicle.com/politics/texas/article/This-place-is-hurting-me-more-than-helping-me-12431592.php.

Warren v. Saenz (Ca. 2001). https://www.ylc.org/wp-content/uploads/2018/11/warrenwrit.pdf.

Washburn, M., and R. Menart. 2019. "Unmet Promises: Continued Violence and Neglect in California's Division of Juvenile Justice." Center on Juvenile and Criminal Justice. http://www.cjcj.org/uploads/cjcj/documents/unmet_promises_continued_violence_and_neglect_in_california_division_of_juvenile_justice.pdf.

Washington, F. 2014. "Regional Juvenile Facility Moving to Old Crockett State School Building." KTRE News, January 23.

Washington Post. 2014. "Texas Leads the Way in Needed Criminal Justice Reforms." Editorial. January 28.

Weaver, T. P. R. 2012. "Neoliberalism in the Trenches: Urban Policy and Politics in the United States and the United Kingdom." PhD dissertation, University of Pennsylvania.

Weaver, V. M. 2007. "Frontlash: Race and the Development of Punitive Crime Policy." *Studies in American Political Development* 21(2): 230–265.

Weir, M. 1992. *Politics and Jobs: The Boundaries of Employment Policy in the United States*. Princeton, NJ: Princeton University Press.

Weisburd, K. 2015. "Monitoring Youth: The Collision of Rights and Rehabilitation." *Iowa Law Review* 297 March 27: 297–341. https://ssrn.com/abstract=2585224.

Weissert, W. 2012. "Troubled Youths Need Help." *Corpus Christi Caller-Times*, March 7.

Wells, C. 2018. "This Malibu Camp Wants Juvenile Justice to Be More Like Rehab Than Prison." *LAist News*, September 27. https://laist.com/2018/09/27/why_la_countys_camp_kilpatrick_is_at_the_center_of_a_debate_over_juvenile_justice_reform.php.

Werth, R. 2013. "The Construction and Stewardship of Responsible yet Precarious Subjects: Punitive Ideology, Rehabilitation, and 'Tough Love' among Parole Personnel." *Punishment & Society* 15(3): 219–246.

Wetzel, J. E. 2012. "Justice Reinvestment Is Key to Reforming Pennsylvania Corrections." *PennLive*, March 17. http://www.pennlive.com/editorials/index.ssf/2012/03/justice_reinvestment_is_key_to.html.

WHYY. 2009. "Pennsylvania: One of the Most Regressive Tax States." December 1. https://whyy.org/articles/pa-one-of-the-most-regressive-tax-states/.

WHYY. 2019. "Beaten behind Closed Doors: A Look into Abuse at Glen Mills Schools." February 25. https://whyy.org/episodes/beaten-behind-closed-doors-a-look-into-abuse-at-glen-mills-schools/.

Willis, D. J., J. Fensterwald, Y. Xie, M. Levin, and J. Osborn D'Agostino. 2018. "States in Motion: Visualizing How Education Funding Has Changed over Time." EdSource, November 14. https://edsource.org/2015/states-in-motion-school-finance-naep-child-poverty/83303.

Wood, M., S. Ward, S. Herzenberg, M. Price, C. Lilienthal, P. Dennis, E. Roberts. 2008. "The Common Good: What Pennsylvania's Budget and Tax Policies Mean to You." Pennsylvania Budget and Policy Center. https://www.pennbpc.org/pdf/PBPC_Tax_Primer_08.pdf.

Woodsworth, M. 2016. *Battle for Bed-Stuy: The Long War on Poverty in New York City*. Cambridge, MA: Harvard University Press.

Yates, R. 2016. "Questions Loom over Fate of Juvenile Murderers." *Morning Call* (Allentown, PA), January 26. http://www.mcall.com/news/nationworld/pennsylvania/mc-scotus-juvenile-life-without-parole-whats-next-20160126-story.html.

Youth Advocate Programs. 2013. "Preventing Youth Violence." http://www.yapinc.org/Portals/0/Documents/Resources/Preventing%20Youth%20Violence.pdf.

Youth Crisis Center. 2022. "SNAP (Stop Now And Plan)." https://youthcrisiscenter.org/our-programs/snap/.

Youth Law Center. 2014. "YLC Files DOJ Complaint over Use of Pepper Spray." July 28. http://www.ylc.org/2014/07/ylc-files-doj-complaint-over-use-of-pepper-spray/.

Youth Law Center. 2018. "Return of Organization Exempt from Income Tax: Form 990." https://ylc.org/wp-content/uploads/2019/09/YLC-2018-990.pdf.

Youth Reinvestment Fund. n.d. "Preventing the Harm of Justice System Involvement." https://a59.asmdc.org/sites/a59.asmdc.org/files/pdf/YRF_Fact_Sheet.pdf.

Youth Should be a Factor. 2010. *The Philadelphia Inquirer*, Editorial, August 2.

Zawacki, S., and P. Torbet. 2004. "Juvenile Detention Capacity and Utilization in Pennsylvania." National Center for Juvenile Justice, Pittsburgh, PA. http://www.ncjj.org/PDF/detcapacity.pdf.

Ziff-Rosenzweig, D. 2020. "'They Are Hurting Them': Advocacy Groups Ask Fed to Investigate Sexual Assaults, Gang Violence in Texas Youth Lockups." ABC KSAT, October 21. https://www.ksat.com/news/texas/2020/10/21/they-are-hurting-them-advocacy-groups-ask-feds-to-investigate-sexual-assaults-gang-violence-in-texas-youth-lockups/.

Zimring, F. E.. and G. Hawkins. 1991. *The Scale of Imprisonment*. Chicago: University of Chicago Press.

Zoukis, C. 2018. "Prisons Don't Damage Only Prisoners; Guards at Risk of PTSD and Suicide, Too." *Prison Legal News*, June 8.

Zuckerman, M. 2014. "Harsh Sentencing, Overstuffed Prisons—It's Time for Reform." *Wall Street Journal*, May 2.

INDEX

For the benefit of digital users, indexed terms that span two pages (e.g., 52–53) may, on occasion, appear on only one of those pages.

Abbott, Greg, 178
Abraham, Lynn, 212n.2
Abraxas, 90, 208–9nn.12–13
abuse of juvenile inmates, 4–6, 39–40, 114–15, 175–76
　in county institutions, 60–62
　privatization and, 94–97
　in state prisons, 40, 175–77, 186
　in Texas, 1–2, 161–62
ACLU (American Civil Liberties Union), 66, 167
Act 21 (Pennsylvania, 2003), 163–64, 165
Act 148 (Pennsylvania, 1976), 118
Act 204 (Pennsylvania, 2012), 152–53
Administration of Justice Commission, 116–17
adult transfers, 148–49, 157–62
　in California, 150–51, 158–60
　in Texas, 150–51, 160–62
AFDC (Aid to Families with Dependent Children), 208n.2
Alameda County, California, 108, 210n.34
Allegheny County, Pennsylvania, 82, 98–99, 153
American Society of Criminology, 136–37
Annie E. Casey Foundation, 11, 54, 80–81, 84, 103–4, 107, 112, 168–69, 187–88, 196, 206n.19, 211n.16. *See also* JDAI
　California and, 10, 85–87
　Juvenile Detention Alternative Initiative, 57, 209n.20
　juvenile justice policy and, 4–5, 13
　Pennsylvania and, 55, 82, 205n.11
　sex offender laws and registries and, 163, 213n.18
antidelinquency, 14, 116, 127–28
　approaches to, 32, 114
antipoverty legislation, 23
anti-recidivism measures, 127–28, 130

antistatism, 6, 7–8, 10, 16, 18, 21–22, 29, 121–22
ARC (Alternative Rehabilitation Communities), Inc., 91
Arena, John, 27
Arnove, R. F., 81
arrest rates, 171, 172
　in California, 50–51
　drop in, 157–59, 172–74
Assessments.com, 143–44, 210n.32, 212n.23
austerity, 12, 46, 70, 142, 186, 191–92
　in California budget, 64
　devolution and, 13–14, 71
　politics of, 7, 12–13, 165–66
　privatization and, 24, 93, 95

Balanced and Restorative Justice Act (Pennsylvania, 1995), 90–91
Barbin, Bryan, 152–53
BARJ (Balanced and Restorative Justice), 45–46, 71–72, 119–20, 140
Barker, V., 109
Beath, Andrew, 84
Biden, Joe, 144–45
bifurcation between low-risk individuals and serious offenders, 148, 150, 183
Big Brothers/Big Sisters, 138, 212n.25
BI Incorporated, 90
Bill and Melinda Gates Foundation, 28
bipartisanship, 7, 209n.17
　in community-based reform, 4–5, 118
　privatization and, 78–79, 109
　on punitive policies, 14–15, 148, 152, 154, 185
　in Texas, 90, 91–92
Black Panthers, 23
Black Power movement, 23

247

INDEX

Black youths, 134–35, 169, 214n.27
   as adult transfers, 160
   in California, 115
   CAPs and, 23
   civil rights of, 204n.6
   DMC of in Texas, 169
   inner-city, 32–33
   juvenile LWOP sentences for, 151
   in post-Katrina New Orleans, 27
   working-class, 23–24
blended sentencing, 160–61
block grants, 46–47, 49. *See also* YOBG
Blueprints Project, University of Colorado, 103–4, 137
bootstraps approach to social problems, 18
brain development research, 87–88
Breed, Allen, 116–17
Breen, Jenny, 30–31
brokerage-based model, 101
Brown County, Texas, juvenile detention centers, 1–2, 3, 58, 92, 141–42, 184, 203n.1, 206n.14
Brown v. Plata, 206n.20
Bucks County, Pennsylvania, 153–54
budget allocations, 48–53
Burrell, Sue, 63

Cain, Camille, 161–62
Calderon, Ron, 64
CalGang, 166–67, 168, 210n.7, 214n.25
Calhoun County, Texas, 66
California, 78–79, 85, 88, 89, 101, 104–5, 116, 128–29, 157, 169, 175, 179
   adult transfers in, 150–51, 158–60
   closures in, 206nn.17–18
   electronic monitoring in, 105–7
   gang-affiliated juvenile offenders in, 165–68
   incarceration rates and arrest rates in, 119, 172
   juvenile justice reform in, 114–15
   juvenile justice system of, 3, 10
   LWOP in, 150–51, 154–56
   nonprofits in, 83, 84
   pepper spray in, 65, 207nn.27–30
   probation in, 57–58, 72–73, 207n.28
   public sector retrenchment in, 42–43
   regionalization in, 67–68, 69–70
   risk assessment tools in, 107–8, 135
   sex offender laws and registries in, 162–63
   solitary confinement in, 62–63, 179–80, 207n.24
   state budget of, 88–101
   state-run prisons in, 59, 60, 177–78
   YOBG in, 48–50, 122
California Board of Corrections, 50
California BPH (Board of Parole Hearings), 155
California BSCC (Board of State and Community Corrections), 48, 83, 205n.5
California Department of Corrections and Rehabilitation, 59–60

California Department of Juvenile Justice, 86, 140, 177, 207n.28
California juvenile justice system, 9–11
Californians United for a Responsible Budget, 84, 208n.7
California Probation Department, 86
California Superior Court, 87
Cambria County, Pennsylvania, 152–53
Cameron County, Texas, 68
Camp Kilpatrick, Los Angeles County, California, 85–87
Camp Scudder, Santa Clara, California, 63
capitalism, capitalist class, 18–19, 28
CAPs (community action programs), 23, 204n.2
carceral expansion, 7, 25
Carnegie Corporation, 31
Carnegie Foundation, 103
Carter, Jimmy, 204n.5
case management software, 107–9
casework model, 101
Cate, Matthew, 59–60
CA-YASI, 135
CCA (Corrections Corporation of America), 91–93, 182, 208n.11
CDCs (community development corporations), 20, 23, 31
Center for the Study and Prevention of Violence, University of Colorado, 103
centralization, 19–20, 21–22
Chan-Zuckerberg Initiative, 88
charitable foundations, 26, 28–29, 31, 76–77, 80–81, 187, 197. *See also* Annie E. Casey Foundation; MacArthur Foundation
   community-based reforms and, 4–5, 10, 40
   growth of, 25–26
   juvenile delinquency and, 14, 32
   juvenile justice developments and, 7–8, 24
   policymaking and, 12, 28, 79, 112
charter schools, 28, 92–93
Chester County, Pennsylvania, 153–54
Chicago, 198–99
Children at Risk, 143
Child Savers Movement, 77–78
Ciavarella, Mark, 76, 95
civil commitment legislation for juvenile sex offenders, 163–64, 213n.21
civil rights and liberties, 20–21, 162, 204n.6
Clear, Todd, 136–37
Clegg, J., 192–93
Clinton, Bill, 21, 27, 35, 204n.4
Clinton, Hillary, 144–45
Cloward, Richard, 32, 116
Cohen, Brent J., 87
Cold War, 31
collective economic security, 18–19, 197–99
Columbia County, Pennsylvania, 207n.35
Commonweal, 83, 208n.4

community, 4, 18, 36
  as concept, 21–24, 37
  control of, 22, 37
  in Texas, 2–3
Community Treatment Program
  (California), 116–17
Conahan, Michael, 95
CoNEXTions, 143–44, 212n.28
conservatives, 2, 21–22
Contra Costa County, California, 63, 207n.24
Conyers, John, 204n.6
Corbett, Tom, 131, 132, 211n.20
Cornell-Abraxas, 90
corporations, 28–29
correctional officers, 86, 178, 195
corrections officers, 94
cost cutting, 95, 132–33, 145–46, 186
  privatization and, 94, 96–97
  rejection of, 192–94
Council of State Governments Justice Center, 184
county consortiums, 69, 70–71
county institutions, 41, 46, 59–60, 63
  abuse in, 60–62
  in California, 48, 49, 50–51, 62, 158
  pepper spray in, 65–66
  in Texas, 51–52
county level, 68, 163, 207n.32
  inequality on, 66–69
county probation, 58
  in California, 64
  in Pennsylvania, 72
  in Texas, 57, 66, 93
crime, 5–6, 18–19, 190–91
Crime Bill (1994), 35
criminal justice reform, 6, 30
  political economy of, 6–8
Crockett, Texas, 58–59, 92
CTU (Chicago Teachers Union), 198
culture of fear, 35
culture of poverty theory, 30, 31, 32, 35, 36–37, 135 36, 189–90
CYA (California Youth Authority), 112, 114–15, 116–17

DAFs (donor-advised funds), 26, 204n.9
Dallas County, Texas, 63, 184
Dauphin County, Pennsylvania, 91
death penalty, 148–49, 183, 190, 199–200, 204n.6
  juvenile offenders and, 5–6, 203n.7
  in Texas, 156–57
deaths in private juvenile prisons, 94, 95–96
decarceration, 10, 12, 17, 162, 172–73, 193
  privatization and, 76, 97–100, 188
  resistance to, 39–40, 41
decentralization, 9–10, 26–27, 30, 76–77, 182
deindustrialization, 22
Delaware County, Pennsylvania, 164

DeLuca, Anthony, 153
democracy, 23, 28–29, 31
democratic accountability, 3, 4, 80–81, 86
Democratic Leadership Council, 22
democratization of community reform, 6, 196–97
Democrats, 18–19, 78–79, 204n.5
  divisions amongst, 19, 20
  in Pennsylvania, 152–53, 164
  in Texas, 84, 91–92, 156
Denton County, Texas, 143
deregulation, 21
devolution of juvenile justice system, 39–40, 42, 62, 76–77, 186–87, 191–92
  in California, 43, 158
  cost cutting and, 71, 194
  entrenched interests and, 71–74
  in Pennsylvania, 39–40, 45–46
  pitfalls of, 186–87
  privatization and, 92–93
  public-sector retrenchment and, 17–18, 74–75
  punitiveness and, 47
  in Texas, 91, 92
devolution of social policy, 9–10, 11–12, 17–18, 19–20, 21, 27, 36, 37, 46–47
  austerity politics and, 13–14
  community-based reform and, 3, 4, 11, 12, 17, 22
  public-sector retrenchment and, 37, 54
  shift to, 18–24
disabled youths, 65, 207n.24
district attorneys, 199–200
District of Columbia, 82
diversion grants, 123–24
DMC (disproportionate minority confinement), 168–69, 173–74
Domhoff, G. W., 28–29
Dream Center, 92–93
drug testing and treatment, 5, 55
Dunnam, Jim, 70

Eason, John, 23–24
economic inequality, 12–13, 22, 67–68
Economic Opportunity Act (1965), 25
education policy, 28, 44
efficiencies, 7–8, 12
electronic monitoring, 49, 50–51, 56, 58, 101–2, 203n.4, 209n.28, 209n.29
  in California, 57–58, 171
  in Pennsylvania, 54–55, 205n.12
  soft-end privatization and, 105–7
  in Texas, 56–57
elites, 196
ESEA (Elementary and Secondary Education Act; 1965), 28
evidence-based programs and practices, 102–5, 122, 123, 130, 131, 145, 187
excessive force, in California, 60, 61, 65

250

INDEX

Fair Defense Act (Texas, 2001), 208n.6
Fair Sentencing for Youth (California), 155
Federal Home Loan Banks, 92–93
FFT (Family Functional Therapy), 138
fiscal conservatism, 118
fiscal policies, redistributive policies vs., 19
Fisher, Scott, 160–61
Florida, 118–19, 152, 153–54
Ford Foundation, 20, 31, 84
Fording, R. C., 35
Forman, James, Jr., 23–24
for-profit prisons, 9–10, 76–77, 93, 188
  rise of, 26–28
Fortner, Michael, 23–24
foundations. *See* charitable foundations
FreeAmerica, 88, 208n.9
Free Venture Program (California), 128
Full Employment Bill (1945), 19

G4S (Group 4 Securicor), 203n.4
gangs and gang enhancements, 14–15, 23–24, 35–36, 148–49, 166–68, 207n.25, 210n.7
Gascon, George, 159–60
GEO Group, Inc., 90, 91–92
"get tough" rhetoric and policies, 150–51, 152, 153, 154, 157, 212n.2
GHAY (Greater Houston Action for Youth), 117
Gilmore, R. W., 42
Google, 88
Gottschalk, M., 109, 131, 162
governance, 26–27, 33, 35, 38, 40–41, 43–44, 186, 191
  post–New Deal, 25, 34–35
  shift in, 26, 29, 34, 120–21
Graham v. Florida (2010), 149, 156, 203n.7
Grasso, A., 134–35
Gray Areas (Ford Foundation), 20
Great Recession, 43, 44
Great Society, 20, 23, 25, 31, 36, 37
group homes, 186

Harcourt, Bernard, 135
hard end of privatization, 79–81, 90–100
Harrell, Will, 177, 180
Harris County, Texas, 46, 57, 63, 143, 209n.16
healthcare, 19, 22–23, 27, 29, 198
Hess, David, 95–96
Hester, Beauford H., 115–16
Hinojosa, Juan, 73–74, 209n.17
Hinton, Elizabeth, 134–35
Hispanics and Latinos, 23–24, 32–33, 160, 169, 214n.27
historical institutionalist approach, 17
Hogg Foundation for Mental Health, 117
Holton, Karl, 112, 114–15
HOPE VI Act, 27

Houston, Texas, 161–62, 167, 210n.5
Houston County, Texas, 92
Howard, Edward, 39
human capital theory, 30–31, 189–90
Humboldt County, California, 69
Humphrey-Hawkins Bill, 204n.5
Hurley, Jim, 181
Hurricane Katrina, 27
hydra risk, 60

incarceration rates, 4–5, 7–8, 14, 34, 59–60, 148, 193, 204n.6
Indiana, 88
individualization of social problems, 6, 11–12, 14, 17–18, 20–21
  community-based reform and, 3, 5
  limitations of, 189–90
individualized behavioral interventions, 2, 11, 17, 36–37, 113–14, 139
  turn toward, 30–34
inequality, 6, 21, 33, 40–41, 43, 59–60, 186–87
  class, 7–8, 18–19, 32
  county-level, 66–69
  culturalist explanations of, 30–33
  economic, 113–14, 168–69
  in punishments, 168–70
  solutions to, 6, 7–8, 22
  in Texas, 44–45, 185
inner cities, 23–24, 32–33
Intensive Community-Based Program (Grant X; Texas), 57
Interbranch Commission on Juvenile Justice (Pennsylvania), 95
IQ tests, 134–35
IRS (Internal Revenue Service), 26
ISP (Intensive Supervision Probation), 5, 57–58
  in Pennsylvania, 54–56, 205n.11

Jails to Jobs (Texas), 127–28
JDAI (Juvenile Detention Alternatives Initiative), 57, 82, 83, 209n.20
Jefferson County, Texas, 92–93
Jessica's Law (California), 155
Johnson, Cedric, 23
Johnson, Lyndon B., 116–17
Jones v. Mississippi, 203n.7
justice by geography, 66–67
juvenile advocacy organizations, 84
  in California, 83, 84
  in Texas, 2–3, 83–84
juvenile delinquency, 12, 14, 32, 115
  solutions to, 3, 14–15, 25, 28
Juvenile Delinquency and Youth Offenses Control Act (U.S., 1961), 116, 210n.5
juvenile incarceration, 77–78, 114–15
  negative effects of, 3–4
  in Pennsylvania, 47, 151

Juvenile Justice and Delinquency Prevention Act (1974), 212–13n.10
Juvenile Justice Crime Prevention Act (California, 2000), 49–50
juvenile justice policy, 4–5, 6
  cyclical nature of, 114–21
  as window to penal policy and American politics, 8–9
juvenile justice system, 5, 14, 38, 114–15, 119–20
  investment in, 194–96
  privatization and, 13–14, 24, 29
  punitiveness in, 3, 34, 35–36
  reform of, 7–8, 17–18, 32
Juvenile Justice System Enhancement Strategy, 123
Juvenile Law Center (Pennsylvania), 84, 95, 96, 153–54
Juvenile Probation and Camps Funding Program (California, 2005), 49–50

Kellogg Foundation, 88
Kennedy, John F., 116, 210n.5
Kern County, California, 63
Kids for Cash scandal, 95, 195
Kimbrough, Jay, 177–78
King, Jane Anderson, 141–42
Krasner, Larry, 199–200

labor movement, 20, 21, 27
  during New Deal, 19, 22
Lafer, Gordon, 28, 124–27
Lake County, California, 69–70
L.A. Model, 85, 86
Lancaster County, Pennsylvania, 61–62, 82, 122, 153
Larson, Lyle, 209n.17
Last Mile, The, 88
law and order policies, 42, 204n.6
Legend, John, 208n.9
legislation
  California, 43, 59–60, 83, 87–88, 101, 155, 158, 159–60, 166–67, 210n.7, 214n.24
  on juvenile sex offenders, 162–65
  Pennsylvania, 90–91, 118, 152–53, 163–64, 165
  Texas, 1–2, 58, 91–92, 141–42, 178, 212n.27
Lehigh County, Pennsylvania, 82
Leija, Luis, 66
Leno, Mark, 64
Levin, Mark, 83, 91–92
Lewis, Oscar, 31
liberalism, liberals, 2, 7, 19
life skills training and programs, 5, 121–22, 123–24, 138, 139
  in Texas, 143, 205–6n.13
LLCs (limited liability corporations), 26, 204n.9
local level, 19–20, 49–51, 73, 113, 191–92
  entrenched interests at, 71–74
  entrenchment of punishment at, 12, 47

Lombroso, Cesare, 213n.16
Los Angeles, California, 23–24, 92–93, 167, 168
Los Angeles County, California, 60–61, 63, 64, 65, 85, 108, 159–60, 167, 207n.24
  Camp Kilpatrick in, 85–87
  incarceration rates in, 67–68
Louisiana, 152, 153–54
Luzerne County, Pennsylvania, 95
LWOP (life without the possibility of parole), 5–6, 14–15, 35–36, 148, 190, 203n.7, 212n.1, 212n.8
  in California, 150–51, 154–56, 212n.5
  limiting of, 148–49, 199
  in Pennsylvania, 9–10, 150–54, 211n.9
  in Texas, 156–57
  U.S. Supreme Court and, 149–50
Lyle B. Medlock Treatment Center, 63

MacArthur Foundation, 11, 54, 80–81, 84, 104, 107, 127, 133–34, 149–50, 168–69, 187–88, 196, 206n.19, 209n.16
  California YACs and, 87–89, 208n.8
  juvenile justice policy and, 4–5, 13
  Models for Change program, 9–10, 82, 211n.15
  Pennsylvania and, 55, 82, 84, 98–99, 127, 205n.11, 211n.15, 211n.17
  sex offender laws and registries and, 163–64, 213n.19
Madden, Jerry, 91–92, 209n.17
mandatory minimum sentences, 149, 152, 204n.6, 212n.3, 212n.4
marketization of education, 28
Mart, Texas, 180–81
Massachusetts, 79
mass incarceration, 5–6, 33, 34–35, 110
  expansion of, 35, 100
  rise of, 7, 38
Mayfield, Alan, 46
MAYSI-2, 107
McCarthyism, 19
McLennan County, Texas, 46, 180–81
McReynolds, Jim, 140
Medina, Estela, 207n.31
Mendocino County, California, 69–70
mental health
  panic of, 141–42
  services for, 60–61, 64, 90
  in Texas, 45, 141–42
mentorship, 5
Mexican youth, 115
Miller, Lisa, 109, 200
Miller v. Alabama (2012), 149, 152, 156, 203n.7, 208n.8
Missouri, 85
Missouri Model, 85–86
Moak, Daniel, 28, 124–27

Models for Change (MacArthur Foundation), 9–10, 82, 127, 211n.15
Moll, Jeanette, 131
Monroe County, Pennsylvania, 153–54
Montgomery County, Texas, 141–42
Montgomery v. Louisiana (2016), 149, 203n.7
Morales, Alicia, 210n.6
Morales v. Turman, 117
moral uplift, 22, 36–37
Moynihan, Daniel Patrick, 32
MST (multisystemic therapy), 104
Multi-Health Systems, Inc., 134
Multisystemic, Inc., 104
Muñiz, Ana, 23–24
Murray, Charles, 32–33

National Council on Crime and Delinquency, 135
Navarro County, Texas, 92
Nebraska, 152
neoliberalism and neoliberal governance, 5, 6, 16, 21, 25, 26–27, 145, 189
  individualist solutions of, 30, 148
  reform and, 38, 136–37
  rise of, 15, 36
neuroscience, 87, 149–50
New Deal, 30–31, 187
  Democratic Coalition in, 5, 17, 18–19, 20, 22, 28, 38, 193
  federalism in, 19–20
New Left, 20, 22, 23, 204n.7
New Orleans, 27
Newsom, Gavin, 69–70, 86, 101
New York City, 23–24
New York Times, 87, 210n.1
New Young Adult Pilot Program, 88
Nixon, Richard M., 204n.4
nongovernmental entities, 7–8
  nonprofits, 7–8, 28–29, 76–77, 88, 149. *See also* charitable foundations
  as advocacy organizations, 79, 82
  in California, 83, 101
  sector of, 25–26
Northwestern Human Services, 91

Obama, Barack, 87
OC (oleoresin capiscum). *See* pepper spray
Ohlin, Lloyd, 32, 116, 210n.5
Oklahoma, 88
opportunity theory, 32
outcome-based models, 100–1
oversight, 185, 194, 195
  in state-run prisons, 177–79

P.A.C.E. (Proper Self-image, Academics, Character Development, Employment), Inc., 143, 212n.26

PACTA (Pennsylvania Association of Career and Technical Administrators), 127
P.A.C.T. tool, 135
partnerships, public-private, 25
PCCD (Pennsylvania Commission on Crime and Delinquency), 132
PCCJPO (Pennsylvania Council of Chief Juvenile Probation Officers), 71–72
penal policy, 8–9, 10–11
Pennsylvania, 9–10, 39–40, 47, 68, 82, 102, 105–6, 107, 118, 119–20, 128–29, 134, 140, 157, 167, 172
  abuse in, 61–62, 175–76
  community-based probation in, 54–55
  DMC in, 169–70
  evidence-based programs in, 103–4
  juvenile justice system of, 3, 9–11, 39, 76, 123
  Juvenile Law Center in, 84
  Kids for Cash scandal in, 95
  local probation interests in, 71–72
  LWOP in, 150–54
  MacArthur Foundation and, 82, 211n.17
  privatization in, 77–78, 90–91, 97–100
  public sector retrenchment in, 45–46
  sex offender laws and registries in, 163–65
Pennsylvania Coalition against Rape, 164
Pennsylvania Commission on Crime and Delinquency, 103, 123
Pennsylvania Council of Chief Juvenile Probation Officers (PCCJPO), 71–72
Pennsylvania Department of Corrections, 132
Pennsylvania Department of Public Welfare, 90–91
Pennsylvania District Attorneys Association, 153
Pennsylvania Juvenile Court Judges' Commission, 103
Pennsylvania Supreme Court, 165
pepper spray, 60–61, 207nn.27–30
  in county facilities, 65–66
  in state-run facilities, 175–76
  in Texas, 180, 181–82, 207n.31
Perry, Rick, 156
Personal Responsibility and Work Opportunity Act (1996), 21, 204n.4
personal responsibility ethic, 117–18
Pfaff, J. F., 99
Phelps, Michelle, 54
Philadelphia, Pennsylvania, 91, 95–96, 152–53, 167, 199–200
Philadelphia County, Pennsylvania, 82, 151, 153–54, 164
Philadelphia Inquirer, 96
Philadelphia Reintegration Initiative, 127, 211n.17
philanthropy, 7–8
philosophy of youth punishment, 15
Phoenix program (Texas), 180–81
policy formation network, 28–29

policymaking process, 17, 79–80, 187–88
  privatization and, 13, 77, 80–85
political context, 28–29, 110
  of reform, 17–18, 39–40, 41–42
political economy, 14, 46, 84, 113–14
  of criminal justice reforms, 6–8
  transformations in, 27, 185, 188
political power, postwar shift in, 28
politics, 36
  of fiscal austerity, 12–13
  of juvenile justice, 8–9, 12
  of prison reform, 7
poverty and the poor, 14, 19–20, 30–31, 32–33, 35
  culture of, 30, 31–32
  solutions to, 12, 28
Powers, Jerry, 64
Presidential Commission on Law Enforcement, 116–17
President's Committee on Juvenile Delinquency, 116
Prison Industry Enhancement program (Texas), 127–28
Prison Rape Elimination Act (Texas), 178
prison reform, 1–2, 77
private sector and private prison companies, 2, 5, 7–8, 13–14, 15–16, 17–18, 24, 49, 91–92, 110
  in California, 7–8, 89
  scandal and abuse in, 76, 94
privatization of juvenile justice, 6, 9–10, 16, 17–18, 29, 36–37, 76–77, 145, 186–87
  community and, 3–4, 13, 17, 24
  consequences of, 11, 28–29
  current forms of, 79–80
  development of, 11–12, 18, 24–29, 77–79
  hard end of, 90–100
  in juvenile justice system, 13–14
  as obstacle to decarceration, 97–100
  in Pennsylvania, 90–91
  problems with, 76, 187–89
  reversal of, 6, 15
  soft end of, 100–9
  in Texas, 10, 91–93
probation, 40, 53–54, 142–43, 171, 172–73.
  See also ISP
  in California, 49, 57–58, 60–61
  community-based, 53–58
  in Pennsylvania, 55
  punitive, 46–48, 50–51
  in Texas, 51–53, 56–57, 143
profit motive, 5
programs and services, as soft end, 79
Progressive Era, 77–78, 134–35
Proposition 8 (Victims' Bill of Rights, California, 1981), 210n.7
Proposition 13 (California), 43
Proposition 21 (California, 2000), 158, 166–67, 210n.7, 214n.24

Proposition 57 (California, 2016), 159–60
Proposition 115 (California, 1990), 210n.7
public defenders, 195
public good and public goods
  as approach to prison reform, 191–96
  commodification of, 25
  declining support for, 36, 37, 186
  equitable distribution of, 29, 39–40
  expansion of, 20–21
  government for, 11–12, 17–18
  marketization of, 27
  as model of governance, 191–92, 195
  universal provision of, 16, 110–11
Public Health Management Corporation (Philadelphia), 95–96
public housing, 27, 29, 193–94
public-private partnerships, 5, 27, 80–81, 82
  nonprofits and, 7–8, 26
Public Safety Committee (California), 108
public-sector retrenchment, 6, 22–36, 37, 38, 42–47, 66, 112, 142, 185, 186–87
Puerto Rico, 82
P.U.L.S.E. (Providing Uplifting Learning Skills to Excel), 122
punishment
  arrest rates and, 172–74
  entrenched at local level, 12, 39–40
  inequality in, 168–70
  in juvenile justice system, 14, 35–36
punitive discipline, 147
punitive model, 199
punitiveness and punitive policies, 10–11, 17–18, 20–21, 24, 66–68, 71–72, 113, 114, 147
  in 1980s and 1990s, 118–21
  bipartisanship and, 14–15, 185
  development and expansion of, 11–12, 16, 34–36
  devolution and, 47
  in juvenile justice system, 3, 5, 35–36
  national developments and, 149–51
  in Pennsylvania, 9–10, 119–20, 151
  persistence of, 14–15, 190–91
  race and, 5–6, 32–33
  seriousness and, 170–71
  in Texas, 10, 119
punitive turn, 19, 34–35

race and racism, 4–6, 23, 32–33, 135, 168, 189
racial inequality, 4–5, 14, 19–20, 28, 32
  failure to solve, 7–8, 12
  naturalization of, 133–36
racial integration, 22
racial minorities, 3, 5–6, 144–45. *See also* Black youths; DMC; Hispanics and Latinos
  gang injunctions and, 165–66, 168
Radack, Steve, 46
Randall County, Texas, 141–42

RDA (regional diversion alternatives) programs, 70–71
Reagan, Ronald, and Reaganism, 21, 22, 35, 204n.4
recidivism, 130, 138, 157–58, 211n.19, 214n.29
 reduction of, 113–14, 131, 132–33, 136–37, 143–44, 145–46
redeemability of offenders, 5–6
redistributive policies
 fiscal policies vs., 19
 upward, 41, 109, 112, 197
Reed, Adolph, Jr., 23, 33
Reed, Touré, 32
regionalization of youth justice programs, 69–71, 73–74
rehabilitation, 5, 117–18, 148
Republican Party and Republicans, 20–21, 78–79, 152, 164
Research Network on Adolescent Development and Juvenile Justice, 87
residential institutions and services, 49, 51–52, 53–54, 79
restitution, 55
Rhode Island, 128–29
right, rise of the, 20–21
Right on Crime, 83–84
rights revolution of 1960s and 1970s, 116
risk assessments, 130, 133–36, 147–48, 168–69, 170–71
 in Pennsylvania, 151, 154
 soft-end privatization and, 107–9
Rockefeller Foundation, 204n.13
Roelof, J., 82
Rogers, Daniel, 30–31
Roosevelt, Franklin D., 204n.1
Roper v. Simmons (2005), 149, 156, 203n.7, 208n.8
Rubin, Ashley, 120
Russell Sage Foundation, 31

Sacramento County, California, 60–61
San Diego County, California, 65
San Francisco, California, 63, 64
 incarceration rates in, 67–68
San Francisco County, California, 87
San Joaquin County, California, 60–61
San Luis Obispo County, California, 69
Santa Barbara County, California, 69
Santa Clara, California, 63
Santa Clara County, California, 85
SB (Senate Bill) 2 (Texas, 2013), 156
SB (Senate Bill) 9 (California, 2013), 155
SB (Senate Bill) 81 (California, 2007), 59–60, 83, 101
SB (Senate Bill) 103 (Texas), 141–42, 178, 212n.27
SB (Senate Bill) 260 (California, 2013), 155

SB (Senate Bill) 653 (Texas, 2011), 58, 91–92
SB (Senate Bill) 1004 (California, 2016), 87–88
SB (Senate Bill) 1106 (California, 2018), 87–88
SB (Senate Bill) 1391 (California), 159–60
Schept, Judah, 23–24
Schlanger, Margo, 60, 206n.20
Schoenfeld, H., 118–19
school choice, 28
Schram, S. F., 35
Schranz, Dennis, 137
Schwarzenegger, Arnold, 49–50
self-help treatment and programs, 121–22, 124, 144, 145
seriousness of crime, punitiveness and, 170–71
sex offender laws and registries, 14–15, 148–49, 155, 157, 162–65, 183, 213nn.16–17, 213nn.18–19
sex offender programs, 205–6n.13
Sex Offender Registration and Notification Act (Pennsylvania), 165
sexual abuse and assaults, 1, 162–63
 in Texas, 2, 61, 176, 178, 182, 206n.22
Sexual Offender Assessment Board (Pennsylvania), 165
Sexual Responsibility and Treatment Program (Pennsylvania), 165
shadow carceral state, 54
Shanblum, Laurie, 91–92
Slack, 88
Sleepy Lagoon trial (1942), 210n.3
Smith, Rogers, 120–21
Social and Environmental Entrepreneurs, 84
social policy shifts, 16
social problems, bootstraps approach to, 18
social scientists, 116
Social Security, 22, 25
social services, marketization of, 25
social structures, inequality of, 4
social welfare policy and programs, 25, 33
 retrenchment of, 34, 40–41, 141
sociopolitical economic system, 15
soft end of privatization, 79–81, 100–9
solitary confinement, 1–2, 41, 62–64, 157–58, 179, 190, 214n.33
 in California, 60, 61, 64, 179–80, 207n.24
 in state-run prisons, 148, 179–82
 in Texas, 10, 147, 180–81, 203n.5, 214n.34
Soss, J., 35
South Texas Chiefs Association, 66
Spriggs, Vicki, 123–24
state budget cuts, 21
state governments, punitive welfare reforms of, 35
state-level juvenile justice reform, 7–8
State Policy Network (Texas), 208n.5
state-run prisons, 4–5, 40, 68–69, 168–69, 177–78
 abuse in, 114–15, 177
 in California, 50–51, 114–15

closing of, 52, 58–59, 79
conditions in, 148–49, 174–82
DMC in, 169
oversight in, 177–79
solitary confinement in, 179–82
staffing in, 177–79
in Texas, 44, 46, 52, 53, 115–16, 143–44, 180, 185
State Sheriffs' Association (California), 72–73
Stedman, Craig, 153
Steinhart, David, 83
Stockton, California, 88
Stoneleigh Foundation, 127
Storm, Jennifer, 153
strip searches, 1–2
structural solutions, 3, 5–6, 28, 36–37
suicide, 157–58, 179, 184
  in California, 179–80, 210n.2
  solitary confinement and, 62, 214n.33
suicide prevention, 60–61
superpredators, juvenile, 4–5, 35–36, 139, 212n.2
surveillance cameras, 177–78
Sussman, Steve, 138
Sutherland, Robert, 117

Taft-Hartley Act (1947), 19, 27
tax cuts, 21
tax policies, 42–44, 45
technocratic approaches to reform, 13
Temple University, 87
Temporary Aid to Needy Families, 25
Texans Care for Children, 178
Texas, 10, 68, 78–79, 90, 94, 100–1, 104, 105–6, 107, 117–18, 119, 122, 123–24, 141–42, 152, 162–63, 169, 172, 175–76, 177, 184
  abuse in, 61, 147
  adult transfers in, 150–51, 157–58, 160–62
  advocacy organizations in, 2–3, 83–84
  community-based reform in, 51–53, 116
  county-run juvenile detention centers in, 2, 3, 206n.14
  death penalty in, 156–57
  devolution in, 58–59
  gang-affiliated juvenile offenders in, 167
  juvenile justice reform in, 3, 9–11, 115–16
  LWOP in, 156–57
  pepper spray use in, 66, 207n.31
  Prison Industry Enhancement program in, 127–28
  privatization in, 91–93
  probation in, 56–57, 72–74, 104–5
  public sector retrenchment in, 43–45
  regionalization of youth justice programs in, 70–71
  sexual abuse and assaults in, 176, 206n.22
  solitary confinement in, 62, 63, 180–81, 214n.34

  state budget and, 51–53
  state-run juvenile prisons in, 1–3, 73, 171, 178, 185
Texas Appleseed, 83, 178, 208n.6
Texas Criminal Justice Coalition, 61, 63, 66
Texas House Corrections Committee, 178
Texas Juvenile Probation Commission, 51, 58, 92
Texas Office of the Independent Ombudsman, 63, 177, 181, 195
Texas Office of the Inspector General, 177
Texas Rangers, 178
Texas State Board of Education, 92
Texas State Employees Union, 178
Texas Training School Code Commission, 115–16
therapeutic communities, 86
Thinking for a Change, 123
Thomas, Curtis, 152–53
Thompson, Michael, 184
TJJD (Texas Juvenile Justice Department), 51–52, 92, 127–28, 141–42, 143, 147, 160–62, 177–79, 205–6n.13
  solitary confinement and, 180–81
totalitarianism, 31
Townsend, Cherie, 141–42
TPPF (Texas Public Policy Foundation), 83–84, 91–92, 100–1, 131, 206n.19, 208n.5
training schools, 117
Transitional Age Youth Pilot Program, 87–88
truancy, 160, 213n.15
TSYDC (Texas State Youth Development Council), 115–16
Turman, James, 210n.6
Turner, Mary Ann, 141–42
TXGang Database, 167
TYC (Texas Youth Commission), 1, 51, 92, 119, 140, 180, 210n.6, 212n.27
Tyler Technologies, Inc., 108

underclass theory and ideology, 30, 32–33, 35, 134, 189–90
unemployment and joblessness, 12, 14, 18–20, 22, 28, 128–29
universal healthcare, 27, 193–94
universal provisions, 18, 192–93, 198
University of Chicago, 30–31
University of Colorado, Blueprints Project, 103
University of Texas, Hogg Foundation for Mental Health, 117
unredeemable offenders, 14–15
Unruh, Debbie, 181
Unsung Heroes for Houston Children's Award, 143
uplift, Missouri Model and, 85
uprisings in Texas state-run prisons, 180
U.S. Centers for Disease Control and Prevention, 103
U.S. Constitution, 152–53

U.S. Department of Justice, 2–3, 60–61, 62, 87, 96, 207n.24
    Office of Juvenile Justice and Delinquency Prevention, 102–3, 134–35, 205n.11
Usmani, A., 192–93
U.S. Supreme Court, 5–6, 149–50, 151, 152, 154, 157–58, 162, 190
    effects of decisions of, 150
    LWOP sentences and, 153–55
    Texas and, 156–57

Ventura County, California, 69
victims rights, 153
Victoria County, Texas, 68
violence, 157–58, 168
    in state-run prisons, 148, 175–76
    in Texas, 2, 175–76, 178–79
visitation, 69–70

Wacquant, Loïc, 34, 46–47, 213n.16
Wagner-Murray-Dingell Bill (1943), 19
Walton Foundation, 28
Ward, G. K., 134–35
War on Crime, culture of fear and, 35
War on Poverty, 20, 31, 32, 78
    CAPs and, 23, 204n.2
Warren, Earl, 114–15
Washington, DC, 23–24
welfare state, 15, 19, 20–22, 26–27, 32–33
    reform of, 25, 35, 44–45
West, Ray, 51–52, 93, 140, 141–42, 206n.15
Wetzel, John, 132
White, James, 178
White, Mary Jo, 212n.4

White House Conference on Children and Youth, 115–16
Whitmire, John, 91–92, 182, 209n.17
WhyTry, 123–24
Wilson, William Julius, 32–33
working class, 5–6, 23–24
World War II, 19
"worst of the worst"
    community-based reform movement and, 157–68
    punishment for, 147–82
    racial and class character of, 166, 190
    in Texas, 181–82

YACs (young adult courts), in California, 87–89
Yee, Leland, 64, 207n.25
YLS/CMI (Youth Level of Service/Case Management Inventory), 122, 134
YOBG (Youth Offender Block Grant), 48–50
    in California, 104–5, 122
Youth Advocate Programs, Inc., 204n.13
Youthful Offender Program (Texas), 161–62
youth incarceration rates, 25, 35–36, 131, 132–33
    in California, 119
    in Pennsylvania, 119–20
    in Texas, 119
Youth Law Center (San Francisco), 63, 206–7n.23
youth prison system, in Texas, 1–3
Youth Reinvestment Fund (California, 2018), 101, 209n.24

zero-sum justice, 152
zero tolerance policies, 35
Zimmer, Mark, 132